Russell Miller is a prize-winning journalist and the author of eleven previous books. He began his career in journalism at the age of sixteen. While under contract to the *Sunday Times Magazine* he won four press awards and was voted Writer of the Year by the Society of British Magazine Editors. His book *Magnum* was described by John Simpson as 'the best book on photo-journalism I have ever read', and his oral histories of D-Day, *Nothing Less Than Victory*, and the Special Operations Executive, *Behind the Lines*, were widely acclaimed, both in Britain and the United States. His authorised biography of Field Marshal Slim of Burma was a bestseller in 2013.

Also by Russell Miller

Uncle Bill: The Authorised Biography of Field Marshal William Slim
The Adventures of Arthur Conan Doyle
Codename Tricycle
Behind the Lines
Magnum
Ten Days in May
Nothing Less Than Victory
Bare-faced Messiah
The House of Getty
Bunny
The Resistance

TRENCHARD

Father of the Royal Air Force: The Biography

RUSSELL MILLER

WEIDENFELD & NICOLSON

A W&N PAPERBACK

First published in Great Britain in 2016
by Weidenfeld & Nicolson
This paperback edition published in 2017
by Weidenfeld & Nicolson,
an imprint of the Orion Publishing Group Ltd,
Carmelite House, 50 Victoria Embankment,
London EC4Y 0DZ

An Hachette UK company

1 3 5 7 9 10 8 6 4 2

A CIP catalogue record for this book
is available from the British Library.

ISBN 978 1 780 22665 1

Typeset by Input Data Services Ltd, Bridgwater, Somerset

Printed and bound by CPI Group (UK) Ltd, Croydon, CR0 4YY

MIX
Paper from
responsible sources
FSC® C104740
FSC
www.fsc.org

www.orionbooks.co.uk

CONTENTS

LIST OF ILLUSTRATIONS

All photographs courtesy of Hugh Trenchard, 3rd Viscount Trenchard, unless stated otherwise. Every effort has been made to acknowledge the correct copyright holders and the publishers will, if notified, correct any errors in future editions.

PREFACE

Rarely has a life been riddled with so many perplexing conundrums as that of Lord Trenchard. Overbearing, tactless, obstinate to the point of insubordination, impatient with all orders except his own, he lacked almost all the social and diplomatic skills required to aspire to high office in the military, yet he rose to the highest rank in the Royal Air Force.

His education was a disaster, not helped by his father being declared bankrupt when he was 16 – the shame of which would haunt him for the rest of his life. He was virtually unable to spell and flunked the entrance exams to both the Royal Naval College at Dartmouth and the Royal Military Academy, Sandhurst. He then failed, three times, to get into the Royal Military Academy at Woolwich. He was finally accepted into the militia – the unpromising 'back door' to a career in the army.

He served first in India, where he did little but play polo, then South Africa, where he was seriously wounded in a Boer ambush. He recovered, returned to South Africa, then spent seven years in the 'white man's graveyard' – seconded to the West African Frontier Force.

At the age of 39 he was a relatively unknown major in an infantry regiment, disillusioned with his life and with very little prospect of further promotion, having twice failed the examination for the Staff College. By the age of 45 he was a general and Chief of the Air Staff, working with Churchill to set up the world's first independent air force.

He owed his meteoric rise to his decision to learn to fly – not because of any passion for flight, but because it offered an escape from the dreary ennui of peacetime soldiering at home. It was at the Central Flying School that he acquired the nickname that would endure for his lifetime – 'Boom', from his powerful voice that could be heard across an aerodrome above the noise of the engines. In fact he turned out to be an indifferent pilot, but he was among the first to recognise that the frail contraptions of wood, wire and fabric puttering about the sky on the Western Front would change the game for ever, that warfare was entering a new and very different age. Although he occasionally expressed regret that aeroplanes had ever been invented, he became the foremost proponent of strategic bombing as a means of winning wars.

Apart from a chronic inability to remember names, of people and places, he suffered from a handicap that would have fatally blighted most military careers – he was famously inarticulate. He would often begin a speech by explaining he was 'not good with words'. It was not unusual for subordinates to gather outside Trenchard's office after a briefing to try and figure out precisely what it was he wanted them to do. Yet he was the driving force in successfully establishing the Royal Air Force as a separate service in the face of savage and persistent opposition from the Royal Navy and the army, both of whom wanted to control their own air services.

He was also able to inspire unwavering loyalty. Many of those who worked closely with him would unhesitantly claim he was not just the greatest man they had ever met, but one of the greatest leaders of the twentieth century. Yet being the combative character he was, it was inevitable he would make enemies. One acidly contended his loud voice compensated for a 'permanently vacant mind'; another asserted in a book that he was a strange, quarrelsome man 'possessed of a hypnotic ability over his protégés similar to those of the Persian magi'. Had he been alive when the book was published he would probably have laughed; anyone less like a Persian magus would be hard to imagine.

He eschewed the social trappings of a service career, avoiding the balls and parties and raucous mess nights and was lonely for much of his life. When he was 45 he confessed that he had never become close enough to anyone to address them by a nickname. His best friend was Maurice Baring, the man who was his ADC when he was commander of the Royal Flying Corps in France. Baring and Trenchard had nothing in common, physically or intellectually. Baring was short, Trenchard was tall. Baring was an aesthete, a poet and an intellectual, fluent in seven languages. Trenchard hardly read a book until he was in his twenties and boasted he could only speak two languages – English and louder English.

Trenchard's other close male friend was equally surprising. He met T.E. Lawrence – 'Lawrence of Arabia' – in 1921 and later broke all the rules by allowing him to enlist in the RAF as an aircraftsman. Trenchard was not quite old enough to be Lawrence's father, but he nevertheless came to treat him like a wayward son he was happy to indulge; Lawrence, on his part, positively hero-worshipped Trenchard. The affection and respect each felt for the other are evident in the frequent letters they exchanged over a ten year period – a uniquely warm correspondence between a man in the highest rank in a service and a man in the lowest. The original manuscript of Lawrence's book about life in the ranks of the RAF, *The Mint*, contained so many laudatory references to his hero that an embarrassed Trenchard insisted most were deleted.

His austere and domineering demeanour led people to assume he was humourless. It was true he could rarely see the point of a joke but he was not without a sense of humour. On one famous occasion, on an infrequent night out with friends, he was invited onto the stage at the Savoy Theatre by an Italian showman whose act comprised picking pockets. Trenchard was determined to protect his wallet and his watch and was unaware the Italian was unfastening his braces. As he went to leave the stage his trousers fell about his ankles. The group he was with was terrified he would explode in a fury, but he roared with laughter, along with the audience.

Until he was approaching middle age Trenchard showed no interest in the opposite sex or in domestic life. He was assumed to be an archetypal bachelor firmly wedded to the military. Then, to the surprise of everyone, possibly including Trenchard himself, he fell in love. He proposed marriage to a war widow friend and was promptly turned down. He believed initially, and incorrectly, that her refusal was connected with his father's bankruptcy – that she did not want to be associated with a family thus stigmatised. It was not in Trenchard's character to accept rejection. He pressed his suit and on the third time of asking she accepted.

Thereafter the towering, impatient figure whose voice echoed along the corridors of the Air Ministry and terrified junior officers, who was in the habit of pressing all the bells on his desk at once to summon subordinates, was transformed, at least in private, into a loving husband, devoted stepfather and father, and genial host. Colleagues who visited him at home could barely believe he was the same man.

Trenchard's friends and supporters argue that his permanent legacy was the creation of the first and the finest air force in the world, engendered with the spirit that won the Battle of Britain. His insistence on a policy of relentless aggression in the air in the First World War and his fervent advocacy of strategic bombing led many people to believe he was indifferent to casualties and the suffering of civilians. The truth was very different. In 1940 he suggested that Germany should be given 72 hours' notice of bombing raids so that women and children could be evacuated. The proposal was turned down.

Trenchard is still commemorated by name in every RAF station around the world and his statue stands in Whitehall. And yet – the final conundrum – he remains probably the least known of Britain's war heroes.

1

A MIRACLE CURE?

Anyone observing the young army officer struggling down the gang-plank from the troopship SS *Assaye*, newly arrived in Southampton from Cape Town, on a cold, wet day in early December 1900, would have had no doubt that his military career was finished. Tall, sun-tanned, with a clipped toothbrush moustache, deep-set blue eyes and a tangle of unruly black hair, he wore the uniform of a captain in the Royal Scots Fusiliers, but it was clear, as he dragged one leg behind the other, that he could only walk with difficulty even with the help of two sticks. Some might have said he was one of the luckier ones: the ship was bringing casualties home from the bloody war in South Africa, many grievously wounded. Twenty-seven-year-old Hugh Trenchard had been shot through the chest in a Boer ambush; he had been lucky to survive and be left with only one fully functioning lung, but the bullet had also damaged his spine, causing him to be semi-paralysed from the waist down.

Trenchard's parents were waiting on the quayside to greet him and were visibly shocked by his condition. Henry and Georgiana Trench-ard had not seen their son for four years and were undoubtedly pleased to have him home safe from the war, even in his wretched state, al-though he was not able to spend long with them: he had been ordered to report to a nursing home in Mayfair being run for the British Red Cross by Georgina, the Countess of Dudley.

Georgina Ward was a vivacious socialite, a noted beauty in the Vic-torian era and a favourite of the notoriously louche Prince of Wales. After the death of her husband, William Ward, the Earl of Dudley, in 1885 she had devoted herself to philanthropy and good causes, in particular the Red Cross, which was working alongside army units to care for the sick and wounded both in South Africa and at home. Like many wealthy people anxious to make a contribution to the war effort, she had turned her large house in Mayfair into a temporary convalescent home for wounded officers.

Shortly after Trenchard arrived he received a note from Lady Dudley promising him that no effort or expense would be spared to ensure his recovery. Trenchard was a notably austere young man, not well versed in the social graces, but even by his standards his reply was lacking in grace: he was not, he frostily pointed out to the lady, in the habit of accepting charity from strangers. In his defence, he was deeply depressed. His career – the only career he had ever known or wanted – was surely at an end. He had no idea what he might do next, or how he might live. His family circumstances added to his distress: his father, a solicitor, had not worked since being declared bankrupt a decade earlier and his mother, despite being increasingly crippled by arthritis, had been obliged to employ her skills as a dressmaker to make ends meet. All their property in Somerset had gone and they were reduced to living in a cheap boarding house in Portsmouth.

Accustomed to dealing with officers struggling to cope with life-changing disabilities, the Countess chose to ignore his rudeness. She called on him the next day, made no mention of his letter, pointed out that four of her six sons were in uniform serving in South Africa and said that their treatment, under similar circumstances, would be no different from his. She said she had arranged for her carriage to take him to see a specialist, Sir Richard Douglas Powell, the following morning. Trenchard, somewhat abashed, felt he had no choice but to agree.

Sir Richard Douglas Powell was Physician-Extraordinary to Queen Victoria and a consultant at the Middlesex Hospital. A tall, spare man with stern, immobile features, he was one of the most respected doctors in the country. He gave Trenchard a thorough examination and then delivered his gloomy diagnosis. He said he was more concerned about Trenchard's injured lung than he was by his partial paralysis. In order for his lung to recover, it was essential that Trenchard should go to Switzerland, where the mountain air would facilitate the healing process. Sir Richard said he could hold out little hope for him if his advice was ignored; there was a considerable risk he would remain an invalid for the rest of his days.

Trenchard left Sir Richard's consulting rooms in a sombre mood. He was perfectly happy to go to Switzerland, except that he could not possibly afford it, neither could his parents, and he was too proud to ask for help from better-off relatives. His dilemma was solved by Lady Dudley. Sir Richard had obviously informed her of his advice, because when Trenchard arrived back at the nursing home she was waiting for him with a cheque to cover all his expenses for his convalescence in Switzerland. Again, he demurred, protesting that he could not possibly accept the money, but she would have none of it. The cheque, she insisted, had been drawn on a special fund that had been set up to assist cases exactly like his. If he refused to make use of the fund, its existence would be pointless. 'She made me feel,' Trenchard would recall years later, 'that I was the one man in the whole army worth looking after. It was impossible to refuse.'[1]

Trenchard arrived in St Moritz by train in the early morning of Sunday, 30 December 1900. By the turn of the century St Moritz 6000 feet above sea level, was a major winter sports resort and health spa, very popular with the British aristocracy. Its origin as a winter resort dated back to 1864 when the legendary local hotelier, Johannes Badrutt, made a wager with four British summer visitors that if they returned in the winter and found St Moritz not to their liking, he would pay for the entire cost of their journey, there and back. If they found it agreeable, they could stay as long as they wished as his guests. The wager marked the beginning of winter tourism not just in St Moritz, but the whole of the Swiss Alps.

A primary attraction, of course, was the traditional winter sports of skiing, skating, curling and ice hockey, none of which were available to Trenchard in his crippled state – torture for someone who had always been keen on sport – but it was not long before he discovered the Cresta Run and the St Moritz Tobogganing Club, which had been founded by a group of British Army officers in 1887. The Cresta Run was first built by Johannes Badrutt's son, Caspar, owner of the Kulm Hotel, in 1884, partly as an attraction for guests and partly to prevent young gentlemen using the steep winding streets of St Moritz for sled racing and putting both themselves, and the good people of the town, at considerable risk. (Members of the St Moritz Tobogganing Club still meet for lunch every year in the Sunny Bar at the Kulm Hotel.) The Cresta is one of the fastest and most dangerous rides in the world. It is a narrow natural ice track, complicated by 12 tortuous bends, which drops more than 500 feet over its 4000 feet length. Experienced riders exit the course at speeds of over 80 miles an hour. Early competitors tackled the run on their backs, feet first, but by the time Trenchard arrived the custom was to go down lying full length on a sled, head first.

He spent some time watching the tobogganers pushing off from the top of the run and realised there was nothing to stop him having a go. He couldn't do a running start, like some did, but once on the toboggan a friendly shove would get him going and he wouldn't be handicapped by his breathing problems. Young British officers in St Moritz to recuperate from war wounds were guaranteed both sympathy and support and Trenchard had no difficulty hiring a toboggan and getting advice on how to negotiate the bends without flying off the track too often. For his first run he had no protection of any kind apart from a woollen cap – no gloves or elbow and knee guards – and no spikes on his shoes to slow himself down. Travelling faster than he had ever travelled in his life, he somehow managed to stay on the track on his first exhilarating run, although when he was taken back to the top by horse sleigh he was reprimanded for attempting the complete run without first qualifying by entering the run lower down, at the 'junction', as the rules of the club required. He was not the kind of man to be bothered by such niceties and promptly went down again.

After that he was hooked on the adrenalin rush provided by streaking down the Cresta. A keen and competitive sportsman, it was only natural that he should want to go down the run faster and faster, which is what he did by the simple technique of trusting to luck and ignoring his instructor's advice to conserve top speed for the stretches between the bends. He just went down the run flat out and hoped for the best. 'Because I was too heavy to get round the corners fast enough,' he explained, 'I had to ride for a win or a fall. The only races I did not fall in, I won.'[2]

But he 'fell' – by which he meant he hurtled off the track on his wooden toboggan – many times, usually sustaining nothing more than bruises, to both his body and his ego. He was often so shaken he had to rely on spectators to help him to his feet and friends to bring his sticks down from where he had left them at the top of the run. On one particular morning he approached the notorious Shuttlecock bend much too fast and knew immediately he wasn't going to make it. He careered up the ice banking and soared over the top of the run, parting from his toboggan on the way, bounced on the frost-hard ground a couple of times and landed in a snowdrift more than 30 feet below.

Family legend has it that it was only when he was picking himself up that he realised feeling had returned to his legs. The accident had somehow jolted his spine and enabled him not only to stand erect without sticks but to walk. He could hardly believe it as he tried out a first few tentative steps. He still had plenty of aches and pains, but there was no doubt that he could walk, if with some difficulty, and as each day passed his mobility improved – as did his lung function in the clear mountain air of the Swiss Alps.

Thereafter Captain Trenchard became an even more enthusiastic member of the St Moritz Tobogganing Club and wore with pride the 'Shuttlecock tie' presented to those members who had come to grief at that famous bend. Several weeks later, at the annual race meeting in March, he won both the Novices' and the Freshman Cups. After the presentation ceremony he was photographed in his Cresta gear (knee pads, elbow pads, gauntlets and boots), standing proudly behind both cups and holding a toboggan, balanced on its end, in his right hand.

By the time he came to leave St Moritz in the spring of 1901 he was already thinking about something that had previously been unthinkable – how quickly he could convince the powers that be that he was fit to return to his regiment and resume his military career.

2

A CHILDHOOD MARRED BY MISFORTUNE

The *Dictionary of National Biography* asserts that Hugh Montague Trenchard came into the world in Taunton, Somerset, at Windsor Lodge, a handsome Grade II listed Victorian Gothic mansion recognised as one of the finest houses in the city. The *DNB* is wrong. Windsor Lodge is number 18 Haines Hill, whereas Hugh's parents, Henry Trenchard and his young wife, Georgiana, occupied a much more modest property further down the road at 6 Haines Hill and it was there that Hugh, their third child, was born on Monday, 3 February 1873, a day on which the *Western Daily Press* reported that a furious gale 'exceeding in severity anything of the kind known for many years' raged across the West Country.

Although Trenchards claimed descent from Raoul de Trenchant, a knight who fought alongside William the Conqueror at the Battle of Hastings, and Trenchards had been feudal landowners on the Isle of Wight and in Hampshire and Dorset for more than seven centuries, the family was unremarkably and irredeemably entrenched in the impoverished gentry by the time Hugh arrived, with his father, grandfather and great-grandfather all having to work for a living, practising as respectable country solicitors in Taunton.

The name Trenchard first makes an appearance in English history with one Paganus Trenchard, who lived at Hord Hall near Lymington in Hampshire and was appointed 'collector of Danegeld' for Henry I on the Isle of Wight in 1135. Little is known about Paganus' successors until 1318 when one of them, a Sir Henry Trenchard, was banished and declared an 'outlaw' for taking part in the rebellion of barons against Edward II, although he somehow managed to stay on at Hord Hall until the sentence was revoked ten years later.

The family occupied Hord Hall for 300 years until 1447 when

another Henry Trenchard made an extremely propitious marriage to the daughter of a very wealthy man and acquired, as part of her dowry, Wolfeton House, a large manor house surrounded by water meadows near Dorchester, which then became the Trenchard family seat for another 400 years. The family fell on hard times in the early nineteenth century and was forced to give up Wolfeton, but it remains standing and is today regarded as one of the most important Tudor mansions in the country, with an interior featuring magnificent Elizabethan and Jacobean oak panelling and ornate plasterwork commissioned by various Trenchards.

In 1483 Sir John Trenchard was unwisely implicated in the Duke of Buckingham's failed rebellion against Richard III. The Duke was tried for treason and beheaded; Sir John escaped with his life but his lands, which by then spread across much of the south of England and included Wolfeton House, were confiscated. When Henry VII seized the throne two years later after defeating Richard III at the battle of Bosworth, Sir John's property, and the family reputation, were restored.

In 1498 John's son Thomas, then High Sheriff of Dorset, was ordered to summon all the troops he could muster and rush to Weymouth, where it had been reported that an armada of ships had appeared offshore and was possibly preparing to invade. In fact the fleet had been assembled by Philip, the Archduke of Austria, and had sailed from the Low Countries bound for Spain, where he intended to claim his inheritance as King of Castile.

Unfortunately the ships ran into a storm and became dispersed; the galleon carrying Philip and his wife, Joanna, the daughter of King Ferdinand of Aragon, was forced to seek shelter in Weymouth. When Sir Thomas arrived and discovered the identity of the unexpected visitors, he invited them to stay at Wolfeton.

Philip and Joanna remained at Wolfeton for two weeks. Neither could speak English and Sir Thomas knew no Spanish, but he solved the problem by calling on the services of a cousin, John Russell, to act as an interpreter. Russell had recently returned from Spain after a business venture had failed and was fluent in the language. After leaving Wolfeton the couple travelled with Russell to Windsor Castle, where they were entertained ostensibly as guests of the King, but in reality held hostage while Henry VII extracted their agreement to a number of treaties and trade agreements before he would consent to their departure. Before they left, they asked Sir Thomas how they could repay his 'attention and civility'. Perhaps, they suggested, they could ask a favour from the King on his behalf? Sir Thomas is said to have replied that he 'thanked God he was quite independent and wanted for nothing' but that he would be greatly obliged if they could ask for something for his young relative Russell, 'who wants for everything, having lately been unfortunate as a Spanish merchant'.[1] Philip had a word with the King and secured for Russell a lowly position in the Royal household. John Russell did well at court – he became a great favourite of Henry VIII, acquired Woburn Abbey after the dissolution of the monasteries and was created Earl of Bedford, a title later elevated to a dukedom.

The radical bent established by Sir John Trenchard's support of the rebellion against Richard III was continued by his descendants. In 1683 another Sir John Trenchard attempted to raise a body of men in Taunton as part of the Rye House Plot to assassinate Charles II; he failed and was obliged to flee the country, to Holland, where he then joined the conspirators led by the Duke of Monmouth, who were planning to overthrow James II. The Monmouth Rebellion ended after the Battle of Sedgemoor in August 1685. Amazingly Sir John escaped being put on trial at the 'Bloody Assizes', where some 300 rebels were sentenced to death, was granted a 'special pardon' by James II in 1687 and served as Secretary of State from 1692 until his death in 1695.

Lord Chief Justice George Jeffreys, who presided over the 'Bloody Assizes' and subsequently became notorious as 'the hanging judge', was invited to dinner at Wolfeton House – a visit that gave rise to a story that Wolfeton had a ghost unique in the annals of haunting inasmuch as it made an appearance before the demise of its bodily counterpart. No sooner had the judge sat down at the dinner table than he turned deathly pale, issued a strangulated cry, jumped up from his chair, swept out of the room, leapt into his carriage and ordered the coachman to make off in haste. Later he claimed he had clearly seen the ghost of Lady Trenchard, standing behind her chair, with her throat cut. This was while Lady Trenchard was still occupying the chair. Before Jeffreys' carriage reached Dorchester a messenger on horseback overtook it with the news that Lady Trenchard had just committed suicide.

Prominent among the family's black sheep was one George Trenchard, a spendthrift who had a 'great partiality for one of his domestics', whom he later gallantly married after she gave birth to a daughter. Some reports assert that Jack Sheppard, the infamous London cat burglar who escaped from prison four times and became a working-class hero before being hanged at Tyburn in 1724 at the age of 22, was a Trenchard, the illegitimate offspring of a wayward daughter of the household who eloped with Sheppard's father, a carpenter.

By the time Hugh Trenchard was born, the family had relinquished ownership of Wolfeton House. After producing a long line of landowners, rebels, members of Parliament, soldiers, lawyers and clergymen, the Trenchards had settled for genteel respectability. Hugh's grandfather, Henry Charles Trenchard, was a solicitor in Taunton (like his father before him) and his only son, Henry Montague Trenchard, was working for him as an articled clerk. Henry Charles was said to be 'extravagant and prone to risk speculation'[2] and at one time was in serious financial difficulties when his managing clerk misappropriated clients' funds, for which Henry was legally responsible. He was obliged to persuade his wife, Mary, to release funds from her marriage settlement to save him.

It appears that Henry Montague, who was born in 1839 and was known as Montague within the family, was keen to follow in the legal footsteps of his father, but he was a sickly young man and after two years working as an articled clerk the family doctor recommended that he should find an occupation which involved a more active lifestyle.

The army was the obvious choice and in 1859 his father purchased a commission for him as an ensign in the 51st Foot. The price was £450, around £35,000 at today's values.

Henry Montague's military career was undistinguished. He served most of his time in India, in a climate that was unlikely to be conducive to his good health, waited four years to be able to purchase promotion to lieutenant and another six years to become a captain, again by purchase. By then he was back home, 30 years old, and engaged to Georgiana Louisa Catherine Tower Skene, the 20-year-old daughter of a captain in the Royal Navy who had moved with her family to Taunton from Scotland after her father retired. Her mother was a Lumsden of Aberdeenshire, a well-known military family which produced two brothers who both rose to the rank of general – both were also knighted and both served in India and Afghanistan with great distinction.

Henry and Georgiana married at St Cuthbert's Church, Wells, in June 1869.

Georgiana became pregnant almost immediately and in January 1870 Henry retired from the army, selling his commission for £1800, just one year before the purchase and sale of army commissions was abolished by Royal warrant. He used the money to buy their marital home at 6 Haines Hill, Taunton (and settle some debts), and resumed his position as a humble articled clerk in his father's legal practice. In April, Georgiana gave birth to a daughter, Catherine, the first of her six children. A son, Alexander, followed within a year and Hugh arrived within two years of his older brother. (Henry possibly suffered some embarrassment about still being an articled clerk in his mid-thirties: on Hugh's birth certificate he described his occupation as 'Late Captain, 51st Foot'.) After Hugh, his mother had a brief respite from childbearing until twins, a boy and a girl, arrived in 1876. A daughter, Dorothy, completed the family two years later, by which time Henry was at last qualified as a solicitor in his home town and was in partnership with a friend, Edgar Watson, with offices at Hammett Street, where many of Taunton's solicitors were based. (In 1874, having passed all the necessary legal examinations, his father had had to employ a QC to apply to the Court of the Queen's Bench to have the two years Henry had spent as an articled clerk before joining the army counted towards the five required to qualify. One judge entertained 'considerable doubt' on the matter, taking the view that entering the army was tantamount to cancelling the articles of clerkship; fortunately for Henry the other two judges disagreed and the application was approved.)

In 1875 Henry moved his family from Haines Hill to Courtlands, a large country house at Norton Fitzwarren, a hamlet three miles from Taunton, perhaps unwisely borrowing the majority of the £3200 purchase price. Courtlands had a kitchen garden enclosed by high brick walls with espaliered peach trees and a dry pond which young Hugh recalled was alive with lizards during the summer. A French governess, Mademoiselle Hongardy, was employed to look after the children and the family enjoyed a very comfortable lifestyle, with no less than seven staff living in the servants' quarters and annual trips to London for 'the season', where Henry and Georgiana had the use of a large house in Roland Gardens, South Kensington. In many ways they were a golden couple: Henry was tall, handsome and had a beautiful singing voice; Georgiana was an accomplished hostess, hopelessly extravagant and a brilliant conversationalist, although she would suffer from chronic ill health in later years. Hugh would remember parties at which his father strolled from room to room with a decanter of port in his hand.

At Courtlands Mademoiselle Hongardy struggled mightily to educate the older children, none of whom was in the least interested in being educated. For the boys the two days a week they were supposed to spend conversing in French or German were nothing but a distraction from what they really wanted to do – riding, shooting rabbits, birds'-nesting, collecting butterflies – anything, in fact, rather than lessons with the despairing Mademoiselle. Hugh was a tall, gangly boy with a shock of black hair and his father's startlingly blue eyes. His father was a first-class shot and expert horseman and taught all his boys to ride and shoot at an early age. Hugh could ride almost as soon as he could walk and his father bought him a small .22 rifle for his eighth birthday. He quickly became, like his father, an excellent shot and never forgot bagging his first hare on his uncle's estate in Somerset. His mother was much more of a disciplinarian than his easy-going father and she was unamused when he commandeered her wickerwork crinoline cage and covered it with muslin as a home for his pet Java sparrows; he never did it again. His principal talent as a boy was in organising complicated games for his siblings which often turned into 'tournaments' that would sometimes last for weeks. Hugh wanted to be the best at everything he did so long as it was what he wanted to do – lessons were rigorously excluded as of no interest.

At the age of ten Hugh was sent as a boarder to Allen's Preparatory School near the small market town of Botley in Hampshire. Unsurprisingly, he failed to thrive academically; his teachers reported to his parents that Hugh was clever, but lazy. After only a year in Botley Hugh was moved to Hammond's, a crammer near Dover named after its principal, a thin-lipped individual with a sallow complexion who could have stepped out of Dickens. Hammond's prepared students for the examinations to enter the Britannia Royal Naval College at

Dartmouth, Georgiana and Henry having decided that Hugh should pursue a career in the footsteps of his maternal grandfather. It was not to be. While Hammond's managed to get him through some subjects he failed, disastrously, when it came to dictation. Hugh's spelling was not just lamentable, it was downright eccentric. He spelled 'why', for example, as 'yi', and 'misdemeanour' as 'Mister Mena' (this despite the fact that, in context, it must obviously have been wrong). He no doubt gave the examiners much wry amusement, but at the same time the door to a career as a Royal Navy officer was slammed firmly shut.

It is possible that young Hugh suffered from dyslexia, a condition that was first identified in 1881 but knowledge of which had certainly not filtered into the general realm of academia, or at least into the kind of third-rate crammers to which he was sent. Thus his teachers tended to consider him either lazy or stupid, or both. His hopeless spelling, his lack of interest in any subjects that involved reading and writing (he was only good at maths), his dreadful handwriting (which would bedevil him for the rest of his life), would all indicate that he was dyslexic, but without diagnosis no one could help him. It would be 15 years before the *British Medical Journal* published a seminal article entitled 'Congenital Word Blindness', but by then Hugh had completed what passed as his education and was a subaltern serving in India, where academic prowess mattered little. Although he would have been unable to put a name to it, Hugh himself clearly recognised he had a problem because later in life, whenever he was called upon to address troops or deliver a speech, he would often preface his remarks by explaining he was 'not good at words'.

Sent home to Courtlands while his parents decided what to do with him, he found the atmosphere subtly changed. His father, normally good-natured and cheerful, was strangely distracted and irritable, his mother was already beginning to suffer from the arthritis that would plague her in later life and his ten-year-old sister, Mary, one of the twins, was very ill. Mary died of diphtheria while Hugh was still at home; he had adored her and cried bitterly as her flower-bedecked coffin was lowered into the ground at the churchyard in Norton Fitzwarren. (Mary's twin brother, Ralph, would die of dysentery during the Boer War.)

After Mary's funeral Hugh was told that his future now lay in the army – he would be joining his older brother, Alex, at Hill Lands school in Wargrave, a village on the Thames in Berkshire. Hill Lands was another crammer set up to get young men the educational qualifications required for a commission in the army. Hugh hated the place from the outset and took an instant dislike to the principal, the Reverend Albert Pritchard, who he decided was an outrageous snob. The only advantage of Hill Lands, as far as he was concerned, was that it was just a mile from the home of some wealthy cousins, the Askews, and he spent most of his time there, often cutting lessons. 'I fear I did no work at all at Pritchard's,' he recalled, 'and I know one term I never even went in there for an hour.'[3]

Hill Lands was divided into three houses: Sandhurst, for the brightest boys with a chance of making it to the Royal Military Academy at Sandhurst; Woolwich, for those destined for the RMA at Woolwich, which trained officers for the Royal Artillery and the Royal Engineers; and Militia House, for those boys too lazy or stupid to get into Sandhurst or Woolwich and whose only hope of acquiring a commission was through the 'back door' offered by Britain's part-time, voluntary reserve army. Hugh was first placed in Woolwich House in the hope that he might knuckle down to his studies, but he did not; he sat the Woolwich entrance examination three times and failed in every subject, except mathematics. So it was he was relegated to Militia House, where he was required to become a militia cadet. He was photographed, at the age of 14, in his uniform – a tall boy staring unsmilingly at the camera, his pillbox hat at a jaunty angle, carrying white gloves and a cane.

Hugh's only happy memory of Hill Lands was learning to play rugby, which he picked up very quickly – he earned a place in the first XV and was soon made captain. He had boundless energy and enthusiasm, was very keen on all sports and loved playing practical jokes. The gardens of Hill Lands bordered the Thames and he once gathered up all the chamber pots, put a lighted candle in each and floated them down the river. During regattas he and his friends would take out a rowing boat and manipulate a capsize near a boat liberally stocked with food and drink so they could be hauled aboard and plied with brandy and champagne to help them recover. That worked well until one afternoon when they 'capsized' near their first victim and were recognised – this time they were left to sink or swim.

The mild-mannered Pritchard was an inevitable target but Hugh realised he had perhaps gone too far when he helped organise the Reverend's fictitious 'wedding' to an equally fictitious bride. Invitations were printed and sent out to all the neighbours and the local bigwigs. The students thought it was an enormous jape, but when Pritchard, who was a confirmed bachelor, inevitably got to hear about it he called the whole school together and delivered a sermon castigating the unknown culprits. He obviously suspected that Hugh was involved, because he took him to one side afterwards and upbraided him for what he described as a 'most ungentlemanly act'. Hugh had the grace to feel guilty.

On his visits home he could not but be aware of the change in his father, who was becoming more and more withdrawn, suddenly old beyond his years. It was, nevertheless, still a shock when, not long after his sixteenth birthday, Hugh received a letter at school from his mother asking him to return home immediately. 'I am sorry to have to tell you,' she wrote, 'that your father is about to be made bankrupt.' By the time Alex and Hugh got back to Courtlands they found the house had been stripped bare and was already on the market. Everything had been sold, even their mother's jewellery. Hugh was distraught to discover that his rifle had also gone, along with his precious album of butterflies, which he had been collecting since he was five years old.

The family's shame and humiliation were complete when the local newspapers reported in detail on his father's public examination before the Registrar at Taunton Guildhall, in July 1889, during which Henry was referred to throughout as 'the bankrupt' and the full shocking extent of his debts was revealed – £11,251 13s 8d, the equivalent to about £1 million today. Under the headline 'Failure of a Taunton Solicitor' the *Western Daily Press* reported that Henry had so many creditors 'there was a large attendance of solicitors representing various interests' at the first hearing. The Official Receiver, the report continued, 'questioned the bankrupt at great length'. Henry denied he had been extravagant in his living and on the advice of his own solicitor refused to answer questions about the whereabouts of a £9000 trust fund that had been settled on him at the time of his marriage, despite a warning from the Registrar that bankrupts were required to answer every question, regardless of whether or not answers might incriminate them. At a subsequent hearing he was forced to admit that the whole of the trust fund was 'exhausted'.

Hugh was greatly affected by his father's bankruptcy, as was his 18-year-old sister, Catherine, who had been due to 'come out' as a debutante that year. All the arrangements had to be cancelled and instead of being 'introduced' to society, Catherine was obliged to start training as a nurse (she eventually settled in South Africa). Hugh never forgot seeing his father snubbed in the streets of Taunton by former friends who would once have greatly prized an invitation to tea or dinner at Courtlands. A neighbour, passing Henry and his son in a carriage, ostentatiously looked the other way when Henry politely raised his hat in greeting.

For a young man who had been proud of his family's illustrious history, his father's downfall was particularly hard to bear. To what extent all this ignominy shaped Hugh's character is unknowable – he certainly grew into an unusually resilient and determined individual – but there was no question he was damaged. When, years later in middle age, he proposed marriage for the first time in his life to a woman friend and was turned down, he immediately assumed it was because she did not want to be associated with someone whose father had been a bankrupt.[4]

As far as Hugh was concerned the one positive outcome of what had happened might have been his escape from Hill Lands, but he was denied even that. The saintly Reverend Pritchard wrote to offer to continue their education at reduced terms. His mother's wealthy cousin, Irwin Cox, owner of *The Field* magazine, stepped in to pay the Reverend's reduced fees and so Hugh and Alex returned reluctantly to school.

Alex's tenure was brief. A rebellious young man, he liked to experiment with explosives and blew up the ornamental fountain in front of the school's main building as a rather foolish prank, after which Pritchard felt he had no alternative but to expel him. Hugh was not particularly sorry to see his older brother leave: they had few mutual friends and had become somewhat estranged since the bankruptcy as Hugh could not understand why Alex seemed entirely unconcerned by their father's disgrace. (When he was 19 Alex followed his sister to the Cape, where he married and raised a large family. Hugh met him once during the Boer War, but only for a day, and never saw him again.)

Despite all Pritchard's efforts, Hugh made no progress with his studies. Perhaps adding to his difficulties were his dismay and embarrassment that he owed his education to the charity of relatives. He twice sat the examination for militia candidates to be granted a permanent commission in the regular army but, to his parents' despair, failed both times in all subjects except, once again, mathematics. Fortunately, the militia itself had much lower entrance standards and he was eventually accepted as a probationary subaltern, at the age of 18, with the Forfar and Kincardine Artillery, a militia regiment based at Montrose in Scotland.

During his preliminary training he managed to make an unfavourable impression on the GOC Scottish Command.

My first official meeting of the General was on parade at Montrose shortly after joining. He had come to inspect us. In those days my hair grew very long and we wore pillbox hats on the sides of our heads. I was very tall and the General was very short and when he looked at me he said 'Oh you don't wear your cap properly' and I had to bend my head down so that he could put my pillbox hat further back on my head. When I stood up and he looked at me and saw my hair was below it, he grunted and said 'That won't do'.[5]

Probationary subaltern Trenchard very soon got a haircut.

Notwithstanding this inauspicious start, Hugh enjoyed his time in the militia immensely possibly because, as he recalled, 'I did no work'. He found it intensely tedious having to endlessly repeat, parrot fashion, the ritual of loading a 32-pound muzzle-loading artillery piece, but he also had plenty of spare time and hired a tandem carriage which he liked to drive around the bay at Montrose in the summer after mess. He was presumably still being supported by relatives, because his parents had by then moved into a very small house at 7 Linden Grove, Taunton, and his mother, perhaps too proud to accept the charity of relatives, was working as a dressmaker to make ends meet. In the 1891 census Henry is still listed as a solicitor, although his practice had collapsed shortly before he was declared bankrupt two years earlier.

Hugh's propensity for practical jokes earned him another rebuke when, in the dead of night, he let down the tent of a deeply unpopular major who had been making their lives difficult. When the major emerged, sleepily, from his collapsing tent, Hugh threw a jug of cold water over him. 'I was hauled out in front of the Colonel,' he recalled, 'who was very kind to me but clearly told me off.'[6] At the regiment's annual training camp, on the Isle of Wight, a confusion with the artillery equipment led to their 10-inch guns being trained on the tug towing their target in the Solent, rather than the target itself. Thankfully their aim was not sufficiently accurate to sink the tug. Then the War Office forgot to provide transport to move the regiment back to Scotland, so they were able to stay on the island and enjoy the Cowes Week regatta.

It was around this time that Hugh's second cousin, Irwin Cox, began to play a more important part in his life. Cox was a Cambridge-educated barrister, writer and politician who would be Conservative MP for Harrow from 1899 to 1906. He and his wife lived at Moat Mount, a 270-acre estate at Mill Hill, which he had inherited from his wealthy father, and where he could indulge his passion for hunting, shooting and fishing. As well as owning *The Field* magazine, Cox edited the annual *Angler's Diary* and was a prolific writer about field sports under the pen name 'I.E.B.C'. The Coxes had no children and looked upon Hugh as a kind of surrogate son. He was frequently invited to Moat Mount for shooting parties. More importantly, Cox encouraged Hugh to make use of his very extensive library and it was at Moat Mount that Hugh learned, really for the first time, the simple joy of reading for pleasure, albeit slowly and with some difficulty.

Hugh recorded that he had 'a great time' at the regiment's second annual camp at Fort Cumberland on Hayling Island, near Portsmouth. 'We were inspected by the Duke of Connaught. He noticed at the sports in the afternoon that all our men were smoking cigars. He asked about it and the colonel said that all our men were very well-to-do people from Dundee, whereas really the night before they had looted a public house and taken all the cigars.'[7]

In March 1893 Hugh made a third forlorn attempt to pass the exam that would enable him to obtain a commission in the regular army. He had little optimism he would succeed, having long concluded that he was destined to fail every exam he sat. He was out hunting with the Askews that summer when a servant brought him an official-looking letter. It contained extraordinary news. Fifty-six of the 225 militia subalterns who had sat the exam had failed – but H. Trenchard

was not among them. He had scraped through with 1673 marks out of
a possible 2400 – just 23 more than the minimum needed for a pass.

On 8 September 1893, Hugh Montague Trenchard was gazetted as
a second lieutenant in the Royal Scots Fusiliers and posted to the Second Battalion, then stationed in India. Few young officers could claim
a more inauspicious start to a military career.

3

POLO AND BOERS

Newly commissioned Second Lieutenant Trenchard sailed for India in October, 1893, on board the SS *Bothnia*, an elderly Cunard liner, outbound from Portsmouth. His uniform and equipment had all been paid for by generous relatives, one of whom had also given him an ancient fowling piece. (He had been advised by another, obviously less sympathetic, relative not to bother to take a gun with him as he would 'never be able to afford the cartridges'.)

The voyage, via the Suez Canal and across the Arabian Sea, was apparently uneventful, or at least did not merit a mention in his autobiographical notes. Karachi, where the SS *Bothnia* berthed, was a bustling port city with paved streets, a network of trams and horse-drawn trolleys, innumerable mosques and temples and a railway connecting it to other major cities in India. When he had disembarked with all his luggage, Trenchard found a porter and made his way through the teeming streets to the railway station, reeling with the culture shock of a young European experiencing India – the sights, the smells, the clamorous confusion – for the first time. With some difficulty he finally found the correct train for the long, hot journey – some 600-plus miles – across the Thar desert to the ancient city of Sialkot, in the Punjab, where the 2nd Battalion, Royal Scots Fusiliers, had been based since the previous year. He finally arrived at four o'clock in the morning exhausted and feeling, he admitted, 'very frightened'.

'I remember I drove from the station in what was called a *tikka gharri*, which was a sort of open Victoria, with a pair of very scraggy horses with sores all over them,' he wrote. 'I noticed that the cushions, none too clean, were covered with faded tartan from the trews worn by the regiment.'[1] At the dusty cantonment he reported for duty to the adjutant and was assigned a bungalow to share with two other young subalterns like himself.

Had Trenchard read Kipling's *Barrack Room Tales* he would have had a good idea of what lay in store for him in Sialkot. After the Mutiny had been crushed in 1858, India settled down to a period of relative calm. Victoria was officially proclaimed 'Empress of India' in 1877 and the only armed opposition to British rule came from the rebellious tribes on the North West Frontier. The Indian nationalist movement would not begin to stir until the turn of the century and so the greatest challenge for young officers was to survive the intense heat in the summer and the tedium of inactivity, while attempting to keep underpaid and unappreciated troops up to scratch to answer rare calls to action. Boredom was inescapable. The official history of the regiment covering Trenchard's years in India only managed to report that it was 'clear from the inspection reports that no battalion in India during these years had reached a higher degree of excellence, especially in signalling, in which it held first place until 1896'.[2]

Not long after his arrival he learned he would soon have to face what would be, for him, a torture. It was a tradition in the regiment that newly arrived subalterns were expected to make a lengthy speech, extolling the glorious history of the Royal Scots Fusiliers, on their first guest night in the mess. Naturally taciturn and reserved, it was more than he could manage. On the dreaded night he got reluctantly to his feet and could say no more than how proud he was to join the regiment and then, after a long pause, he added 'I hope one day I shall live to command it.' He sat down to be greeted with jeers, hoots of incredulous laughter and shouts of 'Thank goodness I shan't be in it then.' His fellow officers all thought it was a tremendous joke, but it was one which the object of their derision might have found it hard to share.

Thereafter Trenchard found it difficult to fit in. He lacked the social graces expected of a young officer, avoided parties, still lived with the shame of his father's bankruptcy and spent much of his spare time alone in his room, reading, in part because he simply could not afford to socialise. The Royal Scots Fusiliers was not a rich man's regiment, like the Guards or the cavalry; nevertheless it was still expected that the officers would have private means and Trenchard did not. He was obliged to live on his pay and it was not easy. Messing had to be paid for and he would occasionally go without lunch to save money; in the mess he drank nothing but water, except for an obligatory glass of port on guest nights.

He was unkindly nicknamed 'The Camel', partly because of his small head and long neck and partly because of his inclination to grunt in answer to a question. Inarticulate, prickly, and a man of notoriously few words, he was notably lacking in tact. If he had nothing to say he would say nothing. But if he thought something, or someone, was wrong he was liable to make his views clear in the bluntest possible terms regardless of the consequences. His gruff disinclination to keep his thoughts to himself often put him at risk of an official reprimand, at the very least.

Even when he won the Viceroy's Gold Medal in the All-India Rifle Shooting Championship he ended up with a rebuke for conduct unbecoming a gentleman. The competition, held annually at Meerut, was open to all officers in the British and Indian Armies. Trenchard knew he was a good shot and thought entering might help his career. In the weeks before the competition he carried his rifle with him everywhere, even to meals, in order, he would explain later, that it 'became a part of me'. He won the Gold Medal with what, at that time, was a record score, but was warned before the presentation that he would be given an empty box because the medal had not yet been engraved with the image of the new Viceroy, Lord Elgin, as he had only recently taken office. Trenchard was not without an impish sense of humour and at the presentation he could not resist opening the box and pretending to be surprised there was no medal inside. He thought it was a harmless prank, but his commanding officer was unamused, considering his behaviour to be 'ungentlemanly'.

He did not continue with competitive shooting. He was put out when he discovered that he was viewed by some of his brother officers as a 'pot hunter', only interested in trophies. It was quite unfair, but he was not of a mind to correct the impression. In any case, he had become disillusioned with what he considered to be an unhealthily combative aura around the sport, with much rumour-mongering and whispering. When he was asked to sign a letter alleging that a particular officer had not shot fairly he became 'disgusted with the whole business' and gave it up.

He may not have been motivated entirely by disillusionment since he had, by then, chanced upon an entirely new passion: polo. Having been loaned a pony by a senior officer on condition he looked after it, Trenchard became obsessed with the idea of setting up a battalion polo team. Polo was considered at the time to be pretty much the exclusive preserve of the cavalry and the commanding officer was deeply unenthusiastic when Trenchard first raised the prospect. The CO did not positively forbid it, but he pointed out that the regiment had no tradition of polo playing, few of the officers owned ponies, there were no stables, there was no suitable ground and no regimental funds were available.

The obstacles were certainly daunting and would have deterred anyone less single-minded. Exhibiting the dogged determination that was very much a part of his character, Trenchard first calculated the precise cost of feeding and grooming a polo pony and then set about convincing those officers with private means (most of them) not only that they could afford it, but they would get great enjoyment from the sport. Major R.K. Walsh was one of the officers who succumbed to his entreaties. Walsh did not even enjoy riding, but nevertheless found himself buying a pony. 'He asked for a show of willingness,' Walsh recalled. 'The actual work we left to him. It was quite extraordinary. Within six weeks we had the equipment, the ground and our own communal stable of good ponies which Trenchard purchased locally. We learnt by trial and error, our form improved with practice, and in six months we had a team which could hold its own against all-comers.'[3] Within three years every officer in the battalion, with the exception of the quartermaster, was playing polo.

An astute judge of horseflesh, Trenchard financed his obsession by buying and selling ponies, sometimes using the services of native moneylenders to raise funds to purchase a likely-looking mount. He was so successful he claimed his polo 'paid for itself'. (By the time he left India he owned a string of no less than nine polo ponies.) It rather appeared his brother officers might have tired of his enthusiasm since he was banned from mentioning the game in the mess, on pain of a fine. 'I played polo for five years on end and on every opportunity,' he said. 'I thought of nothing but polo.'[4] (He certainly did not think much about soldiering, since in his autobiographical notes there is not a single mention of parades, or exercises, or expeditions.)

It was on the polo field that Trenchard first encountered a young officer in the 4th Hussars by the name of Winston Churchill.

Considered to be one of the best polo players in his regiment, Churchill was captain of a team playing the Royal Scots Fusiliers, led by Trenchard. The two men clashed frequently on the field and at one point Churchill was trying to ride Trenchard off the ball using two hands on the reins, instead of one, and resting his stick across his pony's neck.

'Play to the rules,' Trenchard shouted angrily, 'and take that stick out of my eye.'

'If you have a complaint,' Churchill retorted, 'complain to the umpire.'

Trenchard preferred instant justice – he swung his stick up sharply, knocked Churchill's stick out of his hand, sent it soaring through the air and galloped off. In the mess after the match, when tempers had cooled, they laughed about the incident.

All officers in the Battalion were allowed 90 days' annual leave and most of them, Trenchard included, chose to head north to Kashmir, where the climate was less oppressive than the suffocating heat on the plains of the Punjab. He never forgot setting off from Sialkot in a dog cart up the winding road through the hills to Srinagar, known for its gardens, lakes and houseboats as the 'Venice of the East'. On the way he camped overnight in meadows fragrant with wild flowers, waking at dawn to birdsong. The ponies got progressively friskier the higher they climbed into the hills.

In those golden days of the Raj, white visitors to Srinagar enjoyed a vibrant social life. There were picnics, race meetings, shooting parties, dinners, dances, gymkhanas, hunting with hounds for jackal and, of course, polo. 'I played polo most of the time and raced, but I also found time to go out shooting several times in the hills for black bear and red bear and got two black and one red. I also shot Himalayan mountain snipe at 13,000 feet which, when I sent to *The Field* about them, they told me were very rare birds.'[5]

Trenchard was not a great socialiser – he did not dance – but his organisational skills were widely recognised and he found himself much in demand as an arranger of events, so much so that anxious hostesses would often consult him before deciding the date of a party to ensure it did not clash with another function. He organised tournaments and promoted a spirit of competition so successfully among the ladies that on more than one occasion, he recalled, 'opponents on the tennis courts brandished their racquets in each other's faces and I was glad the net separated them'. His talents in this direction earned him another, rather condescending, nickname – 'the man from Cook's'.[6] It did not bother him in the slightest.

Money remained a serious problem and he often sold any cups or trophies that he won at race meetings in order to help his finances. By scrimping and saving he was occasionally able to send money home to help his impoverished parents, who were never far from his thoughts. He also helped raise funds for a local school run by the Reverend Cecil Tyndale-Biscoe, a Cambridge-educated missionary whom he described as 'one of the finest men I ever met'. Tyndale-Biscoe, who had coxed the winning Cambridge crew in the 1884 boat race, was ordained as a Church of England priest after graduation and sent to Kashmir by the Church Missionary Society. Trenchard greatly admired his school – which placed more emphasis on sport and community activities than academic studies – and helped by arranging a race meeting he called the 'Ecclesiastical Stakes', donating all the entry fees to the mission.

Although he tended to avoid dinner parties if he could, when the wife of an officer in an outlying hill station told him that her maiden name was Trenchard and invited him to dinner he felt he could not refuse. It was a mistake. The hostess indicated she would be interested to compare notes to see how closely they were related and over sherry she revealed that her affection for the name was such that she had christened her son Trenchard. A small boy was then ushered into the room and introduced to his namesake, to Trenchard's intense irritation and embarrassment. After the plates had been cleared away at the end of the meal she produced her family tree and began to explain, in great detail, who was who.

Trenchard could finally stand it no longer. 'Madam,' he said, interrupting her in full flow, 'I must tell you this before I go. There are only two branches of the family that concern us. There's the main one to which I belong and there's a second which I've always understood was founded about two hundred years ago by the illegitimate son of an umbrella manufacturer in Manchester.'

With that he took his leave, leaving his hostess still sitting in shocked silence at the table. Next day her outraged husband wrote to Trenchard's commanding officer in Sialkot accusing Trenchard of deliberately insulting his wife. Trenchard was unrepentant and claimed the woman was insufferable, but was again informally reprimanded for ungentlemanly behaviour.

In the autumn of 1896 the 2nd Battalion was due to be sent home to England after 17 years' foreign service. It was relieved by the 1st Battalion, which was so short of officers that volunteers were called for from the 2nd Battalion to transfer. Trenchard, by then promoted to lieutenant, was enjoying his time in India, particularly the polo, and was perfectly happy to stay on. He was less happy when, a few weeks later, his new commanding officer, Lieutenant Colonel J.H. Spurgin, called him into his office and told him he must stop buying ponies because he was spending too much money and setting a bad example to the other subalterns. Spurgin held the view that polo was an indulgence which should only be enjoyed by the cavalry.

Trenchard was furious. He could have perhaps understood that if he had been an officer with substantial private means he might be setting a bad example to less wealthy young officers, but he was not. What he did next was symptomatic of his fierce independence and disdain for authority unfairly wielded – he considered it quite wrong for his commanding officer to tell him how he should spend his own money. Not only did he not stop buying ponies, but the next one he bought, a fine black Arab called 'Australia', was owned by the man who had told him not to buy any more – Colonel Sturgin. It cost him 1000 rupees, which he could ill afford, and to hide his involvement he got a friend in the 11th Hussars to act as middle man and pose as the purchaser. That same afternoon he played polo on 'Australia', unconcerned that Sturgin was among the spectators. After the match Sturgin asked him why he had borrowed 'Australia' from the officer to whom he had sold it that morning. Trenchard immediately owned up that he was the real purchaser, expecting a dressing down. It did not happen. 'The colonel looked at me for a moment,' he reported, 'but did not offer to give back the cheque and I heard no more.'[7]

When the 1st Battalion had settled in, Trenchard was one of seven officers who volunteered to accompany a detachment of two companies to Amritsar, the spiritual centre of the Sikh religion and the site of the famous Golden Temple.[8] There he stayed for 18 months 'playing polo as usual and shooting snipe by the thousand'. In twelve months he said he used 10,000 cartridges shooting the snipe that swarmed in the swamps near Amritsar in winter and spring. He also unashamedly admitted that he 'faked the draw' in a polo tournament so that the two Amritsar companies faced the two companies from the battalion still at Sialkot 'in order to show them that we were much superior to them' – which they did, by winning the tournament.

In the summer of 1897 he had an accident while competing in a gymkhana. He was riding a very small pony when his foot caught the top rail of a jump and unseated him. The fall left him with a hernia and the battalion medical officer strongly recommended that he should return to Britain for an operation. Trenchard hated being ill – and particularly hated other people being ill – but felt he had no option but to apply for sick leave. He had to sell a couple of ponies to pay for the trip and saved money by securing a passage on a cargo ship of the Hall Line from Bombay.

It would prove to be a testing voyage. When he boarded the ship in Bombay, he discovered that the cargo was old animal bones, which filled every corner of the vessel with a nauseating stench that turned his stomach. There were only two other passengers, whom he did his best to avoid, and he spent as much time as possible on the forward deck to escape the smell. Crawling through the Suez Canal the heat was so intense that the reeking cargo began to smell even more horrible, something that he had hitherto considered impossible, then off Algiers the ship ran into a gale and they narrowly avoided being shipwrecked. Two days out from Marseilles, where Trenchard had resolved to disembark, the captain announced that plague had broken out among the crew. Before he was allowed to leave the ship, all his kit had to be 'sterilised' by being baked in an oven at very high temperature, a process that destroyed his boots. He continued his journey by train across France and cross-Channel steamer from Boulogne, eventually arriving in London two weeks late for his hospital appointment.

After his operation, Trenchard was able to spend some time with his parents, although it was upsetting to see for himself, for the first time, their greatly reduced circumstances – they were living in a small boarding house catering for distressed gentlefolk in Eastern Villas Road, Portsmouth. His 58-year-old father had lost everything except, perhaps, the last vestige of his dignity – choosing to ignore his disastrous career as a solicitor he still described himself as a 'retired Army officer'.

While he was still convalescing he learned, to his great frustration, that back in India his battalion was at last in action, fighting Afridi rebels in the Khyber Pass. General Sir William Lockhart, commander of the Punjab Army Corps, included the Royal Scots Fusiliers in the expedition he put together in October 1897 to put down an uprising and recapture the forts along the Khyber seized by the rebels. Trenchard was desperate to see combat and persuaded the War Office Medical Board to reduce his sick leave to three months. He returned post-haste to India and made his way to Landi Kotal in the Khyber Pass, where the battalion was then based, only to discover the campaign had ended with the defeat of the Afridis two days earlier. It was then his melancholy duty, as acting adjutant, to draw up the medal rolls for the battalion, without, he noted bitterly, his name being included.

I resumed my position as secretary of the Regimental Polo Club and we played polo at Landi Kotal on what was really solid rock, which we covered with litter from 4,000 mules we had there as baggage animals. When a bad storm came it blew all the litter away and we had to put down more. Here it was I rode a flat-racing pony called 'The Bun' and won the Regimental steeplechase. The pony had never seen a jump before but it crashed round and over everything, beating all competitors. I was delighted because my best pony, which was a good jumper and ought to have won, I had to sell a week before the race because I was offered a very good price for it, which I could not afford to refuse, but this flat-racing pony beat it comfortably and the owner who had bought the other was very angry.[9]

From Landi Kotal the battalion was transferred to Peshawar, the future capital of the North West Frontier province set in a valley at the eastern end of the Khyber Pass, close to the border with Afghanistan. There, Trenchard predictably recorded, 'we played polo and hunted . . . [and] had many gymkhanas, tent pegging and jumping competitions'. He was lucky to be allocated a pleasant bungalow with a garden full of Marshal Niel roses and violets and large enough to accommodate his polo ponies.

The relaxed tenor of life in Peshawar was only disturbed by a spate of murders committed by *Ghazis*, Moslem religious fanatics seeking a passport to paradise by killing Europeans. The commanding officer of the Hampshire Regiment and a British judge were both assassinated by *Ghazis* in 1899 and the risks came home to Trenchard when a brother officer was shot and killed at a gymkhana one afternoon not three yards from where he was standing. Lord Curzon, the recently appointed Viceroy of India, was concerned that unrest would spread between British soldiers and Indian staff and ordered that any incidents, no matter how trivial, should be reported to Viceroy's House in Delhi without delay.

Trenchard, who by then considered himself to be something of an old India hand, thought this was an absurd overreaction. A few days later, when he was orderly officer and had occasion to rebuke a sergeant in the middle of the night for throwing a lump of mutton fat at a *punkawallah*, hitting him on the nose, he dispatched a lengthy telegram to Delhi with punctilious details. The recipients in Delhi were unamused, as was Trenchard's commanding officer, when he received a chilly note from Viceroy's House asking why it was necessary for Lieutenant Trenchard to report such a footling event. Trenchard was completely unabashed. 'After that,' he recorded, 'only serious incidents were allowed to be reported.'

For many officers in the 1st Battalion, Royal Scots Fusiliers, events in South Africa were engaging more of their attention than what was happening in India in early 1899. The consensus, in the mess at Peshawar, was that war was inevitable and that right was on Great Britain's side. The judgement of history, on the Second Boer War, would be less certain.

The Dutch, German and Huguenot ancestors of the Boers had first settled on the Cape of South Africa as early as 1652. After Great Britain claimed the colony in 1814 to secure a vital port on the route to India, the Boers were reluctant to submit to foreign colonial rule and began leaving the Cape. In 1836 ten thousand Boers headed north in ox-drawn wagons on what was called The Great Trek – still a potent symbol of Boer pride – first to Natal and then to the highlands, where they set up the Orange Free State and the Transvaal Republic, imagining they would at last be free from British imperial ambitions. They were wrong.

In 1877 Britain annexed the Transvaal. Three years later, the Boers, led by the imposing figure of Paul Kruger, rebelled. In December, 1880, the Boers ambushed and destroyed a British Army convoy at Bronkhorstspruit and then laid siege to garrisons across the Transvaal. On 28 January 1881, the Natal Field Force, under the command of Major General Sir George Pomeroy Colley, attempted to break through Boer positions to relieve British garrisons but was beaten back. A month later, at the Battle of Majuba Hill, Colley was killed and the British routed. The first Boer War ended in humiliating defeat on 28 March 1881, when Prime Minister William Gladstone agreed a truce and granted the Boers self-government in the Transvaal.

Six years later the largest goldfield in the world, more valuable even than South Africa's fabled diamond mines, was discovered in the Transvaal, at Witwatersrand, a 60-mile long ridge south of Pretoria. Kruger, by then president, presciently predicted the discovery would lead to disaster. 'Instead of rejoicing you should weep,' he told his countrymen, 'for this gold will cause our country to be soaked in blood.'

Thousands of *uitlanders* (foreigners), mainly British, streamed over the border from the Cape Colony in a migration reminiscent of the great Gold Rush in California nearly forty years earlier. The city of Johannesburg sprang up as a shanty town almost overnight but the churchgoing Boers, nervous and resentful of the presence in their country of so many foreigners, denied the settlers voting rights, obstructed mining developments and imposed swingeing taxes on the gold industry. Great Britain would make the denial of enfranchisement of its citizens in the Transvaal a major issue, but in truth the *uitlanders* were more interested in prospecting than in politics, and Britain was more interested in extending its imperial influence than protecting the so-called rights of the prospectors, described by a contemporary as a 'loafing, drinking, scheming lot' who would 'corrupt an archangel'.

The continuing failure to gain improved rights for the *uitlanders* was used by the British government as spurious justification for a military build-up in the Cape. In September 1899 Joseph Chamberlain, then Colonial Secretary, sent an ultimatum demanding full citizenship rights for British settlers in the Transvaal, only for Paul Kruger to respond with his own ultimatum requiring the withdrawal of all

British troops from the Transvaal border within 48 hours. The British government was certainly not minded to consider ultimata and when the deadline passed with no response from the British, the Boers declared war on 12 October.

In London it was not expected the war would last long. Some newspapers dubbed it the 'Teatime War' (it would all be over by teatime). In fact it proved to be the longest (nearly three years), the costliest (more than £200 million), the bloodiest (at least 22,000 British, 25,000 Boer and 12,000 African lives lost) and the most humiliating war of the century.

The 2nd Battalion, Royal Scots Fusiliers, had fought in the first Boer War. The battalion held out in a fort at Potchefstroom for three months against a force seven times its size and only yielded when their food was exhausted. The Union flag which flew over the fort, made up from the red lining of an officer's cloak, the white lining of a sergeant's cloak and a blue serge coat belonging to a young officer, was proudly displayed in the officers' mess.

The battalion was in Aldershot when war against the Boers was declared for the second time. It was mobilised immediately and arrived back in its old campaigning ground on 23 November 1899, in time to participate in what would later become known as 'Black Week', a series of devastating reversals engineered by incompetent generals who grossly underestimated the fighting abilities of the Boers. On 15 December 21,000 British troops under Sir Redvers Buller VC, commander-in-chief of the British forces in South Africa, set off to relieve Ladysmith, which had been under siege for 44 days. At the village of Colenso, where the Tugela river had to be crossed, Buller ordered a full frontal attack across open ground against entrenched Boer positions in the surrounding hills. Every attempt to cross the river failed and Buller eventually ordered a retreat, abandoning many wounded men, several isolated units and ten field guns. By the end of the battle, 145 British soldiers had been killed and 1200 were missing or wounded. Private George Ravenhill of the Royal Scots Fusiliers won the regiment's first Victoria Cross for going out several times under heavy fire at Colenso to help men trying to withdraw the guns.[10]

When news of what had happened at Colenso reached Peshawar, a call went out for volunteers to replace the lost men and Trenchard, who had yet to see any action in his military career, eagerly stepped forward. To his great delight his application for a transfer back to the 2nd Battalion was accepted and at the same time his promotion to captain was confirmed. He was told to get ready to leave for South Africa, but before he could depart Lord Curzon, alarmed at the drain of officers from India, ordered no more should leave until replacements had arrived from Britain.

Trenchard was not only left in limbo for several months, but his income was significantly reduced. He was greatly disgruntled to discover that since he was now formally on the establishment of a unit no longer in India he no longer qualified for higher pay. (He thought this was grossly unfair and eventually recovered the money after a two-year struggle with the authorities during which he claimed he nearly lost his commission by writing 'insubordinate letters'.)

Kicking his heels waiting for the Viceroy to rescind the ban on officers leaving India was not in Trenchard's nature, particularly as he held a card up his sleeve. Several months earlier he had been asked by General Sir Edmund Elles, then governor of Peshawar District, to rescue a rifle shooting competition which was turning into an organisational shambles. Sir Edmund had obviously heard of Trenchard's formidable administrative abilities and asked him to sort out the problems. The competition went off smoothly and afterwards a grateful Sir Edmund told him that if he ever needed help he should not hesitate to ask.

By then Sir Edmund was military secretary to the Viceroy. Trenchard sent him a telegram explaining his predicament and reminding him of his offer to help. Sir Edmund acted with remarkable dispatch: ten days later Trenchard was informed that permission had come through for him to leave India and rejoin the 2nd Battalion in South Africa. A passage was booked for him on the *Clive*, a Royal Indian Marine steamer which he described as being extremely uncomfortable and 'the worst boat I have ever been on'. On board were 200 native servants and six other British officers. Leaving Bombay they ran into rough weather across the Arabian Sea and once again plague broke out among the crew and as a result when they stopped to refuel at the Seychelles they were refused permission to land.

At Durban they were diverted further south to East London but stayed long enough to learn that Ladysmith had been relieved and that Lord Roberts, who had replaced Buller as commander-in-chief, had captured Bloemfontein and was heading for Pretoria. (Roberts entered Pretoria on 5 June, freeing some 3000 British prisoners, among them six officers and 39 men of the 2nd Battalion, Royal Scots Fusiliers, who had been captured at Colenso.) After ten days' quarantine they were finally allowed to disembark in East London, where Trenchard met his older brother, Alex, whom he had not seen for 11 years and who was now a lieutenant in the Cape Mounted Rifles. Trenchard did not dwell on the meeting in his autobiographical notes, but it did not seem to have been a particularly warm or emotional reunion and in any case he could not linger in East London, having been ordered to proceed to a rest camp at Bloemfontein, 280 miles to the north.

The rest camp was commanded by an overworked major who promptly decided Trenchard would make an excellent assistant and announced he was arranging for him to remain as second in command. The major rather underestimated his man. What Trenchard described as 'great altercations' followed, during which he angrily made it clear he had come to South Africa to fight, and had no interest in remaining at the rest camp but every intention of rejoining his regiment, whereupon the major dug his heels in and, as his superior officer, ordered him to stay. That night Trenchard 'bolted' – he walked out of the camp with his kitbag over his shoulder and hitched a ride on a goods train to Johannesburg, from where it was a short journey to Krugersdorp, where his battalion was stationed. He reported for duty without mentioning the 'great altercations' at the rest camp or the fact that he had deliberately disobeyed orders. If there was great enthusiasm within the battalion at his return, he failed to mention it.

When Trenchard arrived in Krugersdorp the battalion was engaged in routine garrison duties combined with sending out patrols to harass the enemy, although, as he candidly admitted, 'most of the harrying was done by the Boers'. His reputation as a horseman had apparently preceded him because he had only been in Krugersdorp for five weeks when Major General Geoffrey Barton, the district commander, sent for him. He was concerned that his insubordination at the rest camp might have caught up with him but instead the general had the best possible news: he was directed to put together a small section of mounted infantry – a novel concept at the time, much scorned by the cavalry – from the best riders in the battalion. He had barely started recruiting before the Ayrshire Yeomanry was also placed under his command to his great pleasure, since it contained two old friends – Sir James Miller, the owner of Sainfoin, the 1890 Derby winner, and Walter Neilson, amazingly a fellow pupil at Hill Lands. (Trenchard always referred to his old school as Pritchard's.)

Trenchard's new mounted section had carried out two patrols – treks – against the Boers and had had 'a certain amount of fighting and galloping about on the plain' when he was ordered to take over 300 men of the Australian Bushmen's Corps, who had been hanging about in Krugersdorp with no equipment and nothing to do and had, in the process, acquired a reputation as an unruly ill-disciplined mob only interested in drinking, gambling and general debauchery. Trenchard confessed, perhaps with some embellishment, that he was in 'fear and trembling' at his first meeting with the bushmen, whom he described as the most 'slovenly, surly, murderous-looking bunch of ruffians' he had ever seen. But the essence of their grievance was that they had been 'left to rot' rather than fight, a plight guaranteed to ensure Trenchard's sympathy.

Although all the men could ride and shoot from the saddle, they were without breeches, boots or horses. Trenchard won their respect with an act of sheer audacity quite unlike anything they had ever come to expect from a British officer. He had heard there was a goods train packed with equipment in a siding outside Krugersdorp railway station. Commandeering a wagon and recruiting two Australians, whom he swore to secrecy, he simply looted the train in the dead of night and carried away all the gear they needed. 'I remember so well,' he said, 'how pleased they were . . . They thought this was wonderful for what they called an "Imperial" officer.'[11]

Once the bushmen were fitted out with riding gear there was no trouble in finding horses for them – there were plenty available in the local remount depot. Trenchard was impressed by the care and skill with which they selected their mounts. If he had any doubts about their riding abilities they were soon dispelled. He had selected for himself a frisky mare he called 'Zuleika' (the first of many Zuleikas he would eventually own) but quickly discovered she was a buckjumper – she threw him six times in as many minutes. When one of the bushmen claimed he could subdue her, Trenchard handed over the reins. To his amazement, the Australian mounted Zuleika, rode her round without difficulty and later demonstrated how he did it to his dumbfounded commanding officer, who until that moment thought he knew all there was to know about riding a horse.

Just two weeks after the raid on the goods train Trenchard was ready to lead his men into action in a series of skirmishes around Krugersdorp during which, he recalled, 'we thoroughly enjoyed ourselves'. Less enjoyable were the inevitable blunders. In one incident he led his men at a gallop to occupy a hill before it could be taken by the Boers, only for a courier to arrive with orders from General Barton to evacuate the position immediately as it was about to be bombarded by the artillery. Trenchard could see little point in shelling a position he already held, although he had no alternative but to obey. In fact the bombardment opened up before he had completely withdrawn. Luckily none of his men were hurt, but 17 horses were killed. Later that same day he was disgusted to be ordered by Barton to recapture the same hill. When Barton told him he was to avoid casualties he looked at the general in amazement and could not stop himself from snapping 'Do you want the hill recaptured or not?' Thereafter he always referred to Barton as 'Jumpy Geoffrey'.

By the autumn of 1900, with the principal cities in British hands, the nature of the war changed from set-piece battles to a guerrilla campaign waged by Boer commando units conducting lightning raids on the enemy wherever opportunity presented itself and then vanishing before reinforcements could arrive. At the beginning of October Barton assembled a major expedition, including Trenchard's mounted infantry, to clear the guerrillas who had been attacking the railway line on which he relied for supplies. There were daily skirmishes as the expedition moved slowly south-west along the railway line towards Potchefstroom, travelling at night to avoid the heat of the day.

As a young officer, Trenchard frequently teetered dangerously on the edge of insubordination: he was blunt to the point of rudeness, tended to be impatient with all orders but his own, preferred to give loyalty by choice, rather than as a duty, and was inclined to be respectful only to those seniors he admired. It was not, in truth, a recipe for a successful military career. Early on in the expedition a staff officer, a major, arrived to inspect Trenchard's defence dispositions. He announced that the general wanted the largest number of pickets concentrated on the highest points and then enumerated in great detail how many men should be stationed on each position, pointing out that the general was very keen on such details. Trenchard listened in silence and then, in a voice heavy with sarcasm, inquired 'In that case will you ask the general from me what kind of men he'd like me to put up there, fat men or thin men?' The affronted major stalked off, promising to report Trenchard for insolence, but nothing came of the incident.

On 17 October the expedition made camp near the village of Frederikstad, in a valley where the railway ran alongside the Mooi river. It was evident that Boers were in the neighbourhood in large numbers since foraging parties were frequently attacked and occasionally cut off. After a night march during which the Australian bushmen acted as rearguard, Trenchard was ordered to bring his men to the front of the column.

I got the order that the advance guard was held up and that there were a lot of Boers in front of us. I was to take the whole of my command and go straight up through the column and take charge of the advance guard with my men and drive the Boers off. It was dark but just getting light when I got to the head of the column. I heard a certain amount of firing and I gave the order to re-mount. We spread out and galloped forward. The enemy galloped and re-treated. We galloped after them. After going ten miles full blast, with a good number falling in the bad light, coming to grief in holes and ant-hills, the Boers got on a big ridge in front of us about 200 yards ahead. Our horses were dead beat and so we jumped off and ran forward trying to lead our horses.

Under constant rifle fire from the Boers on the ridge, Trenchard, his senior NCO Sergeant Gilbert Lewis, his groom Private Donald McDermid and two Australians took cover in a farmhouse which they found occupied by a young woman and two small, frightened children. The coffee the Boers had left on the table was still hot. One of the Australians picked up a jug of milk and made to drink it, but was curtly ordered by Trenchard to put it down and leave it for the children.

Sergeant Lewis would later describe what happened in a letter to his father. Trenchard, he said, was 'roused to a fury' and almost 'sobbing with rage' when he saw the Ayrshire Yeomanry, who were attacking the Boers on the right of the ridge, had inexplicably halted. 'He stamped around calling them damned cowards and in his anger he went beyond the wall of the farm. I said "Look out, sir, they hit that corner stone a minute ago" and he replied "Shows what damned bad shots they are" and as he said it he was shot through the chest.'[12]

Lewis carried his CO, with blood gushing from his mouth, back into the farmhouse, where he passed out. 'I remember very well thinking "This is the end",' Trenchard recalled later. When he came round, only ten minutes later, he saw the young farm woman dancing with delight that he was not dead. He could hear the battle still raging outside the farmhouse and lay there all night, slipping in and out of consciousness. As he was carried out of the house the following morning, after the Boers had retreated, the woman leaned over him and asked 'Live?'

'Yes,' he grunted. No one else was as confident.

'I happened to be with my machine gun in the vicinity when he [Trenchard] was brought in and laid down on the veldt,' said Private William Robertson of the 6th Scottish Yeomanry. 'His face was the colour of paper and he looked like a corpse, so much so that a Scots Fusilier next to me said "That bugger's dead".'[13]

At the field hospital in Krugersdorp doctors removed six pints of blood from his lung and did not expect him to survive. Miraculously, he slowly began to pull through, although his life was at risk a second time when the hospital caught fire and he had to be lowered from a first-floor window tied to a mattress. After a month in Krugersdorp he was transferred to a regular hospital in Johannesburg and then to Cape Town, from where he was put on a Red Cross hospital ship bound for England, by which time he knew he had been partly paralysed by the Boer bullet in his chest and knew, too, that his military career was over.

BACK TO SOUTH AFRICA

After three months' convalescence in St Moritz, Trenchard was convinced he was fit enough to rejoin his regiment and when he returned to England in April 1901 he immediately applied to have his year-long sick leave reduced to six months. Whether he explained to sceptical doctors at the Army Medical Board that he was 'cured' by soaring off the Cresta Run is not known, but in any case his application was turned down, to his intense irritation.

Trenchard privately admitted to himself, and perhaps to his parents, that he was only 'fairly well'. Although he could walk again, his damaged lung left him short of breath and he would never recover complete control of his right hand – for the remainder of his life whenever he had to sign his name he held his right wrist with his left hand to steady it. His handwriting, always far from copperplate, inevitably became even worse.

Determined to get fit, he took up tennis again in order to try and strengthen his weak lung. During an extended visit to his parents, who were still living in a boarding house in Portsmouth, he entered two tennis tournaments in nearby south coast resorts and although he was only able to play one set before retiring, exhausted, his participation was reported in the local newspapers. It gave him an idea. He sent the cuttings to the Medical Board with a covering letter pointing out that if he was fit enough to play in tennis tournaments he was surely fit enough to return to duty. It worked. He was invited to attend the Medical Board for a second examination, after which his application to have his sick leave reduced was approved.

Trenchard arrived back in South Africa in July 1901 to find much had changed. Lord Kitchener of Khartoum, the hero of the Battle of Omdurman, had replaced Roberts and introduced ruthless measures, which would later be much criticised, to finally defeat the Boers. His 'scorched earth' policy required crops and livestock to be systematically destroyed to deny sustenance to the enemy. Homesteads and farms were burned to the ground and tens of thousands of women and children were moved into tented 'concentration camps' – the first time the world had ever heard that gruesome designation. Poorly administered, the camps became increasingly overcrowded and ravaged by disease while concern mounted at home about what was happening – the Liberal MP David Lloyd George angrily accused the government of a 'policy of extermination' directed against the Boer population.

It had been Trenchard's intention to rejoin his battalion, but in Pretoria he was assigned to command a company of the 12th Mounted Infantry Battalion, which had been formed from Scots regiments six months earlier in response to Lord Roberts' directive to increase the number of mounted infantry units available to the British Field Force. Among the recruits was Private Donald McDermid, his former groom, who was astonished – and delighted – to see him. 'Blimey, sir,' he said cheerfully, 'we thought you'd been buried long ago.'

Trenchard's company was sent to Zandrivierspoort in the Northern Transvaal to chase Boers in an area between Potgietersrus (now Mokopane) and Pietersburg (Polokwane). For three months they mounted daily patrols, virtually living in the saddle, only returning to base to refit and then going out again.

'My idea of hell,' Trenchard confessed later, 'was riding through Zandrivierspoort every morning being sniped at, returning to camp getting sniped at again and then doing it all over again next day.' In August his commanding officer, Lieutenant Colonel Cecil Vandeleur, Scots Guards, was killed in a Boer ambush when the train on which he was travelling was blown up – he was shot as he struggled out of a wrecked carriage.

Trenchard was still greatly troubled by the wound in his chest, which had not properly healed.

Trenchard frequently fainted clean away at the end of a day's trek [a young officer in his company said], and had to be lifted bodily off his horse. He never complained, just as he never explained. Nor was he ever heard to thank anyone for fussing over him when he recovered. On the contrary, 'Leave me alone' he would growl and stagger to his feet as though nothing was wrong. It soon became part of the drill to lift him down and leave him to regain consciousness at his own pace. With the help of a finger or two of whisky, he would usually be himself again within five minutes.[1]

He was perhaps not displeased when in September he was ordered to report urgently to General Headquarters in Pretoria, where he was ushered into the presence of Lord Kitchener himself looking, he recalled, 'tall and fierce'. Kitchener explained that his name had been put forward, as a stern disciplinarian, for a special, and difficult, task. A mounted infantry regiment newly arrived from Britain had run into a Boer ambush on its first patrol and lost a lot of men and equipment. Its morale was rock bottom and its organisation was in chaos. Trenchard was to make an inspection of the unit and take whatever steps were necessary to restore its fighting capability, even if he had to assume temporary command. 'Remember you are acting on my personal authority,' Kitchener is said to have told him. 'Do what is necessary and report directly to me.' It was an extraordinary assignment to give a 28-year-old captain; fortunately Trenchard never courted popularity or shirked making difficult decisions.

There can be little doubt that everyone knew what he was about when he arrived at the regiment (which he discreetly never named in his autobiographical notes) and his reception was hardly likely to have been warm. His first decision was that the commanding officer was 'no good' and should be removed, which happened very swiftly. He then decided two company commanders should also be removed, which led to what he described as 'an amusing incident' – the telegram agreeing to the dismissal of the company commanders warned him that he had been sent there to 're-organise the unit, not to disband it'.

If Trenchard hoped he would end up in command, he was disappointed. A new commanding officer was appointed and he was ordered to return to Pretoria where Kitchener, who had apparently decided to use him as a kind of roving troubleshooter, had another job for him. This time he was to go to De Aar, in the Northern Cape, to speed up the formation of a new corps of mounted infantry.

It took me a month to organise it [Trenchard noted breezily], and we were then asked to guard a convoy of about 8,000 donkeys over the Kalahari desert . . . We did this successfully though it was the

most awful work as the donkeys never went more than three quarters of a mile in an hour and they strayed all over the place. When
this was completed I got another telegram ordering me to hand over
to the next senior officer and proceed to Pretoria again.[2]

He was no doubt hoping for a slightly more glamorous assignment
than escorting 8,000 donkeys across a desert and he got it – Kitchener wanted him to capture the Boer government. Intelligence sources
had reported discovering a secret hideout, beyond Middelburg, east of
Pretoria, where senior members of the Boer government were believed
to have taken refuge. Previous attempts to capture the government
with a large body of troops had failed because their approach had always been detected in time for their quarry to flee. Kitchener thought
a raid with a handful of men would have a good chance of success and
put at Trenchard's disposal a small group of troops with an intimate
knowledge of the terrain. There were eight or nine of them, Trenchard
recalled, 'mainly half castes', and their leader rejoiced in the unlikely
name of Fleur-de-lys.

Trenchard considered the mission carefully and concluded, in
direct contradiction of Kitchener's view, that it was an impossible task with so few men. Not many temporary captains would
have dared to disagree with the commander-in-chief but Trenchard
had no hesitation in asking to see him again and telling him that
he did not want to undertake the operation unless he could have
more men. Kitchener, perhaps amazed by this young officer's brass
nerve, offered him a column of National Scouts, then camped at a
village called Streams, not far from Middelburg. National Scouts
were renegade Boers of doubtful repute who had surrendered and
been persuaded to change sides and fight on the side of the British
against their fellow countrymen,[3] but Trenchard appeared to have no
doubts about them. 'I was delighted,' he recalled. 'I thought this was
splendid.[4]

He set off immediately on horseback with just a servant and his
groom, McDermid, and a letter signed by Kitchener requiring him
to be given whatever assistance he required. He reported first to the
general in command of Middelburg district who, when apprised of his
mission, muttered 'God help you.' Trenchard was unclear whether he
was referring to the prospect of commanding a column of National

Scouts, or attempting to capture the Boer government, but either way it was hardly encouraging. The general also flatly refused his request for spare horses, despite being shown Kitchener's letter. Trenchard had no time to argue or appeal to Kitchener and went without.

When he arrived at the Streams encampment he ordered his new command to be drawn up on parade and addressed the men through an Afrikaans interpreter. He briefly explained their mission and warned them they would be travelling light and should be prepared to leave at dusk the following day. His words were greeted with a sullen silence. That afternoon he agreed to receive a deputation from the men, seeking assurance that they would be taking with them plenty of provisions. Trenchard could give them no such assurance; when he said they would be travelling light, he told them, he meant it. An hour later the deputation returned to ask if they would be accompanied by carts and spare horses. Trenchard again shook his head – the essence of the mission was speed and surprise; he did not want to be slowed down by carts. The deputation departed, much aggrieved.

At sunset the next day, as the column prepared to leave, a head count revealed that no less than 170 men had disappeared. Trenchard was unconcerned – the 500-plus remaining were more than enough for his needs. A greater problem was the language. Kaffir[5] guides hired for the expedition could understand Afrikaans but not English, which meant that Trenchard was entirely reliant on National Scout interpreters to understand what the guides were saying. The first night passed without incident. The column hid in a *kloof* (gorge) during the day and the interpreters assured Trenchard that the guides were saying they were heading in the right direction and nearing the Boer hideout.

They set off again at dusk. As the column pressed on through the inky night, Trenchard was getting more and more perturbed by the nervous behaviour of both the guides and the interpreters.

In the middle of the night I heard a donkey bray, but the Kaffirs said it was nothing and guided us on. In another hour, two men let off their rifles, accidentally so they said, but it made me still more suspicious. We moved on for another half an hour when two Kaffirs came in to tell me we were where we were supposed to be. There was a heated altercation between the Boer interpreters and I

was anxious about what was happening. I felt the Boers were interpreting what suited them and not correctly what the Kaffirs said.[6]

Told that the Boer government was holed up in a *kloof* a short distance away, Trenchard deployed his force to surround the area and
then dismounted and crawled cautiously forward to find the kloof was
filled with well-fed cattle. Furious, he immediately ordered the entire
column to proceed at a gallop back to where he had heard a donkey
bray in the middle of the night in the faint hope that might be where
the Boer leaders were encamped. The National Scouts were having
none of it – most of them wheeled their horses and headed off in
the opposite direction towards a distant railway line, leaving Trenchard with a small force of around 30 foreign mercenaries, among them
Americans and Canadians who had made their way to South Africa to
fight and somehow ended up enlisted in the National Scouts.

As the first grey light of dawn lit the horizon to the east, rifles
opened up from the surrounding hills and Trenchard found himself
in the middle of a fierce fire fight. They had clearly been led into a
trap and several of his men were wounded before they could reach
cover. They managed to seize a Boer wagon to carry the wounded
and withdrew slowly, fighting all the way, to a gorge with a narrow
entrance which they could easily defend. After a while, to Trenchard's
great relief, the Boers, apparently uninterested in continuing the fight,
made off.

When he finally got back to Middelburg two days later, he discovered that his treacherous Scouts had preceded him and reported that
he had been caught in a Boer ambush and was either dead or captured.
He concluded later that his column was not so much interested in
capturing the Boer government as capturing the cattle. 'It was,' he said
with characteristic understatement, 'a bad show.'

By then he had had quite enough of being Kitchener's troubleshooter and fired off a telegram to Pretoria asking once again to be allowed
to return to his battalion. Three days later, while still waiting for a
reply, he read in a newspaper, to his utter astonishment (he put it that
he was 'much surprised'), a report that the entire Boer government
had narrowly escaped being captured in an operation involving the
National Scouts. He then received a telegram from Kitchener congratulating him and ordering him to return to Pretoria. 'I went back to

be told by a staff officer that we had done very well,' he noted, adding 'but I did not think so.'[7] Trenchard was frankly mystified that anyone should think the operation was anything but a fiasco.

Kitchener blithely ignored Trenchard's request to return to his battalion and sent him off to be second in command of a swashbuckling unit known as the Canadian Scouts, which had been formed from volunteers by an officer of the Royal Canadian Dragoons in December 1900. When he was killed in action two months later, his place was taken by Major Charles Ross, a colourful character with a magnificent handlebar moustache who had run away from home as a child to live with Indians in the United States and later was a scout for the United States Army in three Indian wars. Under Ross, the Canadian Scouts gained a reputation for disdaining standard military discipline at the same time as being hard-riding, courageous soldiers who could usually be found in the thick of the action.

Ross was the kind of maverick figure Trenchard liked instinctively. By the time he arrived the regiment had evolved into an irregular mounted corps of four squadrons, a machine-gun battery, a troop of black South African scouts and a transport column, in all about 475 men, not all Canadians by any means but drawn from all parts of the Empire. All they had in common was a burning desire to fight the Boers. Trenchard called them 'great-hearted ruffians and magnificent fighting men'.

The Canadian Scouts took part in the great sweeps to round up the 25,000 Boer fighters still in the field in the final stages of the war in early 1902. Trenchard reported that they 'lost a few men' but rounded up a good number of the enemy. 'After one drive with about six British columns, when we got into the railway line to re-equip for another drive, all the columns were wired by Lord Kitchener to ask when they would be ready for the next drive. We wired "Ready at once". All the other columns wanted a week or ten days and we knew we could not be sent out by ourselves so we had a week to ten days as well.'[8]

The last of the Boers surrendered in May 1902 and the Second Boer War was brought to an inglorious conclusion with the signing of the Treaty of Vereeniging at the end of that month. Some 75,000 lives had been lost, including 22,000 British and Allied soldiers, most of whom died from disease. Even with peace Trenchard was still not allowed to return to his regiment, but was posted as temporary commandant of

the 9th Mounted Infantry and ordered to move as rapidly as possible
to Pietersburg[9] in the North Transvaal where a native uprising was
expected. 'I trekked up through the Orange Free State, through all
the country I knew so well, to Waterberg, Potgietersrus to Pietersburg,
where I made my headquarters, but the natives soon gave up any idea
of any rising and we settled down to a peaceful life.'[10]

Trenchard stayed in Pietersburg for around three months, played a
lot of polo, hunted, organised gymkhanas and 'did not have too bad
a time'. While he was there the Low Veldt was opened for gold prospecting and with two friends he pegged out 500 claims near the town
of Louis Trichardt, at the foot of the Soutpansberg mountains, north
of Pietersburg. They hired two Australian prospectors who they were
assured were honest, hard workers and equipped them with wagons
and mules and all the equipment they needed. (In his notes Trenchard said they were given all the 'impedimenta' necessary.) Sadly, his
dreams of untold riches would come to naught. 'They worked at our
claim trying to find gold for two and a half years, even though I had
left South Africa for good. No gold in big quantities apparently was
ever found and eventually the men were paid off . . . that was the end
of my gold prospecting.'[11]

In the late summer the 9th Mounted Infantry was ordered to move
south and set up station close to the town of Middelburg, a trek of
some 170 miles. En route Trenchard managed to upgrade the unit's
horses and to acquire several for himself. With the end of the war
many columns were being disbanded and thousands of horses were
being handed in to remount depots. At every station they passed as
they trekked south they stayed two or three days to check on the
horses, exchanging their worst for the pick of what was available. By
the time they arrived in Middelburg, he reported, the unit was 'magnificently mounted'.

The government was also selling horses and Trenchard bought
'ten or eleven very good ones', never paying more than £20 for any
of them. One, another Zuleika, became a first-class polo pony and
flat racer and won every race for which she was entered, except on her
first outing when she was three stone overweight, being ridden by her
14-stone owner. Trenchard claimed that Zuleika won him £1267 in
prize money before he eventually sold her for £250.

In October, shortly after arriving in Middelburg, he was gazetted as brevet major 'in recognition of services during operations in South Africa'. He was surprised, because it was his understanding that no brevets were given as a reward for active service without the recipient being mentioned in dispatches and he had never been mentioned since he had never served under any individual general for more than two months. He assumed, probably correctly, that Kitchener, who had left South Africa to become commander-in-chief in India, had pulled strings on his behalf. He would tell his children later in life that he would look down at the crown on his shoulder and ask himself 'How did that happen?'

While Trenchard was in Middelburg, the station was inspected by Lieutenant General Neville Lyttleton, the new commander-in-chief. He was asked to mount the general and his staff during their visit, not an easy job, he recalled, since one of his staff officers weighed 22 stone. The visit culminated with a ceremonial march past at which Trenchard was determined to make an impression. The 9th Mounted Infantry was at the rear of the parade, following the 16th Lancers. Trenchard held back until the dust kicked up by the Lancers had settled and then, sword in hand and mounted on Zuleika, he led his men past the saluting base at a full gallop, hoof beats thundering and the gun carriages bouncing madly in clouds of red dust. 'We really did gallop,' he said. 'It was no question of a gentle canter, we went as hard as we could, much to the amusement and consternation of everybody else. . . . It was a fine sight.'

In August 1903 Trenchard's tour of duty in South Africa came to an end and he was finally posted back to the 2nd Battalion, Royal Scots Fusiliers, then stationed in Aldershot, although Colonel Thomas Hickman, the station commander in Middelburg, had done his best, unsuccessfully, to keep him with a glowing testamonial.

Major Trenchard is, I consider, the best Mounted Infantry Officer of his rank I have met during the war [he noted in a report]. He is equally good in camps as in the field and his Institutions and General Disposition for the comfort of his men are superior to any other Regiment of any arm in the Command: this is entirely due to his personal attention. His horses are the fittest and best I have seen in South Africa. I am strongly of the opinion that if this officer reverted to his Infantry Regiment it would be a great loss to the M.I. and that when we have found such an exceptionally good man for the work, we should stick to him. I attribute the high state of efficiency of the 9th M.I. entirely to him.[12]

On the long voyage home Trenchard had plenty of time to consider his future. He was 30 years old and back on regimental duty he would revert to his substantive rank of captain. Although he was happy to be rejoining his regiment, peacetime soldiering at home – with its tedious drills, parades and exercises – held little attraction for him. He had enjoyed his time in South Africa and liked the country. The more he thought about it the more inclined he became to resign his commission and return to South Africa to try his luck as a gold prospector. The 500 claims he had staked out in the Low Veldt had yielded little in the way of gold at that point but there was always the tempting possibility of a life-changing lucky strike transforming both his fortunes and those of his family.

He was due a month's leave before he had to report to Aldershot. After visiting his parents in Portsmouth he went to stay with a family he had first met in St Moritz and with whom he had stayed in contact. The Hargreaveses owned a large country house in Hampshire – John Hargreaves was Master of the Blackmore Vale hunt – where they hosted frequent weekend shooting parties and entertained their many society friends. Trenchard recalled that the house always seemed to be full of languid young women, friends of the Hargreaveses' daughter, Violet, who, he rather ungallantly asserted, 'monopolised' the best chairs in the drawing room. Violet's brother had recently acquired a Wolseley Voiturette motor car in which he taught Trenchard to drive and together they spent many happy hours careering up and down the Basingstoke–Winchester road, blithely ignoring the 20 miles an hour speed limit recently imposed by the passing of the Motor Car Act 1903 in Parliament.

Through the Hargreaveses, Trenchard became friends with another local family, the Pocklingtons, and it was at the Pocklingtons' house in Romsey that he was introduced to a Colonel Gilman, who had recently been appointed by the War Office to recruit officers for the West African Frontier Force, which had been raised by the Colonial Office in 1897 to garrison the colonies of Nigeria, Gold Coast (now Ghana), Sierra Leone and Gambia and counter the threat of French and German colonial expansion in the area.

They fell to talking after dinner one evening and Trenchard revealed his tentative plans to return to South Africa. The older man, possibly with an eye to a new recruit, was dismissive. Why, he demanded, was Trenchard squandering his military experience in pursuit of a chimera? There was 'real work' to be done in Nigeria, where professional, experienced officers were desperately needed. Gilman hinted that the calibre of the West African Frontier Force officer corps left much to be desired, that drinking, gambling and consorting with local women were rife. The sultry climate was partly to blame, he explained, but what was required was a disciplinarian prepared to risk extreme unpopularity to bring them to heel. The more he talked about the challenges of West Africa, the more interested Trenchard became. 'I've often found,' he told Gilman, 'it's a sign you are working on the right lines when everyone detests you.'

A week later Trenchard found himself in the Colonial Office being interviewed by Brigadier General George Kemball, the Inspector General of the West African Frontier Force. Kemball was 44, a veteran of the Second Afghan War whose father and uncle were both generals in the British Army and whose grandfather had been the Surgeon-General in Bombay. After lengthy service in India he transferred to West Africa and led a number of expeditions into the interior, for which he was awarded the DSO and a CB. He was the sort of no-nonsense military man to whom Trenchard immediately responded and by the end of the interview Trenchard had agreed to accept the post of Deputy Commandant of the Southern Nigeria Regiment. (Within the WAFF a single regiment was allocated for the defence of each country, with the exception of Nigeria, which was given separate regiments to cover the north and south of the country.)

One of the attractions was that with care he would be able to live on allowances and save most of his pay; he was also assured that polo and game shooting would be available. On condition that he would serve at least six months, Kemball acquiesced to Trenchard's demand that he should be given the right to command all the regiment's expeditions into the interior. It was a foolish promise that would cause problems almost as soon as Trenchard had arrived.

5

THE WHITE MAN'S GRAVEYARD

At the turn of the century the hinterland of Nigeria, the most populous country in Africa, was largely unexplored, a pestilential wilderness inhabited by more than 500 different ethnic groups, many of them in thrall to Ju-Ju witch doctors, who frequently resolved tribal disputes by ordering human sacrifices. Tribal warfare was continuous; slavery, human sacrifice and cannibalism were common. In 1901 one of the largest ethnic groups, the Aros, rose up against British imperialism. The Anglo-Aro war culminated in a series of major battles in the east of the country before the Aro people were defeated, but tension remained high across the territory.

The climate along the coastal belt was humid and steamy; the interior was very hot and dry. In the rainy season, tropical deluges descended in torrents and between December and March a dry dusty wind, the *harmattan*, blew in from the Sahara sometimes blotting out the sun. Malaria, blackwater fever and a host of other unpleasant tropical diseases were endemic.

Not for nothing was West Africa known as 'the white man's graveyard'.

Trenchard had little idea of the cauldron into which he was to be pitched when he boarded a steamer at Liverpool in October 1903, for the three-week voyage to the west coast of Africa. On his first night at sea he was surprised to find he was the only passenger who had dressed for dinner. He continued to do so, blithely ignoring the advice from someone who claimed to be an old Africa hand that dinner jackets were 'much too dressy for the Coast'. (He noted with some satisfaction, however, that by the end of the voyage four men had joined him and when he returned to the UK for good seven years later all the male passengers dressed for dinner.)

Trenchard disembarked at the ramshackle port of Bonny, on

Nigeria's south coast, the capital of an ancient kingdom which, until comparatively recently, had worshipped the iguana lizard as a sacred deity. At Bonny his baggage was transferred to a small, rust-flaked coastal steamer for the slow 40-mile journey further along the coast and up the muddy Cross river to Calabar, the former slave trading post where the Southern Nigeria Regiment was headquartered. Trenchard stood on the deck to try and escape the stifling heat as the steamer chugged up the Cross river, bordered on both banks by dense tropical rainforest and the occasional rickety landing stage indicating the presence of a village – usually no more than a small cluster of crude huts with thatched roofs and naked children staring solemnly at the passing steamer. His fellow passengers were largely traders and various missionaries, one of whom seemed unusually pleased to inform him that the British presence barely extended beyond the river banks. The interior was extremely treacherous, he warned, with many tribes practising cannibalism.

It was late by the time he arrived in Calabar. The night was very hot and humid – he called it 'sticky' – and he was sweating profusely as he made his way to the officers' mess, followed by native porters carrying his baggage on their heads. The mess turned out to be a two-storey wooden building with a row of cannons lined up in front of a verandah; there was no one around to greet him and so he went straight to bed after a servant had shown him to his room.

When he arrived punctually for breakfast in the dining room the following morning he was surprised to find the place deserted. Over the course of the next hour his brother officers drifted in and casually introduced themselves. Trenchard was appalled: most of them were still in their pyjamas, few had bothered to shave or brush their hair and several were obviously nursing monumental hangovers. At least the commandant, Lieutenant Colonel Arthur Montanaro, emerged properly dressed in crisp khaki drill, but he sat apart and seemed untroubled by the distinctly unmilitary demeanour of his officers, who were soon engaged in a heated debate about the unorthodox sexual talents of local women, while their newly arrived second in command glowered over his coffee.

At a briefing in Montanaro's office immediately after breakfast, Trenchard felt obliged to raise his concerns about his slovenly fellow officers but was brusquely dismissed. Things are very different on the coast, Montanaro explained: the debilitating climate affected every-one and he (Trenchard) could not expect the same standards to apply as in Britain or even India. His deputy was unpersuaded, but un-characteristically held his tongue. Forty-one-year-old Montanaro was a very experienced and unusually literate officer, having co-authored a book, *The Ashanti Campaign of 1900*, which had been published two years earlier. Frederick Hodgson, the British governor of the Gold Coast, had sparked a war by unwisely demanding, in the name of the Queen, to sit on the Golden Stool of the Ashanti people. The Golden Stool had great spiritual and symbolic significance for the Ashantis and they responded to the governor's demand by laying siege to the garrison in the city of Kumasi. Montanaro led the relief expedition which recaptured the city in September 1900, and then wrote a first-hand account of the episode. His co-author was Cecil Armitage, the governor's private secretary, who was in the besieged city. The same year the book was published Montanaro commanded a major coun-ter-insurgency operation to capture Arochukwu in the Anglo-Aro war. A natural writer, his dispatches from the field described grisly scenes of mutilated corpses piled on sacrificial altars at the behest of Ju-Ju priests.

Closer contact with his fellow officers over the next few days gave Trenchard no cause to think better of them. He was genuinely shocked by their louche behaviour, even though he had been forewarned by Colonel Gilman, that weekend at the Pocklingtons', about what was going on. Some of them thought nothing of starting the day by gulp-ing a tumbler of gin before breakfast, often after having played poker all night for stakes they could not afford. A few were thorough repro-bates – Trenchard called them 'bad hats' – who had 'left their country for their country's good', but most had volunteered because they were hard up and attracted by the higher pay and allowances. Even the most enthusiastic arrivals were soon brought low by the heat, the bore-dom and the bad example of their fellow officers.

Trenchard felt no need to hide his disapproval and his relationship with Montanaro quickly became strained, particularly when Montan-aro announced his presence would not be required on an upcoming expedition into a remote area in the north, where serious intertribal warfare needed to be quelled. Trenchard protested vigorously, remind-ing Montanaro that General Kemball had promised him command of all expeditions into the interior. Montanaro was unimpressed and refused to change his mind.

'The fact was that the Colonel did not want me in West Africa at all,' Trenchard wrote later, '. . . he said I was not fit to command anything until I had been in the country for two or three years.'[1]

Montanaro was not, in reality, being unreasonable. His sensible view was that his newly arrived deputy needed to become acclimatised and more experienced before taking command of any expedition. Perhaps to get his bad-tempered deputy out of the way, he ordered Trenchard to take a detachment of 40 men up-country and stand guard at Owerri, a town some 100 miles to the north-west of Calabar. Trenchard was so angry he seriously considered resigning on the spot – neither the regiment nor the country held much attraction for him – but reason prevailed and he realised that, for the moment, he had no alternative but to obey his orders.

Still fuming when he arrived at Owerri, he ascertained by chance that General Kemball was on the Gold Coast. Officers with more finely tuned discretion might have hesitated before complaining about a superior officer to an even more superior officer, but Trenchard had a strong sense of right and wrong: he felt he had a genuine grievance and had been let down. He thus suffered no misgivings dispatching a telegram to Kemball explaining what had happened and adding that he was thinking about going home as he did not think he was 'going to do any good'[2] in Nigeria. Kemball, possibly irritated Montanaro had ignored his instructions that Trenchard was to command expeditions into the interior, wired Sir Ralph Moor, the High Commissioner of Southern Nigeria, advising him to recall Montanaro and replace him with Trenchard. Sir Ralph was in poor health, suffering from malaria, about to retire and had no wish to get involved; he wearily accepted Kemball's advice and forwarded a telegram to Trenchard ordering him to join the expedition and take over command.

As soon as he received the glad news Trenchard returned, posthaste, to Calabar only to discover the expedition had departed three days earlier. He had only a vague idea of Montanaro's ultimate destination but he was determined to catch him. He rounded up a couple of porters, hired a local guide and chartered a launch to take them up the Cross river to the small town of Ito. From Ito they set out through the rain forest in single file, following a 'track' – not much more than a rabbit run through a tangle of tropical vegetation, vines and creepers – which the guide assured Trenchard would lead them to the expedition. They spent the night in a clearing beside a clump of cotton trees, Trenchard sleeping fitfully on a camp bed set up by his servant, and continued their journey at daybreak. By early afternoon the guide seemed confident they were getting close. In broken English he explained to Trenchard that he believed the expedition was only about an hour ahead.

Colonel Montanaro was astonished when, later that afternoon, his deputy appeared at the expedition's makeshift camp, emerging from the jungle with his uniform soaked in sweat.

'What the devil are you doing here?' the colonel demanded angrily.

'I've been sent to relieve you,' Trenchard replied, reaching into his pocket and handing Montanaro the crumpled telegram from the High Commissioner.

Montanaro scanned it quickly, his features expressionless. If he was surprised he gave no indication. Instead he simply looked up, muttered 'I'll be leaving in the morning' and stalked off. News of the sudden change of command spread quickly around the camp and was not received with enthusiasm. That night, while Trenchard was trying to get to sleep in a bush hut he was disturbed by a group of officers standing directly outside and loudly complaining about the 'long-legged bastard' who had usurped their commander and how they did not intend to put up with it. Trenchard listened to them griping for a few minutes, then jumped out of bed, stormed outside in his pyjamas and told them to clear off. If they were not gone in two minutes, he said, he would send the lot of them back to Calabar. They quickly skulked away. (His threat might have been a somewhat empty one, since a number of them would undoubtedly have been delighted to be sent back to Calabar rather than face the rigours of an expedition into the interior.)

As he had promised, Montanaro departed very early the next morning without a fuss. (To his great credit, he bore no grudge against his deputy and later submitted fulsome reports to the Colonial Office about Trenchard's conduct on operations.) After breakfast Trenchard called all the officers together for a briefing. Ignoring the palpable aura of morose hostility, he made no mention of the incident outside his hut the night before but concentrated on the upcoming expedition, attempting to exude a confidence he certainly did not feel. The objective was to bring intertribal violence to an end in a huge area of uncharted territory around 100 miles to the north and persuade defiant tribal chiefs to accept the authority of the government, but Trenchard was acutely aware – how could he not be? – that he was about to lead troops he did not know into country he did not know against opposition he did not know. He indicated he was going to follow the general plans drawn up by his predecessor, with one exception. Drawing on his experience in South Africa, he had decided that they would all march at night and rest during the heat of the day. This decision was accepted with a barely perceptible shaking of heads. If those present had little confidence in their new commander, they could hardly be blamed.

Apart from a light-artillery company, almost all the 250 troops now under his command were locally recruited Yoruba and Hausa volunteers, and Trenchard quickly discovered they were well trained and well disciplined. (Although he would later put an end to their custom of cutting off the genitals of men they had killed and producing them as evidence of their deaths.) Trenchard divided them into three columns, each of which was to operate as an independent patrol and make its way separately through the jungle. They were to link up at the base camp at Ibibio in ten days' time. Trenchard took command of the largest of the patrols. On the second day he encountered, for the first time, a gruesome victim of the Ju-Ju priests – the blackened naked body of a young woman hanging upside down from a tree. The political officer accompanying him said it was likely she had given birth to twins, a terrible misfortune since one was always stigmatised as the child of an evil spirit. As it was impossible to tell which was which, both babies were usually taken into the jungle and left to die and the mother was sacrificed – hung upside down by her feet until she died.

Trenchard was shocked, but he would soon become familiar with even more bestial practices – men or women crucified or tied to a stake in the ground, their genitals, mouths and eyes smeared with a honey-like substance to attract swarms of ants which ate them alive. There were many other sacrificial rites, he noted, 'too horrible to mention'.[3]

Three days into the patrol, his column was halted at a huge spiked stockade that had been built across the track. Trenchard ordered his men to fan out and hack a path through the jungle on each side. He remembered, later, being aware of a curiously ominous silence, only broken by the machetes slashing at the undergrowth, when suddenly hordes of screaming Igbo tribesmen leapt out from behind the trees brandishing spears and blowpipes and blindly firing ancient shotguns. In the bloody skirmish that followed the tribesmen were hopelessly outgunned by the disciplined and well-armed troops and they fled after 20 or 30 of them had been killed and many more wounded. Only a handful of Trenchard's men suffered superficial wounds.

Having established a base camp at Ibibio, Trenchard began the task of pacifying the area, sending out punitive patrols to warn tribal chiefs that continued fighting would result in their villages being burned to the ground. 'Several engagements took place,' he reported to Montanaro in Calabar, 'in all of which the enemy was routed.'[4] In the same dispatch Trenchard described the tactics he had developed in the field: 'I found night surprises in the bush were most successful, and had an excellent effect on the enemy. Also, I tried rushing the enemy directly they opened fire, with very good results and to these two causes I attribute the fact of my having no casualties.'

One after another, the chiefs were summoned to Ibibio where Trenchard dictated the four simple terms under which he intended to impose peace: murdering people on government roads must cease; all firearms were to be given up and banned in the future; summonses to meet the white men must be obeyed; government roads must be maintained and kept open. To drive home each point he held up his left hand with the fingers extended and grabbed each finger in turn and waggled it. Those chiefs who refused to accept the terms were warned their villages would be burned, as were the villages of those chiefs who refused the summons to meet Trenchard. He had no regrets, at first, about destroying entire villages – the natives, he noted dismissively, were 'really nothing but savages or monkeys'[5] – although he would later change his views.

When news of the expedition reached London, there were concerns about British officers employing such apparently brutal tactics. Thomas Russell, a Liberal Unionist MP, raised the issue in the House by asking on 'whose authority and for what reason Major Trenchard attacked the natives of the Opopo country and burned six villages . . . and what is the object to be attained by the sacrifice of human life and the expenditure involved'. Alfred Lyttelton, the Colonial Secretary, replied that the operation had been sanctioned by his predecessor. 'The country traversed is a very wild one,' he continued. 'The object was to take away the war guns and arms of precision in the hands of the natives, to open the district to trade, and to bring it under Government control, the natives having refused to give up criminals, and any attempt to arrest an offender being immediately met with armed resistance.[6] Lyttelton admitted that 'it had been found necessary' to burn a number of villages but pointed out that the huts destroyed could be easily reconstructed and that casualties were minimal. Russell, apparently satisfied, chose not to pursue the matter further.

Trenchard would return to the area several times during the next two years. Expeditions were usually only undertaken during the dry season, from September to April, the summer months being too hot and too wet. (During the rainy season the Niger river was two miles wide at some points and was navigable by river steamers; during the dry season it was possible to wade across it. Trenchard never forgot watching porters cross a river with their loads held over their heads, getting into deeper and deeper water until they were, for a few yards, completely submerged with their loads still held above the water. He was impressed.)

He was blithely unconcerned by questions being asked in Parliament about his conduct, but it did not take him long to realise that punitive reprisals against entire villages achieved little but stoke resentment, so he banned, as being counter productive, the practice of burning villages and carrying away livestock. Instead he simply set up camp in the 'market square' – usually a clearing with a clump of cotton trees where surrounding villages sent their products for sale – and announced that he was not going to leave until the local chiefs did what he wanted. It usually worked. He also stopped flogging natives to obtain intelligence, firstly because it was degrading and secondly because it produced no worthwhile results as they inevitably lied. As an alternative, he explained, he searched the faces of the tribesmen to find 'one less blank and unintelligent than the rest, usually a teenage boy', who was then brought into the camp, given a singlet (much prized) and other trinkets, and in this way persuaded to talk. These young men became known as 'Trenchard's Mustn't Touch 'Ems' after Trenchard warned of severe retribution if any of them were punished for helping the white men.

After some time in the field Trenchard became aware that the Arochukwu tribe – the Aros who had fought the British a few years earlier – exercised a peculiar dominance over the area. They were physically bigger and markedly more intelligent than some of the other tribes and because they knew the country so well they were invariably hired as guides during Southern Nigeria Regiment expeditions, marching prominently at the head of the column. 'This had the effect,' Trenchard noted, 'of making the other natives believe that these Aros always brought white men to punish them . . . they could blackmail the whole country by threatening to bring the white man.'[7] Aros, said by legend to be a lost tribe of Israel, also wielded formidable Ju-Ju and promised a village riches and prosperity in return for the sacrifice of one of their men, who would be taken away and slain to appease the gods. (Trenchard later found out that human sacrifices were, in reality, rare. What usually happened was that the individual taken away for sacrifice was sold as a slave – generating income for the Aros.)

Trenchard suggested to the political agent who always accompanied expeditions that it might be an idea to employ other tribes as guides, but was warned it would be absolute folly. Typically, he completely ignored the man's concerns and, as an experiment, began hiring Igbos as guides. 'The result was instantaneous and miraculous,' he reported. 'People came in much more often to meet us. I could talk to them about the horrible customs they must give up and it was very seldom necessary to shoot.'[8] Igbo tribesmen admiringly called him *Trenchard Nwangwele* – young lizard.

In the first weeks of the New Year he established a permanent garrison at Bende, a small town founded on the trade of palm oil, in Abia state, between the Cross and Niger rivers. It was at Bende that a runner arrived from Calabar with orders for him to proceed at once to Aba, 60 miles to the south, where the natives were rioting and on a rampage of killing. Trenchard set off almost immediately with a large party of troops to deal with the trouble. The track to Aba, alongside the Iwo river, was wide and well maintained and three days of forced marching brought the troops to the outskirts of the village, where they were met by a pompous local district commissioner who immediately raised Trenchard's hackles (not a difficult feat) by introducing himself as 'the representative of the King'. He announced that the troubles had died down but he wanted the troops to stay while he looked into what had happened and dealt with the troublemakers.

Trenchard was preternaturally disinclined to be given orders by a district commissioner. He tersely informed the man that while he might represent the King, he (Trenchard) was in command of the expedition and he would remain in command. If he was not needed in Aba, he was certainly needed elsewhere and would depart in the morning. The district commissioner could accompany him, if he so wished, but Trenchard had no intention of leaving any of his men to protect him. The district commissioner fulminated at this slight to his authority and dispatched an indignant formal protest to Sir Walter Egerton, the newly arrived High Commissioner. Egerton replied, to Trenchard's undisguised delight, that the commander of a military expedition in the field should be regarded as a chief political officer and that all district commissioners were subordinate to him.

Trenchard would later describe Egerton as one of the greatest men he had ever met. He never forgot the High Commissioner's simple recipe for modernising Nigeria: 'The country must be opened by proper communications. Roads must be made through the thick bush, straight and broad, as that is the best civilising influence on any country.'[9] It was Sir Walter who insisted that every expedition into the hinterland should also carry out a survey. After he took office, troops cutting through the bush were invariably followed by a man with a measuring wheel. In this way much of the country was mapped.

Even in the bush, Trenchard made no concessions to the harsh conditions and enervating climate and maintained rigorous standards. A junior officer invited to dine with him would be expected to put on a clean shirt and a clean pair of shorts and would find Trenchard standing before his tent in a newly laundered shirt and collar and tie. Whisky and water would be offered, along with five grains of quinine, the compulsory daily dose, and dinner would be served on a table set up in the shelter of a cotton or mahogany tree. Conversation was usually stilted.

In March 1904 a native uprising in neighbouring Cameroon, to the south-east of Nigeria, quickly spread over the border. Cameroon had been annexed by Germany in 1884 and an iron-fisted system of forced labour instituted to improve the country's infrastructure. When the natives rebelled and massacred an entire German garrison, reports began reaching Government House in Calabar that the Southern

Nigeria Regiment outpost in the border town of Aparabong was under threat. An advance party was sent up the Cross river towards Aparabong in steel canoes and Trenchard was ordered to follow and take command.

His first problem was acquiring transport – the only vessel he could find was a heavily laden missionary launch on charter to a trader which was heading upriver and willing to take him as a passenger. En route Trenchard was curious about the cargo and the skipper was so evasive he became suspicious and ordered the tarpaulin covers to be removed. 'On that launch,' he recalled, 'were a lot of Dane guns[10] – four or five hundred of them – and kegs of gunpowder which were going to be sold to the very natives that I was going up to suppress!'[11] Trenchard never explained exactly what happened to the cargo, only that it never reached its destination and as a result there was a 'terrible row' which, in the end, the High Commissioner was obliged to sort out.

Trenchard linked up with the troops at a village about 30 miles south of Aparabong and learned that all the expedition's porters had bolted the previous night after rumours had spread that the garrison was going to be overrun and that a major battle was in the offing. In the absence of porters the gun carriages were the only transport available. He ordered three of the guns to be dismounted and the stores and munitions loaded onto the three carriages.

Leaving a small contingent behind to protect the remaining baggage and equipment, they set off at daybreak next morning, dragging the heavily laden gun carriages with them. When they arrived on the outskirts of Aparabong they came under desultory fire, but there was no real sign of any organised defence, and as night fell Trenchard directed a 'star shell' to be loaded into their one gun and fired over the town as an experiment to see what would happen. The effect was dramatic and far exceeded his expectations – the natives besieging the town panicked and fled en masse. Trenchard was able to lead his troops into Aparabong without firing another shot. He found the garrison's commanding officer in bed with malaria and a very high temperature and the other officers feeling 'rather sorry for themselves but otherwise all right'. (Such was the success of his ruse with the star shell that Trenchard subsequently had a consignment of Brock's fireworks sent out from England. The rockets and firecrackers, in particular, came to be regarded by the natives as fearsome Ju-Ju.)

Next day he sent a runner across the border asking the German commander to meet him. He was amused when the German arrived in a native canoe shortly afterwards wearing a spotless white dress uniform with full medals, including, Trenchard noted, an Iron Cross won in the Franco-Prussian war. They compared notes and discussed plans perfectly amicably. The German, a Colonel Muller, complained of the difficulty of getting any information from the tribesmen; Trenchard forbore to point out that the likely cause was the extreme brutality with which they were treated by their German colonial masters.

Within a month the rebellion on the Nigerian side of the border had collapsed. (Trenchard was incensed when he learned much later that after the uprising had been put down in Cameroon thousands of natives had been rounded up and forcibly driven into the desert, where many of them died of thirst and starvation. A United Nations report in 1985 revealed that the Herero tribe, predominantly cattle herders, were reduced from a population of 80,000 to some 15,000 starving refugees between 1904 and 1907 – the first case of genocide in the twentieth century.)

In the summer of 1904 Colonel Montanaro retired and Trenchard, as the next senior officer, was appointed temporary commanding officer. In his final dispatch to the High Commissioner, Montanaro praised Trenchard's tactics in the field:

> The energetic way in which he moved his troops through the country enabled him to visit and bring to reason many towns which up to now have been hostile to the Government. I consider he fully justified his selection for the command of the expedition. He laboured at times under great difficulties from want of a sufficient number of troops to carry on operations over an extended area, owing to an outbreak of guinea worm among his men, but he showed the greatest self-reliance and resource in meeting these difficulties.[12]

Since it was the rainy season and expeditions were curtailed, Trenchard set about 'cleaning up' the regiment in his role as temporary CO. He called the officers together and announced that he expected standards of discipline, dress and punctuality to be greatly improved. Henceforth there was to be no gambling, no consorting with native

women and no drunkenness. (Trenchard never touched alcohol during the day, but at six in the evening allowed himself a single whisky
and water with which he took his quinine tablets.) Anyone breaching
the new orders, he warned, could expect to be sent back to the UK
in disgrace. Trenchard recognised he was going to be unpopular, but
it was not in his nature to court popularity and he was completely
indifferent to the widespread belly-aching that ensued. In reality it
was short-lived: he had by then earned the respect of his fellow officers
by his conduct in the field and most soon accepted the new regime
with reasonable grace.

When he found five young officers playing poker he resolved to
make an example of them and send them all home. They protested,
claimed they were being treated unfairly and demanded to know on
what basis they were being sent home. He replied that he had decided
they were 'temperamentally unsuitable'.

'What does that mean?' one of them asked.

'It's a funny thing,' Trenchard replied, 'but King's Regulations don't
explain what it means. It just says that a Commanding Officer has the
power to order a man home if he is temperamentally unsuited.'

With that they had to be satisfied. (Some years later one of them
wrote to Trenchard to say that being sent home was the best thing that
could have happened to him because he was losing far more money at
the card table than he could afford.)[13]

'Major Trenchard is only disliked by the worst,' one young officer
wrote home, 'because he makes them work. I don't know what Calabar would do without him, for he keeps everything up to the top
standard . . . Everyone is inclined to be irritable, but he's the best we
have got out here.'[14]

Only the regimental medical officer, an alcoholic, challenged the
acting CO. One morning Trenchard accidentally tripped over his
black bag and spilled the contents, including an empty whisky bottle,
onto the floor. He was incensed to see the man's medical instruments
were filthy – actually rusty – and dismissed him on the spot. The doctor, perhaps bolstered by drink, insisted he could only be dismissed
by a court martial and wrote to both the High Commissioner and
to General Kemball claiming that Trenchard had exceeded his
authority and was 'probably insane'. Unfortunately the credibility
of his claim was somewhat blunted when, a few days later, he burst

into the sergeants' mess wearing nothing but a singlet, boasted that the King had appointed him governor of an island in the Mediterranean and invited the regimental sergeant major to join him as his chief staff officer in the pagoda which the King had been pleased to give him. It was his final appearance before being put on a ship back to England, destined for an asylum; in fact he died a few weeks later.

In July 1905, Lieutenant Colonel Harry Moorhouse arrived in Calabar to relieve Trenchard and take over command of the regiment. Moorhouse, who was only a year older than Trenchard, was a Royal Artillery officer who had been serving with the West African Frontier Force since 1900, most recently in northern Nigeria. He was an amiable, easy-going personality and a fine cricketer who had played regularly for the MCC at Lord's, enough in itself to warmly recommend him to the man he was replacing. They would later become great personal friends.

By the time of Moorhouse's arrival, Trenchard was finalising plans for a major expedition into the Bende-Onitsha hinterland as soon as the dry season arrived. The area to be covered was huge – the size of Belgium – one into which few white men had ever ventured and was closed to trade. He had no illusions about the risks.

'This expedition was expected to have a lot of hard fighting as most of the country [was] very thickly populated by truculent natives who were in a state of rebellion. They had been murdering people in villages, killing and eating them.'[15]

The plan, which Moorhouse approved, was for two columns, the larger one under Trenchard and the other commanded by Captain George Mair, a Boer War veteran like Trenchard, to set out from different locations, marching on a compass bearing which would bring them to a rendezvous in the heart of the area, where they would set up a base camp and send out patrols to 'bring the country under rule and order'. Trenchard's column comprised ten European officers and NCOs, 325 native soldiers and 600 porters.

After three days of marching in single file, cutting a path through the bush with machetes, a native runner arrived from the south with the disturbing news that the regimental doctor, who had been sent from Calabar to catch up with the column, had been kidnapped and the whole area through which they had passed was up in arms. Doctor

Stewart's fate was unknown, but Trenchard had little doubt that he was very unlikely to survive. He elected to press on and meet up with Mair's column as soon as possible and then return to look for the unfortunate doctor and deal with the uprising. His only method of communicating with Mair – there were no wireless or telegraph facilities at that time in the field – was by firing a star shell into the sky after dark and hoping for a similar response from Mair. That night his signal was answered by a star shell fired, he judged, some 40 to 50 miles distant.

They made good progress the following day and that night Trenchard directed two star shells to be fired in rapid succession – a pre-arranged distress signal he hoped Mair would interpret as an instruction to link up as rapidly as possible. At around four o'clock the next afternoon, 30 November 1905, he ordered a gun to be fired and was relieved to hear an answering shot fired relatively close by. An hour later, the two columns met.

Trenchard and Mair conferred and agreed to set up a base camp in the bush and return in strength the following day to the area where Dr Stewart had vanished. They left at first light, Trenchard setting a rapid pace and urging the men to keep up, despite the difficult conditions and the heat. The sun was low in the sky when the column was halted by an enormous trench dug in the red soil, some ten feet wide and at least six feet deep.

Reconnaissance parties were sent out left and right to ascertain its length and they reported back that it extended at least half a mile in both directions.

While Trenchard was still deciding which route to take, the forest on the other side of the trench erupted with hundreds of screaming Igbo tribesmen emerging from the trees. A hail of bullets, spears and arrows tore into the leading troops. 'Behind that trench,' Trenchard noted, 'was the most awful scene. Dane guns firing at us and the whole place seemed in an uproar. It sounded as if there were thousands and thousands of natives.'[16] His troops were returning fire and sweeping the forest with their Maxim machine guns with deadly effect, but the natives were undeterred. Trenchard was concerned that the tribesmen might attempt to circle round behind his position in the fading light and trap him against the trench, so he shouted to his artillery officer above the din, ordering him to fire a salvo of star shells. Although it was a trick he had tried before he had little confidence it would work again – he thought it quite likely the natives had got wise to it. He was wrong.

As the first star shell burst above the trees Trenchard could see, in its eerie glow, hundreds of startled black faces turned skywards. A second and third shell quickly followed and a strange silence suddenly fell over the forest as the warring tribesmen began slinking away through the trees to put as much distance as possible between themselves and the white man's menacing Ju-Ju in the sky. Trenchard was amazed.

The troops stayed on guard at the trench through the night and the following morning skirted round it and entered a native village which appeared to have been hastily – and recently – abandoned. There was not a man, woman or child to be seen. (Villagers often fled on the approach of troops and occasionally left booby traps behind – like covered earthenware cooking pots filled with angry bees.)

Trenchard and Mair were standing in a clearing in the centre of the village when an elderly man appeared, apparently intent on giving himself up. Under interrogation, he revealed the doctor's dreadful demise. Dr Stewart, a newcomer to Nigeria unaccustomed to the hazards of travelling alone in the bush, had attempted to catch up with the column on a bicycle. He promptly lost his way and fell into the hands of rebel tribesmen. He had been kept alive for three days and slowly dismembered as he was paraded, naked and tied to a pole, through all the nearby villages. His fingers, toes, ears and nose had been cut off and eaten. He was finally decapitated in the very clearing where they were standing.

Trenchard knew that the doctor's death presaged trouble. The Igbos believed that eating a white man fortified them with the white man's Ju-Ju – thus they were likely to be more aggressive than usual and more inclined to attack the expedition. For the next four weeks his patrols were constantly at risk of ambush and under fire from snipers with Dane guns. Trenchard was frustrated by his inability to confront the tribesmen and worried that porters who lagged behind patrols were often captured and eaten. On one occasion three porters were taken at once and by the time he realised they were gone it was too late – he turned back to try to rescue them but found only three headless corpses trussed up for roasting.

The breakthrough came one night when a native crawled into their

camp on his hands and knees with the information that some five
thousand armed Igbo tribesmen were hiding in a swamp only about
a mile away. It was the opportunity for which Trenchard had been
waiting. He gathered together half his force, with three Maxim machine guns, ready to mount an attack at dawn. What followed he
described as a 'brisk little fight' in which large numbers of tribesmen
were killed by the machine guns and many more captured. The tribesmen fought with fanatical courage but their antiquated and primitive
weapons were no match for the machine guns and it was all over in
half an hour.

> Of those captured [Trenchard wrote], I let them go at the rate of
> two or three a day, having spoken to them that they had better
> make peace terms, but the only peace terms that I could accept
> were that they must hand over the Doctor's head and every bone of
> his body. I knew that if I did not get that, they would say they had
> killed a white man and had got the white man's Ju-Ju in them and
> therefore they were as strong as the white man and would always
> be fighting. I said the war would go on until then, and no mercy
> would be shown.[17]

Three months of what he recalled as 'desultory scrapping' went by
before a skull was brought in which the replacement medical officer
certified was almost certainly a European not long dead, and bit by bit
other bones were delivered. In the end Trenchard considered he had
collected all the doctor's remains with the exception of 'the hands and
the left lower part of the leg'.

As a punishment for his murder, he pressed thousands of Igbo
tribesmen into forced labour to build the roads that Sir Walter Egerton, the High Commissioner, believed would be the first step to bring
civilisation to the interior of the country.

> After they had surrendered the remains of Doctor Stewart, I pro-
> ceeded to make roads, broad roads, forty feet wide, absolutely
> straight up and down hill. We cut down the bush, we dug out
> stumps, and the natives were made to do it as one of the condi-
> tions of peace . . . Many years afterwards, on seeing that country
> with my wife when we drove through it in a motor car, what

struck me enormously was how the natives had grown in stature, were physically now fine men, walking about in thousands on the roads, doing their business, happy and contented, instead of looking like monkeys, fleeing on the bush paths from each other as though they were wild animals. It pleased me more than I can say to think that those years, when I had wondered if I was doing any good in making what I called the Egerton roads, had pacified the country and brought home the truth of 'communications make civilisation'.[18]

By the end of the expedition in April 1906, the two columns had marched more than 1100 miles, most of it across unexplored country, and in the process had discovered a previously unknown range of hills rising out of the jungle. Nearly 3000 guns had been surrendered and the regiment's casualties were extraordinarily light – only one soldier had been killed, and five officers and 58 other ranks wounded. Years later, when he was an unsuccessful candidate for the Staff College, Trenchard would write: 'Any officer with a little gumption can march a column through most of these savage, badly armed people, losing a few men every day; but it requires enormous energy, careful plans and a cool head on the part of the officer and great marching powers on the part of the men to inflict a crushing defeat on the elusive enemy.'[19]

The Bende-Onitsha expedition was an undoubted success but by then Trenchard was suffering from the first stages of blackwater fever, a serious complication of malaria with a high mortality rate among Europeans, which induced a high fever, vomiting and jaundice. Characteristically, he had refused to admit that he was ill until he was on the point of collapse. He was taken back to Calabar on a litter, immediately hospitalised and then sent home on sick leave. Sir Walter Egerton's report to the Secretary of State at the Colonial Office on military operations during the dry season of 1905–6 made special mention of him: 'Brevet Major H.M. Trenchard, Royal Scots Fusiliers, has commanded a column of 800 men in the field for five months and shown energy, resource and powers of organisation far above average. I wish to bring his services specially to Your Excellency's notice . . .'[20]

6

TAMING THE TRIBESMEN

Soon after returning to England Trenchard learned that both he and Mair were to be awarded the DSO 'in recognition of services during the operations in the Bende-Onitsha hinterland, Southern Nigeria, November 1905 to April 1906'.[1] He was not the kind of man to set much store by what he liked to describe as 'baubles', but he nevertheless must have been secretly pleased and proud that his exertions in Nigeria had been officially recognised and rewarded.

Back home in time to enjoy the tranquillity of an English summer after the debilitating heat of Africa he soon recovered his health. He rented a house near Ross-on-Wye in Herefordshire and invited both his parents to stay. Their financial position had not improved. They had moved from Portsmouth to London and were living in cramped rooms in a dismal boarding house in Earls Court after his mother, despite her poor health, had found a job with the Church Army as an 'investigator', ensuring that people seeking the charity's relief really needed it.

Trenchard could not but be moved by their difficult circumstances and it was partly in the hope of making some money to help them that he began to look into the possibility, unofficially, of exploiting Nigeria's commercial potential for trade. After three years' service with the West African Frontier Force he could have honourably retired and returned to his regiment but he had already decided to go back, preferring action, even in the 'white man's graveyard', to the ennui of peacetime soldiering in the UK.

He first approached Sir Thomas Lipton, the Scots tea baron and owner of a chain of grocer's shops across Britain, with a proposal to import tea into Nigeria. Sir Thomas heard him out at his City Road office in London, but remained unpersuaded that a market existed in West Africa. Undeterred, Trenchard next sought an appointment with Richard Burbidge, the managing director of Harrods. Burbidge, perhaps intrigued to know why a serving army officer would want to see him with a business proposition, agreed to meet him in his office at the upmarket Knightsbridge store. Trenchard came straight to the point. He explained he had an intimate knowledge of Nigeria, the country and its people, and claimed he could open the Nigerian market to Harrods by acting as an agent, on commission, for the import of a whole range of goods, including bicycles, tinned food and textiles, for which there was enormous demand. Burbidge was, understandably, sceptical, particularly when Trenchard admitted that he had no commercial experience, no capital, no authority from the Colonial Office to set up a business on the side of his official duties and spent half the year more or less out of touch on expeditions into unexplored territory. Nevertheless, he agreed to put Trenchard's proposal to his board, while holding out no promises.

Trenchard was not hopeful and was both pleased and surprised when, a week later, he received a letter from Burbidge saying the board had agreed to a trial period of 12 months. It was arranged that the first consignment of goods on approval (including the first motorcycles ever seen in Nigeria) would be shipped out in the hold of the vessel on which Trenchard was booked to return to duty. To celebrate, he treated himself – although he readily admitted that he could not afford it – to an expensive tiffin carrier from Drew's, the Piccadilly silversmith. It was enormously heavy and came complete with blue and gold china coffee cups and liqueur glasses, but he was inordinately proud of it and it would accompany him on all his future expeditions into the Nigerian interior.

He had only been back in Calabar for a few weeks before he was called upon to undertake another mission, this time to open up the country occupied by a mysterious tribe, the Munshis (now known as the Tiv people), in the far north of the territory. The most elusive of all the peoples of West Africa, they were distinguished by strange facial markings and their savagery. 'This tribe had a legend grown up around them,' Trenchard noted. 'That they were the most hostile tribe of enormous numbers . . . That they were the most fierce fighters, that they used poison arrows. That they wiped out and massacred all the people from many villages . . . Sketchy drawings were made of what they were supposed to look like, showing curious markings on their faces, but nobody had ever seen them.'[2]

When Joseph Chamberlain had been Secretary of State for the Colonies several years earlier, plans had been discussed in London to send out an entire infantry brigade supported by artillery to assist local troops in subduing the Munshis, but nothing had come of it. Trenchard knew this, but when Sir Walter Egerton asked him if he needed additional troops for the expedition, he nonchalantly replied that he was confident the Southern Nigeria Regiment could handle it without any assistance from England.

He set up a tented base camp at Abakaliki, a town within a few miles of Munshi territory, and sent out patrols to gather intelligence on the Munshi people. What he got back was a lot of confused and fearful gossip. 'We were told how they would eat us up, how there were millions of them, and how you got killed by poison arrows from which you died in nine minutes in awful agony . . . and that we needed many more men.'[3] (The native troops were terrified of poisoned arrows, although in the whole of his service in Nigeria Trenchard only saw one man die from one, albeit in great agony.)

Frustrated by the lack of solid intelligence, Trenchard had what he described as a 'brainwave'. He asked his political officer to inquire among the locals in Abakaliki if any of them were married to Munshi women. To the amazement of everyone, they found some. 'This was a tremendous surprise. Everybody was flabbergasted at the idea that Munshi women had been living in our midst all the time.' Not only that, but one of them had a brother who visited her frequently. Arrangements were made for Trenchard to meet him. He turned out to be very much like the drawings that Trenchard had seen in intelligence reports – he was short, squat, virile and intelligent-looking, with identical markings on his face. After interrogating him for some time with the help of an interpreter, Trenchard came to the conclusion, as he had suspected all along, that the Munshis were nothing like as warlike as their reputation suggested. 'I concluded there was nothing to be unduly alarmed at, if only one showed no fear and a determination to do what was necessary.'

Ignoring dire warnings from his political officer that he was courting disaster, Trenchard changed his plans and decided to enter the area leading a small column comprising himself, four other white officers, a doctor, an interpreter and 25 men (plus three machine guns as an insurance in case he had got it wrong). They set off at dawn, marching on a compass bearing that would take them across Munshi territory towards the Katsina river, at a point where there was an outpost of the Northern Nigeria Regiment on the far bank. The country was an open, undulating plain dotted with high scrub bushes and native villages of thatched huts.

As they approached the first village, Trenchard could see that the natives, most of them naked, their bodies covered with pigment and oil and carrying bows and arrows, had formed up to block their path. His options were few – he could stop and try to negotiate, he could change course and skirt round the village, or he could march straight through and hope they would step aside. True to form, he chose the last option. 'I put two machine guns with three British officers in charge of them at the head of my column and we then marched straight through the village after I had given them orders not to open fire unless I gave the word. The natives fell back on either side of us, some of them looking very sour. Many of them had bows and arrows, but no one had shown any sign of using them.' This became the routine at every village; occasionally the Munshis would follow the troops after they had passed through, but when the interpreter shouted at them to stay away they turned back.

> Where to camp the first night was a problem . . . Late in the af-
> ternoon we halted on a mound with a clear view all round and we
> cut a few thorn shrubs as a protection for our camp. I do not think
> anybody slept that night. It was a bright, moonlit night, and we
> could see almost as clear as day. The natives shouted and kept beat-
> ing their tom-toms and from the noise they could not have been
> more than a couple of hundred yards away.[4]

But there was no attack, neither that night nor any other night. When the column reached the outpost of the Northern Nigeria Regiment on the Katsina river, no one could believe it had crossed the entire territory of the Munshi without firing a shot. Soon after arriving at the Katsina river Trenchard sent emissaries back down the trail with gifts – singlet vests, hand mirrors and other trinkets – for the chiefs and a message to say he wanted to meet them. Three days later he was meeting Munshi chiefs in his tent at the spot where they had first camped overnight: none of them brought their bows and arrows.

Trenchard's first impression of the chiefs was that they were a 'bloodthirsty-looking gang' but he was encouraged that they did not seem disposed to violence and they listened carefully as he explained why the government wanted to open the territory to trade and bring an end to intertribal warfare. He offered to take them to see where the white man lived and promised they would be returned safely to their villages. Four of them took up the offer and were given a guided tour of Abakaliki and treated as honoured guests. Abakaliki, once a major slave trading centre, was a thriving market town at that time, trading in yams, cassava, rice and palm oil. The Munshi chiefs had never seen such prosperity and were clearly impressed. By the end of their visit Trenchard was convinced that the rumours about the Munshi were 'bunkum' and that their territory could be opened without bloodshed, which was what he reported to the High Commissioner.

The expedition then moved south to an area where a different tribe was causing trouble. After what Trenchard insouciantly described as 'a certain amount of fighting' he learned from captured prisoners that the principal troublemaker was the 'second chief', a man said to be of great height and physique, a terrifying warrior who had vowed to kill all white men. Everything Trenchard heard about him indicated that such a man was not interested in making peace and he made a decision of which he was later ashamed. He sent a message to the 'second chief' guaranteeing his safe conduct if he would agree to a meeting, but at the same time made plans to kidnap him. Breaking his word to the natives was, he knew, a terrible risk, but he could see no other way of ending the fighting – tribesmen were getting pointlessly killed every day. Taking the Munshi chiefs to see the world of the white men had worked wonders, but he had little doubt that this individual would refuse such blandishments, so his plan was to force him to do what the Munshi chiefs had done voluntarily in the hope it would make him see reason. 'I hoped for the best,' he admitted. 'I did not want to go on killing people.'

Trenchard's plans were complicated by the 'second chief' arriving with his two sons – all three of them tall, magnificent-looking men quite unlike the others in their tribe. Trenchard reported that all three were 'collared', but only after a 'terrific fight'. After they had been overpowered they were each tied into a hammock and sent downriver in a government launch to Calabar under close guard. Trenchard did not accompany them, but left instructions that they were to be given 'honoured guest' treatment and shown everything – the big ships in the harbour, the hospital, the schools – and taken shopping to buy whatever they wanted with money supplied by the government.

His gamble paid off. 'Within a month,' Trenchard reported, 'he [the second chief] was brought back to my camp . . . he rushed towards me and had already learned to hold out his hand and shake hands with me and was delighted with what he had seen down country . . . The war was over.'[5] Trenchard told him to send a message to his people to say he was back and to call a meeting in three days' time. Trenchard estimated that some 80,000 tribesmen turned up. Through an interpreter he outlined the government's peace terms and then formally presented the 'second chief' with a Birmingham-made smoking cap, in blue velvet, stitched with gold and silver braid, with a long gold tassel.

The 'second chief' soon took over as ruler of the tribe – Trenchard presumed he killed the leading chief – and was, as far as the government was concerned, co-operative in every way. (Trenchard was saddened to learn, some years later, that he had been murdered by a jealous rival, not for his position, or his land, or his wives – but for his hat.)

In March 1907, Colonel Moorhouse's stint as commanding officer came to an end and he was replaced by the next most senior officer – Trenchard. Around this time the headquarters of the regiment was transferred from Calabar to Lagos, now the largest city in Nigeria but then an unhealthy depressing place on a low-lying island surrounded by a malodorous lagoon. It was not a popular move, as one young officer noted in a letter home: 'I haven't really slept since I arrived. You lie surrounded by mosquito nets in a sort of pool of perspiration until from sheer weariness you slide into a state of lethargy and welcome the dawn to get up and have a bath . . . We've a rotten mess here, not a patch on Calabar.'[6]

Trenchard, who was promoted to temporary lieutenant colonel the following year, did his best to improve things. He had the decrepit barracks pulled down and rebuilt; he transformed a desolate patch of ground into a sports field which was later said to be 'the envy and admiration of all who visit Lagos';[7] he improved the racecourse and offered trophies for soccer, golf, tennis and polo; he had a small motor cruiser, the *Oyster*, shipped out from England to make patrolling the creeks and waterways easier; and he built a house for himself on the edge of the lagoon which he claimed to be the finest in Lagos, despite the doubtful skills of the construction team. (He had a sapling bougainvillea planted in front of the officers' mess and was delighted, many years later when visiting Nigeria as a businessman, to see that it had grown enormously.)

His private importing business was also flourishing, despite objections from local merchants that he was undercutting their prices. Unquestionably many individuals looked askance at a British officer running a business on the side. There were certainly raised eyebrows in the Colonial Office and an official complaint was lodged with the High Commissioner, but Sir Walter Egerton, a great supporter of Trenchard, ruled that he had broken no rules. The agency's turnover in its first full year of trading was in excess of £10,000 and Trenchard took great pride in the window dressing of the agency's newly opened shop in Lagos.

In his autobiographical notes he made virtually no reference to his entrepreneurial activities, except to mention casually towards the end of his tour that he was 'bringing out motor cycles from England' – and then only because of an amusing incident when he allowed his cook to have a go on one on the barrack square. Trenchard reported that he went round and round in circles, gripping the handlebars tightly with his eyes starting out of his head, until the petrol ran out. No one had thought to tell him how to shut down the throttle.

With the situation in Southern Nigeria greatly improved compared to when he had first arrived, Trenchard had time to play polo – he bought a string of ponies on the strength of his import business profits – organised regular horse races and enjoyed playing tennis with the High Commissioner. He only undertook one further expedition, when several tribes began fighting over a river with clean water. He set up a base camp at the source of the river and announced that henceforth it was the white man's water, but as the white man was kind and generous, he would give the water away for free. That settled all further disputes.

By the beginning of 1910 Trenchard had served in Nigeria for more than seven years and his health was suffering in the unforgiving climate. He had gone down with blackwater fever several more times, he had been warned by his doctor that his blood count was alarmingly low, he had no energy or appetite and was enduring crippling headaches. One morning his servant, John Ewoh, entered his quarters and found him lying unconscious in bed. A doctor was called, diagnosed an abscess on the liver, and advised him to return home immediately. Trenchard recognised that he could not continue and that he had no real alternative but to relinquish his command.

At the time he left the Southern Nigeria Regiment he was proud to note that the officers no longer lounged about the mess in their pyjamas. They dined off mahogany tables resplendent with the regimental silver and wore mess kit every evening. And the country was sufficiently peaceful for him to take a memorable cycling tour, with the High Commissioner and without military escorts, along some of the roads he had caused to be built.

'I am not a religious man,' he wrote later in his 'jottings' about Nigeria, 'and I have a very simple rule which I try to follow and which is certainly not unique. I want to leave my little bit of the world better than when I found it.'[8]

Friends and family were shocked by Trenchard's appearance when he returned to Britain. He was drawn and gaunt, his short cropped hair emphasising the unhealthy pallor of his complexion; he had lost weight and looked much older than his 37 years. It was months before he was fully able to recover his health; thus it was November 1910 before he was posted back to the 2nd Battalion of the Royal Scots Fusiliers, then based at Ebrington Barracks in Londonderry, as a company commander with the reduced rank of brevet major.

He had been away from the regiment for so long that he managed to mark his return by turning up on his first church parade in full dress uniform wearing his bearskin back to front. A subaltern, too nervous himself to tell the company commander, detailed a reluctant sergeant to break the news. Trenchard took it in surprisingly good part. Ordering the company to stand at ease, he said: 'Take two minutes' laughter while I fix this thing, then let's forget about it.' Actually, no one dared laugh, but then no one forgot about it either.

The men of F Company soon discovered their new company commander was a strict disciplinarian.

We were at first inclined to be terrified of him [Colour Sergeant C.F. Judge wrote]. He came to us with such a reputation and we did not know quite what to expect. One day soon after he arrived we were doing arms drill on the green outside the barracks. 'Colour sergeant!' he shouted. I ran up to him and saluted. 'That man over there is slacking,' he said, 'bring him to me.' I called to the man and he marched up. 'You're a colour sergeant and you ran,' the Major said to me. 'This man's a private and he walks. Why?'

I said something about me being an old soldier and therefore always moving at the double when summoned by an officer. The major stared at us for a minute and then said to the man, 'See that tree over there? Double to it and come back here.' The private soldier did so and when he returned, panting, the major said to me 'Send him back and let him keep it up for an hour.' After that, we all ran when he called us. But he was not a bully; he was hard but fair and thought of nothing but strict duty at all times. Only shirkers and lead swingers needed to fear him and once the slate was cleaned it was forgotten.[9]

Junior officers in the battalion tended to be in awe of Trenchard, both because of his extensive experience – it was well known he had recently been in Africa fighting rebellious tribes armed with spears and poisoned arrows – and his brusque demeanour. Uncommunicative, monosyllabic when he could be persuaded to enter into a conversation, he hated gossip and lax discipline. He was almost always the first to sit down for breakfast in the officers' mess. A 'Good morning' from a younger officer would only be answered with a grunt, but anyone who failed to greet him would be bluntly asked where he had 'mislaid his manners'.

When Second Lieutenant Robert Barton arrived in the battalion fresh from Sandhurst he found himself sitting opposite the imposing figure of the F Company commander at dinner on his first night. Trenchard fixed him with a glare and demanded to know if he liked riding.

'No, sir, not very much,' Barton replied truthfully, having fallen off his mount at Sandhurst riding school no less than 72 times, by his own count.

'Good,' Trenchard barked. 'Meet me at the stables tomorrow afternoon and we'll go for a ride.'

Those present swore the colour drained from Barton's face at this news, but he returned from the dreaded ride next day amazed by Trenchard's skill and patience teaching him how to handle a horse. Having been thrown at the first fence they reached, he eventually cleared it under Trenchard's watchful eye.

'He seemed to know exactly when my mount would grow weary of trifling with me,' he told his friends later.

Some senior colleagues found Trenchard, frankly, tiresome. He was accepted as an experienced, professional and energetic officer, but he was tactless and abrasive, with a tendency to speak his mind in the most forthright, if not always the most articulate, terms without regard to possibly causing offence. He was also inclined to interfere, irritatingly, making unsolicited and unwelcome suggestions to fellow officers about how they could better carry out their duties. He carped about the drudgery of form-filling and offered to demonstrate the system he had devised in Lagos which cut paperwork by half. Unsociable in the mess, the damning verdict, by and large, on the newly arrived officer in the battalion was that he was 'unclubbable'. Even the easy-going commanding officer, Lieutenant Colonel Donald Stuart, who claimed to like Trenchard, was under no illusion about the strength of his personality and observed more than once that he wondered if there was sufficient room in the regiment for both of them.

One of the few friends Trenchard made in the battalion was Captain the Honourable James Boyle, the younger son of the Earl of Glasgow, and his wife Katherine, who lived with their two small children in a rented lodge four miles from the barracks. Katherine, known to friends and family as Kitty, always remembered her husband coming home one day and saying 'a most unusual customer' had arrived in the battalion and was creating quite a stir. 'His name is Trenchard. He's a major and a holy terror. He has the Colonel looking like a ghost and he's only been in the place a couple of days. He seems determined, in a nice but irresistible way, to turn the place completely upside down.'

'What an odd-sounding creature,' Kitty said.

'Yes,' her husband agreed. 'I've invited him to lunch tomorrow.'

Trenchard turned out much as Kitty had pictured him. 'Big, loud

voice, slightly aggressive manner. Older than I had imagined but with
a sense of humour. I could see why the younger officers shrank back
from him in terror.'[10] After lunch they went for a stroll through the
grounds of the lodge and Kitty suggested to her husband that he bring
over some of the subalterns for a shoot.

'What do you want them cluttering up your grounds for?' Trenchard growled.

Kitty fixed him with a piercing look and snapped 'They are OUR
grounds, you know.'

When he discovered a disused polo ground not far from the barracks, he had it mowed and laid out in no time and 'encouraged' the
young officers to get involved by issuing an outrageous edict, as Mess
President, that no officer would be allowed to drink in the mess unless
he kept at least one pony. It caused enormous resentment. Trenchard
was entirely unconcerned and would stretch out of an evening in front
of the smoky fire in the mess anteroom with the newspapers or a book,
apparently unaware of the glum atmosphere. But before six months
were up, no less than 16 officers were playing polo regularly in the
summer and hunting with the Londonderry Harriers in the winter,
perhaps a record for an infantry regiment. Trenchard by then was the
officer in charge of Battalion sports, football and the Regimental Polo
and Hunting Club.

'He made us all play polo whether we liked it or not,' one unnamed
young officer grumbled. As obsessive about polo in Londonderry as he
was in Sialkot, Trenchard bought his own pony, called The Nipper,
in Dublin and was always ready to advise his brother officers looking
for a horse, or willing to haggle with dealers to drive down the price.
He took responsibility for managing the battalion's communal stable
and was sympathetic to any young officers finding it difficult to meet
the cost of stabling. In the mess if someone ordered a drink at the bar
he liked to point out that 'the price of a glass of port is the price of a
pony's feed'.

Kitty Boyle's opinion of Trenchard was not improved by watching
him play polo. His behaviour on the field seemed to her to be exces-
sively impatient, excitable and inconsiderate. He charged about on his
pony, shouting, exhorting and admonishing the other players on his
team. When the ball shot towards him with several players in pursuit
and he bellowed 'Leave it to me!' Kitty muttered to a friend standing

nearby that she hoped he missed it. After the game Trenchard heard about the incident and taxed her about it. Kitty, who was as plain-spoken as Trenchard himself, did not dispute it and 'ticked him off' for being selfish, showing off and bullying the subalterns.

'Was I being too noisy?' Trenchard asked.

'Yes,' Kitty replied. 'Don't be too hard on these beginners.'

Trenchard was taken aback by such candour from a woman and tried to explain that as he had been playing with novices they needed to be told what to do.

Later, despite this inauspicious start to their relationship, they became firm friends, so much so that when Kitty gave birth to a daughter, Belinda, her third child, she asked Trenchard to be the baby's godfather. Kitty recognised that Trenchard was uncomfortable with women and did her best to bring him out, discovering in the process that she liked him, that behind the brusque facade was a man with considerable charm who laughed immoderately at his own jokes. In the summer of 1911 the Boyles invited Trenchard to join them grouse shooting on the family estate in Ayrshire, staying with the Earl and Countess of Glasgow in Kelburn Castle, which had been in possession of the Boyle family since the sixteenth century. One afternoon on the moors Trenchard received a charge of shot in the back of the knee from another guest, a Royal Navy captain. The guest was distraught, but Trenchard brushed it off.

Polo, hunting and shooting were pleasant enough pastimes, but the truth was that Trenchard found peacetime soldiering monotonous and unrewarding, although he remained punctilious in carrying out his duties. When organising manoeuvres he would dictate his plans to Colour Sergeant Judge for upwards of three hours and the unfortunate Judge would have to try and make them intelligible on paper, a far from easy task given that his company commander's words usually came too slowly for his flying thoughts.

As he approached 40, still only a substantive major, Trenchard recognised his future in the army was problematic. He had twice applied for Staff College and twice been turned down. (He suspected his poor command of English in his dispatches and memoranda had probably counted against him.) Accepting that promotion within the regiment was unlikely, he scoured for opportunities in the Colonies, firing off applications to the Egyptian army, the Colonial Defence Force, the

Macedonian Gendarmerie and the mounted defence forces in South Africa, New Zealand and Australia. No one wanted him. He even wrote to Richard Burbidge, the elderly managing director of Harrods, with whom he had set up the import agency in Nigeria, asking if a job might be available, but Burbidge could offer him nothing.

'I wonder when you and I will meet again,' he wrote despondently to his newly married sister Catherine, who was about to leave home for South Africa in early 1912. 'I should so like to have come across to see you off, but it's really impossible. I have no cash. I wish I could have sent you more, but I have not got it now. [As it was, the cheque he sent for her wedding represented half his monthly salary.] I shall probably come out one day to South Africa to see you if I can only stick out the service for another twelve years.'[11]

In fact he had already more or less decided that he would not stick it out and was seriously considering resigning his commission when, in the spring of 1912, he received a letter from a friend, Eustace Loraine, with whom he had served in Nigeria. Loraine, then a lieutenant in the Grenadier Guards, had been on the headquarters staff of the Southern Nigeria Regiment in Lagos and had taken part in Trenchard's Munshi expedition as a section commander. While still in Nigeria he had read reports of Louis Blériot's historic flight across the English Channel in 1909 which had stirred his interest in aviation and on his return to Britain he asked to be seconded from his regiment in order to learn to fly. He earned his aviator's certificate in November 1911.

In his letter Loraine was full of the wonders of aviation and urged Trenchard to follow his example. 'You've no idea what you're missing,' he wrote. 'Come and see men crawling like ants on the earth from above.'

It was a letter that would change Trenchard's life.

TAKING TO THE SKIES

In 1901 the English writer H.G. Wells contributed a remarkably prescient series of articles to the *North American Review* under the title 'Anticipations: An Experiment in Prophesy', in which he predicted that command of the air would be decisive in future wars. Once a flying machine had been perfected, he wrote, 'the new invention will be most assuredly applied to war'.

Two years later, on 17 December 1903, the most famous date in the history of aviation, Orville Wright made the first powered, sustained and controlled flight in a heavier-than-air machine on a bitterly cold day at Kitty Hawk, North Carolina. (An achievement still celebrated on vehicle licence plates in the state: 'First In Flight'.) Curiously, the event failed to excite much media interest at the time. In Britain it merited a single paragraph in the *Daily Mail* and only 16 lines in the *New York Times*, which reported that the unnamed inventors were anxious to sell their device – 'an adaptation of the box kite idea' – to a government for 'scouting and signal work'. The story was sandwiched between a long piece about an unfortunate young British girl who had arrived in the United States only to discover her fiancé had been killed in a train crash and that of an even more unfortunate lady who had perhaps unsurprisingly dropped dead after eating three dozen Christmas cakes.

Undeterred, the Wright brothers, Orville and Wilbur, remained convinced that in the absence of any obvious commercial market, their best chance of making money from their invention lay with a 'great government'.[1] It was disappointing that their own government showed no interest but their hopes rose when a British officer, Lieutenant Colonel John Capper, turned up at their home in Dayton, Ohio, in the autumn of 1904 to discuss the military potential of their flying machine. (Capper was attached to the British Army's experimental

School of Ballooning in Aldershot and would pilot Britain's first military airship flight over London in 1907. In fact he was in the United States to see the aviation exhibits at the World's Fair in St Louis, but having heard about the Wrights' work made a detour to see them.) Welcome as he was, the secretive Wrights were not willing to show him their machine or talk business although they were prepared to discuss their work at length and made a very favourable impression, judging by the persuasive report Capper filed on his return to England.

> I do not think they are likely to claim more than they can perform . . . [They] have satisfied me that they have at least made far greater strides in the evolution of the flying machine than any of their predecessors . . . If carried to a successful issue, we may shortly have as accessories of warfare, scouting machines which will go at a great pace, and be independent of obstacles on the ground, whilst offering from their elevated position unrivalled opportunities of ascertaining what is occurring in the heart of the enemy's country.[2]

Capper had extracted a promise from the Wrights that when they were ready to talk business they would 'give Great Britain a chance'. In March 1905 the Wrights wrote to the War Office offering to supply an 'aerial scouting machine' capable of carrying two men and sufficient fuel for a flight covering at least 50 miles at 30 miles an hour. The trouble was that the brothers wanted the War Office to sign a binding contract *before* they were willing to provide a machine or reveal its secrets, something that the bureaucrats in Whitehall were very reluctant to do. Negotiations continued for several months, with the War Office insisting it wanted to see the machine fly before signing any contracts and the brothers equally insistent that a contract must be forthcoming first.

In the early summer of 1906 the War Office tried a different tack and asked the Wrights how much they would charge for all the rights to their invention. Orville and Wilbur had no doubts about the value of their work. For the staggering sum of $100,000 (around £1.75 million at today's values) they offered to supply a machine, train a pilot to fly it and grant the British government the right to manufacture further machines based on their patents. For a further $100,000 they were willing to sell all their formulas and tables. Capper's view was that the price was 'out of all proportion to the benefits to be gained'[3] and recommended that the Wrights' offer should be turned down.

By then other inventors were experimenting with flying machines similar to that of the Wrights. In October 1906, the Brazilian aviation pioneer Alberto Santos-Dumont, who had become famous after piloting an airship around the Eiffel Tower in 1901, coaxed a fixed-wing aircraft of his own design and construction off the ground in the Bois de Boulogne and flew for 722 feet – the first heavier-than-air flight to be certified by the Aéro-Club de France. The event was covered in a faintly uninterested fashion by the *Daily Mail*, prompting the exasperated proprietor, Lord Northcliffe, to send a furious memorandum to the editor. The story was not that Santos-Dumont had flown 722 feet, he fumed, it was that 'England was no longer an island . . . It means the aerial chariots of a foe descending on British soil if war comes.'

Less than 12 months later the *Daily Express* excitedly reported 'BRITAIN'S FIRST AEROPLANE EXPERIMENTS WITH AERIAL FIGHTING MACHINES – SUCCESS ASSURED'. An enterprising reporter equipped with a pair of powerful field glasses had been sent to Scotland to observe the official testing of Britain's first military flying machine, which was being carried out in great secrecy on the Duke of Atholl's estate in the Highlands. The pilot was Lieutenant John Dunne, an officer who had been invalided home from South Africa and assigned to the Army Balloon Factory, where he designed and built gliders. Regrettably, the newspaper's forecast that success was assured was misplaced – Dunne's glider, fitted with two engines for its maiden flight, was launched from a specially laid track and immediately dived, nose-first, into the ground.

In the summer of 1908 Wilbur Wright, now pursuing a contract with the French government, staged a series of flying demonstrations on the Hunandières racecourse near Le Mans which caused a sensation. At the controls of a Wright Flyer, Wilbur was able to climb to 90 feet, stay aloft for 30 minutes and effortlessly perform manoeuvres other aviators could only dream about – circles and turns and figures of eight. He proved beyond doubt, to sceptics and rivals alike, that he and his brother had finally solved the conundrum of flight. 'We are as children compared to the Wrights!' the French pioneer aviator René Gasnier exclaimed with dismay.[4]

Belatedly prompted by events, in Britain the Committee of Imperial Defence (CID) set up an Aerial Navigation Sub-Committee to investigate 'the dangers to which we would be exposed on sea or on land by any developments in aerial navigation reasonably probable in the near future' and to determine what, if any, military benefits might accrue to Britain from the use of airships or aeroplanes.[5] General Sir William Nicholson, Chief of the Imperial General Staff, was certain he knew the answer to both questions: 'None at all.'

While many senior officers wanted nothing to do with these frail contraptions of spruce, wire and fabric wallowing about in the sty and ridiculed the notion of air warfare, there was a school of thought (not including General Nicholson) that flying machines could be useful for reconnaissance purposes – to be able to 'see over the hill' – if a reliable, reasonably easy to fly machine could be developed. But few could see military potential beyond that. At a lecture on aviation at the Royal United Services Institute in London a staff officer warned that the public should not be carried away with 'wild ideas' about battles in the sky. The hypothesis of air to air combat, he pointed out, was particularly absurd since it would mean 'certain death' for both combatants.[6]

The fact that the development of aviation was largely in the hands of enthusiastic amateurs and empiricists hardly endeared the emerging science to military men, neither did the fact that the first successful heavier-than-air flight in Britain was piloted by a flamboyant American showman with a preposterous 12-inch waxed moustache and questionable past. Samuel F. Cody arrived in Europe in the early 1890s with a touring 'Wild West' show in which he gave demonstrations of his horse riding, shooting and lassooing skills, allegedly learned from his youth as a cowboy in Texas. In fact he was born in Iowa. Much of his past was pure invention – he variously claimed his entire family was massacred by Indians or that he was the son of Buffalo Bill Cody (he wasn't – his real name was Cowdery). But he was certainly versatile – his later stage show, *The Klondyke Nugget*, a melodrama in which he played the villain and performed with his common-law wife and her children, became a big success in British music halls.

Sometime towards the end of the century he became fascinated by kite flying and experimented with huge box designs capable of lifting a man at ever increasing heights. He made several demonstration 'flights' in and around London and held an exhibition of his designs at Alexandra Palace in 1903. The following year he was hired by the Admiralty to look into the military possibility of using man-lifting kites for observation and in 1906 he was appointed 'Chief Instructor in Kiting' on a two-year contract at the army's School of Ballooning in Farnborough, where he rode about on a white horse with a revolver at his hip and long hair flowing below his wide-brimmed Stetson hat. By then his interest had turned to 'motorised kites' which he intended to develop into an aeroplane with the backing of the War Office. On 16 October 1908, the British Army Aeroplane No. 1 – designed and built by Cody – took off from Farnborough Common with a Union flag fluttering proudly from a wing strut and its designer at the controls. It flew nearly 1400 feet – Britain's first powered and sustained flight – before crashing when Cody attempted a left turn to avoid a clump of trees. He was luckily unhurt and lauded in the newspapers next day as a hero.

His achievement clearly did not impress members of the Aerial Navigation Sub-Committee. In February the following year the committee, having listened to the testimony of innumerable experts, recommended that all government-funded experiments with heavier-than-air machines should cease and that development of aviation should be left to the private sector. Cody's contract was cancelled but he was allowed to keep the damaged British Army Aeroplane No. 1, which he repaired and modified and continued to fly. (On 7 August 1913 he was test-flying his latest design when it broke up at 500 feet and both he and his passenger were killed. Cody was buried with full military honours in Aldershot Military Cemetery and his funeral procession was said to have drawn a crowd of 100,000 people.)

Not many months passed before it became evident the committee's decision was distinctly out of step with the rest of Europe, where military aviation was being embraced with enthusiasm. 'The sky is about to become another battlefield,' an Italian aviation pioneer, Giulio Douhet, predicted in 1909, 'no less important than the battlefields on land and sea . . . In order to conquer the air, it is necessary to deprive the enemy of all means of flying, by striking him in the air, at his bases of operation, or at his production centres. We had better get accustomed to this idea, and prepare ourselves.'[7]

In July 1909, Louis Blériot claimed a £1000 prize offered by the *Daily Mail* for the first aviator to fly across the English Channel. He took off from Calais shortly after dawn in a monoplane of his own design and landed behind Dover Castle 37 minutes later. It was a feat that made headlines around the world and turned Blériot into an international celebrity. The day after Blériot had been handed his cheque at a luncheon at the Savoy, H.G. Wells warned of the dire implications in a long xenophobic article in the *Daily Mail*:

> This event – this foreigner-invented, foreigner-built, foreigner-steered thing . . . – puts the case dramatically. We have fallen behind in the quality of our manhood . . . Within a year we shall have – or rather they will have – aeroplanes capable of starting from Calais . . . circling over London, dropping a hundredweight or so of explosive upon the printing machines of the *Daily Mail* and returning securely to Calais for another similar parcel.

In August the first international air show, the Grande Semaine d'Aviation, was held at Reims in France and marked the coming of age of heavier-than-air aviation. Blériot was among the leading aviators who took part and the event attracted around 250,000 paying spectators. An American, Glenn Curtiss, set a new world speed record of 47.1 miles an hour and Henri Farman, one of three brothers who would set up a successful aircraft manufacturing company, established a new distance and duration record, flying more than 100 miles in just over three hours. So excited were the crowds that customers in nearby open-air cafés were said to have stood on their tables to cheer as the aircraft flew by. After Reims, aviators became the new superheroes, daredevil masters of the sky soaring aloft in their flimsy contraptions and exercising a romantic allure among their adoring followers, particularly women.

Despite the continuing scepticism of senior military men – General Nicholson expressed the view that 'aviation is a useless and expensive fad' and his counterpart in France, Marshal Ferdinand Foch, declared that aviation was fine as a sport but as far as military use was concerned '*l'avion c'est zéro!*'[8] – by 1910 at least 50 aircraft were in use by different armies around the world. In the autumn of that year a Bristol biplane flown at his own expense by a Captain Bertram Dickson[9] appeared at the British Army's annual manoeuvres for the first time, 'to the chagrin of the cavalry, who saw dimly in his strange lumbering machine an indication that one day their occupation would be gone'.[10]

In 1911 aircraft were deployed in combat for the first time when Italy went to war with the Ottoman empire for control of Libya. Captain Carlo Piazza, flying a Blériot XI, made the first wartime reconnaissance flight near Benghazi and on 1 November Lieutenant Giulio Gavotti carried out the first aerial bombardment in his Etrich Taube monoplane. Flying at a height of 600 feet over Ottoman positions, he screwed the detonators into four grenades and tossed them out. It was reported that no one was hurt.

By the summer of 1911 it was at last clear to the War Office that military aviation could no longer be ignored and in November a young British officer, Captain Frederick Sykes of the 15th Hussars, was sent to France to observe the autumn manoeuvres of the French army and report on the role of aircraft in the operations. (At that time the British Army was said to have only 11 trained pilots in its ranks, whereas the French boasted more than 200 and were already experimenting with aerial photography.) Sykes was an exceptionally 'air-minded' officer, having obtained a ballooning certificate in 1904 and recently qualified as a pilot. His report was unequivocal, estimating that a single aircraft could achieve in a few hours what a cavalry patrol would take four days to accomplish. 'There can no longer be any doubt,' he wrote, 'as to the value of aeroplanes in locating an enemy on land and obtaining information.' But he went further, pointing out that aircraft could also be used to attack an enemy's 'vital points' and provide assistance to the artillery by spotting the fall of shells fired by guns on the ground and enabling the gunners to adjust their sights.[11]

In November 1911, another sub-committee was set up by the CID to examine the question of military aviation and in February 1912 the same committee which had recommended three years earlier that no further funding should be forthcoming for military aviation now recommended the formation of a flying corps comprising a naval wing, a military wing, a flying school and an aircraft factory. The recommendations of the committee were accepted and on 13 April 1912 King George V signed a Royal warrant establishing a new component within the British Army – the Royal Flying Corps.

For Hugh Trenchard the prospect of learning to fly, suggested by his friend Eustace Loraine, was not so much a great adventure as an escape route from the dreary regime of peacetime soldiering with his regiment. Once he had decided to apply, he was immediately presented with two problems – his age and his size. Typically, he was deterred by neither.

The War Office had decreed that the maximum age for training pilots was 40 – and Trenchard would be 40 in a few months, so he had no time to lose. And then there was his size – he was 6' 3" tall and heavily built. Some suggested, somewhat unkindly, that with him on board a heavier-than-air machine would prove just too heavy to take off. His response was that there was only one way to find out.

When he formally applied for leave of absence from the regiment to undertake pilot training, his commanding officer, Colonel Stuart, initially tried to talk him out of it. Stuart was not, in truth, particularly sorry to lose the difficult commander of F Company but at the same time he did not want aero him to kill himself, which he considered was a likely outcome. But once having made up his mind about anything, Trenchard could rarely be persuaded to change it and so Stuart reluctantly forwarded his application to the brigadier in command of the Londonderry area, who was even more dismissive. He held the view that aviation was 'quite useless' and that Trenchard was wasting his time. Although he consented to forward his application to the War Office he refused to endorse it. Trenchard imagined that not having the brigadier's support would probably mean refusal and so he was surprised when, in early July 1912, he learned his application had been approved.

Officers wishing to join the Royal Flying Corps at that time had first to obtain, initially at their own expense, an aviators' certificate from the Royal Aero Club. The standard charge for a course at a private flying school was £75 (nearly £6000 in today's money) which covered lessons, insurance and breakages, but which was reimbursed by the War Office if the officer was accepted into the RFC for further training at the newly established Central Flying School at Upavon on Salisbury Plain. Trenchard never explained how he raised the money, but since only a few months earlier in a letter to his sister he was complaining about being hard up, it can be assumed he somehow obtained a loan, perhaps from his mother's wealthy cousin, Irwin Cox.

He left Londonderry without fanfare and first travelled to London to visit his parents. (His mother had recently written to say that his

73-year-old father had suffered a minor stroke.) On the day he arrived, he picked up a newspaper and was shocked to read that his friend Loraine had been killed the previous day in a flying accident – the first Royal Flying Corps officer to die in an air crash. He was flying a French Nieuport monoplane out of Larkhill aerodrome on a routine training sortie when he attempted to execute a tight turn and the machine side-slipped and dived into the ground from 400 feet. His observer, Staff Sergeant Richard Wilson, was killed instantly; Loraine died hours later in hospital.[12] Later that day an order was issued stating 'Flying will continue this evening as usual', thus inaugurating a service tradition that operations were never interrupted by accidents.

Trenchard was obviously distressed by the news, but was still determined to go ahead with his plans. After a brief stay with his parents he made his way to Brooklands in Surrey, where an aerodrome had been laid out inside a recently opened motor racing circuit and had attracted a number of private flying schools and oddball aircraft manufacturers, among them a Russian prince, one Serge de Bolotoff, who was struggling, unsuccessfully, to build a huge tandem triplane in one of the many sheds dotted about the place. Trenchard sought out the Sopwith School of Flying, to which he had been recommended, and demanded of the surprised owner: 'You Sopwith? Can you teach me to fly in ten days?'

Twenty-four-year-old Tommy Sopwith was already a well-known name in aviation. He had taught himself to fly in 1910 and within months won a £4000 prize for the longest flight from England to the Continent in a British-built aeroplane, flying 169 miles from the Royal Aero Club's Eastchurch flying field to Beaumont in Belgium, in 3 hours and 40 minutes, setting a new British endurance and distance record. He used the prize money to launch the Sopwith School of Flying at Brooklands and in 1912 set up the Sopwith Aviation Company, which would produce more than 18,000 aircraft for the Allies during the Great War, including some 5000 Sopwith Camels, a single-seat fighter.

'Trenchard impressed me the moment he walked in,' Sopwith later recalled. 'He said the War Office had given him a fortnight to get his aviator's certificate, and that if for any reason he missed the test by then he would be over age. I promised to do my best for him.'[13]

Either Sopwith's memory of his first meeting with Trenchard was faulty or Trenchard had other reasons for being in a hurry – in July 1912 Trenchard was still some eight months from his fortieth birthday, so there was plenty of time for him to obtain his aviator's certificate. In fact he had rented a room in a house near Brooklands for two months as he had been told that it often took 'five or six weeks to get a ticket' [certificate]. It may have been that he wanted to speed up the process because he did not want to miss the first course at the Central Flying School, which was due to start on 17 August.

The Sopwith School of Flying was equipped with a Howard Wright biplane and an American Burgess Wright, both fitted with dual controls for elementary instruction. In the Howard Wright (the designer, Howard T. Wright, was British and no relation to the Wright brothers) pilot and student sat side by side in front of the engine, which drove two pusher propellers connected to the engine by lengths of chain. Trenchard remembered being shown the machine on his first day by Sopwith's partner and chief engineer, Fred Sigrist. From where you sat, he said, there was absolutely nothing in front. 'You sat looking out over empty space.'[14]

Early flying machines were incredibly fragile – basically wooden airframes covered with linen and held together by wire – and in those days no aircraft was sufficiently robust to fly in a strong wind; no one went up, certainly not on a training flight, if the aerodrome flag was fluttering, even half-heartedly. Trenchard was initially lucky with the weather. Every day at dawn he walked from his lodgings to Brooklands, impatient to get into the air as quickly as possible. On his first day he made two short flights with his instructor, Evelyn Copland Perry, who cheerfully pointed out the sewage farm where more than one trainee, unable to get back to the aerodrome, had landed.[15] Trenchard managed to avoid the sewage farm and was soon flying solo; after seven days he was completing shaky figures of eight in the sky. The school's flying log records his dogged progress, along with three days when there was no flying because of the weather. While the log notes that 'Major Trenchard . . . passed tests in really excellent style', the reality was that he was far from a natural pilot and his success was more due to determination than to a talent for flying.

On 13 August, after a total of only one hour and four minutes in the air, flying solo, Trenchard was awarded a Royal Aero Club certificate, number 270, and thus became eligible for the first course at the

Central Flying School. The test for the certificate was to complete five figure-of-eight patterns above the aerodrome, land within 50 metres of a specified point, then take off again and repeat the landing in a glide descent without the engine. Trenchard was very proud of getting his 'ticket' in such a short time, but candidly admitted it was 'more [by] luck than judgement'.[16]

'It was no light accomplishment,' Tommy Sopwith noted, 'but Major Trenchard tackled it with wonderful spirit. He was out at dawn each morning. He was dead keen to do anything that would expedite tuition – a model pupil from whom many younger men should have taken a lead.'[17] Privately, Sopwith admitted to reservations about Trenchard's skill as a pilot. 'I think it was just as well he didn't go on flying himself for very long,' he said later, 'he would never have been a very good pilot.'[18]

If Sopwith was not overly impressed, Trenchard's family certainly was. 'Hugh has gone in for flying and joins the Royal Military [sic] Flying Corps on the 16th of this month,' his father wrote to Trenchard's sister, Catherine, in South Africa. 'He went to Brooklands to learn, never telling us a word . . . He is very pleased about it and hopes to get on rapidly. It's much better than plodding on in his regimental duties.'[19]

The Central Flying School had been established in a collection of weatherboarded huts on a windswept hillside near the village of Upavon on Salisbury Plain in Wiltshire, a location which was deservedly unpopular with both students and staff alike. 'Taking its bad points first,' a correspondent of *The Aeroplane* magazine observed sourly, 'the school has been located on the top of a mountain, where it is open to every wind that blows . . . One may expect that those aviators who survive the gorges and ridges, the upward and downward *remous* [turbulence], the arctic frigidity and saharic parchedness of the Upavon School will develop into aviators of unsurpassed hardiness.'

Ten army pilots and five from the Royal Navy had qualified for the first course, which was due to last four months and included practical training in advanced flying, navigation and engine maintenance and written exams on subjects like the theory of flight, map-reading, meteorology, signalling and aerial reconnaissance. Pupils were first taken up as passengers, then allowed to feel the controls, slowly progressing to short flights with frequent landings, followed by circular flights at increasing altitudes and cross-country trips.

Among the officers on the first course was John Salmond, then a captain recently seconded from the King's Own Royal Lancaster Regiment and a future marshal of the Royal Air Force. He remembered his arrival at Upavon officers' mess as being

> a very wet day with wind and rain scurrying over the Downs making the windows of the wooden mess rattle. There were several people there and it is interesting to realise how a strong personality will leap across and hit on you immediately. For in the corner, sitting rather apart, was a dark, glowering man with a parchment coloured face, and a light behind his eyes, whom I was soon to know as Trenchard, and it was not long before I knew what that fire meant.[20]

(Trenchard and John Salmond would become lifelong friends.)

To the intense frustration of all the students, flying was delayed for a week by the bad weather during which time the commandant of the school, Captain Godfrey Paine, RN, decided to co-opt Trenchard, as the oldest and most experienced of the students, onto the permanent staff as adjutant, although he continued training as a pilot. One of his duties was to set the examination papers and then to mark them – his own included. 'Needless to say,' he noted laconically, 'I passed!'[21]

Trenchard's flying instructor was a naval officer, Lieutenant Arthur Longmore, a brilliant pilot well known for his calm confidence in any situation. Trenchard would test this attribute to the limit when Longmore was observing his first solo flight. The school was woefully short of aircraft – only eight of its expected complement of twenty-five had arrived – but two Farman Longhorn biplanes, so named for their curiously prominent frontal elevators, designed to prevent the machine tipping onto its nose in the event of a botched landing, were reserved for beginners. The pupil sat behind the instructor on the petrol tank with his feet dangling in the air and could reach round his instructor to operate the control column, but not the rudder bar. Trenchard and Longmore had completed a couple of circuits together in a Farman Longhorn, Longmore piloting the first and Trenchard the second, when Trenchard persuaded his instructor he should be allowed to go solo. Longmore watched, with his heart in his mouth, as Trenchard's machine tore across the grass and lurched into the air 'like a kite in a gale'.[22] He managed to complete an uncertain figure of eight and then landed with a thump. Longmore's analysis was that his pupil 'lacked finesse' and was over-confident. 'At best he was an indifferent flier,' Longmore recalled. 'His age told against him, though he showed enviable pluck and perseverance.'[23]

At the end of September, Royal Flying Corps aircraft participated for the first time in the army's annual manoeuvres in East Anglia – the biggest event in the military calendar, watched by King George V, a Russian delegation under Grand Duke Nicholas, defence ministers and other dignitaries. Longmore was one of the pilots selected to take part and he chose Trenchard to be his observer. They took off from Upavon in a Farman en route for Norfolk. 'Our first stop was a meadow in Oxford,' Longmore recalled. 'We should not have landed there because it was too small to take off again. Next morning I had to discard Trenchard in order to hop the hedge at the far end at low height and pick him up on the proper landing ground.'[24]

The scenario for the exercise was that the Red army, under the command of Lieutenant General Sir Douglas Haig, was assumed to have landed in Britain intent on advancing on the capital. The Blue army, under Lieutenant General Sir James Grierson, was to repel the 'invaders'. Haig was expected to be the victor since his staff all came from Aldershot command and were accustomed to working together with superior organisation and training, whereas the Blue army was a 'scratch team' put together from disparate units and territorials.

Longmore's and Trenchard's Farman was assigned to the Blue army. On the first day of the battle Longmore took the Farman up at dawn to report on 'enemy' movement and within an hour he and Trenchard had spotted the Red army's main advance. Grierson was dismayed when they reported back, since he immediately realised he had sent his cavalry in the wrong direction. At a hastily convened field conference it was Trenchard – already 'air-minded' – who suggested that new instructions could be delivered by air to the misdirected Blue cavalry. Grierson leapt at the idea, quickly consulted with his staff officers and wrote out new orders which he gave to Trenchard to deliver personally to the cavalry commander, Major General Edmund Allenby. Five minutes later the Farman was back in the air, flying at 50 feet along the route taken by the Blue cavalry, looking for a column of horses, the glittering lances of the Blue cavalry and the red tabs of a major general at its head. It did not take long to find them. On the ground, every face looked up as the Farman puttered into view and circled overhead. Longmore banked steeply and put the machine down in a field alongside the road. Trenchard leapt out, ran across the field and along the column to where General Allenby, his curiosity aroused, was waiting astride his horse. Trenchard saluted and handed over the new orders signed by Grierson, which would change the course of the 'battle'.

For the next four days Longmore and Trenchard spent an average of six hours in the air on reconnaissance, sleeping at night under hedgerows or behind haystacks, with the Farman parked nearby in a stubble field.

At the end of the manoeuvres the Blue army was declared the clear winner and the 'intervention of aircraft' was judged to be a significant factor in the 'victory'. Aviation historians would later credit the 1912 manoeuvres as the moment that the aeroplane transformed for ever the science of war, although it was still the view of many senior officers that aeroplanes 'spoiled things'.

On the return journey to Upavon, they again made a stop near Oxford but Longmore misjudged the landing and damaged the Farman's tailplane. A local blacksmith was summoned to forge a metal sheath to repair the damaged strut, but it was dark before he had completed the job. In the air next morning the imperturbable Longmore asked Trenchard to check behind them to make sure the tailplane was still there and Trenchard did so before he realised Longmore was joking.

They arrived back at Upavon to find the funerals taking place of two young aviators who had crashed days previously. Serious accidents were part of life at the Central Flying School. Machines were difficult to fly, they not infrequently fell apart in the air and young trainee pilots, fuelled with adrenalin, often tended to be overconfident. (The inquest into the death of Eustace Loraine concluded that he was too low when he attempted a manoeuvre and his lack of flying experience had engendered 'an excess of confidence in his ability to control his machine'.)

On 25 October the *London Gazette* reported that Brevet Major Trenchard had been appointed an instructor at the Central Flying

School, 'vice [replacing] Captain E.B. Loraine, deceased'. Trenchard was never a *flying* instructor at the CFS but with his genius for administration he practically ran the place with untiring energy. He drew up the training schedules and dealt with a thousand and one problems, ranging from housing to rations to camp guards to the shortcomings of the cooks in the mess. He made it his business to know what was going on in every part of the school. By its nature the place attracted raffish characters looking for excitement and prepared to take risks. As adjutant Trenchard had to balance maintaining discipline while at the same time encourage the school's burgeoning *esprit de corps*. Acutely aware that flying was a very dangerous business and that the young men at Upavon were being trained for something infinitely more dangerous – to fight a war in the air – he had no time for show-offs or prima donnas and made no concessions to thrill-seekers who flouted the rules: they were promptly returned to their units.

Eugene Gerrard (a future Air Commodore) was a flight commander at the school.

We had men of every type in the C.F.S., men from nearly every unit and civilians, too. Trenchard's method stood the test because of his personality and drive and his really amazing knowledge of human nature. He didn't believe in standing on ceremony. He could smell out difficulties as they arose. We seldom questioned his proposals or decisions. He didn't mind criticism and enjoyed a constructive argument. But we could be sure he'd have [new arrivals] taped from the moment they arrived until they left the school as disciplined, accomplished airmen.[25]

While he was at the school Gerrard set a new altitude record, achieving a height of 10,000 feet in a prototype RE7 biplane with Trenchard squeezed into the forward cockpit. (A curious choice, since Trenchard was certainly among the heaviest of the officers at the school.) A year earlier Gerrard had broken the duration record with a flight of four hours and thirteen minutes in a Short biplane.

Trenchard continued to fly himself as often as he could. On windless days, shortly after dawn or shortly before sunset, the best times to go up, he could often be found on the tarmac in front of the hangars, muffled in flying kit and clambering into a machine to go for a spin.

When Robert Barton, the young subaltern in the Royal Scots Fusiliers whom Trenchard had taught to ride in Londonderry, arrived in Upavon as a trainee pilot almost the first person he met was his former company commander. 'Meet me at 6.15 tomorrow morning,' Trenchard said, 'and I'll take you up.' In the grey light of dawn next morning Barton found his mentor making routine checks on a machine which Barton described as a 'singularly frail-looking object'. He was about as enthusiastic to fly with his former company commander as he was to get on a horse and go riding with him, but their short flight passed without incident.

Not long afterwards Trenchard took part in a fly-past staged at Tidworth for the benefit of Sir John French, the new Chief of the Imperial General Staff. On the way back, flying alone in a Farman, petrol began gushing from a cracked pipe in the engine and he was forced to make an emergency landing. Several days later, on a flight back from Farnborough, the same thing happened. He landed in a field near the village of Whitchurch, found a telephone and called Upavon to send a salvage party. Upavon was only 25 miles distant but patience was not Trenchard's strong suit. There was a friendly blacksmith in the village willing to repair the pipe, which he accomplished in no time. Trenchard should then have waited for the salvage party to assist him take off, but the temptation to manage it himself was too great. The propeller in the Farman was located behind the pilot's seat between the longitudinal struts attaching the tailplane and rudder. It had to be swung by hand to fire the engine and the more Trenchard thought about it the more convinced he became he could manage it alone. He set the throttle back as far as he could, then swung the propeller. As the machine started to move forward he ducked under the struts and somehow managed to scramble aboard, with great difficulty, grab the controls and take off just before the machine careered into a hedgerow at the end of the field. As he banked towards Upavon he saw the salvage party, far below, turn into a lane leading to the field.

His luck only deserted him once when, on a misty spring morning, he decided to test an experimental Bristol machine recently delivered to the school. He took up with him a new pupil, Henri Biard,[26] and very nearly killed him.

The wind was worse upstairs than on the ground [Biard recalled], but Trenchard completed the tests and had turned the machine homewards when an unusually severe gust flung us completely over on our side. He took the one slender chance there was of saving us from disaster. Twisting round and round, we dropped like a comet towards the earth. I for one thought we were both booked. As we fell headlong into the opaque mist, Trenchard straightened out the machine. Almost simultaneously it hit the ground. Even with my slight knowledge of flying I knew that an almost perfect landing had been made under merciless conditions.[27]

After inspecting the damage Trenchard stalked off, 'fierce faced and without a word', according to Biard, to complete an accident report. He never spoke of the incident to Biard again. Biard had had his first meeting with Trenchard a few days earlier.

One afternoon, soon after my arrival on the Plain, when I was an exceedingly shy young second lieutenant, I had occasion to take in to the Major a special sum of money – eight pounds and some odd shillings. I did not have the exact amount and innocently took in two five pound notes. He looked up from his papers, stared at the notes, then at me. 'I'm not a clerk! Get out and get change!' he said in a tone which made me vanish again as quickly as ever I have done in my life. Later I returned with the exact amount and apologised rather nervously for my error. Major Trenchard put a friendly hand on my shoulder. 'That's all right, my boy,' he said. 'I happened to be very busy.' Something in the tone, and the fact that the man who *was* so busy was able to find time to take away all the sting from a well-deserved rebuke delivered to a young sub-altern, sent me out of the room glowing. If he had asked me then to fly straight into a brick wall, I would have done it with a singing heart.

It was at Upavon that Trenchard acquired the nickname that would stay with him for the rest of his life – 'Boom'. Trenchard himself liked to say that he spoke only two languages – English and louder English. He certainly had a deep, powerful voice and if he saw a student bungle a landing he would call out 'BAD LANDING' loud enough for the luckless pilot to hear it over the roar of his engine. He became known as Boom not just throughout the Royal Flying Corps and later the Royal Air Force, but to friends and family as well. Actually many of the younger officers at Upavon called him, behind his back, 'Umph', which was the grunt he made behind his newspaper at breakfast in acknowledgement of a morning greeting. Trenchard was well aware of it. At the end of the first four-month course he was scheduled to speak after Captain Paine, the commandant, at a formal dinner in the mess. Paine was extremely long-winded; some students later said they wondered if he would ever sit down. When it came to Trenchard's turn, he got to his feet, stared around the room for a moment, cleared his throat, then said 'Umph' and sat down again. The mess erupted in laughter.

Trenchard rarely talked about his years in Nigeria, but he was obliged to explain when he refused to allow a Roman Catholic priest to visit the bedside of a young pilot seriously injured in a crash. Sub-Lieutenant Joseph Smyth Pigott nose-dived into the ground less than a month after arriving at Upavon. 'Trenchard told me later,' Smyth Pigott said, 'that as he walked to the scene of the accident he passed me as I was being carried off on a stretcher. The leader of the stretcher party halted and asked if he should take me to the mortuary. Trench-ard told them that in case I was still alive the sick bay might be more appropriate.' A telegram was sent to his mother, a devout Roman Catholic, informing her of what had happened. She replied saying she was leaving immediately for Upavon but in the meantime she asked for a priest to be sent to her son's bedside. The priest duly arrived and asked permission to visit the young man, which Trenchard, mindful of an incident in Nigeria when one of his officers had a heart attack and died when he found a padre kneeling by his bedside, refused. Nothing the outraged priest could say or do would persuade Trench-ard to change his mind. 'When my mother arrived she was furious,' Smyth Pigott said. 'I would have loved to have been present at the interview twixt them – the two people who frightened me more than anybody in the world.'28

By chance Trenchard's friends, the Boyles, moved to Salisbury, not far from Upavon, in 1913 when Boyle was appointed ADC to General Horace Smith-Dorrien, GOC Southern Command. Boyle installed his wife and family in a comfortable house in St Ann Street, close to the cathedral, where Trenchard became a frequent visitor for the luxury of a hot bath or a game of tennis. When he could find the time he hunted with Blackmore Vale and could also be occasionally observed, on weekend afternoons, pushing a pram containing his godchild, Belinda, around the cathedral precincts.

Kitty Boyle noticed a considerable change in her friend.

> He obviously lived for flying now and talked of little else. One day he told me he had been 'flying higher than the birds'. My husband was interested in the subject. Alan Boyle, his brother, had been the first amateur pilot in Britain to make a cross-country flight in his own Avis monoplane. There were frequent arguments about the uses of aircraft in warfare and here Hugh Trenchard held extremely advanced views. He used to assert that the aeroplane would one day transform the battlefield, and did so one evening at table in the hearing of General Smith-Dorrien. His words were coldly received.[29]

In September 1913 Trenchard was promoted to temporary lieutenant colonel and appointed assistant commandant of the Central Flying School. By then the tenor of the training had subtly changed to emphasise the roles – mainly reconnaissance and artillery spotting – that the Royal Flying Corps would undertake in support of the army in an upcoming war. Learning to fly – and the nascent art of aerial warfare – suddenly became a much more serious business.

Trenchard was among those, in 1913, who believed that war with Germany was inevitable. It was a view he shared with Winston Churchill, then First Lord of the Admiralty, who was also convinced that aircraft would have a major role and was himself learning to fly, with limited success. Trenchard remembered seeing him 'wallowing about the sky' and thinking that he probably was not exactly a natural pilot.

> He seemed altogether too impatient for a good pupil, and I could sympathise. He would arrive unexpectedly, usually without pyjamas or even a handkerchief, see what he wanted to see, and stay the night – or what was left of it when he'd finished talking. Everything,

including flying, was subordinated in his mind to a single purpose
– getting the fleet ready for a war in which Germany would be the
enemy.[30]

On 28 June 1914, the heir to the Austro-Hungarian throne, the Archduke Franz Ferdinand, and his wife, Sophie, Duchess of Hohenberg,
were assassinated by a 19-year-old Serbian student while on a visit
to Sarajevo, the capital of Bosnia. A wave of horror and indignation
swept through Europe in its wake. 'It shakes the conscience of the
world,' *The Times* declared. The *Daily Chronicle* described it as a 'clap
of thunder' over Europe. In Vienna students staged anti-Serbian
demonstrations and the foreign minister, Count Leopold von Berch-
told, spoke of dealing with the 'Serbian wasp's nest', even at the risk of
provoking European 'complications'.

While these great events were unfolding, Trenchard was dealing
with unhappy family matters. On 1 July his father died, aged 75. He
had never really recuperated from the stroke he had suffered two years
earlier and he succumbed to endocarditis, a heart infection, complicated by pneumonia. Trenchard could not but reflect that his father
had not enjoyed a happy life. He had not worked since being made
bankrupt, never recovered from the shame of it and he and his wife
had been reduced to living in a series of boarding houses for many
years. (After her husband's death, Trenchard's mother, Georgiana,
went to stay with family friends in Biggleswade, but she was to die
within months at the comparatively young age of 66. One of the causes of her death was noted as 'exhaustion'.)

On 5 July, Kaiser Wilhelm II reaffirmed Germany's alliance with
Austria. On 23 July, the Austrian government issued an ultimatum
giving Serbia 48 hours to agree to a series of drastic and humiliating
demands. Events then evolved with bewildering speed. Serbia rejected
Austria's ultimatum and ordered its army to mobilise. In St Petersburg
the Tsar warned Germany that Russia would not remain indifferent if
Serbia was invaded. On 28 July Austria declared war on Serbia. Great
Britain's attempts to mediate were rejected by the Kaiser as 'insolent'.
On 1 August the Tsar declared war on Germany, on 3 August Germany
declared war on France and on 4 August Britain declared war on
Germany.

As news of the war spread, cheering crowds gathered outside

Downing Street and Buckingham Palace, and young men flocked to the recruiting offices, anxious to see action for fear it would be 'all over by Christmas'.

8

WING COMMANDER IN FRANCE

Trenchard not unnaturally assumed he would be going to France with the Royal Flying Corps on the outbreak of war and was dismayed when he discovered he was to be left behind. He was told he would be replacing Major Frederick Sykes as commandant of the RFC's Military Wing at Farnborough. Sykes, for whom Trenchard would soon develop a visceral loathing, *was* going to France – as chief of staff to Brigadier-General Sir David Henderson, who was to be commander of the RFC in the field.[1] Trenchard secured an interview with Henderson at the War Office and pleaded with him to change his mind. Henderson, a likeable Scot and experienced soldier, was sympathetic, but regretted there was nothing he could do. Trenchard left the War Office, he recalled, in a mood of 'rage and despair'.[2]

Desperate to see action, he applied for a transfer from the RFC to rejoin his regiment: both regular battalions of the Royal Scots Fusiliers were destined for the Western Front. But harassed staff officers at the War Office had no time to deal with the complaint of a single disgruntled officer and his application was rejected. So it was he arrived at Farnborough, thoroughly depressed, on 7 August 1914, to take over command of the Military Wing. There was, in truth, not much to take over. The four RFC squadrons preparing to leave for France had commandeered all the serviceable aircraft and useful personnel. The Military Wing was left with one clerk, one typewriter, one orderly, a large number of unpaid bills incurred by various officers who had disappeared to the front and a row of empty sheds with a few decrepit aeroplanes unfit for service.

Trenchard could hardly have been more different, both physically and temperamentally, from the man from whom he was taking over. Trenchard was a big man with a big voice, brusque, impatient, boundlessly energetic, intolerant of human weakness and unawed by authority. Although he often confused people he was trying to enlighten, he had an extraordinary ability to arrive at the right decision after an apparently erroneous thought process. Crucially, he had an innate talent to inspire loyalty. Few people seemed to have a good word for the hapless Sykes. A former cavalry officer, he was slight in stature, a deep thinker, shrewd in argument and a competent staff officer. But he was a cold fish – 'an intriguer with a fine conceit of himself' was one characterisation – with a personality that 'strongly engendered mistrust'.[3] Too calculating and aloof to kindle loyalty, he was generally unpopular and never really won the confidence of his men.[4]

Some blamed Sykes for deliberately stripping the Military Wing to make things difficult for his successor. Bertie Fisher, one of Henderson's staff officers, had lunch with Lady Henderson before he left for France and told her that Sykes was hated by all the soldiers as a mean and narrow-minded officer and that 'all he wanted was to make a fine show for himself in France and didn't care a hang how he left things in Farnborough'.[5]

According to Trenchard, a curious incident happened in Sykes' office while he was handing over to his successor. With some reverence he gave Trenchard a key to a locked box which he said contained top secret plans to deal with a potential invasion of Britain by German airships. Trenchard put the key in his pocket and slept with it under his pillow that night. Next morning, after Sykes had departed, he discovered the box contained nothing but a dirty pair of tennis shoes. It was extremely unlikely that Sykes, not a man known for his sense of humour, was joking and indeed he had a different version of events. Writing years later he claimed that the box actually contained detailed records of the formation of the Military Wing which someone had either hidden or destroyed while he was absent.[6] The mystery of the locked box remained just that.

On 15 August Trenchard and Sykes had a final meeting at Farnborough before Sykes left for France. Sykes' purpose was to brief Trenchard on what he (Sykes) perceived as the other man's duties. Trenchard firstly resented being briefed by a man for whom he had little respect and secondly he fundamentally disagreed with what Sykes had to say. Sykes insisted that the Military Wing's first function was simply to provide machines and pilots as and when they were needed as reinforcements in France and that there was no need for any new squadrons to be formed as it would 'all be over by Christmas'.[7] Trenchard told him he was talking 'damned rubbish' and that his (Trenchard's) job was to put together new squadrons. 'I informed him,' he recalled, 'that it was nothing to do with him what we did in England and that I proposed to begin raising 12 new squadrons at once.'[8] Sykes, increasingly irritated, argued his case; Trenchard, red-faced, stood his ground. The meeting degenerated into an acrimonious shouting match and ended with both men disliking each other even more than they had before. Sykes later let it be known he thought Trenchard's loud voice compensated for a 'permanently vacant mind'; Trenchard viewed Sykes as arrogant, conceited and duplicitous and would make little attempt to conceal his animus towards the other man right through the war and long afterwards.

Meanwhile, the RFC had suffered its first casualties before the Corps had even arrived in France. Lieutenant Robert Skene[9] and his mechanic, Ray Barlow, were killed on 12 August when their overloaded Blériot crashed at Netheravon on their way to a rendezvous with the rest of the RFC near Dover. On the following day 56 patched-up machines, their crews equipped with inflatable inner tubes in the event of an engine failure over water, set off across the English Channel to Boulogne, then flew down the coast to the bay of the Somme and followed the river to Amiens, where the RFC was establishing its headquarters. Miraculously, all the crews eventually arrived safely, although not always with their machines. The leader of No. 4 Squadron had an engine failure as he crossed the French coast and began to glide down, frantically waving to the other pilots to carry on. Unfortunately they mistook his hand signals and followed him down onto a newly ploughed field. A number of the fragile machines were too damaged to take off again.

Although pilots of those days enjoyed a glamorous image in the public's mind, there was very little glamour in the reality of getting a flimsy contraption of fabric, wood and bracing wires off the ground, sitting in the open cockpit blasted by winds, spattered by castor oil used to lubricate the rotary engine, deafened by its roar, manipulating the controls with freezing hands while trying to see where you were going, then putting the thing down on the ground in one piece. And this was before anyone started shooting at you.

At the outset of the war it was generally agreed that if the Royal

Flying Corps had any use at all (not a universal view by any means) it was only to provide the army with reconnaissance behind the enemy lines and spotting for the artillery – reporting the fall of shells to enable the gunners to improve accuracy. This last was problematic in the early days because of the difficulty of communicating with the ground – wireless equipment was far too heavy to be carried, signalling methods were crude and sometimes dropping a scribbled note over the guns was the best early pilots could manage.

On 19 August, in France, the RFC attempted its first aerial reconnaissance at the front with two machines, both of which ran into poor weather and got lost. But on 22 August, during the battle of Mons, 12 reconnaissance sorties were flown and reported extensive German troop movements attempting to outflank the British Expeditionary Force, which enabled Sir John French, the commander-in-chief, to realign his forces and prevent his army being encircled by the enemy, saving the lives of 100,000 soldiers. On 7 September, in his first official dispatch, French was lavish in his praise of the RFC:

> I wish particularly to bring to your Lordships' notice the admirable work done by the Royal Flying Corps under Sir David Henderson. Their skill, energy, and perseverance have been beyond all praise. They have furnished me with the most complete and accurate information, which has been of incalculable value in the conduct of operations. Fired at constantly by friend and foe, and not hesitating to fly in every kind of weather, they have remained undaunted throughout. Further, by actually fighting in the air, they have succeeded in destroying five of the enemy's machines.[10]

Back at Farnborough, Trenchard did not let his chagrin about not being in France prevent him from getting on with the job with his usual dauntless gusto. Since there were no rules to work to, he simply made up the rules as he went along. 'We had no power to enlist men,' he wrote, 'no rates of pay for them, no kit, no clothing, and nowhere to put them, but we made our own terms of enlistment and our own rates of pay.'[11] He requisitioned Brooklands aerodrome, where there were a number of aircraft in various stages of construction, some useful, some not. To provide accommodation he bought a neighbouring pub and all the contents, including bed sheets, table linen, a piano and numerous kegs of beer. Then he sallied off to Harrods and bought their entire stock of ready-made overcoats for uniforms.

Bureaucrats at the War Office were soon fretting about his activities, warning him he had no authority to lay down rates of pay or go shopping in Harrods or buy the contents of public houses. Trenchard blithely responded by pointing out a directive from Lord Kitchener, then Secretary of State for War, requiring all commanding officers to use their initiative to ensure the comfort and equipment of their men.

Fortunately Trenchard established a good working relationship with Major Sefton Brancker, who was in charge of supply and equipment at the newly established Directorate of Military Aeronautics. A dapper little man with a foppish manner, a Charlie Chaplin moustache and monocle, he was actually an extraordinarily effective and efficient administrator and was a great admirer of Trenchard's unconventional, not to say abrasive, methods.

> Trenchard was magnificent. Although thirsting to go and fight with his own regiment, the Scots Fusiliers, he was in his element in those first months of the war . . . He conjured a new squadron into existence out of practically nothing in a way that took my breath away. He combined tremendous power of getting through work with the ability to apply his energy to none but the essential factors. His dominating personality swept aside difficulties and tore red tape into shreds. Woe betide the shirker and the faint-hearted – they withered under the blast of his searching vehemence and were lost. He was a master of detail without losing any greatness of mind thereby; [yet] verbally he was one of the most incoherent men I have ever met. Later on in the war I had many and endless discussions with him on policy and on the happenings of the moment; his brain and his mind were full of ideas, but he could not express them, and often I have come away after an hour or two's talk with him quite tired with my efforts to understand exactly what he meant. . . .[12]

Within a month of the outbreak of war, Trenchard had put together the nucleus of three or four new RFC squadrons. He bought every aircraft he could lay his hands on to provide machines for pilot training and urged the Royal Aircraft Factory, also at Farnborough, to increase production. With Brancker's help, he set up a recruiting office in the

West End of London to hire vital technical personnel and by mid-September more than 1000 men had been enrolled to train as riggers, fitters and mechanics.

He also recruited an old friend from home, Charles Lee, a retired officer of the 60th Rifles and master of fox-hounds at Taunton Vale, to join him as adjutant. Smart and hard working, Lee had a dry sense of humour. When Trenchard was loudly complaining that the telephones had broken down, Lee murmured 'That won't make any difference to you, sir. I think you will still be able to make yourself heard', making Trenchard laugh.

Promoted, somewhat to his surprise, to Brevet Lieutenant Colonel, Trenchard remained very much a law unto himself. He was extremely irritated, for example, by army and navy vehicles driving at speed past the Royal Aircraft Factory, kicking up great clouds of dust. When repeated orders failed to slow them down, Trenchard took matters into his own hands and instructed two men to dig a trench across the road. 'After four cars had come to grief in it,' he noted with some satisfaction, 'I had no more trouble.'[13]

Talking to pilots returning from France, Trenchard came to the conclusion that the RFC under Henderson was not being sufficiently aggressive. There were stories early on in the war of British pilots smiling and waving cheerfully at their German counterparts in the air; Trenchard believed that instead of greeting each other as fellow aviators they should be shooting at each other, difficult though that was in a machine which required the pilot's full concentration just to stay in the air. He considered it essential that the Allies should win ascendancy of the air and that it had to be fought for, whatever the cost. His conclusion – actually quite unfair – was that RFC pilots were being 'wrapped in cotton wool'. In reality the RFC had so few aircraft available by the end of the battle at Ypres in November that Henderson could not risk losing further machines to secure command of the air. Of the 63 aeroplanes that had finally flown to France, more than 40 had been destroyed.

Trenchard undoubtedly attempted to make his views clear when Henderson visited him at Farnborough, and at the end of what he described as 'a long talk' – during which he lectured his superior officer on the dangers of the enemy achieving air supremacy – he once again asked to be returned to his regiment. Henderson, who was a man of unusual forbearance, brushed his request aside and revealed he had some good news. The RFC was being reorganised into three operational wings, one for each Army Corps in France: he wanted Trenchard to take over command of the First Wing.

It was Trenchard's long-awaited opportunity to see action in France, but he hesitated, fearing that he might find himself under the command of Sykes, which he would find intolerable. When he was assured that he would work directly under Henderson and would be second in seniority in the RFC he accepted the offer and immediately started to make plans to hand over the Military Wing to his as yet unnamed successor.

Trenchard left for France by sea on 18 November. He was met at Boulogne by Henderson's ADC, Captain Maurice Baring. 'I had never seen Colonel Trenchard and I wondered how I should recognise him. I arrived at Boulogne, went to the fish market and bought fish. Then I waited for the boat. The boat came in about half past four. Standing quite by himself on the deck of the boat was a tall man with a small head and a Scots Fusiliers' cap on. That, I said to myself, must be Colonel Trenchard. It was.'[14]

After introductions and some difficulty finding petrol for the second-hand Rolls-Royce that Trenchard had brought with him as a staff car, they set off in the dark for the RFC headquarters, which had been established in a small château, the Château des Bruyères, in Longuenesse, on a hill between St Omer and the aerodrome on the local racecourse. Unfortunately Baring, who was the most unmilitary of men, did not notice the driver had taken the wrong turning outside Boulogne and that they were heading north, towards Calais, rather than east, towards St Omer. Although he claimed 'a certain intuition' warned him they were going the wrong way, he only realised his mistake when they were stopped at a road block and told that if they continued along the same road they would soon cross into the German lines. It was eight o'clock before they arrived at the hard-pressed RFC headquarters, where a constant stream of pilots were coming and going with reconnaissance reports and a bevy of clerks were clattering at typewriters in the flickering light of candles. That night Trenchard slept on the floor of the guest room, along with a number of other visitors.

Almost as soon as he arrived in France, Trenchard received bad news. Major General Samuel Lomax, commander of the 1st Division, had been very seriously wounded during the closing stages of the first battle of Ypres when German artillery shelled the château being used as divisional headquarters. Trenchard learned to his dismay, on 22 November, that Sir John French had promoted Henderson to take over the 1st Division in place of Lomax and that command of the Royal Flying Corps had been handed to his nemesis, Sykes, whom he not only detested but who was also ten years his junior.

It was an utterly unpalatable proposition for Trenchard. He went straight to French's headquarters, buttonholed the most senior staff officer he could find, curtly explained why it was absolutely impossible for him to remain in the Royal Flying Corps and insisted on a telegram being sent to the War Office at once, laying out his position and requesting an immediate transfer back to his regiment. He then drove to the First Wing headquarters at Merville, 20 miles to the east, to await developments.

Whether Trenchard's telegram had any influence on subsequent events is uncertain, but what is known is that a few days later Kitchener refused to sanction Sykes' taking control of the Royal Flying Corps on the basis of his inexperience. (In fact Sykes probably had as much experience of aerial warfare as any man in the British Army. Kitchener, of course, knew Trenchard reasonably well from the time they had served together in South Africa during the Boer War.)[15] Kitchener ordered that both Henderson and Sykes were to return to their previous posts, scotching Henderson's hopes of promotion and high command in the regular army. Trenchard, no longer insisting he wanted to return to his regiment, remained in place as commander of the First Wing at Merville. On 18 January his promotion to Brevet Lieutenant Colonel was confirmed by the *London Gazette*, ensuring he retained seniority over Sykes.

A few days earlier, Trenchard had been summoned to meet Sir Douglas Haig, commander of the newly formed First Army.

This was the first time I had ever seen Sir Douglas Haig. I was very nervous at meeting him, as I had always heard that he was very reserved, austere, severe, and that he did not believe a great deal in Air.[16] He ordered me to go round to his H.Q. about 5 o'clock one evening and he asked me about the use of aircraft in battle.

I tried to explain what I thought Air could do in the future beside reconnaissance work, how it would also have to fight in the
air against German machines, and how we should have to develop
machine-guns and bombs. He was interested, and then he told me
he was going to tell me something that only three or four people in the world knew, that we were going to attack the Germans
somewhere in the neighbourhood of Merville and Neuve Chapelle
in March, and that I was not to tell anybody. I explained about
artillery observation, reporting to batteries by morse, signal lamps,
and trying to get wireless going to report back to the batteries. I
outlined where I had the few squadrons and what their several tasks
would be on the map. I remember very well when his chief staff
officer, General John Gough,[17] came in and began to talk Haig said
'Don't interrupt, I am listening to Trenchard describing Air.'

I explained all I could, rather badly and nervously, and he said
'Well Trenchard, I shall expect you to meet me on the day or the
night before the attack to tell me whether you can fly, because on
your being able to fly and observe artillery and reconnaissance will
depend the battle. If you cannot fly because of weather, I shall probably have to put off the attack.'

Trenchard was both surprised and encouraged by Haig's apparent con-
version to the notion that the Royal Flying Corps could make a real
contribution towards the war effort, since only a few months previously he had expressed the view that it was 'foolish' to think aeroplanes
could be usefully employed in war.[18]

'I could not help feeling then and for years afterwards that Haig
said what he did to give confidence to me and the whole RFC. Though
he did not understand very much about it, he believed in the Air. And
he accepted what I said.'[19]

Towards the end of January 1915, an officer by the name of John
Moore-Brabazon was posted to First Wing. A keen photographer, he
had set up a photographic unit at RFC headquarters and Sykes had
sent him to First Wing to develop practical aerial photography. It was
sorely needed – observers on reconnaissance sorties had to balance
sketch pads, maps and notebooks on their knees and scribble in the
blast of propellers as best they could. Trenchard, always open-minded
to new ideas, was enthusiastic. He could see that aerial photography

had great potential; in fact only a few weeks earlier he had dispatched an officer to London to buy hand cameras to test on machines in France.

Lieutenant Moore-Brabazon was already a well-known figure in aviation circles. He had learned to fly in France in 1908 in a Voisin biplane, won a £1000 prize offered by the *Daily Mail* to the first man to fly a circular mile in October 1909, and the following month proved that 'pigs could fly' by taking off with a very unhappy piglet strapped to the wing of his biplane in a wastepaper basket. On 8 March 1910 he became the first person to qualify as a pilot in Britain and was awarded Aviator's Certificate No. 1 by the Royal Aero Club.[20]

Trenchard would certainly have known who Moore-Brabazon was, but the fact that he happened to be a protégé of Sykes would have done him no favours. Their first meeting, over lunch in the First Wing officers' mess, did not go well. Moore-Brabazon spoke up when one officer gave another the incorrect time. For some reason having this new arrival announce the correct time irritated Trenchard and the following exchange took place:

'You're Moore-Brabazon, aren't you?'
'I am, sir.'
'And you only got here today?'
'I did, sir.'
'Well remember this, Moore-Brabazon. The time is what I choose to make it.'

'Colonel Trenchard, as he then was, was a tremendous personality, quite terrifying,' Moore-Brabazon recalled. '"The time is what I choose to make it" was the first thing I heard him say and was a shattering utterance. I collapsed, crestfallen, determined not to say another word during luncheon.'[21]

So it was he said nothing when, a few days later during lunch in the officers' mess, he was served a cutlet which reeked of paraffin. 'I played about with it on the side of the plate without saying anything and watched out of the corner of my eye what would happen when the Colonel got his chop and paraffin. He exploded with fury, turned to me and said "Why didn't you tell me?" I did not really know what to answer, so I just said "I thought I'd spoken quite enough during lunch the first time."'

It was perhaps hardly surprising that Moore-Brabazon felt 'as welcome as measles' when he first arrived at First Wing, but he soon discovered that Trenchard's overbearing manner belied his enthusiasm and willingness to embrace new ideas and he gave Moore-Brabazon unqualified support and encouragement when he began experimenting with aerial photography.

> He was a very hard worker, more enthusiastic about air than anybody else was, and tried to preach the gospel of air, even in the early days, to the unbelieving generals ... What we would have done without him I do not know. Not a very communicative man, very difficult for a junior officer to talk to in any way, not particularly clever, but extremely wise. After all, you can get clever people at two a penny – wise ones are very rare.[22]

In February, photographs taken with a plate camera through a hole in the floor of a B.E.2c biplane over a brickworks at La Bassée revealed the presence of a hitherto unsuspected trench system and contributed to the success of a subsequent raid which captured the area – a minor, but morale-raising, action at a time when good news was in short supply.

Later Moore-Brabazon was in hot water again when he upset the 'maps section' at GHQ by circulating, on his own initiative, a map compiled from photographs of the entire German trench system opposite the First Army. He was hauled before Trenchard and given a bruising dressing-down, told he had no right to interfere with other people's business, that it was a disgraceful thing to do and he should be ashamed of himself. As he turned to leave, thoroughly chastened, Trenchard suddenly beamed, slapped him on the back, said something like 'You know what the Army's like' and proceeded to tell him how delighted he was with what he had done. Outside Trenchard's office, a puzzled Moore-Brabazon concluded that his commanding officer must have been ordered by GHQ to 'strafe' him.

In the days before the battle of Neuve Chapelle – the first planned British offensive of the war – RFC machines flew up and down the front, despite bad weather, taking photographs which enabled the attack front to be mapped in detail to a depth of up to 1500 yards. It was the first time the Allied commanders had been supplied with irrefutable photographic evidence of the enemy's front-line dispositions.[23] First Wing set up an advanced headquarters in a small house in the centre of Merville, next door to the First Army's intelligence centre. On 7 March Trenchard was warned the offensive would be launched two days later, weather permitting.

In his autobiographical notes, Trenchard claimed he was summoned to meet Haig at one o'clock in the morning of 10 March. Haig greeted him wearing a greatcoat over his pyjamas and together they walked across the village square to a bridge over the canal. It was a very dark night, Trenchard recalled, with light rain. Haig wanted to know if the RFC would be able to take to the air at five o'clock. Trenchard said he had arranged for a machine to go up that night if conditions allowed and if it flew overhead within the next few minutes it would mean they could fly. Almost before he had finished speaking they heard the engine of an approaching aircraft. It may be Trenchard's recollection was faulty as Haig recorded in his diary that a machine made a short reconnaissance flight at about 6 a.m. and reported low clouds but fairly satisfactory visibility, as a result of which he ordered the attack to go ahead as planned.

The battle of Neuve Chapelle began with a massive artillery bombardment at 7.30 followed by an infantry attack 35 minutes later, which would set the terrible pattern of trench warfare on the Western Front – troops advancing into tangles of barbed wire and machine-gun firestorms. Wave after wave of infantry was mown down as communication between various army commanders disintegrated and confusion spread. RFC machines 'spotting' for the artillery were frequently ignored, sometimes because of the technical difficulties of air–ground communication. An infuriated Trenchard later reported to Haig that a senior gunnery officer had told him during the battle he was 'too busy fighting to deal with your toys in the air'. Attempts at bombing German positions behind the lines were largely ineffective – all three machines briefed to carry out a night bombing of a rail junction at Lille crashed before reaching their target. A German counter-attack on 12 March failed, but by then the First Army was running short of ammunition and Haig was obliged to call off the offensive. Of the 40,000 Allied troops who took part, more than 11,500 were killed, wounded or missing, at the cost of gaining 100 yards of territory. Trenchard was distressed to learn that one of the units which had suffered heavy casualties was the 1st Battalion, Royal Scots Fusiliers.

After Neuve Chapelle Trenchard spent much of his time touring First Wing squadrons, haunting the hangars at all hours talking to the pilots and observers. He was usually accompanied by his orderly, Air Mechanic Cecil King.

We were all a little bit scared of him. He was very, very severe and his manner was quite frightening. If you were his orderly he used to tell you what you had to do. 'You'll follow 20 paces behind me wherever I go. If I go in a door and I want you to come, I'll beckon you. If not you'll wait at the doorway until I come out and if I call you you'll come at the double to receive your orders.' He never said anything that was unnecessary. If he called 'Orderly!' you jumped to attention and went off at the double. He gave the impression of being a bit of an ogre.

If he went down to the aerodrome I used to follow him and he'd watch the flying. One day he said to me 'There's an aeroplane over there that's just landed. Go over and tell the pilot to report to me immediately.' I went over and said to the pilot 'Colonel Trenchard wants to see you, sir.' He looked very anxious and said 'Do you know what he wants?' I said 'I'm sorry, sir, I don't.' He went up to Colonel Trenchard and the Colonel said 'You will catch a train back to your unit and I will send your report afterwards.' The pilot said 'But, sir . . .' and he said 'That'll do.' It was no wonder they were frightened of him.

He used to fly occasionally. He would say 'Orderly start such and such an aircraft up and get it ready' and he'd say 'Get in with me' and he'd fly around for ten minutes or so, land and get out and walk away. He just used to fly around to see if he could handle it all right. We used to call him Harry Lauder because he still wore his old Scots Fusiliers uniform with the red and white band round his hat, like Harry Lauder.[24]

In terms of living conditions the men of the Royal Flying Corps were very comfortably off compared to those in the trenches – they had beds to sleep in at night, regular meals which they ate off tables, reasonable washing facilities and even the occasional opportunity to visit an *estaminet* (small café-bar). Occasionally Trenchard shrugged on a greatcoat without badges of rank and walked through the trenches alone, both to watch the air battle from the ground and to hear what was being said about his pilots by troops in the front line. He concluded, perhaps unsurprisingly, that most of the remarks he overheard were ignorant and unhelpful and made by 'people who did not understand air'.

He was determined that the air crew should be aware of the wretched conditions on the ground.

I made my pilots go and see the men in the trenches [he wrote] and see what an awful life it was for the infantry, where they had trench feet, were up to their waists in water, with dead Germans all around them, rats and everything else. The courage required of airmen was a different type of courage from what was required of the infantry, as in those days there were no parachutes and whenever you were hit you came down in flames. You were by yourself with nothing to keep up your courage. They were attacked in the air by Germans, shot at by anti-aircraft guns and engines were always going wrong . . . yet how magnificently those airmen did their work.[25]

With every week that passed Trenchard's admiration for his air crew increased. More effective anti-aircraft fire was forcing pilots up to 8000 feet (2400 metres) – twice as high as they had been flying six months earlier – and making life particularly difficult for observers, leaning over the edge of the cockpit with the wind whipping at their goggles, trying to make sense of what they could see far below on the ground.

On 26 April 1915 four B.E.2 aircraft each loaded with a 100lb bomb set off from First Wing to bomb the railway yards at Courtrai in Belgium, which were being used to bring German reinforcements up to the front during the second battle of Ypres. Only one machine, flown by Second Lieutenant William Rhodes-Moorhouse, reached the target. Rhodes-Moorhouse accepted before he took off that he was probably on a suicide mission.

'I am off on a trip from which I don't expect to return,' he wrote to his wife on the night before his departure, 'but which I hope will shorten the war a bit. I shall probably be blown up by my own bomb, or, if not, killed by rifle fire.' On reaching Courtrai he ignored his flight commander's advice to bomb from altitude and made his run below 300 feet through a hail of machine-gun fire from a church tower and rifle fire from the ground. A shell tore through his seat into his left thigh and a piece of shrapnel took off three fingers from his right hand. He was able to release his bomb and could have landed and perhaps saved his life, but although grievously wounded he chose to return. On the 30-minute return flight across the Ypres battlefield he was hit by a stray bullet which ripped through his abdomen. He somehow managed to make a perfect landing at Merville and when ground crew rushed to lift him from the cockpit there was so much blood they thought his leg had been severed. He insisted on being carried to the squadron office to make his report and dictated it from a stretcher in Trenchard's hearing before being taken to the casualty clearing station, where he died next day. 'It's strange dying, Blake old boy,' he had said to his flight commander, Maurice Blake, 'unlike anything one has ever done before.' On Trenchard's recommendation, Rhodes-Moorhouse was awarded a posthumous Victoria Cross, the first to be won by the Royal Flying Corps.[26]

In the face of the dangers they all faced, pilots and observers kept up their spirits by affecting a laconic disdain for the enemy and the risks they were taking. Missions behind enemy lines were called 'shows' and anti-aircraft fire was referred to throughout the war as 'Archie', although not everyone knew why. It derived from a Lieutenant Amyas 'Biffy' Borton, said to be something of a dare-devil, who developed a technique for avoiding anti-aircraft fire by slipping sideways and rapidly changing height; every time the enemy missed he would triumphantly shout out 'Archibald, certainly not!' – a line from a faintly risqué music hall monologue made famous by the comedian George Robey.[27] Abbreviated to 'Archie', it became standard RFC vernacular.

An easy informality distinguished life in the RFC from the rigid discipline imposed in the regular army, possibly because so many pilots and observers were free spirits recruited from public schools and were drawn to flying from a sense of adventure. 'Any sportsman will realise,' ran a letter in Westminster School's newspaper, 'that, apart from fighting, there is absolutely nothing to touch flying as a sport . . .' Almost all pilots had nicknames, very often uncomplimentary. One rather rotund officer was called 'Pregnant Percy' and another poor fellow who suffered from chronic haemorrhoids was known to everyone as 'Piles'. Brigadier General John Higgins, commander of the 3rd Brigade, was known throughout the RFC as 'Bum and Eyeglass' because he walked with a limp, having been shot in the backside during the Boer War, and wore a monocle. Many kept pets, which invariably featured in group photographs showing smiling young men draped casually around an aircraft in a variety of often scruffy uniforms. Parties in the mess, with boisterous games, raucous singing and heavy drinking, helped relieve the stress of constantly losing friends who failed to return from 'shows' over the German lines.

In early May three squadrons from the First Wing were assigned to fly defensive patrols to deter enemy reconnaissance before the battle of Aubers Ridge, part of a Franco-British offensive intended to exploit the German diversion of troops to the Eastern Front. During the battle itself they switched to reconnaissance and bombing enemy rear areas. Heavy rain and dense mist delayed the start of the attack but the weather then miraculously cleared, although the outcome was, once again, a disaster for the Allies, with no tactical advantage gained and more than 11,000 casualties sustained on the first day, the majority within yards of their own front-line trench.

Trenchard had hoped for more, much more, and admitted to a rare moment of self-doubt.

The battle took place on a cloudless day, lovely sun, and I thought the Air would come into its own and do great work. But the battle turned out to be another setback and then I wondered if what I thought Air could do was right, or wrong. Here we had perfect [flying] weather, but it had not influenced the battle. But I believed . . . that we did not have enough Air to make it widely felt and we did not know how to use it enough.[28]

His conviction was growing that reconnaissance and artillery spotting were not enough, that the Royal Flying Corps needed to adopt a policy of unflinching aggression, that the battle had to be taken to the enemy and that, almost regardless of the cost, the Allies needed to achieve and maintain supremacy in the air. This would clearly involve air to air fighting, but experiments in arming machines for what would become known as 'dogfights' were proving difficult and in the early days of the war German pilots were often disinclined to fight and chose to flee rather than engage in aerial combat.

In truth, aerial combat remained highly problematic. Captain Louis Strange of 6 Squadron, flying a single-seater Martinsyde S1 Scout over enemy lines in May, had an extraordinarily lucky escape when he attempted to engage an enemy fighter with a Lewis machine gun he had mounted experimentally on the top wing of his aircraft. The drum of the gun promptly jammed and when Strange stood up to replace it, his machine stalled and flipped over, leaving him clinging to the drum praying it would not now disengage and dangling in mid-air as his plane descended upside down in a flat spin. He somehow managed to hook his feet into the cockpit, get the stick between his legs and right the machine 500 feet. When he returned to base he was reprimanded by his CO for causing 'unnecessary damage' to the instrument panel in his efforts to regain the cockpit.

On 17 May Henderson arrived in Merville to see Trenchard and was surprised to find him lying fully clothed on his bed, laid low by a crippling migraine attack. (He had been plagued by bouts of migraine, usually brought on by overwork or worry, ever since being wounded in South Africa. It accounted, in part, for his brusque manner, although most people who encountered the rough edge of his tongue simply assumed he was naturally cantankerous.) Henderson was sympathetic, sat at the end of the bed, and talked about changes he was planning to introduce into the RFC. One of them was that he had decided to replace Sykes – some reports alleged that he had discovered Sykes had been plotting to succeed him (Henderson) while he was at home on sick leave. He wondered if Trenchard would take the job. Trenchard shook his head. The last thing he wanted, he said, was to become a staff officer. It was nothing to do with his frequent, and sometimes caustic, criticism of the organisation of the Corps; he wanted to remain a commander in the field.

Three months later Henderson reluctantly decided he would have to relinquish command of the RFC in France to redress serious supply difficulties in London. The Royal Navy had its own air service able to purchase the best engines and airframes from private manufacturers, whereas the RFC was contracted to buy often inferior machines from the Royal Aircraft Factory. Brancker was doing his best but did not have the seniority to change the system, the result of which was that the Royal Naval Air Service was far better equipped than the RFC. Henderson had become convinced the only way to resolve the problem was for him to return to London and take charge personally at the Directorate of Military Aeronautics.

Kitchener approved Henderson's decision and also warmly approved his recommendation for his replacement. On 25 August 1915, Brevet Lieutenant Colonel Trenchard was promoted to temporary brigadier general and appointed Officer Commanding the Royal Flying Corps in France.

BOOM AND BARING

Among the staff officers Trenchard inherited when he took over from Henderson was the man who had met him in Boulogne when he had first landed in France back in November 1914 and very nearly delivered him into the arms of the enemy – the Honourable Maurice Baring. 'I always intended sacking him,' Trenchard said, 'as I did not know him and I could not think he was doing any good.'[1] In the event he grudgingly allowed him to stay on for a month on trial with the warning that if he was no good – as Trenchard strongly suspected – he would have to go. Baring was embarrassed. 'I felt adrift,' he wrote to a friend, 'like a stranded bondsman face to face with a new Pharaoh, and a bondsman who felt he had no qualifications.'[2]

One of the many reasons Trenchard was wary of Baring was that they had absolutely nothing in common. Baring was an intellectual and an unashamed aesthete; many of his colleagues assumed he was gay, or, in the terminology of the time, 'queer'. A poet, novelist, essayist, dramatist, linguist and critic, he could speak seven languages, including Russian, had read Dante in Italian and Montaigne in French and could quote Homer in the original. He had been born into one of the grandest and most influential families in England – his father was Lord Revelstoke, Edward Baring of the Baring banking family, one of five Baring peers in the House of Lords. His mother was the granddaughter of the second Earl Grey. Only a year younger than Trenchard, he was educated at Eton and Trinity College, Cambridge, where he got a first and from where, predictably, he joined the Foreign Office.

Posted as an attaché to Paris at the height of the Belle Époque, he befriended Anatole France and Sarah Bernhardt, and was then transferred to Copenhagen where he was taken up by the Russian ambassador and his wife, the Count and Countess Benkendorf. He resigned the diplomatic service in 1904 to become a journalist, travelled widely, particularly in Russia, and reported on the Russo-Japanese war for the *Morning Post*. By 1914 he had published ten books – travel writing, short stories, novels and poetry – and was well known in social and literary circles, being a friend of G.K. Chesterton and Hilaire Belloc and a leading light of The Coterie, a fashionable set of aristocrats and intellectuals, including Lady Diana Manners, the most famous beauty in England, notorious for its extravagant parties at the Café Royal and the Cave of the Golden Calf, London's first night club, which promoted itself as 'a place given up to gaiety'.

No, Trenchard and Baring had absolutely nothing in common – neither intellectually nor physically – no mutual interests, no shared experiences, no similar tastes. Yet unlikely as it seemed at the outset, there quickly grew up between them a strong bond of genuine affection, reciprocal admiration and the utmost respect. Not only did they get along famously, they became lifelong friends, so close that Trenchard chose Baring to be best man at his wedding after the war. Later in his life Trenchard would describe Baring as 'the greatest personal friend I ever had'.[3]

Among Baring's huge circle of influential friends before the war was David Henderson. He was probably the most well-connected military man that Baring knew at the outbreak of war and so it was to Henderson he went to ask for a job. Despite his age and distinctly unmilitary demeanour, he was fluent in so many languages that Henderson thought he might be useful as an interpreter and so he was taken on as a junior staff officer attached to RFC headquarters and arbitrarily awarded the rank of lieutenant. On the night before they left for France Baring tried on his uniform for the first time at their hotel in Folkestone and discovered he had absolutely no idea how to put on his puttees. Henderson was obliged to get down on his knees to show him.

Baring quickly proved his usefulness in France not just as an interpreter, but as a personal assistant and general factotum to Henderson, so much so that when Henderson left for London he wrote to Trenchard that it 'broke his heart' to lose the services of his ADC. Trenchard was perhaps unsympathetic but began to warm to Baring after a trivial incident in the mess. Only a few days after he had taken over command he expressed a liking, in Baring's hearing, for Oxford marmalade. Next morning he found a pot of Oxford marmalade on the breakfast table. 'I see you've got a memory, Baring,' he grunted. 'Don't worry, I shall use it.'

Baring quickly discovered that his primary function was to trail around after his boss with notebook in hand as Trenchard toured RFC aerodromes, talking to squadron commanders and pilots to assess their needs and problems, listening to countless complaints and suggestions. Trenchard so frequently barked 'Make a note of that, Baring,' that it became a joke, a catchphrase, throughout the RFC. Wherever Trenchard went with Baring in tow – 'the general, tall and straight as a ramrod, covering the ground quickly with huge strides, forcing his shorter aide to move in a quaint kind of turkey-trot at his side, trying to keep up with him'[4] – everyone would be waiting for him to instruct Baring to 'make a note of that'. Afterwards pilots would create ludicrous scenarios, imitate his voice and bark at each other 'Make a note of that, Baring' and fall about laughing.

The General's system of note-making was like this [Baring explained]. On visits he took someone – me – to take notes about anything he wanted. In the evening the notes used to be put on his table, typed, and then he would send for various staff officers who dealt with the matters referred to in the notes and discuss them. The first thing he would ascertain was if the matter mentioned in the note had a real foundation; for instance, whether a squadron which complained they were short of propellers had not in fact received a double dose the day before. If the need or complaint or the request was found to be justified and reasonable, he would proceed to hasten its execution and see that the necessary steps were undertaken. If the requests were found to be idle or baseless, the squadron or petitioner in question would be informed at once.

But where the General differed from many capable men was in this: he was never satisfied with investigating a request or a grievance or a need or a suggestion. After having dealt with it he never let the matter rest, but in a day or two's time he would insist on hearing the sequel. He would find out whether Squadron B had received its split pin, or what Mr A had answered in England when asked for it. This did not conduce to our repose, but it did further the efficiency of the RFC.[5]

Anyone who wanted to see Trenchard was well advised to check first with Baring.

'Trenchard was a very difficult person,' Lieutenant Brabazon, still working to perfect aerial photography, recalled, 'and when you wanted to see him you had to choose the right moment, and nobody ever dared go and see him until they had consulted the great Maurice Baring, who was always in his confidence. Maurice used to tell you whether it was a good or bad moment. Only when you got his O.K. did you go into the presence.'[6]

It was also incumbent on Baring to waste no time becoming an expert in interpreting Trenchard's sometimes less than coherent thoughts. 'I can't write what I mean and I can't say what I mean,' he announced to Baring early in their relationship, 'but I expect you to know what I mean.' Baring usually did and as a natural writer was able to transform his chief's convoluted instructions into lucid, measured prose.

Long after the war, Robert Brooke-Popham, a future air chief marshal and long-time friend of Trenchard, tried to analyse his problems with words:

I regarded him as one of those people who had the facility of seeing the essence of a problem at once, and of realising the things that really matter. Some people would say that Boom had an instinct for knowing what was right. I'd say it was more passing over the intermediate stages of thought so rapidly that he didn't have to register them in his brain and more or less jumped at once to the right decision. This had the disadvantage that Boom often found it difficult to explain to others why he acted or thought as he did; he just knew he was right but had not memorised how he got there. So, like Kitchener, he sometimes passed for being a stupid man because he couldn't explain his reasons. Added to this, Boom usually found difficulty in choosing the right words or phrases in speech or writing. The latter was also indecipherable except after long practice and his speeches when reproduced usually read badly, but an audience was always perfectly clear what he meant because his conviction and personality alike were so impressive.[7]

Sir John Slessor, a future Chief of the Air Staff, agreed:

> His mind always worked quicker than his tongue; he was almost
> physically incapable of expressing his thoughts on paper – his hand-
> writing had to be seen to be believed – his dictating was a nightmare
> to his stenographers, and his instructions were often a cause of puz-
> zlement (and sometimes amusement) to his staff officers. His closest
> friends (or worst enemies) could hardly accuse him of being an in-
> tellectual type of officer. But he had a flair, an instinct, for getting
> at the really essential core of a problem.[8]

As far as Baring was concerned, Trenchard's tangled syntax was
simply a part of his character, as was his notoriously prickly comport-
ment, which gave Baring plenty of opportunities to deploy his gift
for smoothing ruffled feathers. If Trenchard was bellowing at some
unfortunate pilot and frightening the life out of him, Baring would
often smile and wink behind his chief's back and in this way diffuse
animosity and resentment. He once described his role, picturesquely,
as 'bottling a mountain torrent while yet preserving the tingling fury
of its natural state'.[9]

He also devised a hilarious system of 'Field Punishments for the
General'. If he thought Trenchard had behaved unreasonably or treated an individual or a squadron too harshly, he would later inform the
victim which 'field punishment' he had imposed in retribution. Field
Punishment Number 4, for example, might be inflicted as they drove
away from an aerodrome. Baring would suddenly lean forward in his
seat and look intently out of the window up at the sky.

'What is it, Baring?' Trenchard, his curiosity aroused, would
demand. 'What is it? What are you looking at up there?'

'Oh nothing, sir,' Baring would reply dreamily. 'Just some birds.'

All the field punishments were numbered and were specifically
designed to irritate the general:

> Field Punishment Number 1 was to get out of the staff car slowly.
> Field Punishment Number 2 was to present a map to him upside
>   down.
> Field Punishment Number 3 was to smoke French cigarettes in the
>   car.

Field Punishment Number 5 was to bang the car door, allegedly
   hard enough to smash a window.
Field Punishment Number 6, 'the most severe punishment, imposed very rarely', was to hide the General's pipe.

Baring's list of 'Field Punishments for the General' circulated widely.
No one took them very seriously but even if they only provided imag-
inary redress for some perceived grievance they undoubtedly boosted
morale. They also contributed to Baring's popularity with younger
officers, as did his party piece in the mess which was to lie flat on the
floor with a glass of port balanced on his bald head, then get to his
feet without spilling a drop. On special occasions he performed the
same trick with a bottle of champagne and proceeded to strip to his
underwear while it remained balanced on his head.

'Field punishments' notwithstanding, Baring made it clear, in
frequent letters to his aristocratic and literary friends, how much he
admired Trenchard, referring to him sometimes as simply T, sometimes 'the G' and sometimes Boom.

'You cannot overestimate the pedestal I put him on,' he wrote after
the war. 'He was and is one of the few *big men in the world* and incom-
parably finer and bigger than anyone I have met in my life in any one
of the services, army, navy, air, or politics, in any country; and a big
brain, lightning intuition as well as his obstreperous overwhelming
character, personality and drive . . .', and then he added '. . . only it is
not good for him to have this dunned [sic] in his ears.'[10]

Trenchard in turn described Baring as 'truly the best character' he
ever knew.

He was a genius at knowing the young pilots and airmen. He also
knew about what mattered in war, how to deal with human nature,
how to stir up those who wanted stirring up, how to damp down
those who were too excitable, how to encourage those in need of
it and telling me when I was unfair. He was a man I could always
trust. He was my mentor and guide, and, if I may say so, almost
my second sight in all the difficult tasks that came in future years
. . . He never once failed me and only twice lost his temper with
me, though I must have tried him sorely. He was the most unselfish
man I have ever met or am ever likely to meet.[11]

The fact that the British and French air services worked together in harmony and with complete trust owed much to Baring's skill as an interpreter and diplomat and it was largely due to Baring that Trenchard was able to establish a warm working relationship with his French opposite number, Commandant Paul du Peuty, despite the fact that neither could speak the other's language. Engaging and charismatic, five years Trenchard's junior, du Peuty was a fighter pilot who took to the air at every opportunity. During prolonged conversations, with Baring sitting between them interpreting, both men agreed that the aeroplane was a weapon of attack, not defence – a philosophy to which both adhered – leading to a joint doctrine on the most effective use of air power that was to dictate the strategies of both air forces for the remainder of the war.

Trenchard's two priorities, his guiding principles, remained virtually unchanged throughout the war. The first, and most important, was that the RFC's *raison d'être* was to support the army. 'No call from the Army,' he drummed into his subordinates, 'must ever go unanswered.' The second was that air superiority was essential for victory and had to be fought for and sustained. To him, the arithmetic was clear. 'If I thought that sacrificing an entire squadron would shorten the war by just one day,' he often told his pilots, 'I would do it.'

Shortly after taking command of the RFC, he was invited to attend a major conference convened by Kitchener in St Omer to discuss the future course of the war. 'I remember well sitting on the window-sill while they all sat round a table. I was never asked a single question or spoken to, but I listened . . . The government was very anxious for some victory for political reasons and therefore they wanted action after the failure of Neuve Chapelle and Aubers Ridge.'

The action proposed was a major new Anglo-French offensive – it would become known as 'The Big Push' – to break through the German defences in Artois and Champagne in an attempt to restore a war of movement. The British contribution was for Haig's First Army to attack the mining town of Loos across ground overlooked by German-held slag heaps and colliery towers. To improve their chances of success Field Marshal Sir John French agreed to allow poison gas to be used, for the first time, by the BEF.

In his autobiographical notes, Trenchard related a story that seemed very much at odds with his usual assertive disposition. As the meeting

to enjoy more or less uninterrupted air supremacy. Some RFC pilots thought it a great joke to drop pairs of boots onto German airfields with a note suggesting they could use the boots to run away, as they would not come out and fight. The joke soon turned sour when the first Fokkers appeared in the skies over the Western Front fitted with synchronisation gear which enabled their machine guns to fire through the spinning propeller without hitting the blades – the gun was synchronised with the rotation of the engine so that it only fired at the instant the propeller blades were not in the line of fire – and making it much easier for the pilots to aim at enemy aircraft.

What became known in the newspapers at home as 'the Fokker Scourge' effectively began at five o'clock in the morning on 1 August 1915, when two B.E.2c machines from 2 Squadron bombed a German aerodrome at Douai, waking the sleeping pilots, among them two aviators who would become legendary aces later in the war – Oswald Boelcke and Max Immelmann, 'the Eagle of Lille', both of whom had recently been flying prototype Fokkers fitted with forward-firing machine guns. Orders had been given that the new machines were not to be flown over Allied lines to avoid the risk of the revolutionary synchronisation gear falling into enemy hands. But the opportunity to test the Fokkers in combat proved irresistible and both pilots rushed to take to the air. Boelcke's gun jammed and the B.E.2 he was chasing escaped, but Immelmann caught and engaged the other machine, which was being flown by Lieutenant William Reid.

'Like a hawk I dived and fired my machine gun,' Immelmann wrote afterwards in a graphic letter to his mother. 'For a moment, I believed I would fly right into him. I had fired about 60 shots when my gun jammed. That was awkward, for to clear the jam I needed both hands – I had to fly completely without hands . . .'[14]

Immelmann cleared the jam and continued firing. Reid fought back courageously, flying his aircraft with his left hand and firing a pistol at Immelmann with his other, but his aircraft was peppered with bullets and he was hit four times in his left arm. When his engine spluttered and died, he was forced to make a crash landing. Immelmann followed him down, landed nearby, took Reid prisoner, arranged for him to be taken to hospital and later flew over British lines and dropped a note to say he was alive. Chivalry had not yet died, at least among aviators.

(Immelmann was shot down and killed in June 1916, but his name is immortalised in the famous Immelmann turn – a difficult manoeuvre he perfected by which he was quickly able to gain altitude and position his aircraft for another attack. In an Immelmann turn the pilot accelerates and pulls the aircraft into a climb as if to loop, then turns sideways over the vertical and is ready to dive again on his disconcerted opponent from the opposite direction.)

The news that enemy aircraft capable of firing forward had appeared on the Western Front caused consternation among RFC pilots, since it was clearly obvious that the game had changed for ever, that with the aircraft itself doing the aiming aerial combat would henceforth be very different and they would all be horribly vulnerable whenever they encountered a Fokker. The RFC workhorse, the B.E.2, was totally unsuited to meet the Fokker threat – it was slow and under-armed and was never designed as a fighter aircraft since the mass of struts and bracing wires holding the machine together made it difficult for observers to get a clear field of fire in a dogfight.

There were not, in reality, many Fokkers available to German aviators, but their number was disproportionate to the psychological effect on RFC morale. Gloomy rumours – completely untrue – spread that the Fokker could fly at twice the speed and climb faster than any RFC machine and pilots began to believe that they were 'as good as dead' if a Fokker appeared on the scene. In fact the Fokker was by no means an outstanding aircraft – it was only its armament that gave it an advantage. Trenchard, tirelessly touring his squadrons with Baring in tow, did his best to keep up morale, but the small group of Fokker pilots began shooting down increasing numbers of Allied aircraft. Their technique was to gain altitude and swoop down out of the sun, often attacking before their hapless opponents had seen them and giving birth to the aphorism 'Beware the Hun in the sun'.

With RFC losses starting to exceed replacements, Trenchard bombarded the War Office with demands for more machines and more pilots trained in aerial combat. He even at one point suggested to Henderson that the Naval Air Service might spare him some of their under-used pilots, only to suffer the humiliation of being told that navy pilots were unwilling to fly RFC machines in action as they considered them 'unsuitable'.[15]

He also wanted to know what was being done to equip the RFC with machines that would enable his pilots to meet the Fokkers on equal terms.

> It may be asked [Baring noted in his diary], why we had not got the equivalent of the Fokkers in great quantities at this time, and the answer is that everything in aviation during the war was a compromise between progress and supply. As it took more than nine months for anything new in the shape of a machine or an engine to be available in any quantity, it generally happened that by the time a machine or an engine or the spare parts of both were available in sufficient quantities, the engine or machine or spare parts in question by that time were out of date.[16]

Another worry was the poor standard of pilot training. Although there were plenty of volunteers for the RFC, there were insufficient instructors; many of them were pilots who had been sent home for a rest after cracking up under the strain of operations in France and held a jaundiced view of the joys of flying. The result was that newly qualified pilots arriving in France after the statutory 15 hours of solo flying were far from ready to face action. Trenchard complained to Henderson that they were often more of a liability than an asset to their squadron commanders. 'A reserve pilot has just smashed his fourth machine,' he wrote despairingly to Henderson, 'so I'm sending him back for further training.'

By late 1915 the Fokkers had enabled the Germans to achieve air superiority on the Western Front. Between November and early January 1916, almost 50 RFC pilots and observers were killed – the worst flying months of the war so far. Some people assumed, because of Trenchard's reputation as a martinet, that he was indifferent to casualties. Nothing could have been further from the truth, as Maurice Baring frequently testified. Baring said his chief could never forget he was 'seated on the ground in complete safety' while his men were risking their lives on a daily basis and had to steel himself against the losses. Although Trenchard rarely spoke about his feelings, Baring saw the anxiety and pain etched on his face as he watched so many young men go out and not return.

On 7 November Trenchard and Baring drove to the aerodrome at

St Omer to see a newly arrived French Morane biplane fly against a Bristol Scout. 'The General watched the two machines go up,' Baring wrote. 'It was rather cloudy and after they had been up about half an hour he began to grow uneasy. Like all people who have an intimate experience of aircraft, he hated watching flying and hated still more waiting for people to return.'[17] On that occasion both aircraft returned safely.

In December, Haig replaced French as commander of the British Expeditionary Force, a move Trenchard greatly welcomed. The two men had by then established a close working relationship, held very similar views about the conduct of the war and had a good understanding of each other – Haig naturally approved of the fact that Trenchard made supporting the BEF his priority and Trenchard believed, like Haig, that no matter how difficult it was to accept, a general should not allow himself to be influenced by the cost, in lives or material, of obtaining victory. The bond between the two men strengthened as the war progressed, with Haig always ready to accept Trenchard's advice on the deployment of air power while Trenchard's admiration of Haig bordered on hero-worship.

By the turn of the year RFC losses at the hands of the dreaded Fokkers forced Trenchard to act and on 14 January 1916 he issued an order making the provision of escorts for reconnaissance flights a matter of established practice:

Until the RFC are in possession of a machine as good as or better than the German Fokker, it seems a change in the tactics employed becomes necessary. It is hoped very shortly to obtain a machine which will be able to successfully engage the Fokkers at present in use by the Germans. In the meantime, it must be laid down as a hard and fast rule that a machine proceeding on reconnaissance must be escorted by at least three other fighting machines. These machines must fly in close formation and a reconnaissance should not be continued if any of the machines become detached. This should apply to both short and long distance reconnaissances.[18]

This new strategy helped cut losses, but Trenchard remained very concerned.

Trenchard as a militia cadet, 1889, aged sixteen

In India, 1893. He introduced his brother officers to polo.

A formal portrait of the officers of the 1st Battalion, Royal Scots Fusiliers, Sialkot, India, 1896. Trenchard is standing 4th from left.

Posing with his cups at the Cresta Run in St Moritz, 1901

(*left*) In South Africa, as a young major, pipe in hand, at the end of the Boer War

(*below*) Officers of the Southern Nigeria Regiment in Calabar, circa 1905. Trenchard is seated middle row 2nd from left.

In Nigeria, 1907, while Trenchard was serving with the West African Frontier Force.

The house Trenchard had built in Lagos.

Colonel Moorhouse (*left*), with Trenchard in Nigeria, 1907. They later became close friends.

The pilot's licence that reinvigorated Trenchard's career.

Students on the first course at the Central Flying School, Upavon, 1912. Trenchard is on the right, middle row.

Château des Bruyères, RFC HQ in France, 1914

With Queen Mary during her visit to France, July 1917 (Trenchard on right)

Pencil sketch of Trenchard, France, 1917

I cannot believe you know the seriousness or something would have been done [he wrote to Henderson in February]. I have repeated this so often but nobody believes it now . . . Every FE2, FE8 and de Havilland Scout we have got in this country will be practically wiped out directly the fighting gets serious . . . There is no doubt that even Flying Corps people and people who believe in the Flying Corps have seen our machines completely outclassed . . . I am not trying to get at you or anybody else. What I am trying to point out is that I cannot fight the offensive really successfully from what I see of the Huns at present with what I have got now.[19]

Trenchard was exasperated to read reports of a Parliamentary debate on the air services in February during which one Honourable Member saw fit to raise the fact that most of the senior officers in the Royal Flying Corps had very little flying experience and that only one had flown at the front since the beginning of the war.[20] 'I see they have lately been talking in the House as if I was afraid of being shot at and stating that I never go over the line,' he wrote in another letter to Henderson. 'I hope when you get a chance you will ask these political people whether they are prepared to come as my passenger if I take them across the line.'

Tact was not, by far, his strongest suit and what he called 'stupid orders' from the War Office would rouse him to a fury. When Brancker forwarded a set of orders detailing what officers should, and should not, wear on leave, he asked sarcastically if he could be given two months' warning so that he could be sure his officers were 'properly dressed' when their leave came around. Again, when it was decreed that RFC officers at the front should wear identifying armbands and Brancker asked if one could be sent home for his inspection, Trenchard's response was less than respectful: 'Why not get all your lady friends to make them for you? I'm having a stock of them made ready, so that you can put them on both arms and legs when you arrive. How many hundreds do you want? Can you send out some sailmakers to cope with the extra work?'

Although Trenchard always insisted that the RFC's primary role was to co-operate with the army, he did not want to be seen as an integral part of the army and was impatient with army 'bull'. He tore a strip off an overzealous officer who decided to punish his men for

some misdemeanour by making them go on a cross-country run before breakfast. 'Get this into your thick head,' he bawled. 'This is a
technical corps. Our job is to shorten the war. You're not in the Army
now, you know.'

Among the recruits arriving at St Omer that spring was 17-year-old
Cecil Lewis, who would later write a First World War aviation classic,
Sagittarius Rising. Lewis had lied about his age to enlist and had just 14
hours' flying time when he got to France. His squadron commander
told him he 'wouldn't stand a chance' in action and kept him out of
the line to get more experience before he was sent out. 'It's absolutely
disgraceful to send pilots overseas with so little flying . . .' he protested. 'My God, it's murder!'

As the size of the RFC in France grew and the intensity of the air
war increased, so did the volume of paperwork, including the production of a weekly communiqué, widely known as 'Comic Cuts',
detailing all RFC operations on the Western Front. Maurice Baring
described the hectic day to day life at RFC headquarters at the Château des Bruyères:

> A study office, full of clerks and candles, and a defining noise of
> typewriters. A constant stream of pilots arriving in the evening
> in Burberries with maps, talking over reconnaissances; a perpet-
> ual stream of guests and a crowd of people sleeping on the floor; a
> weekly struggle, sometimes successful, sometimes not, to get a bath
> in the town, where there was always a seething crowd of suppli-
> cants, and a charming capable lady in charge who used to call one
> '*Mon très cher Monsieur*'; hours spent on the aerodrome, which were
> generally misty; small dinners in the flight messes in the various
> billets round Longuenesse; almost every day some inquiry or dis-
> pute with regard to a billet; and a tense feeling the whole time that
> the situation was not satisfactory, but that it would somehow come
> out all right in the end.[21]

In between his duties, Baring somehow found the time to write to his
friends, usually extolling his boss.

Yesterday afternoon I was with Trenchard at Ypres [he wrote to
Ettie, Lady Desborough, a celebrated London hostess before the

war], in the deathly silence of the deserted ruins and gutted houses – broken every now and then by the barking of French guns, and sometimes the scream of German shrapnel out of sight, and the whistling of whistles warning one that a German aeroplane was in the sky . . . I have such an interesting time now. T suddenly sends for me and says 'You have got common sense, tell me what you think of this' and he is so dog quick that he has understood before one has got half the answer out. He is a v. wonderful man, I think. Nothing – no detail – escapes him and he never forgets. His mind registers like a camera.[22]

With his impeccable French, Baring was required to deal with innumerable problems, not all of a military nature, as when two elderly ladies arrived at the headquarters with a serious complaint about the behaviour of two officers billeted with them. They stressed they would only speak to General Trenchard since it was a matter of '*grave indélicatesse*'. Eventually they were ushered into Trenchard's office and, with Baring translating and trying to keep a straight face, they explained that their lodgers had had the effrontery to wash their socks in the kitchen sink.

On another occasion, conferring with a French general with Baring interpreting, the Frenchman remarked '*C'est impossible.*' Impossible was one of the few French words Trenchard understood, so he barked at Baring: 'Tell him impossible is not a word that exists in the English language as far as I am concerned.' Baring did as he was told. The Frenchman looked surprised, shook his head and walked away. As he did so, Baring heard him mutter: '*Cet homme avec un nez qui ressemble à la nacelle d'un avion, dit que "impossible" n'est pas un mot anglais.*'

In March a fundamental reorganisation of the RFC was completed with the Wings being transformed into brigades, each commanded by a brigadier general, requiring Trenchard to be promoted to temporary major general. (He might well have paused to marvel at his meteoric rise – only four years earlier he had been a major with very little chance of further promotion.) That same month RFC headquarters moved into larger premises, the Château St André, close to the village of Hesdin, east of St Omer.

The Château St André was approached along a long avenue of lime trees leading to a fine archway with a coat of arms which had been

mutilated in the French Revolution.[23] Built in the style of Louis XIII
the château itself was massive, with stonework let into the pink walls
and a grey slate roof. Beyond the house was a large kitchen garden and
an orchard. Trenchard had an office on the first floor with a south-
facing window overlooking the surrounding forests, a bedroom off to
one side and an *escalier dérobé* (a hidden staircase) leading from it to
the ground floor.

After his years in West Africa he felt the cold keenly and one of the
first things he did on moving in was to get a big iron stove installed
by the main staircase with a flue leading straight up through the roof.
It was ugly but effective; visitors often reported that his office was always uncomfortably hot. Meals in the officers' mess at St André could
be an ordeal, particularly for younger officers. Trenchard would sit
behind his personal mustard pot with a whisky and soda and would
lay his watch on the table beside his plate to ensure the break did not
last a moment longer than he decreed. During the meal he would fire
questions at more junior members of his staff and expect full, and
knowledgeable, answers. As soon as he had finished his food he would
leave, to everyone's relief, and they could relax for a few minutes until
a bell summoned them back to work.

By then everyone knew his nickname and innumerable stories of
Boom's booming circulated around the Corps. A favourite had him
sitting in his office at the Château St André on a warm summer day
with all the windows open discussing with his chief of staff the move
of three squadrons to new airfields and the equipment they would
need. After the chief of staff left, Trenchard rang the bell on his desk
for his equipment officer, who entered promptly, saluted and said: 'The
stores are on their way to the airfields, sir.'

'How the devil did you know?' Trenchard is said to have shouted.
'I've only just agreed it with the chief of staff.'

'Sir, I was walking from the village and heard you as I was coming
up the drive.'

Most mornings Trenchard drove in his Rolls-Royce staff car to
GHQ, just down the road in Montreuil, sometimes to confer with
Haig, to whom he had direct access, sometimes just to find out what
was going on, sometimes to attend the C-in-C's weekly meetings, at
which he listened intently but said little. Afterwards he would tour
squadrons in daily contact with the enemy. Sometimes his visits were

completely informal – which he much preferred – and a commanding officer would not even be aware that the general was on the aerodrome talking to the men; others were more akin to an inspection, more nerve-racking, and known as 'Boom alerts'.

> We had been warned of the advent of Trenchard and a 'Boom alert' had been ordered in the 2nd Wing [Lieutenant Thomas Hughes recalled], and so there was a feeling of considerable unrest all morning. We got half hourly telephone messages from victims of his previous visit, reporting his progress and the sort of questions he was asking, for which we then proceeded to get up the answers. The CO was in quite a panic. At about 12.30 the great man arrived. I sat tight in the office and all the pilots and observers stood by their machines. Trenchard went booming around asking pertinent questions. He asked why we hadn't got double Lewis drums. The reply was 'It takes time.' Trenchard's riposte was 'Well, it oughtn't take time.'[24]

(It was a variation on his usual response. If someone said he would see to something as soon as possible, he would invariably demand 'What's wrong with now?')

Trenchard listened intently to what the pilots had to tell him, their complaints and ideas. They were all obsessed with the performance of their machines and usually had suggestions as to how performance could be improved or how a new piece of equipment could be incorporated. He decreed that every squadron should set aside one machine on which modifications could be tested and encouraged squadrons to examine, analyse and criticise each other's ideas. Much of the talk, he confessed, was 'unmitigated rot, but if you combine all the views you will find a thread of sound common sense running through all the criticism'. He estimated that 5 per cent of all the suggestions proved really useful and were at once incorporated into operational machines.[25]

His dedication to the job took a toll on his health. Baring recalled that the general was often 'white with fatigue' at the end of the day, but his presence on an aerodrome unquestionably bolstered morale. Everyone knew he could be brusque and short-tempered – many people were physically frightened of him – but at the same time, paradoxically, he was able to inspire ferocious loyalty. No one doubted he had the best interests of the RFC at heart. 'We all worshipped him,' said Robert Barton, the young subaltern he had taken flying at Up-avon, by then a staff officer at St Omer.

After a prolonged spell of bad weather at home prevented flying for several weeks, Henderson wrote to Trenchard to warn him that he would not be receiving the replacement pilots he was expecting. 'I am sorry for this but the combination of bad weather and casualties has brought us down for the moment to bedrock in pilots. . . . The casualties must give you a lot of worry. I am trying to ginger up the political crowd here to see that casualties are inevitable and that the only surprising thing is that we escaped them for so long.'

Henderson's attempt to 'ginger up the political crowd' was not markedly successful, particularly with Noel Pemberton-Billing MP, who styled himself as 'the Air Member' and assumed authority to speak on all air matters in Parliament. Bombastic, eccentric and am-bitious, before the war he had won a £500 wager that he could learn to fly within 24 hours of first sitting in an aeroplane. The following year he joined the Royal Naval Air Service as a pilot but resigned his com-mission to stand for Parliament, winning a by-election in Hertford, standing as an independent 'Air candidate', in March 1916. In his maiden speech he announced that he had resigned from the RNAS so that there would be 'at least one person in the House able to speak on air matters'. Several days later he launched an immoderate attack on the air services, claiming they were in disarray and that the solution was to amalgamate them into a joint force under one political chief.

> I do not intend to deal with the colossal blunders of the Royal Fly-ing Corps [he continued], but I might refer briefly to the hundreds, nay thousands, of machines they have ordered and which have been referred to by our pilots at the front as 'Fokker fodder' . . . I do not wish to touch a dramatic note, but if I do, I would suggest that quite a number of our gallant officers in the Royal Flying Corps have been rather murdered than killed.[26]

Pemberton-Billing's intemperate speech produced howls of out-rage in the House and predictably made headlines the following day with 'Fokker fodder' and 'murder' featuring prominently, al-though Stanley Spooner, the editor of *Flight* magazine, dismissed his 'unnecessarily vehement language' as 'the irresponsible ravings of third-rate sensational journalism'.[27] Trenchard absolutely agreed and suggested to Henderson that Pemberton-Billing should be made to fly his own machine on the front every day for a year. 'He would not fly for more than two days . . . because he would either be killed or broken up.'[28]

Sefton Brancker, recently appointed Director of Air Organisation in London, fired off a furious letter to Trenchard: 'I get more and more impressed with the rottenness of our system and our institutions . . . The Boches will beat us yet unless we can hang our politicians and burn our newspapers and have a dictatorship.'

Trenchard agreed. 'Our institutions badly want revising,' he replied on the following day, 'and I am afraid we shall not move on until things get worse.'[29]

After the government had been prodded by the media furore to set up a judicial inquiry, Trenchard grudgingly informed Henderson he was willing to supply facts and figures but added that he was 'not going to give information for political agitators to pull to pieces unless I am ordered to'. He attached a typically indiscreet postscript: 'I suppose that mountain of conceit G.N.C. [George Nathan Curzon, Lord Curzon] will be put in as head of it. He is an able man, but he does not like me and I do not like him.'[30]

(The previous month Trenchard had travelled with Lord Curzon, a former Viceroy of India, on a cross-Channel steamer from Boulogne and had endured a pompous monologue during which Curzon had asserted the urgent need for an Air Minister within the government, making it quite clear he considered himself the right man for the job. Trenchard listened in silence, but with mounting irritation, increasingly convinced that Curzon was the last man he would have wanted in the job.)

The judicial inquiry was not, in the end, headed by Curzon. It would eventually exonerate Trenchard completely and dismiss Pemberton-Billing's claims as 'extravagant and without foundation', but not before he had launched another thinly disguised attack on Trenchard in the House. Waving a bundle of letters he claimed to have received from airmen in France, he accused the War Office of being 'guilty of supplying our officers with machines that are inefficient and if they meet their deaths in consequence . . . it is very difficult to find a word with which to describe the behaviour of those who are primarily responsible'.

Hugh Cecil, MP for Oxford University, leapt to his feet to defend the RFC.

Nothing is more stimulating [he cried], than reading the tales of aerial combat as they come in . . . You have as much a combat between two individuals as it used to be in the days of knights of old – but all done when flying at 80 or 100 miles an hour thousands of feet above the ground. Nothing in fiction is so inspiring to the imagination than these thrilling dramas of courage and dexterity played without spectators. Taking all considerations into view, our Royal Flying Corps is the best and most efficient in the world.[31]

Cecil sat down to loud cheers.

'I don't know who makes the silliest remarks in the papers,' Trenchard wrote to Henderson. 'Pemberton Billing, who thinks everybody is sent up to be killed, or members of the inquiry, who think war can be conducted without any risk.'[32]

Ironically, while British newspapers and politicians were getting into a lather about the 'Fokker scourge', new aircraft were at last beginning to arrive in France, notably the two-seater F.E.2b and the D.H.2 single-seater fighter, which would prove to be more than a match for the Fokkers. Although neither had synchronisation gear, both were 'pushers' (with the propellers behind the pilot), enabling them to fire forward.

By June the 'Fokker scourge' was effectively over. Even though, on average, one machine, with its pilot and observer, was lost every day during the first six months of 1916, the front-line strength of the RFC had grown to more than 400 machines and RFC pilots with improved aircraft were holding their own in the skies over the trenches. It was not a moment too soon, for the battle which would become a metaphor for the horrors of the Great War was about to begin . . . in the Somme.

10

THE SOMME

An unfailing way to earn Trenchard's instant respect, paradoxically, was to refuse to be browbeaten and stand up to him. It was a lesson 23-year-old Archibald James learned when, a few days before the battle of the Somme, he was summoned into the great man's presence at RFC's forward headquarters, a house that stood at the junction of five roads in the centre of a small village called Fienvillers, 12 miles east of Abbeville. James had joined the RFC from the 3rd Hussars, answering a call for 'lightweight' volunteers willing to train as observers. His first job was taking photographs through a hole cut in the floor of the fuselage holding a big box camera between his knees; later he learned to fly and qualified as a pilot. A flight commander with 2 Squadron, he had no idea what Trenchard wanted when he arrived in Fienvillers.

I was shown into Trenchard's room on the first floor. On the wall was a big map and Trenchard said 'As you probably know, a great battle is going to start on 1 July. A glance at the map will show you that this straight main road in the centre of the battle area is the key to German supplies. The road runs from Albert to Baupaume. In order to deal with this situation I am forming a special squadron of eighteen machines by drawing two from each of the BR2c squadrons on the northern front that won't be involved in the battle. They will operate here under my direct hand, with no Brigade or Wing between the squadron commander and myself. You are in charge and you are in charge of the timetable. The machines will fly single-seater unescorted at 3,500 feet to get out of the reach of small arms fire and they will carry 112-pound bombs with which they will put the road out of action. It's my pet project. I've told Sir Douglas Haig what I'm going to do. I have made out an establishment for the operation and here it is.' He handed me a typescript and said 'Now go for a walk. We lunch at one o'clock. Immediately after lunch come up here and you will tell me if there's anything more needed to make the scheme a success.' So I said 'Thank you, sir' and went out. It was a lovely summer's day and I hadn't gone very far before I came to a big fallen tree. I sat down and read the paper and did a bit of thinking. I then went back. With Trenchard lunch last-ed no more than 20 minutes and when we finished he said 'Come with me.' I went upstairs behind him.

According to an account lodged by James in the Imperial War Muse-um[1] the following exchange then took place:

TRENCHARD: 'Have you read the paper?'
JAMES: 'Yes, sir.'
'Is there anything more that I haven't put on paper that is required for a success?'
'No. I can see nothing required at all.'
'Then you are satisfied?'
'With one exception.'
'What's that?'
'I want to go back to my regiment.'
'What on earth do you mean?'
'Well, sir, several times over the last few years you have ordered me not to argue with you, and I don't propose to do so now. I'm a sec-onded officer and I propose to go back to my regiment.'
'I *order* you to argue with me!'
'You are quite clear, you are ordering me to argue with you?'
'Yes!'
'Well, sir, the reason why I won't take on the assignment is that in my opinion it is doomed to failure. The machines are to fly single-seater unescorted and they will be shot down one after the other. The Fokkers will see to that. And when the first six or eight have been shot down the others will run cunning. They'll jettison their cargoes. The whole thing is bound to be a failure and I am not prepared to be associated with a failure, because you have to sack the commanding officer of a failure.'
'You will not go back to your regiment!' Trenchard snorted. 'You

will go back to your squadron!'

'With that,' James recalled, 'I was bundled out and went back to my squadron.'[2]

Despite his fearsome reputation, Trenchard was always ready to listen to junior officers even if he ultimately ignored what they had to say. James was not reprimanded for his impertinence, neither was his career blighted, possibly because his foreboding turned out to be justified, as he explained: 'Trenchard then appointed a fellow named Dowdeswell to command the squadron, which he did. And the thing turned out exactly as I had predicted. It was a total failure.'[3]

The mission aligned closely with Trenchard's unflinching determination to take the air battle to the enemy. It was a strategy, supported to the hilt by Haig, that would result in an unprecedented level of casualties and which would leave him open to bitter criticism, both during the war and after it. Critics claimed the policy was ill-conceived and placed the RFC at a severe disadvantage, not least because fighting over enemy territory meant both machine and pilot were lost if they were forced down. The official history of the War in the Air concluded that the offensive on the Somme which was 'relentlessly pursued by the British air service' was about four times more costly in lives than the defensive strategy adopted by the Germans.[4] Trenchard himself never appeared to suffer a moment of doubt that he was doing the right thing.

In the weeks leading up to the Somme offensive, he ordered enemy observation balloons to be attacked all along the front – a difficult task which required pilots to dive on the target at full throttle and fire a rocket from a distance of 100 feet, made even more difficult by the fact that the balloons were heavily defended by anti-aircraft guns and enemy fighters.

'We had our great strafe today,' Trenchard wrote to Brancker on 25 June. 'Three Nieuports met their balloons with rockets and brought them down, a fourth missed . . . One phosphorous bomb hit a balloon as it was being hauled down very quickly . . . There was one hell of an explosion which blew everything into the air . . . Just heard that another has been seen burning.'[5]

Trenchard exhorted his pilots to fly reconnaissance sorties ever deeper into enemy territory, believing their presence would establish a 'moral ascendancy' over the enemy, although the direction of the prevailing wind meant that machines usually had to return to base head on into the wind, slowing their progress and making them more vulnerable to attack.

> To him, as to his staff, and most of his senior commanders [wrote Lieutenant Arthur Lee, an RFC pilot, after the war], for a British aeroplane to be one mile across the trenches was offensive; for it to be ten miles over was more offensive. But distance behind the line was largely irrelevant in a three dimensional sphere. In air fighting it was not the plane's position in relation to the front line that measured offensive spirit but the aggressive will of its occupants to attack the enemy when he was encountered, whatever the odds.[6]

Lee considered the High Command's persistence in sending virtually obsolescent[7] machines far behind the lines was incomprehensible, and amounted to 'irrational obduracy'.

On the eve of the battle Trenchard toured the squadrons with Baring. It was in many ways baffling that a man so often accused of being inarticulate had a natural ability to lift the spirits of his men with a simple pep talk. Cecil Lewis was with 3 Squadron, whose aerodrome was just outside the village of La Houssoye.

> Sitting on his shooting stick, he called us all up round him, gave us a bird's eye view of the whole attack, and in his pleasant, masterful way congratulated us all on our work. It had contributed, he said, more than we knew to the success of the preliminary bombardment. Artillery observation, photography, reconnaissance, all received their commendation. 'Boom' infused men's enthusiasm without effort by a certain greatness of heart that made him not so much our superior in rank as in personality. When he left we were all sure that victory was certain, that the line would be broken, the cavalry put through and the Allies sweep on to Berlin.[8]

Would that it had been so. Rather than opening the gates to Berlin, the battle of the Somme became one of the bloodiest in human history. On the morning of the first day, 1 July 1916, 100,000 troops from the BEF's Fourth Army went over the top. By nightfall 19,240 men had been killed and more than 38,000 wounded. They had been told that after a week-long artillery bombardment of the German trenches the attack would be a 'walkover'. Instead it was a bloodbath.

Baring spent the first day of the battle at the RFC airfield at Vert Galant, north of Amiens.

> I saw the pilots of No. 60 Squadron start, and then one waited and waited . . . Who would come back? Who would not come back? At 4.30 Ferdy Waldron came back with his machine riddled with bullets. I went home at 4.30 and reported to the General, and then went back again at six and stayed until 6.30. This time I saw a lot of pilots hot from the fighting and in a high state of exhilaration, as if they had had a grand day.[9]

Cecil Lewis was not one of them. He had been out on two 'contact patrols' over the battlefield to look for flares marking the line of advance; his observer would then scribble a note of the co-ordinates and drop a message bag onto a white groundsheet spread out at brigade headquarters. But he had seen nothing worthwhile to report. 'I was bitterly disappointed. For months we had been preparing, hoping and believing that at last the Air could do something valuable and definite for the wretched men who were carrying forward the line, and in effect it was a complete washout.'[10]

Although the RFC lost 20 per cent of its flying strength during the first few days of the battle, Trenchard was pleased with the performance of his men and remained optimistic, but admitted that his pilots were finding it 'a bit of a strain'.

> I have lost a good many machines lately and a certain number of pilots [he wrote to Brancker on 5 July], but really they have done splendidly. We have crashed a good number of Fokkers and brought down a good many more than they admit. We have done 1,200 hours' flying a day, which makes you think a bit, and a lot of pilots have done five to six hours' flying a day, and this is going on day after day which is a bit of a strain with so many hostile machines and anti-aircraft guns about. I have lost, as you know, eight machines at low bombing and I am afraid that some of the pilots are getting a bit rattled and it is not popular . . .[11]

It was entirely understandable that the pilots were getting 'a bit rattled'. With aircraft flying continuous patrols over enemy terri-tory from dawn to dusk, casualties mounted alarmingly, as did the number of aircraft lost. By the end of July, 210 machines had been 'struck off the list', 97 by enemy action. In 70 Squadron, flying long-distance reconnaissance and fighting patrols in Sopwith 1½ Strutters – the RFC's best two-seater – only nine of the original 36 pilots and observers were left after nine weeks. The remainder, including 20 re-placements, were either dead, missing, captured or wounded. They ranged in age from 17 to 22.

Ground attack sorties at low level – strafing enemy trenches with machine guns and light bombs – were proving very effective but incredibly dangerous. One hit from small arms fire could bring a ma-chine down and the tactic became even more hazardous when troops on the ground learned the technique of deflection shooting (aiming ahead of the target) to hit relatively slow-moving enemy aeroplanes. 'Pilots go down so low now that they can tell which are our infan-try and which are the Germans in the trenches,' Trenchard wrote to Brancker, 'as they can easily distinguish their uniforms.'

Philip Gibbs, one of five official war correspondents with the British Army, described the toll it took on the nerves of the air crew.

Some young men complained to me, bitterly, that they were ex-pected to fly or die over the German lines, whatever the weather, or whatever the risks. Many of them, after repeated escapes from anti-aircraft shells and hostile craft, lost their nerve, shirked another journey, found themselves crying in their tents, and were sent back home for a spell . . . or made a few more flights, and fell to earth like broken birds . . . They were mostly boys – babes, as they seemed to me when I saw them in their tents or dismounting from their machines. On 'dud' days, when there was no visibility at all, they spent their leisure hours joy-riding to Amiens or some other town where they could have a 'binge'. They drank many cocktails and roared with laughter over bottles of cheap champagne, and flirt-ed with any girl who happened to come within their orbit. If not allowed beyond their tents they sulked like baby Achilles, reading novelettes, with their knees hunched up, playing the gramophone, and ragging each other . . .

On a stormy day which loosened the tent poles, and slapped the wet canvas, I sat in a mess with a group of flying officers, drinking tea out of a tin mug. One boy, the youngest of them, had just brought down his first 'Hun'. He told me the tale of it with many details. They had manoeuvred round each other for a long time. Then he shot his man, *en passant*. The machine crashed on our side of the lines. He had taken off the Iron Crosses on the wings, and a bit of the propeller, as mementoes . . . and told me he was going to send them home to hang beside his college trophies. I guess that he was less than 19 years old. Such a kid!

A few days later, when I went to the tent again, I asked about him. 'How's that boy who brought down his first "Hun"?' The squadron commander said 'Didn't you hear? He's gone west. Brought down in a dog fight. He had a chance to escape, but went back to rescue a pal . . . A nice boy'.[12]

Gibbs saw no need to attribute responsibility to Trenchard, whom he lyrically described as a 'Napoleon in this war of the skies, intolerant of timidity, not squeamish of heavy losses if the balance were tipped against the enemy'.

While Trenchard unquestionably drove his men hard, he was surprisingly sympathetic when young pilots burned themselves out or lost their nerve, as many did. He accepted as a given that a percentage of pilots and observers would crack up under the strain of constant patrolling behind enemy lines with anti-aircraft fire bursting all around them and enemy fighters waiting to dive on them out of the sun. Many of the pilots and observers prayed that luck would get them through, and carried mascots or lucky charms whenever they set out. The main fear of all the air crews was a direct hit, causing their machine to disintegrate in the air in a ball of fire – a dreadful death.

(Parachutes were only supplied to airmen in static observation balloons. It was widely rumoured that Trenchard, with his reputation as a hard-hearted disciplinarian, refused to allow air crew the opportunity of parachuting from a stricken machine lest it diminish their fighting ardour and encourage them to abandon a machine they might otherwise have brought home, but there was no truth in it. The issue was one of weight and space – there was too much of the first and not enough of the second in First World War aircraft to allow parachutes, which were heavy and cumbersome, to be carried. In fact Trenchard had suggested experimenting with parachutes early on in the war.)

In his private correspondence with Brancker, Trenchard's concern for the welfare of his pilots was always evident. Explaining why he was sending one of his pilots home, he wrote: 'He is not "tired" but he has been out here a long time and I think he had better go home as I do not want to run the risk of breaking him up.' A few weeks later he was writing about another officer who was suffering very badly from nerves after his observer had been killed. 'They tried to make him pull himself together but it was no good, and whenever he went out to work he returned without doing any work. He stated to his squadron commander that he did not want to fly any more.'[13]

It was Trenchard who introduced the 'no empty chairs' philosophy in the squadron messes, insisting that casualties were replaced immediately to avoid conspicuous empty chairs at the dining table.

> I always looked on the RFC as a family [he explained]. When your family is seated around you your courage is high. I tried to put myself in the others' places and to consider the feelings of those who flew as if they had been my own. If, as an ordinary pilot, you saw no empty seats at table then you didn't tend to dwell on the losses the Squadron had suffered and the fate of your friends who had disappeared. Instead your mind is taken up with buying drinks for the newcomers and making them feel at home. It was a matter of pride and human understanding.[14]

Nevertheless, it was inevitable that morale was affected. Major Oliver Stewart, a pilot with 27 Squadron, admitted to heretical talk in the mess.

> There was hardly an evening when the same people gathered in the mess. It was here that a certain amount of frank and free comment on our casualty rate could be heard . . . Our commanding officer discouraged it, but it continued. We did not believe the losses we were suffering were helping the Allies in their war effort. This feeling, although officially looked on as defeatist, was prevalent among operational pilots . . . Officers of the higher command, from Major General Trenchard down to the commanders of Wings, according

to the critics, were throwing away aircraft and lives for no distin-
guishable purpose. At any rate, they did not convince their pilots
that there was a purpose. The aim seemed to be to contrive the
greatest number of confrontations of British and German aircraft
and to have the greatest number of battles in the air. To us junior
officers there was no discernible military objective.[15]

It was not a subject that any of them would have dared raise with
Trenchard himself, who did not react well to hints that his strategy
of all-out aggression might be flawed. Hugh 'Stuffy' Dowding, the
commander of the 9th (Headquarters) Wing and the future hero of
the Battle of Britain, almost ended his career during the Somme by
asking Trenchard for permission to rest his pilots, who had suffered 50
per cent casualties and were exhausted by non-stop duty. Trenchard
grudgingly complied but in a letter to Brancker described Dowding as
a 'dismal Jimmy' who was 'obsessed by the fear of further casualties'
and who he had decided to send home when the opportunity arose.
Dowding was later duly dispatched back to Britain to command a
training squadron and never returned to the Western Front.

(Dowding's relationship with Trenchard was already strained.
When he was commander of 16 Squadron, Dowding had complained
to Trenchard about being sent the wrong propellers for his Maurice
Shorthorn machines. Trenchard told him to try and adapt them to
fit. Dowding attempted to do so, but after a test flight decided it was
too dangerous and informed the RFC commander. Trenchard was
irked by what he viewed as Dowding's 'pernickety primness' while
Dowding condemned Trenchard's 'technical stupidity'. Trenchard
later recognised he had misjudged Dowding).[16]

In the end, Dowding joined the list of Trenchard's admirers and
liked to tell a story about walking one evening with a friend recently
posted into the area down a village street past RFC Headquarters.
'Flying was over for the day and it was getting dark. We passed a
house from the open window of which came the sound of tremendous
shouting and bellowing. "What on earth is that?" exclaimed my companion. "Oh, that's Trenchard talking to the 12th Group," I answered.
"Good gracious," said my companion, "why on earth doesn't he use
the telephone?"'

Throughout the long Somme offensive Trenchard tirelessly toured the aerodromes and depots to try and bolster the spirits not just of the aircrew but of the mechanics and riggers and technicians toiling on the ground to keep the machines in the air. He often talked about being 'condemned' to ride about in a Rolls-Royce and being 'forced' to sit out the fighting in an office – words that would undoubtedly have been greeted with considerable cynicism if spoken by anyone else, but his gruff sincerity got through to the men: they believed him and they believed in him. When visiting casualty clearing stations he would bark at wounded men 'Get well soon – I hate sick people.' It was true – he had no time for illness – but somehow he managed to say it without causing offence.

The effect that Trenchard's visits had on the morale of those in the squadrons was almost magical [Major Sholto Douglas, commanding officer of 84 Squadron, recalled]. He was a tall man of a commanding presence which was coupled with a personality that was extraordinarily inspiring. And yet that personality itself, or perhaps I should say the quality of it, is difficult to analyse. He was far from being what could be called articulate, and on paper he was almost chaotic. When he spoke it was nearly always in a manner that was strangely disjointed, and sometimes it appeared that what he did manage to say was quite off the point. Perhaps it was the spirit and the great humanity of the man that counted, for those qualities shone through all the awkwardness. It gave him the unique ability of being able to raise the morale of those with whom he came in contact in a manner that was out of all proportion to the visible or audible manifestations of the spirit of the man.[17]

'The General made a speech to the air mechanics who have been working like slaves ever since the battle began [Baring noted in his diary]. He told them he knew well how fed up they must be with the work they were doing at such high pressure and how disheartening it must be sometimes owing to the way aviation had of letting you down. They enjoyed the speech immensely and I nearly cried.'[18]

On the way to a routine squadron visit Baring reported on one occasion that the general's suitcase 'made of Wilton canvas containing his razor, his new coat, his trousers, his shoes, his favourite buttonhook and an advance copy of the *News of the World*' had fallen from the back of their Rolls-Royce and rolled into a ditch. Baring's little *en-tout-cas* (parasol) 'bought in St Petersburg' also suffered the same fate. A messenger had to be dispatched to find them.

Willie Fry, a 20-year-old newly arrived pilot with 11 Squadron, which was bombing targets behind the German lines, remembered a visit from Trenchard:

> A day or two after I arrived he visited the squadron to give what would have to be called a 'pep talk'. I can see him now, sitting on a tree trunk at the edge of the aerodrome with the pilots standing around him. He told us there had been casualties in the squadron in the last few weeks and that there would be many more in the weeks to come, but that we must carry out the bombing tasks set us at all costs as our bombing was of the utmost importance to the offensive. While we were pleased to be assured of the importance of our contribution to the offensive it was perhaps lucky for our morale that we did not pay too much attention to all he said – especially about casualties and the seriousness of the military position. As was the way with young pilots, we thought he was an old buffer talking the usual blather.[19]

Early on the morning of 14 September, Trenchard and Baring arrived by road at the aerodrome at Vert Galant, where 60 Squadron was based. It was the day before Haig's second 'big push', when tanks were to be used on a battlefield for the first time. Trenchard called the pilots together and told them that overnight the enemy had hoisted three observation balloons which might be able to overlook the British tank parks. It was essential, he said, that the balloons were destroyed before zero hour. Only 60 Squadron had the machines – Nieuport fighters equipped with Le Prieur rockets – close enough to do the job. Before calling for three volunteers, he emphasised the gravity of the mission in typically candid Trenchard style. 'Remember,' he said, 'it is far more important to get those balloons than to fail and come back.' The pilots could have been forgiven if they thought that Boom was sending them on a suicide mission, but they knew, and understood, it was not his way to mince words or sidestep an unpalatable truth.

Trenchard and Baring watched the three Nieuports take off and then endured the interminable wait, at the aerodrome, for news. At last a telephone rang. It was army headquarters reporting that the three balloons had just fallen to earth in flames. Shortly afterwards, all three machines returned, bullet-scarred but safe. (Euan Gilchrist, one of the volunteer pilots, met Trenchard years after the war and, more as a 'respectful leg-pull' than anything else, reminded him of his farewell that morning. 'He had not forgotten. Indeed, the look of pain that crossed his face, betraying for once that sensitiveness which he took such trouble to hide, made me wish I had kept my mouth shut.')[20]

Baring's affection and admiration for his chief remained undiminished.

Although what I do is infinitesimal and utterly insignificant [he wrote to Dame Ethel Smyth, the composer and suffragette], I am conceited enough to believe that I can fill that particular role – given the fact of T. and his idiosyncrasies, temperament, ideas – as well as anyone else. I think I understand what he is driving at better than most people; and I sympathise with the overtones of his mind and his character. He is one of those people who have such swift intelligence, such lightning-like grasp, that they don't make themselves clear when they write. I mean they jump to the end of their sentence when they have hardly got the first word out of their mouth . . . I have never met a man or woman with intuition to beat his. So long as I can be of the faintest use to him I shall feel perfectly contented.[21]

Even when Trenchard was in a foul mood, Baring was cheerfully unbothered. 'The G. is in a raging temper this morning of the silent, mumbling kind' he noted in his diary at one point. Then, on another day: 'The G. has just come into the room like a tornado, shouting . . . certainly not about some memorandum written for him of which he has only read one sentence.'

As RFC casualties mounted, so did public concern, much to Trenchard's exasperation, and he continued to bombard the War Office with demands for more and more replacement pilots.

With regard to the number of pilots that we have had and are asking for [he wrote to Brancker on 21 September], I admit that the demand has been enormous. I cannot understand, however, why the demand calls forth letters of protest. We are fighting a very big battle, and fighting in the air is becoming intense. The fighting will increase, I regret to say, not decrease, and it is only a question of our keeping it up longer than the Hun. If we cannot do that, then we are beaten; if we do it, we win . . .

He continued with a gloomy prediction:

I must warn you that in the next ten days, if we get fine weather, I anticipate a very heavy casualty list. There are many more German machines than there were and much better pilots have appeared on our front. I hope you will take this letter very seriously, but what is to be chiefly remembered is that whatever we suffer the Huns are suffering more, and it is only by keeping up the pressure that we can hope to keep the Huns under to the extent that we have them under now.[22]

Trenchard was only partly correct about the suffering of 'the Huns' – the Germans lost far fewer pilots at the Somme than the Allies, although there was no doubt that the RFC onslaught in the early days of the battle caused considerable concern in the German High Command, which would later categorise July and August 1916 as 'the blackest days in the history of German war aviation'. General Fritz von Below, commander of the army which bore the brunt of the Allied attack, admitted that RFC machines were inflicting severe material and psychological damage on his troops:

The enemy's aeroplanes enjoyed complete freedom in carrying out distant reconnaissance. With the aid of aeroplane observation the hostile artillery neutralised our guns and was able to range with the most extreme accuracy on the trenches occupied by our infantry. By means of bombing and machine-gun attacks from a low height against infantry, battery positions and marching columns, the enemy's aircraft inspired our troops with a feeling of defencelessness.[23]

But by September the Germans, reorganised and re-equipped, were fighting back. Faced with Allied air superiority, the German air service, the Luftstreitkräfte, had set up specialist fighter squadrons called Jagdstaffeln, with hand-picked pilots trained in aerial combat, which were swarming up to engage incoming RFC machines with deadly effect. Oswald Boelcke, commander of one of the first Jagdstaffeln, shot down no less than 20 British and French machines in September and October flying a new Albatros D1, which not only had an excellent rate of climb and a top speed of 110 miles an hour, about ten miles per hour faster than the best British and French machines, but was armed with twin synchronised machine guns. The Lewis guns fitted to British machines could only fire 500 rounds before the drum had to be changed – a tricky business at the best of times, let alone in mid-combat.

Trenchard, alarmed at the prospect of the enemy adopting the RFC's tactics, circulated what would become an historic memorandum urging that the air offensive should be pushed even harder. This document, entitled 'Future Policy in the Air' and undoubtedly finessed by Baring, clearly articulated for the first time the basic principles of air power as envisaged by the the RFC commander in France:

> Owing to the unlimited space in the air, the difficulty one machine has in seeing another, the accidents of wind and cloud, it is impossible for aeroplanes, however skilful and vigilant their pilots, however powerful their engines, however mobile their machines, and however numerous their formations, to prevent hostile aircraft from crossing the line if they have the initiative and determination to do so.
>
> The aeroplane is not a defence against the aeroplane. But the opinion of those most competent to judge [Trenchard undoubtedly included himself, not without some justification] is that the aeroplane, as a weapon of attack, cannot be too highly estimated . . . On the British front, since the operations which began with the battle of the Somme, we know that although the enemy has concentrated the greater part of his available forces in the air on this front, the work actually accomplished by their aeroplanes stands, compared with the work done by us, in the proportion of about four to one hundred. From the accounts of prisoners,[24] we gather

that the enemy's aeroplanes have received orders not to cross the lines over the French or British front unless the day is cloudy and a surprise attack can be made, presumably in order to avoid unnecessary casualties.

On the other hand, British aviation has been guided by a policy of relentless and incessant offensive. Our machines have continually attacked the enemy on his side of the line, bombed his aerodromes, besides carrying out attacks on places of importance far behind the lines. It would seem probable that this has had the effect of compelling him to keep back or to detail portions of his forces in the air for defensive purposes . . .

The question which arises is this: Supposing the enemy, under the influence of some drastic reformer or some energetic leader, were now to change his policy and follow the example of the English and French . . . Should we abandon our offensive, bring back our squadrons behind the lines to defend places like Boulogne, St Omer, Amiens and Abbeville, and protect our artillery and photographic machines with defensive escorts, or should we continue our offensive more vigorously than before? . . .

It has been our experience in the past that at a time when the Germans were doing only half the work done by our machines their mere presence over our lines produced an insistent and continuous demand for protective and defensive measures. If the Germans were once more to increase the degree of their activity even up to what constitutes half the degree of our activity, it is certain that such demands would be made again. On the other hand, it is equally certain that were such measures adopted they would prove ineffectual . . . If the enemy were aware of the presence of a defensive force in one particular spot, he would leave that spot alone and attack another, and we should not have enough machines to protect all the places which could possibly be attacked behind our lines, and at the same time continue the indispensable work on the front . . .

But supposing we had enough machines both for offensive and defensive purposes. Supposing we had an unlimited number of machines for defensive purposes, it would still be impossible to prevent hostile machines from crossing the line if they were determined to do so, simply because the sky is too large to defend. We know from experience how difficult it is to prevent a hostile vessel, and still more a hostile submarine, from breaking a blockade when the blockade extends over a large area. But in the air the difficulty of defence is still greater, because the area of possible escape is practically unlimited and because the aeroplane is fighting in three dimensions.

The sound policy would seem to be, if the enemy changes his tactics and pursues a more vigorous offensive, to increase our offensive, to go further afield, and to force the enemy to do what he would gladly have us do now.[25]

The tacit acceptance of the doctrine of attrition enshrined in 'Future Policy in the Air' formally brought the Royal Flying Corps into alignment with Haig's own concept of modern warfare and it would exercise a powerful influence over strategic thinking about the deployment of air power between the wars. Critics would claim Trenchard's offensive policy was too blunt an instrument applied too indiscriminately, 'a product of its creator's intuitive but unsystematic mind',[26] and was forced through blindly with too little regard for the cost in lives. Frederick Sykes, who was hardly likely to be sympathetic, described it as 'stubborn stupidity'.[27] Some argued that Trenchard's early success in establishing air supremacy was as much the result of the enemy's disorganisation as it was the battering being administered by his pilots, and that he was deluded into believing it was his strategy alone that gave the RFC initial command of the skies above the Somme.

In accordance with 'Future Policy in the Air', Trenchard continued to urge his pilots to 'shoot all Hun machines on sight and give them no rest'. No German machines were to be allowed close enough to the Allied lines to carry out artillery observation; bombers were to harass enemy lines of communication; infantry and transport were to be attacked by machine-gun fire from the air; reconnaissance missions were to be completed at all costs if there was the slightest chance of bringing back useful information. In 'BRING DOWN YOUR HUN', a leaflet distributed to RFC pilots, they were told that the enemy was easily intimidated by a bold show of aggression: 'Only very occasionally does one meet a good enemy pilot . . . When a Hun is attacked on our side of the lines, he is nervous and his chief idea is to get back to his own side where he can get aid.' It was an assertion that hardly accorded with the toll being exacted daily by the Jagdstaffeln.

Meanwhile in London Brancker was so close to despair in his attempts to meet Trenchard's never-ending demands for more machines and spare parts that he asked to be allowed to return to his regiment. He was refused. There were unceasing troubles – continuing technical problems with engines, labour disputes holding up production and the difficulty of trying to keep abreast of fast-moving technology. Trenchard was relieved his friend was staying in post. 'Keep going and don't be depressed,' he wrote. 'Do not forget that your work influences work out here as a whole more than anything else I can think of.'

But while Trenchard complained constantly and vigorously about unsatisfactory aircraft and the poor standard of training of air crews arriving in France, he did not, it appears, consider modifying his strategy. With his already inadequate resources severely strained he found himself trapped in a pernicious spiral of increasing losses and falling training standards. New pilots were arriving at the front barely able to take off and land without damaging their machines.

In October Haig warned Trenchard that a number of generals were complaining that his strategy of fighting behind the enemy lines meant that the RFC was not providing sufficient air cover for the troops in the trenches. Trenchard agreed to address a meeting of top brass at Second Army headquarters near Ypres to explain his tactics. He arrived to find a large group of senior officers assembled, he recalled, 'pretty morosely' in a tent. He stepped up onto a small box so they could all see him and began his remarks in classic Trenchard style. 'Well I have come up here because I understand you are all squealing,' he boomed. 'I want to tell you I am very much surprised and to explain that my tactics are not aimed at preventing you from squealing, if that is what you feel inclined to do, but to make the Germans squeal even louder. That is the way to win the war and even protect you . . .' He continued in a similarly truculent vein: his audience was said to have been stunned.[28]

That same month Geoffrey Dawson, the editor of *The Times*, spent an afternoon with Trenchard at RFC HQ during an official visit to the front. Trenchard made no secret of his dislike of newspapers, newspapermen and publicity, but he must have been on his best behaviour because Dawson was very impressed.

A wonderful organisation and a wonderful set of men . . . I came
away with no doubt that he himself [Trenchard] was a really remarkable man. Everyone testified to the spirit which he had infused
into the Flying Corps and I was specially struck by the generous
attitude towards people who must have been serious thorns in his
side . . . He is obviously nervous about the future. At the present
moment our supremacy in the air is absolute. During the whole
time I was in France I never saw an enemy machine. Our own
'sausages' sit in the air all day long just behind the fighting and our
aeroplanes are backwards and forwards over the German lines from
dawn to dusk . . .[29]

Dawson's assertion that Allied air supremacy was 'absolute' was highly questionable. In fact by the time of Dawson's visit to the Somme
the German air service, equipped with new, faster fighters, like the
Albatros, was showing strong signs of recovery. During four weeks in
September 276 RFC pilots and observers had been killed or reported
missing behind the lines.

When the Air Board, which had been set up in London earlier that year under Lord Curzon ('that mountain of conceit') to
co-ordinate general policy in relation to air matters, expressed
concern about the 'grievous' RFC losses on the Somme, Trenchard retorted that the RFC had only one casualty for every 100
times a machine crossed enemy lines, compared to one in three
for the infantry. It was an analogy that did not bear too close an
examination.

RFC pilots knew better than most what was going on on the
ground, since they had a bird's view of the apocalypse below.

The war below us was a spectacle [Cecil Lewis wrote]. We aided
and abetted it, admiring the tenacity of men who fought in ver-
minous filth to take the next trench thirty yards away. But such
objectives could not thrill us, who, when we raised our eyes, could
see objective after objective receding, 50, 60, 70 miles beyond. Indeed the fearful thing about the war became its horrible futility,
the mountainous waste of life and wealth to stake a mile or two of
earth. There was so much beyond. Viewed with detachment, it had
all the elements of grotesque comedy – a prodigious and complex

effort, cunningly contrived and carried out with deadly seriousness, in order to achieve just nothing at all.[30]

A few weeks before the end of the battle Haig dispatched a private letter to General 'Wully' Robertson, the CIGS, which had almost certainly been written by Trenchard, enclosing details of RFC casualties.

I would like to point out [he wrote], that during the last month the majority of casualties have been in the last fortnight, the period when the new German fighters have appeared. The result of these casualties is that we are not doing as much fighting far behind the enemy's lines as we were, with the result that an increasing number of German machines now come up to our lines and a few cross them, whereas practically no German machines crossed the lines in the first two months of the battle. It is fighting far behind the lines which tells most.

The RFC began the battle with 421 aircraft and 426 pilots. By mid-November, when the offensive teetered to its inglorious end, 363 British aircraft had been destroyed or written off, 190 were missing and 308 pilots and 191 observers were either killed, wounded or missing. Trenchard described them, rather movingly, as 'Young men, almost boys, boys who were poets, boys from universities, boys with great mental capacity and boys with only courage . . . I used to say after the Battle of the Somme that every pilot was looked upon as a hero of honour.'[31]

After 141 days of fighting, the Allies had advanced 6 miles along a 16-mile front at a cost of 419,654 British and 202,567 French casualties. The Germans also suffered terrible losses – 465,181 dead or wounded.

A German officer, Friedrich Steinbrecher, summed up the battle: 'Somme. The whole history of the world cannot contain a more ghastly word.'

11

BLOODY APRIL

In his autobiographical notes Trenchard characterised 1917, with some justification, as 'an unhappy year'. It was a year dominated by a melancholy rising toll of casualties, continual production and supply problems and the nadir of the RFC's fortunes – a grim month during which so many machines were shot down it would become known in the Corps' history as 'Bloody April'. Trenchard was particularly irritated to learn that some senior generals thought he had got 'jumpy', worrying that the Germans would do to the RFC what the RFC had done to them the previous year, which was precisely what happened.

Before the 'unhappy year' had begun Haig, at Trenchard's urging, had asked the War Office for a further 20 squadrons of fighters and in December Trenchard travelled to London to appeal in person for the extra machines. He addressed the Air Board on 12 December 1916 in the aftermath of a political crisis during which the vacillating Asquith, overwhelmed and exhausted by the war, had resigned as prime minister and been replaced by David Lloyd George, with the nation demanding he take vigorous charge.

As he felt members might well have been distracted by events, Trenchard circulated a memorandum to the war cabinet, the War Office and the Admiralty summarising his position:

The British forces from the Somme to the sea comprise 36 squadrons, including the naval squadron recently lent by the Admiralty, or about 700 machines in all. Of these 36 squadrons, eighteen are fighting squadrons and eighteen are artillery squadrons. Opposed to us the enemy have from 500 to 600 machines of all sorts, but their proportion of artillery machines to fighting machines is considerably higher than ours.

Three months ago, it was discovered that the Germans were in possession of two or three very fast types of aeroplane. One of these has now come into our possession and has been proved, by trials, to be faster than the majority of fighting machines at our disposal. The number of these fast enemy machines has increased with great rapidity, and it is estimated that 150 of them are now employed against us.

The R.F.C. has at this moment one fighting squadron, besides the naval squadron lent to it, of a performance equal to that of the German machines. It is hoped that nine further squadrons of equal performance will be available before the end of March, making a total of eleven squadrons. This is the most that can be expected from army sources and falls far short, as will be seen, of the Commander-in-Chief's request for twenty additional squadrons.[1]

While new Allied fighters – the Sopwith Pup, the Sopwith Triplane and the SPAD S.VII – were coming into service their numbers were small and they were very slow reaching the front. Fortunately the weather in January – gale force winds and low cloud – kept most aircraft on the ground and afforded the RFC a brief respite from the war, but when Brancker informed Trenchard that an industrial dispute would delay the delivery of the new, urgently needed, Bristol fighters, Trenchard fired off a bitter letter of complaint: 'You are asking me to fight the battle this year with the same machines as I fought it last year. We shall be hopelessly outclassed, and something must be done. I am not panicking, but the Hun is getting more aggressive . . . All I can say is that there will be an outcry from all the pilots out here if we do not have at least these few squadrons of fast machines, and what I have asked for is absolutely necessary.'[2]

Haig added his voice to that of his RFC commander, warning the War Office that the RFC was at least seven squadrons under establishment and would be unable to support the spring offensive if supplies did not rapidly improve. 'Our fighting machines will almost certainly be inferior in number,' he wrote, 'and quite certainly in performance to those of the enemy.'

When repeated letters to Brancker and his boss, General David Henderson, the Director General of Military Aeronautics, appeared to fall on resolutely deaf ears, Trenchard went over their heads and appealed directly to Lord Cowdray, who had replaced Curzon as chairman of the Air Board, earning a reprimand from Henderson, who was irked by what he saw as an unwarranted breach of protocol. Trenchard replied that he had only acted because of the seriousness of the situation. 'I would emphasise once more,' he added, 'that if everybody thinks I am attacking them when I say the supply is hopeless, and they begin to defend themselves instead of trying to improve the supply, I am afraid we shall never get the supply to what we ought – and the result is we shall continually fall behind the Hun.'

Although his previously warm relationship with Henderson definitely cooled after this incident he was not in the least repentant, as he spelled out to Brancker:

> Henderson apparently objects to my writing to Cowdray, so in reply I thought I would bombard him with letters on the subject of machines to see if I can get anything satisfactory. If not, I shall go on writing to Cowdray. Things are too hopeless. To think that we are in the middle of the war and the only letter I get for six months from the man responsible does not mention machines at all but only remarks about my conduct and military usage and 'the usual channels of communication'. It really is as good as a comic opera and, as you say, we deserve to lose the war.

'I still apparently cannot make myself understood,' he wrote again to Henderson on 19 March, 'which I am afraid must be my fault. My point is that I am <u>not</u> trying to find fault: I am only criticising and pointing out things which I ask to be expedited and improved . . .'[3] (His relationship with the War Office was never anything other than testy. When an officer at the Directorate of Aeronautics ventured to suggest which machines were needed in France, Trenchard rounded on him as 'a blithering idiot'.)

Towards the end of March Trenchard went down with German measles, ignored his doctor's orders to stay in bed and developed severe bronchitis, which laid him low for several days. (There was much hilarity among the pilots that their chief had managed to catch 'German' measles.) It could not have happened at a worse time, since the big Arras offensive was about to be launched. Planned in conjunction with the French, who were to embark on a similarly massive attack along the Aisne river some 50 miles to the south, the objective was to achieve a strategic breakthrough on the Western Front and force the numerically inferior enemy to engage in a war of movement on open ground. There was ludicrously optimistic talk that success could end the war in 48 hours.

A few days before the battle Trenchard had circulated orders to brigade commanders emphasising, once again, the need for constant aggression:

> The aim of our offensive will be to force the enemy to fight well behind, and not on, the lines. This aim will only be successfully achieved if offensive patrols are pushed well out to the limits of army reconnaissance areas, and the General Officer Commanding looks to brigadiers to carry out this policy, and not to give way to requests for the close protection of Corps machines except in special cases when such machines are proceeding on work at an abnormal distance over the lines.

In line with Trenchard's 'no empty chairs' philosophy, it was considered morale-boosting for air crew to let off steam at the end of the day and so impromptu raucous parties in the mess, no matter how incongruous in the middle of a bitterly fought battle, were not uncommon. On Easter Sunday, 8 April – the day before the ground assault was launched at Arras – Trenchard and Baring drove to 60 Squadron's base at Filescamp Farm outside Arras to attend a party being thrown to celebrate Canadian pilot Billy Bishop[4] becoming an 'ace', having that day shot down his fifth enemy aircraft. Bishop was said to be acutely embarrassed when he was congratulated by Trenchard, who told him gruffly: 'If everyone did as well as you've done, my boy, we'd soon win this war.' The party was a boisterous affair, with much champagne being consumed and 23-year-old Bishop tap-dancing on the piano and reciting a famous RFC ballad:

Oh the bold aviator was dying
And as 'neath the wreckage he lay, he lay,
To the sobbing mechanics about him
These last parting words did he say

Two valves you will find in my stomach
Three sparkplugs are safe in my lung, my lung,
The prop is in splinters inside me,
To my fingers the joystick has clung

And get you six brandies and sodas
And lay them all out in a row,
And get you six other good airmen
To drink to this pilot below

Take the cylinders out of my kidneys,
The connecting rod out of my brain, my brain,
From the small of my back take the crankshaft
And assemble the engine again.[5]

His recitation was vigorously booed, as was the tradition, and Trenchard, smiling, advised him to 'stick to flying'. When the pianist complained his piano was drying out Bishop promptly poured a quart of champagne into it. The party finally broke up at around three in the morning, although Trenchard and Baring left much earlier. Many of the partygoers would be in the air within hours; many would die in the forthcoming days.

By the time Allied troops began advancing across no man's land at Arras behind a creeping artillery barrage before dawn on 9 April it was snowing hard, with winds gusting at 60 miles an hour blowing squalls of sleet and hail into drifts. If the weather made conditions difficult for the RFC pilots, what they discovered once they were airborne was infinitely worse. They were, as Trenchard had gloomily predicted, 'hopelessly outclassed' by highly trained and motivated enemy aviators in vastly superior machines. During the first four days of the battle alone the RFC lost 75 aircraft and 105 air crew. A further 56 machines crashed due to the inexperience of their hapless pilots.

Trenchard, still not recovered from bronchitis, sent Baring out to tour the aerodromes and report back to him. 'The General sent me out by myself to see the squadrons,' he wrote. 'The battle was now upon us. Fighting in the air on a battle scale had begun. We had not got the necessary number of fighting machines . . . It was evident we should not get through the battle and do the work of the armies without severe loss.[6]

Few of the new generation machines for which Trenchard had pleaded had arrived by then. Fighter squadrons were equipped with obsolete 'pushers' like the F.E.8 and DH.2, which were no match for the German Albatros D.II and D.III, while the RFC's lumbering two-seater bombers and reconnaissance machines – the B.E.2c, F.E.2b and Sopwith 1½ Strutter – were equally vulnerable. (The Sopwith 1½ Strutter was rumoured to be under-stressed and liable to break up in mid-air, spooking the pilots of 48 Squadron to such an extent that they lodged a formal complaint with Trenchard. The squadron commander, Major Sholto Douglas,[7] settled the matter by taking his adjutant Thomas Purdey, of the gunsmith family, aloft on his twentieth birthday in a Sopwith 1½ Strutter and performing no less than 12 consecutive loops while the rest of the squadron, 'suitably impressed', watched from the ground.) Only the SPAD S.VII and the Sopwith Triplane could compete on anything like equal terms with the Albatros, but they were few in number and widely dispersed along the front. A few Bristol fighters had arrived but made a disastrous debut – four out of six machines were shot down on their first patrol.

RFC losses forced squadron commanders into a self-perpetuating predicament – having to deploy more and more pilots with less and less flying time and consequently less chance to acquire the skills needed to stay alive. Many of them would only survive a day or two, pitted against the specially trained pilots of the Jagdstaffeln, among them legendary aces like Manfred von Richthofen, the 'Red Baron', whose Jagdstaffel would dispatch 89 RFC machines in dogfights during the battle. On 29 April, patrolling the skies over Arras at the controls of his famous red-painted Albatros, Richthofen shot down four RFC aircraft in a single afternoon.

While the fighting was at its height Trenchard had to deal with a serious morale crisis in a squadron equipped with the R.E.8, a two-seater biplane which was said to be jinxed, being both difficult to fly and cumbersome in the air, with a tendency to stall or spin out of control. The first production machines had arrived in France towards the end of 1916. Several pilots were killed attempting to land the new aircraft and the R.E.8 quickly acquired an unhealthy reputation as being inherently dangerous. On 13 April six R.E.8s from 59 Squadron, sent out on a long-range photo reconnaissance mission, were intercepted by enemy fighter pilots and shot down within five minutes. A few days later Trenchard arranged to visit the squadron – and arrived sitting in the observer seat of an R.E.8. He clambered out, glared at the pilots standing stiffly to attention by their machines and boomed 'Who arranged this parade? I want lunch and so do you.' After lunch, during which he seemed in unusually good humour, he thanked his hosts, told them to 'give the Hun hell' and then departed, waving cheerfully from his seat behind the pilot as his R.E.8 taxied for take-off. He could not have delivered a clearer message.

The poor standard of pilot training remained the RFC's Achilles heel. Brigadier General Percy Groves, director of flying operations, made a tour of RFC training establishments at home and reported to the Air Board that pilots were being dispatched overseas before they had acquired even the minimum standard of proficiency needed for active service, that their standard of aerial gunnery was such that they had 'only the remotest chance' of hitting another machine in the air, that their flying experience was so limited they could neither manoeuvre nor keep formation and that many left for the front without having ever flown the type of machine they would be called upon to take over in France. One squadron commander told Groves that his pilots 'went west' so rapidly that he never had the time to get to know them.[8]

Trenchard did not need to be told all this – he knew it only too well. Critics would later claim that he should have modified his relentless offensive strategy to accommodate the inexperience of his pilots and that the moral ascendancy gained by long-distance patrols was not worth the cost in lives. But while he could be flexible on many issues, on this he was ruthlessly inflexible and remained so for the duration of the war, although he admitted in a letter to Brancker on 19 April that the battle was turning into 'a heart-breaking game': 'I am very hard put to it to get through the work and I feel sometimes I am very ungrateful for what you do for me. I am having a very strenuous time of it . . . our machines are being driven back behind Arras and cannot get out to work in front of Arras . . . Do not think I am ungrateful but it is a heart-breaking game . . .' (Trenchard's admission that he was ungrateful probably struck a chord with Brancker. A month earlier he had written to complain that a squadron of de Havillands had arrived without bomb racks or bomb sights, adding furiously: 'I must say I do not know what you do at home. You have got a huge staff and they cannot even see to a simple thing like that.'[9])

Although he was still recovering from bronchitis he refused to relax his schedule. 'The G has surpassed himself,' Baring noted in his diary on 21 April, 'carrying everybody on a whirlwind of enthusiasm and energy and electric vitality in spite of his having been ill. He is better now, quite well, I hope.'

On 29 April Trenchard and Baring drove to Vert Galant to talk to Hubert Harvey-Kelly, the commander of 19 Squadron, who had the distinction of being the first RFC pilot to land in France back in August 1914 (and the even rarer distinction of still being alive). They discovered when they arrived that he had gone up that morning to engage a German patrol. Baring described the long and agonising wait for him to return. 'We stayed there all the morning. By luncheon time he had not come back. He was due and overdue. When we went away the General said "Tell Harvey-Kelly I was very sorry to miss him" but I knew quite well from the sound of his voice he did not ever expect this message would be delivered. Nor did I. Harvey-Kelly never came back.' Using the innocent terminology of the age, Baring said Harvey-Kelly was the 'gayest of all gay pilots'. He always took a potato and a reel of cotton with him when he went over the lines, claiming that if he was forced down the Germans would be sure to treat him well when they found he possessed such useful and scarce commodities.

Two weeks later the initial battle of Arras ground to a halt with the troops on the ground having made a significant advance, notably at Vimy Ridge, but without achieving the hoped-for breakthrough and the stalemate resumed, with Allied casualties amounting to some 158,000 men. The French, on the Aisne, fared much worse. The disastrous failure of their offensive, with 40,000 casualties on the first day, led to widespread mutinies in the French army which spread to nearly half the French infantry divisions on the Western Front before order was restored.

Siegfried Sassoon grimly commemorated Arras in his poem 'The General':

'Good morning, good morning,' the general said,
When we met him last week on our way to the line.

Now the soldiers he smiled at are most of 'em dead,
And we're cursing his staff for incompetent swine.
'He's a cheery old card,' muttered Harry to Jack
As they slogged up to Arras with rifle and pack.
But he did for them both by his plan of attack.

The average life expectancy of an RFC pilot during the battle of Arras
was a shocking 18 flying hours, or 11 days. German pilots largely confined themselves to operating over their own lines, meaning they could
stay in the air longer, could pick and choose their targets and were less
likely to be captured if forced down. The Germans lost 66 aircraft
during April 1917, compared with the RFC's loss of 245 machines, with
211 aircrew killed or missing and 108 taken prisoner. Almost a third of
British losses were accounted for by von Richthofen's Jagdstaffel.

It was Trenchard's fervent belief that a general could not allow himself to be influenced by the cost in lives or machines of any operation
and that if he did so he was bound to lose. His personal philosophy
was simple: when he had assured himself a certain course of action was
right, he stuck to it rigidly regardless of what anyone else might say
or think. He was particularly contemptuous of politicians, and complaints from politicians about RFC casualties. He could rightly claim
that the enemy had failed to prevent the RFC carrying out its prime
objectives of supporting the army, but the cost had been horrendous.
Between March and May 1917, no less than 1270 aircraft were lost.
This, coupled with the production crisis at home and the difficulty of
providing sufficient trained pilots to replace those losing their lives in
France, for a time threatened the viability of the Royal Flying Corps
as an effective fighting unit.

The battle of Messines Ridge in June was the first faint indication
that the dark days of 'Bloody April' were coming to an end. Small
numbers of improved aircraft – the Bristol F.2 fighter, the Royal Aircraft Factory's S.E.5, the de Havilland 4 and the Sopwith Triplane
– had at last been brought into service and proved their worth by
dominating the air, keeping the enemy behind their own observation
balloons, six miles behind the front, and directing Allied artillery fire.
Improved ground to air communication allowed areas threatened by
German bombardment to be warned and enemy artillery-spotting
aircraft to be attacked. Long-range bombers targeted German-occupied

airfields and railway junctions while two squadrons were reserved for close air support on the battlefield and low-level attacks on the trenches, enemy transport and machine-gun nests.

Baring was exultant that things were at last looking up. 'It all went like clockwork and the air reports read like fairy tales,' he wrote in a letter dated 7 June. 'I think the Boches must be thinking long and bitter thoughts . . . It is the finest day in the air we have had. Our people entirely prevented the Boche Flying Corps from working, and our artillery work in co-operation with aircraft went without a hitch.' Being the man he was, he could not refrain from adding: 'It is hot. The summer is arriving in great strides, bearing in one hand a poppy and in the other a basketful of strawberries.'

Trenchard did not share his friend's optimism. On 10 June he was forced to circulate an order to brigade commanders to 'avoid wastage of both pilots and machines for some little time. My reserves at present are dangerously low. In fact, in some cases barely exist at all . . .' He added a paradoxical rider: 'It is of the utmost importance, however, that the offensive spirit is maintained.'

In a letter to Brancker marked 'Private and Very Urgent' and dated 26 June, he laid out his concerns:

There is a good deal of panic going on at present out here about the strength of the Flying Corps. Many people are saying we are getting the worst of it . . . I am not grousing but I would ask you to do your level best to divide my requirements into two parts, one to carry me through the next six weeks and the second to complete the final programme [of aircraft production]. Things are moving and I must say at present that really level-headed people who have never panicked before are panicking now on the subject of the number of German machines against us.[10]

William Joynson-Hicks, a Tory MP and persistent critic of air defence policy (and of Trenchard), had cause to change his mind after an official visit to the front with a Parliamentary delegation in June 1917, during the battle of Messines Ridge. Reporting to the House of Commons, Joynson-Hicks admitted that the 'General was never a friend of mine' but went on to praise his extraordinary mastery of detail and ability and his extraordinary effect, both moral and spiritual, upon the force in France . . . General Trenchard was not galloping about on a white horse. He was in the upper room of a chateau far behind the lines, surrounded with maps, with telegrams pouring in, and the telephone going, and there we had the opportunity of sitting, without interfering, of course, while the battle was in progress, and watching the effect of every movement made by the enemy as it came in, and we had the opportunity of watching the effect of the orders given by General Trenchard and observing the extraordinary grip and mastery of that man over every detail of the fighting.[11]

In July, Trenchard was invited to attend a dinner hosted by Haig at GHQ in honour of General Pétain, recently appointed commander-in-chief of the French army. 'After dinner,' Haig noted in his diary, 'Pétain had a great discussion with Trenchard regarding the principles of employment of aeroplanes, i.e. the relative advantage of close protection of artillery machines, or (our method) of distant attacks to draw off his machines. Trenchard had the best of the argument.'[12]

That new aircraft were finally arriving in France was largely due to the efforts of an energetic Scottish industrialist by the name of William Weir. After Lloyd George had succeeded Asquith as prime minister, one of his first appointments was that of Weir to the crucial post of controller of aeronautical supplies at the Ministry of Munitions, with a seat on the Air Board. Weir's Clydeside factory manufactured artillery shells; he was a man who understood industry, understood the vital need for new machines in France. He galvanised aircraft production to such an extent that 37 of the 51 RFC squadrons in France had been equipped with new machines in time to support the offensive at Passchendaele and RFC fighters began operating in ever larger formations, with as many as 60 machines engaged in lengthy dog fights behind the lines. By the autumn of 1917 Trenchard was at last receiving regular deliveries of new, much more sophisticated machines all fitted with forward-firing synchronised machine guns – the Sopwith Camel, the S.E.5a and the French SPAD S.XIII – which began to tip the scales in the air war back in favour of the Allies.

The standard of pilot training also greatly improved when the instruction regime devised by Major Robert Smith-Barry began to pay dividends. A minor Irish aristocrat who had been expelled from Eton for laziness, Smith-Barry was one of the many mavericks attracted to the RFC. As commanding officer of 60 Squadron in France he was appalled by the incompetence of newly arrived pilots, many of whom had only a hazy idea of how a flying machine took to the air. He was convinced that the way to inculcate student pilots into coping with the mysterious hazards of aviation was to deliberately expose them to potentially dangerous manoeuvres, in a controlled environment during dual flight instruction, in order for them to learn how to recover from errors of judgement.

Smith-Barry pestered Trenchard with his ideas until Trenchard finally agreed to send him home to try them out. He set up a new training school at Gosport with a radically revised curriculum combining academic classroom lessons with extensive dual-control flight instruction during which instructor and pilot communicated through voice tubes fitted into their helmets. It quickly became clear that his theories worked – the number of accidents in training began dropping steadily. Smith-Barry's revolutionary methods would gain worldwide recognition and what became known as the 'Gosport system' was soon adopted by other combatant nations. Trenchard liked to describe Smith-Barry as 'the man who taught the air forces of the world how to fly'.

Through the summer of 1917 Trenchard continued to drive himself hard. 'Yesterday and the day before we visited nine squadrons and three kite balloons,' Baring wrote to a friend. 'The G. spoke to all the pilots and saw everything. He rides the whirlwind and directs the storms and kindles in everyone he sees an undying spark. But he was white with fatigue afterwards. I can't tell you how tiring it must be for him since I myself, who only look on, am worn to a shred.'[13]

Charles à Court Repington, a well-connected Old Etonian and war correspondent for *The Times* and the *Morning Post*, came away very impressed after a visit to RFC headquarters at St André, describing Trenchard as

one of the few indispensable men in the Army. He has done wonders and deserves immense credit . . . His policy is to seek out the German airmen and either drive or draw them away so that our artillery scouts may carry out their mission. This has led to heavy

fighting and many casualties, but he has persevered . . . A pilot takes
two months of fighting to become adept, but his nerve usually only
lasts for three, six or nine months afterwards and a man who has
had a rest is seldom good for much else again. . . .[14]

Initially Trenchard had been reluctant to allow the exploits of his
fighter pilots to be publicised, fearing it would overshadow the equally
dangerous, but perhaps less glamorous, 'shows' being flown every day
by other pilots. But intense public interest and the newspapers' thirst
for heroes persuaded him to change his mind on the correct assumption that publicity would boost morale both in France and at home.

At a time when there was rarely any good news from the Western
Front, newspapers leapt at the opportunity to report the gallant exploits of RFC 'aces'. They were feted by the media as heroic figures
and became lodged in popular imagination as gladiators of the air,
fearless heroes with goggles and white silk scarves dicing with death,
craning their necks in open cockpits in search of prey, then swooping
and rolling through the air in deadly one-to-one combat.

The darker side of being an RFC pilot in France was ignored by the
media – officially compiled 'wastage' figures assumed the average life
span of a bomber pilot was four months, a reconnaissance pilot could
expect to live three and a half months and a fighter pilot two and a half
months. The utterly terrifying stress of aerial combat manifested itself
in stomach ulcers, insomnia, nightmares and shattered nerves. Pilots
affected to pretend that aerial combat was not dissimilar to 'rugger',
but few of them could tolerate much more than six months of active
duty without cracking up. They also reacted with 'cynical amusement'
to their portrayal in the media. 'Bar-room brawling, bicycle chains
and broken bottles,' an RFC pilot wrote after the war, 'have a closer
affinity to early fighting in the air than the chivalrous, formalised,
knightly encounters with lance and épée to which it has been likened.'
The principal objective of a fighter pilot, he asserted, was to sneak up
unobserved close behind his opponent and 'shoot him in the back'.

Nevertheless British aces like Albert Ball, Edward Marnock and
James McCudden – all of whom won VCs – became national heroes.
When 21-year-old Lieutenant Ball crashed to his death in a field in
France in May 1917, after notching up 44 'kills', the news sparked a
wave of national mourning and large crowds gathered for a memorial

service in Nottingham, his home town. Trenchard later described Ball's death as 'the greatest loss the Flying Corps could sustain at that time'. He was saddened to receive a bitter letter from Ball's grieving father accusing him of being 'a murderer', this despite the fact that Ball himself had told fellow pilots that 'Boom' had earlier saved his life by transferring him to a home posting when he was 'getting too big for his boots'.[15]

> To belong to the RFC in those days [wrote Cecil Lewis], was to be singled out among the rest of the khaki-clad world by reason of the striking double-breasted tunic, the Wings, the little forage cap set over one ear, but more than this by the glamour surrounding the 'birdmen'. We who practised it were thought very brave, very daring, very gallant: we belonged to a world apart ... The RFC attracted adventurous spirits, the devil-may-care young bloods of England, the fast livers, the furious drivers – men who were not happy unless they were taking risks.[16]

In November the RFC underlined its growing status on the battle-field, at Cambrai, the last major battle of 1917, where tanks were used effectively in large numbers for the first time, smashing through enemy fortifications thought to be impregnable. Despite operations being hampered by fog and mist, RFC pilots were able to develop close support and battlefield co-operation tactics with the ground troops, and low-flying fighter aircraft worked effectively with the advancing columns of tanks and infantry, but the lethal mixture of low-level operations and inexperienced pilots again resulted in severe losses – 115 casualties, including 68 dead and missing, and 77 aircraft destroyed.

At the end of 1917 it was time to count the cost of the year's operations – 2094 RFC aircrew killed in action, or missing. Trenchard was obliged to order brigade commanders to reduce patrols over the lines to a minimum and refrain from operations in bad weather in order to husband resources in preparation for the spring offensive in 1918.

Meanwhile, the air war had moved much closer to home.

12

A FORETASTE OF THE BLITZ

At 11.30 on the morning of 13 June 1917, a beautiful English summer day, 14 Gotha heavy bombers, twin-engined biplanes with a wingspan of 72 feet and a payload of 13 bombs, appeared over London without warning and began dropping their bombs from a great height, well out of the range of anti-aircraft fire from the ground. Liverpool Street railway station was severely damaged, as was the Royal Mint, next door to the Tower of London, and a school in Poplar. Ninety-two RFC aircraft were scrambled but by the time they had climbed to the height of the enemy invaders the raid was effectively over. Two RFC observers were killed – the Gothas carried a rear-facing machine gunner in the underside of the fuselage which made them very difficult to shoot down.

All 14 bombers returned safely to their base in Flanders, leaving Londoners stunned by the sheer effrontery of the raid; that such a thing could happen in broad daylight and that the war could be brought to their very doorsteps seemed inconceivable, as was the apparent inability of the RFC to prevent it. Some 162 people were said to have been killed (figures vary) and 432 injured – the highest casualties from a single raid during the whole of the war. The most devastating loss was at Upper North Street school in Poplar, where a bomb smashed into the infants' classroom, leaving 18 children dead and 30 severely injured. According to 'Wully' Robertson, the CIGS, the war cabinet reacted with panic 'as if the world was coming to an end'.[1] In some ways, it was. The appearance of Gothas over London indicated that the 'nature of warfare had changed in a manner which could only spell danger to Britain's long-enjoyed "insular fastness"'[2] and seemed to put at risk the very seat of government.

But it was the needless deaths of so many innocent children – and newspaper pictures of their little coffins in a procession of horse-drawn carriages – that most inflamed public opinion and fuelled calls for vengeance. Lloyd George, inspecting the damage the following day, promised 'We will give it all back to them soon . . . with compound interest', but the newspapers called for immediate action, publishing front-page maps of Germany pinpointing major cities allegedly within range of RFC squadrons in France. A few days later the *Daily Express* sponsored a mass meeting at the Royal Opera House in Covent Garden to protest 'the brutality and horror of high explosive bombs being dropped upon small children who were blown about like bundles of bloody rags'. The Lord Mayor of London was in the chair and moved a resolution urging Lloyd George and the war cabinet to 'initiate immediately a policy of ceaseless attacks on German towns and cities'.

C.G. Grey, the combative editor of *The Aeroplane* magazine, called for the strategic bombing of Germany, not as a retaliation for the raid on London but as part of the war effort: 'Behind Germany's army lie the sources from which it is fed. The iron mines, the steel works, the armament factories . . . lie within reach of the weapons of war . . . Instead of bowing to popular clamour for reprisals – mere retaliatory raids in revenge after every enemy attack – let us take the invasion of Germany from the air as a serious problem of the war.'[3]

On Saturday, 7 July, the Gothas returned – 22 of them this time, flying in fan formation over London. By the time the 'All Clear' sounded, 57 people were dead and a further 193 injured, all but 5 of them civilians. Although 95 naval and RFC aircraft took off to engage the Gothas, only one invader was shot down. This time public fury spilled onto the streets – a large mob rampaged through the East End, smashing the windows of shops with vaguely foreign names. A boisterous crowd gathered on Tower Hill and petitioned the King to 'instruct your Ministers at once to make vigorous and continual attacks on German towns and cities' or else 'dissolve Parliament and appoint Ministers who will do their duty'. Lord Derby, Secretary of State for War, promised the House of Lords that nothing would be left undone to protect the country against 'aircraft invasion' but the public remained unconvinced. A few days later all the mayors of the metropolitan boroughs met at City Hall, Westminster, and called for 'attacks on the largest possible scale against German cities and towns without distinction'.

In a leader, *The Times* declared: 'The experience of Saturday makes it abundantly clear that . . . all our arrangements in connection with air campaigning, both offensive and defensive, require fresh investigation.' In the United States, which had joined the war the previous April, the *New York Times* called for restraint, hoping 'a competition in savagery may be avoided . . . The bombing of undefended German cities promises no better result than the depriving of the Allies of a moral superiority they now possess. And that is not worth while.'

In fact the attacks on London should not have come as a surprise since small-scale air raids had been going on for more than two years. The first strategic bombing operation in history took place in January 1915, when two massive German navy Zeppelins crossed the Norfolk coast and dropped 24 50-kilogram high explosive bombs and a number of ineffective incendiary devices on Great Yarmouth, Sheringham, King's Lynn and the surrounding villages, or wherever they saw clusters of lights, killing four people, injuring sixteen and causing £7500 worth of damage. It was the first, but very far from the last, direct aerial attack on civilians in war. In May London was targeted for the first time, the Zeppelin pilots scrupulously avoiding the west of the city on the orders of Kaiser Wilhelm out of respect for his royal cousins, resident in Buckingham Palace.

Zeppelin raids continued through 1915 and 1916, usually at night and creating considerable paranoia both among the public and in Whitehall, which found itself facing a barrage of criticism about government defence policy. War cabinet meetings discussed spreading a 'blight' on German crops from the air, or burning them with incendiary bombs, in retaliation. In Parliament there was fanciful talk about massed raids on Germany's industrial centres and in the *Daily Express* H.G. Wells proposed a mass attack with 2000 planes to destroy Essen, arguing that even if 1000 machines were lost the cost would be cheaper than the battle of Neuve Chapelle or the loss of a battleship.

During 1916, Zeppelins dropped 125 tons of ordnance in 23 raids, mainly in the south-east of England, killing 293 people and injuring 691. In February 1917 operations escalated considerably when the Kaiser authorised Gotha bombers to attack urban centres in England with the express intention of 'intimidating the morale of the English people and crushing their will to fight'.[4] Gothas were redeployed from other theatres to airfields in Belgium where they formed 'The England Squadron'. (Gothas were the first heavier-than-air machines to be used for strategic bombing and were much more cost-effective than Zeppelins. They would be followed, later in the war, by formidable four-engined R-type 'Giants', with a crew of seven. All told, bombing raids throughout the war would kill or injure 4003 civilians, compared with 146,777 in the Second World War.)

In May 21 Gothas raided the Kent coast, crossing at Folkestone, and in the space of ten minutes killed 95 people and injured 192. It was described by *The Times* as a 'well-planned and disastrous air attack'. The newspaper concluded 'the only means of coping effectively with this prospect is by an aggressive aeroplane policy of our own . . . in the air, far more than in any other sphere of modern fighting, the overwhelming advantage is always with the attack'. It was a leader that could have been written by Trenchard himself and certainly one with which he wholeheartedly agreed.

After the first daylight Gotha attack on London in June, Trenchard, now recognised as the foremost authority on air power, was recalled urgently from France to discuss this alarming new development. He arrived with a detailed appreciation of the situation in the air, made cogent with the help of Baring, which he presented to an emergency meeting of the Cabinet in Downing Street on 20 June. The most effective way to defend Britain, he argued, would be to capture the Belgian coast which would increase the distance German bombers had to travel and force them to cross territory occupied by the Allies, making them vulnerable to attack before they could even head out across the Channel. The second option was to inflict the 'utmost damage' on enemy aerodromes and aircraft behind the front, although the RFC was limited by the number of machines and pilots available.

He made it clear he did not believe that fighter patrols over the Channel would work, since they would only be able to intercept incoming bombers by 'sheer luck' and 'the number of pilots and machines required would be entirely beyond our present power of supply.'

Turning to the question of retaliatory attacks on German towns he was circumspect.

Reprisals on open towns are repugnant to British ideas [he said], but we may be forced to adopt them. It would be worse than useless to do so, however, unless we are determined that once adopted they will be carried through to the end. The enemy would almost certainly reply in kind – and unless we are determined and prepared to go one better than the Germans, whatever they may do and whether their reply is in the air or against our prisoners or otherwise, it will be infinitely better not to attempt reprisals at all.[5]

In any case, he concluded, the RFC did not presently have suitable bombers to carry out sustained and effective reprisals.

When Lloyd George suggested bombing Mannheim immediately, perhaps to appease public opinion as much as to retaliate against Germany, Trenchard was obliged to point out that Mannheim was not within the range of any of his aerodromes in northern France and barely within striking distance of French bases in the east. Privately, he was not against bombing Germany in principle, but while every RFC machine in France was needed to support the army he was convinced the army should have priority.

At a second meeting the following day, Trenchard was astonished to learn that a decision had been taken that aircraft manufacture was suddenly to be given priority over all other forms of weapon production. The size of the RFC was to be increased from 108 to 200 squadrons and 40 of the new squadrons were to undertake the bombing of German cities. He had little confidence in the extra squadrons materialising any time soon, and neither did Haig, who sourly wrote to Henderson to inquire if 'these mythical bombers' were to get priority over the 'fighters and other machines' for which he had been waiting for months.

Despite Trenchard's advice that trying to intercept enemy bombers on their way to Britain would be fruitless, the war cabinet decided that two 'crack' fighter squadrons should be detached from the RFC in France to carry out daylight defensive patrols over the English Channel. Trenchard protested that every machine was needed in France and argued that the best way to stop the bombing of London was to knock out the enemy's aviation capability from France, but he was overruled. It was perhaps for this reason that he was reported to be in a 'savage mood'[6] when he returned on 27 June to St Omer, to where he had moved his advanced headquarters in preparation for Haig's new offensive in Flanders. Fortunately his demeanour had greatly improved by the time Queen Mary arrived on an official visit to the front a few days later. Trenchard was required to escort her on a tour of the airfield and stand alongside her as she watched a flying display.

Deeply concerned by the rising levels of public alarm, four days after the second Gotha raid in July, Lloyd George asked General Jan Smuts, the South African representative in the Imperial War Cabinet, to investigate the arrangements for home defence against air raids and the organisation of the air services. (Smuts fought against the British in the Second Boer War and contrived by his tactics to make British generals look inept and foolish, but later led the fight against German colonies in Africa and had been invited to join the Imperial War Cabinet earlier that year.) It took Smuts just eight days to conclude that London could become 'part of the battlefield' within 12 months and to recommend urgent measures to create a unified command of air defence fighters, guns, searchlights and observation posts.

A month later Smuts' Committee produced a second report, largely written by General David Henderson, who had been seconded to Smuts as an adviser, which criticised the friction and inefficiencies resulting from the competition between the RFC and the RNAS and called for the establishment of a unified air service and raising the status of the Air Board to a Ministry. (It was this report which would eventually lead to the establishment of the Royal Air Force in April 1918 and prompt Trenchard to assert that it was Henderson, not himself, who was the real 'Father of the RAF'.)

The RFC and the RNAS had been at loggerheads since the start of the war, largely because of production problems. The Admiralty persistently outbid the War Office for new machines and engines, leaving RFC pilots in France stuck with obsolescent machines, often unsuitable for the roles they were required to carry out. While the RFC was always short of pilots, the RNAS often had more pilots than it needed. It was hardly surprising that relations between the two air services were sour.

Smuts' report envisioned the Western Front moving forward at a 'snail's pace' in the summer of 1918 while the air battle was being fought far behind the Rhine with attacks on industrial centres and lines of communication likely to be the 'determining factor' in ending the war. He warned that the enemy was making 'vast plans to deal with us in London if we do not succeed in beating him in the air and carrying the war into the heart of his country'. He also argued, presciently, that 'the day may not be far off when aerial operations, with their devastation of enemy land and destruction of industrial and populous centres on a vast scale, may become the principal operations of war . . . to which the older forms of military and naval operations may become secondary and subordinate.'[7]

On 24 August, the war cabinet, mesmerised by the notion that the war could perhaps be won in the air as an alternative to the ghastly slaughter in the trenches, approved in principle the setting up of a separate independent air service. Trenchard, who received an advance copy of the report, dismissed the war cabinet's hopes. 'The contention on which the whole argument for a separate air service is based,' he wrote, 'is that the war can be won in the air as against on the ground. Nothing but bare assertion is urged in support of this contention.'[8]

He also did not think the time was right for setting up an independent air force, just when the RFC was winning plaudits for its growing contribution to operations on the ground and beginning to feel it was part of the army. Further, he doubted that the long-range bombing of Germany – one of the arguments being advanced for the new service – would either be justifiable or would make a significant contribution to victory. 'I thought that if anything were done at that time to weaken the Western Front,' he explained, 'the war would be lost and there would be no air service, united or divided. I wanted to unify it, but later on at a more suitable opportunity.'[9]

Haig noted Trenchard's concern in a diary entry dated 28 August:

> The War Cabinet has evidently decided on creating a new department to deal with air operations on the lines of the War Office and the Admiralty. Trenchard is much perturbed as to the result of this new department just at a time when the Flying Corps was beginning to feel that it had become an important part of the army. The best solution would be to have one Minister of Defence with the three offices under him, viz: Admiralty, War Office, Air.[10]

Unseasonably bad weather – days of torrential rain – was hampering progress of operations in France. Trenchard had agreed during his visit to London to negotiate with the French for a lease on an aerodrome in the French sector from which the RFC could mount bombing raids on Germany when machines became available. In fact the French were extremely reluctant to co-operate – they were opposed to the bombing of Germany for fear of instant reprisals against French towns and were reluctant to let him have any facilities. But after difficult and protracted negotiations Trenchard was finally able to lease an airfield at Ochey, near Nancy, close to the German border.

In London, arguments continued about the wisdom or otherwise of bombing Germany in retaliation for the continuing raids on southern England. One member of the Air Board, Rear Admiral Mark Kerr, circulated a 'bombshell memorandum' citing intelligence sources and claiming the enemy was building a fleet of 4000 heavy bombers – huge six-engined machines each capable of carrying five tons of explosives – with which they planned to destroy most of London. To counter this threat he urged the creation of an RFC bombing force of not less than 2000 aircraft. His was an apocalyptic view of the war: 'The country who [sic] strikes first with its big bombing squadrons of hundreds of machines at the enemy's vital spots, will win the war.'[11]

In late August the Germans switched tactics from daylight to night bombing of targets in southern Britain, mainly London. For three successive nights beginning on 2 September, Gothas launched raids, with London the main target on 4 September. On the following day the war cabinet agreed a motion that 'we must carry the aerial war into Germany, not merely on the ground of reprisals'. There was a short lull in raids, but they resumed on a larger scale on 14 September and continued every night, with the exception of 26 and 27 September, until the end of the month, further fraying the nerves of Londoners and increasing the clamour for retaliation. Public morale began to crack, with people staying overnight in tube stations or sleeping rough in parks. Lloyd George summoned a meeting of newspaper editors and ordered them to stop publishing photographs of bomb damage.

There was also much criticism that the RFC had no machines comparable to the Gotha.

What has happened [C.G. Grey wrote caustically in *The Aeroplane*], is simply that the Germans have developed a special branch of warfare which we have neglected in a manner which can only be described as idiotic. Until quite recently it was never worth the while of any designer to design a machine specially for bombing because the authorities did not want it . . . And yet we are surprised

when the German goes to the trouble of building as good a bombing machine as he knows how, and proceeds to use it for the purpose
for which it was built.[12]

On 1 October General Robertson dispatched a cipher telegram to
Haig in France:

Continuous aircraft raids on England are causing interruption in
munitions work and having some effect on general public. Cabinet
desire immediate action against those German objectives which can
be reached from neighbourhood of Nancy. Send Trenchard over at
once to me to discuss scale on which you can undertake these operations and necessary arrangements for them. Cabinet wish for
at least one line squadron to be employed and with least possible
delay.[13]

After being briefly held up by heavy mist, Trenchard left next morning from St Omer aerodrome in the passenger seat of an R.E.8.
Baring travelled in a second R.E.8 and a clerk in a third. It was a
journey not without drama. Visibility worsened as the three aircraft
crossed the English coast. The pilot of the first, carrying Trenchard, lost contact with the second, carrying Baring, as they entered
a thick blanket of cloud. Anti-aircraft units along the coast were already jumpy after enemy air raids on four successive nights; a general
alert was sounded at the approach of three unidentified aircraft and
spasmodic firing broke out. Trenchard's pilot made an emergency
landing at Lympne in Kent while the other two machines continued to
Croydon.

When the general failed to arrive at Croydon, Baring feared the
worst. He described the journey and the subsequent anxiety in his
diary:

We flew at about 3,000 feet. It was fine as far as the coast, but
slightly hazy. Over the Channel it was quite fine as far as Folkestone.
We flew along the railway line, I could see both the other machines.
Then when we got near Tonbridge some small clouds began to
appear in the distance like small pellets of cotton wool. More and
more of them gathered, until suddenly we were enveloped in a

thick wet blanket of white cloud. We lost sight of both the other machines at about 800 feet. Reeves [Baring's pilot] went down quite low, and trees appeared out of the mist. He went down to 30 feet, reconnoitred the railway line and then went up again. We soon left the whole bank of cloud to the south-west of us.

We landed at Croydon safely; there were no signs of the General. About a quarter of an hour later the machine with Bates [the clerk] landed; there were still no signs of the General. I telephoned to Hounslow. No machine had landed there. Then to Lympne; no machine had landed there either. Then suddenly the air raid alarm was given, and all further telephone communication became impossible. Machines were turned out and stood by. I waited about an hour and then I borrowed a car and motored to London with the two pilots; we arrived in a deserted city. The population was sheltered from the supposed raiders. I went to the Hotel Cecil [designated HQ of the proposed Air Ministry between the Thames Embankment and the Strand]; it was quite empty, partly because of the alarm and partly because it was the belated luncheon hour. I could not find a single soul. I went down into the basement to the telephone exchange and asked if I could telephone France. They got me on to our Headquarters at once. There I learned the General had gone back to Lympne. He motored up, and I found him later at the Army and Navy Club. I was exceedingly anxious, especially as his clerk told me he had seen a crashed machine in a field and First Aid being brought.[14]

Trenchard was 'less than amused' to discover that it was their aircraft that had triggered a general alert, the sound of their engines in the clouds being mistaken for Gothas. The 'All Clear' was not sounded until 2 p.m. – he was amazed that a few unidentified aircraft could virtually paralyse the capital for several hours.

At a meeting with the Cabinet later that afternoon Lloyd George emphasised the need to start replying in kind to the enemy's attacks on Britain 'for the morale of the people' and raised Admiral Kerr's warning about London being attacked by 4000 bombers. 'Nonsense!' Trenchard snorted. 'Forty at the most.' The prime minister, perhaps unaccustomed to being told he was talking nonsense, was taken aback and asked Trenchard to explain. 'I replied,' he recalled, 'that even if the Germans had 4,000 aeroplanes to bomb London with, which I did not believe, it would take them months to organise aerodromes and the whole paraphernalia of preparation. I gave him practice, not theory.'[35]

Trenchard was asked when RFC bombers would be able to start operating from Ochey. Six days, he replied, after they had arrived. Uncharacteristically tactful, he forbore to mention how much he disliked conducting a campaign to satisfy political demands, but he did warn the prime minister not to expect too much – success would very much depend on the size of the force he was able to assemble and would be subject to the vagaries of the weather. Privately he would still have preferred to concentrate his forces in supporting the army rather than divide his limited resources between two unrelated bombing campaigns. He did not believe that bombing Germany would either spare London or win the war.

While he was in London he had a long meeting with General Smuts, whom he had previously met only briefly. The two men recognised qualities in each other – integrity, common sense and candour – they both shared. Trenchard spoke enthusiastically about the 'boundless possibilities' of aircraft in future wars but at the same time warned Smuts about the extent of the production and supply problems that he faced and that he was still waiting delivery of squadrons that had been promised a year earlier.

Smuts realised that his estimates for future aircraft production were grossly over estimated – on the over-optimistic advice of Lord Cowdray he had predicted a 'great surplus available for independent operations' in the spring of 1918. He penned a chiding memorandum to the war cabinet which very much reflected Trenchard's views and in which he declared himself to be 'somewhat alarmed' by the backwardness of their preparations.

General Trenchard is quite clear that the enemy has never been stronger in the air than he is today, and that relatively we are not so strong as we were some months ago ... General Trenchard, therefore, presses for an acceleration of our aircraft production programme so that this position may be improved instead of worsened before the winter ... As regards the bombing campaign of next spring and summer, the fear amongst officers is chiefly that the enemy is making very great preparations to recover ascendancy in the air, and that success for him in that respect may have far-reaching consequences on the course of the war.

Even from a purely defensive view, therefore, we are called upon to make a very great effort in the air. But our preparations should be on such a scale as not only to make our defensive position secure, but to enable us to gain a decisive superiority on the battle fronts so that the road may be cleared for our offensive bombing policy against the industrial and munition centres of Germany.[16]

Trenchard returned to France – by destroyer – with orders to transfer a day and night bombing squadron to Ochey and 'as soon as possible, undertake a continuous offensive, by air, against such suitable objectives in Germany as can be reached by our aeroplanes'. It would become the 41st Wing, under the command of Lieutenant Colonel Cyril Newall, a future air chief marshal. On 17 October, exactly six days after the first RFC bombers had arrived in Ochey, two flights took off on the first long-range bombing mission into Germany, hitting factories, railways and the Burbach iron foundry near Saarbrücken. A week later Handley Page bombers carried out the first night-time raid and operations continued into November with the loss of only five aircraft, giving the citizens of Saarland a taste of what Londoners had had to cope with at the hands of the Gothas and Zeppelins.

There was still considerable opposition to the policy. Winston Churchill, then Minister of Munitions, was among the sceptics.

It is improbable that any terrorisation of the civil population which could be achieved by air attack [he wrote in a report to the Cabinet], would compel the Government of a great nation to surrender . . . In our own case we have seen the combatant spirit of the people roused, and not quelled, by the German air raids. Nothing that we have learned of the capacity of the German population to endure suffering justifies us in assuming that they could be cowed into submission by such methods, or, indeed, that they would not be rendered more desperately resolved by them.[17]

Trenchard was not intrinsically against the idea of bombing Germany, but believed it should wait until there were a sufficient number of machines available to carry out massed attacks. 'I am in no way trying to upset the policy of the War Cabinet for bombing Germany with a large number of machines . . .' he wrote in a memorandum to the war cabinet, 'but please remember that if we lose half our machines in doing so, the good morale effect, which is three-quarters of the work, will be on the German side and not ours.'[18]

While the third battle of Ypres was grinding to an inconclusive end in the mud at Passchendaele and the grim list of casualties, killed and wounded, already exceeded 200,000 (it would later be described by Lloyd George, who had little respect for Haig as a military commander, as a 'senseless campaign' and 'one of the greatest disasters of the war'[19]) the government was pressing ahead with establishing an Air Ministry and considering the major changes that would be required at the top of the Royal Flying Corps in preparation for the establishment of an independent air service.

The obvious candidate to become the first Chief of the Air Staff was Henderson, but his health was poor and he had lost the confidence of Lord Derby, the Secretary of State for War, and had alienated many of his military colleagues by his support for an independent air force. There was also a salacious rumour that his son was having an affair with an actress who was thought to be a spy. In fact Derby had attempted to replace Henderson with Trenchard earlier in the year. He had suggested the move to Trenchard on a visit to France and was left in no doubt about Trenchard's robust opposition. His language was so immoderate that Baring, who was present, rebuked his boss afterwards for his rudeness to the Secretary of State. In the end Haig put an end to the matter by refusing to release him.

In October Henderson was replaced as DGMA by Major General John Salmond and Brancker, who had essentially run the Directorate under Henderson, was rewarded for his years of selfless loyalty and hard work by being posted to take command of an obscure aviation brigade in Egypt. Brancker blamed the CIGS – 'Wully' – for his downfall and was unable to hide his bitterness in a letter to Trenchard:

They have got me all right at last. I am to go to Egypt. It's very clever and I don't know how far you have helped them indirectly . . . Wully (backed by you) is up against the Air Ministry – he *thinks* I am an ardent supporter of it (I am not very much really). His first effort was to try to put Capper in [Major General Sir John Capper, the officer who had met the Wright brothers in the US before the war] – I frustrated that and got myself disliked in consequence. This is a brilliant stroke. He has never seen Salmond and knows nothing about him, but he gets rid of D.H. [Henderson] and side-tracks me with one blow . . . It makes me smile. Of course, your everlasting criticism of everything at home has given them a good lever – and as I always told you, everybody's sins have eventually fallen on my head.[20]

Trenchard did not reply, whether out of guilt, sadness, or embarrass-ment is not known. But he did find time to write what he described as a 'long sermon' to his friend Jack Salmond, briefing him on what he could expect in his new post. Salmond, the former Director of RFC Training, was only 36 and had little staff experience and, like so many senior officers who owed their position to Trenchard's patron-age, would look to him for advice and support.

Remember in your dealings with the War Office [Trenchard wrote], that we are part of the army and that we are not trying to run a separate show at their expense. Although at times the Flying Corps conflicts with other arms, at the same time remember that there are two sides to every question and be certain that what you ask for is really necessary . . . Don't forget that you must decide in favour of a machine or engine, etc, which some technical experts are against. No two technical experts agree. I listen to one and am guided only by one and never more than one, and sometimes go against his opinions . . .

You can do nothing with a rush. Take your time over everything and make up your own mind and keep to it, unless there is a sound argument against your decision which you had not thought of before . . . The Progress and Allocation Committee is a perfect dis-grace. Most of it is due to there being too many people and nobody responsible and it ought to be knocked on the head . . . Anyhow you might attend two or three meetings and listen to the bunkum and then make Cowdray attend one . . .[21]

He concluded by wishing Salmond good luck and advising him, for some reason, to burn the letter. Salmond had only been at his new post for a matter of weeks when he began to despair of ever getting anything done and let Trenchard know he was on the point of tendering his resignation. Trenchard was unsympathetic and advised him to stick it out. 'You can't resign in a war,' he said. (Four months later Trenchard would blithely disregard his own advice and do just that, war or no war.)

It was widely believed that Lord Cowdray, who was said to have performed well as president of the Air Board, would be appointed the first Air Minister, but during a visit to France he had a meeting with Trenchard who brusquely disabused him.

'Lord Cowdray came out to see me and I said "Do you think you will be the first Air Minister?" He looked at me rather queerly and asked what business it was of mine. I told him that I asked him simply because I believed he thought it, and I then told him that he wasn't going to be. This surprised him very much indeed and he did not like it.'[22]

Trenchard had apparently heard, somehow, that Lloyd George wanted the newspaper baron, Lord Northcliffe, to take the job. Alfred Harmsworth, the 1st Viscount Northcliffe, dominated the British press, owning the *Daily Mirror*, the *Daily Mail* and *The Times*. He had always taken a strong interest in aviation matters from the start. The *Daily Mail* had offered thousands of pounds in prizes to encourage flying and the prime minister thought his drive and energy made him the perfect candidate to be the first Air Minister, not to mention the power he wielded through his newspapers. Over a private lunch at Downing Street Lloyd George claimed to have 'sounded out' the newspaper proprietor but without making him a definite offer. Be that as it may, Northcliffe claimed he left the lunch convinced that the job was his.

On 16 November, while the Air Force Bill was still going through Parliament, *The Times* published a copy of a gratuitously insulting letter which Northcliffe had sent to the prime minister the day before declining what he called the prime minister's 'repeated invitations' that he should take charge of the new Air Ministry. 'I feel that in present circumstances,' he wrote, 'I can do better work if I maintain my independence and am not gagged by a loyalty that I do not feel towards the whole of your Administration.'

Lloyd George understandably viewed the letter as a gross breach of confidence and an embarrassment.[23] Cowdray was incandescent and deeply insulted that the first he knew of the prime minister's intention was when he read about it in *The Times*. He immediately resigned and never forgave Lloyd George, writing to him that 'it ought not to have been left to me to receive from Lord Northcliffe's letter to *The Times* the first intimation that you desire a change at the Air Ministry'. (He retained his affection for the air service, however, and later, with great generosity, donated the funds necessary to acquire and furnish the handsome mansion in Piccadilly which is still the Royal Air Force Club.)

The Air Force Bill passed into law on 29 November, by which time, to widespread astonishment, Lloyd George had persuaded Northcliffe's younger brother Harold, Lord Rothermere, also a newspaper baron, to accept the position of Air Minister. It would turn out to be a disastrous appointment. Rothermere, who would be widely criticised in the 1930s for using his newspapers to support the appeasement of Nazi Germany, had done his bit for the war effort in 1916 by becoming director general of the army clothing department and had a reputation for financial acumen, but popular gossip held his major qualification for the role was being Northcliffe's brother.

Rothermere had been persuaded that the best man to occupy the important post of Chief of the Air Staff was Trenchard. The trouble was, Trenchard did not want the job.

ROWS WITH ROTHERMERE

As the most experienced air commander in the field, Trenchard was an obvious choice to be the first Chief of the Air Staff, but he was otherwise ill equipped for the role. He loathed politics and political manoeuvring, he had had very little contact with Whitehall or the War Office, having spent only four of his 24 years of service in Britain, he was accustomed to running his own show, he was under fire for the grim toll of casualties resulting from his policy of relentless aggression and he was deeply sceptical about plans for creating the Royal Air Force in the middle of a war. He also detested the media, and the man with whom he would have to work most closely was a newspaper baron.

Harold Harmsworth, Lord Rothermere, and his older brother, Alfred, Lord Northcliffe, had bought the London *Evening News* in 1894 for £25,000 and founded a newspaper empire which wielded enormous political and social influence. Rothermere, a large well-built man with a high forehead and a walrus moustache, was widely recognised as a pioneer of popular journalism. At the time of his surprise appointment as Secretary of State for Air he was living in a variety of London's finest hotels, moving regularly from one to another, and it was in his suite at the Ritz that he set up a meeting in December 1917 at which he intended to persuade Trenchard to accept the post of Chief of the Air Staff. Also invited was his brother, Lord Northcliffe and Major John Baird, the Permanent Under-Secretary designate.

Trenchard, with the faithful Baring at his side, crossed the Channel by destroyer from Boulogne in the early hours of 16 December and motored directly to London from Dover, arriving at the Ritz at 3 o'clock for what he assumed would be a relatively brief meeting. He knew what was on the agenda and he firmly intended to refuse whatever blandishments Rothermere was intending to offer him, since he had not the slightest desire to become Chief of the Air Staff.

Both Harmsworth brothers greeted Trenchard effusively, but the atmosphere quickly soured when they began to criticise Haig's leadership in France and revealed that they intended to use their newspapers to agitate for the sacking of both Haig and Robertson. This was like a red rag to a bull as far as Trenchard was concerned. The argument that followed, he recalled, was 'bitter and unpleasant'.[1] Trenchard was a Haig man through and through; he had worked closely with the commander-in-chief, whom he admired and respected, and they shared identical views about the conduct of the war. He would never countenance being a party to any campaign against him, but at the same time it was made clear to him that if he refused to accept the post he was being offered, his refusal would be used as further ammunition to attack Haig. It seemed to him that 'all they really cared about was not beating the Germans, but beating Haig and 'Wully' Robertson. They seemed to think that getting rid of Haig would be the first step in winning the war, whereas I thought exactly the opposite.'[2]

'The impression left on my mind by this interview – and I am perfectly certain it was the correct impression,' he noted later, 'was that if I refused to come home, or Sir Douglas Haig did not wish me to, then the Air would be used in the Press campaign against Sir Douglas. There is no doubt whatsoever that this was intended to be conveyed to me.'[3]

As the argument dragged on, Trenchard, who was exhausted, admitted that 'many points arose which should not have been stated'. He said he did not want the job because he had no desire to fight 'both the Army and the Navy' and he was also fundamentally at odds with Rothermere over the newspaperman's well-known views about reprisal raids against Germany. Rothermere wanted to bomb Germany on a scale 'not hitherto dreamed of', using between 100 and 150 machines carrying enough bombs to lay waste to two or three towns in retaliation for every raid on Britain and creating terror among the population. Trenchard sarcastically pointed out that it was much easier to bomb Berlin in headlines than it was from the cockpit of any machine likely to be constructed for years. The exchanges became 'hotter and more unpleasant' as the night wore on. At the end Trenchard decided he had no choice but to accept the position if for no other reason than to 'head off' Rothermere's intemperate plans to lobby for

Haig's dismissal. When he left the Ritz at half past three the following morning he had agreed, reluctantly, to take the job, providing Haig agreed.

> I thought I might be of more use to the nation, the RFC and the RNAS if I accepted the post [he wrote later]. At the same time I knew I should have to fight Rothermere and Northcliffe from the day I took the job. I remember well saying 'All right, I will agree to come home, but don't forget that I am not the man you think I am, also don't forget that I am neither a good writer nor a good talker [a familiar refrain always delivered to divert precocious expectations]. But I knew what I wanted and I was determined to get it with the help of my wonderful staff and the wonderful pilots of the RFC. I thought of what they wanted and I knew I could help them.
>
> I can remember driving down to Dover that night with Maurice Baring on our way back to France. I remember so well that I was most annoyed. We had been told to get to Dover at a certain time or we would miss the tide, which we did. Then we found, when we got to the other side, it was low water and we could not get in. Nobody had even thought of looking up the tides of the port we were putting in to.[4]

When he finally got ashore in France he drove direct to GHQ to see Haig, tell him what had happened and seek his permission to leave his position as commander of the RFC in France. When Trenchard arrived, Haig's ADC tried to intercept him by saying the C-in-C had asked not to be disturbed but Haig poked his head out of the bathroom door and said 'Trenchard, is that you? I'll dress and come down in a moment.' Trenchard described his interview with Rothermere without mentioning the brothers' threats to mount a press campaign against him – he could see no point in adding to Haig's worries and in any case there was nothing either of them could do about it. When Trenchard concluded by saying 'I think I had better go home,' Haig suggested a compromise. He saw no reason, he said, why Trenchard could not remain in command of the RFC in France while combining it with his duties as Chief of the Air Staff. Trenchard thought it would be totally impractical, but Haig, very reluctant to lose his friend and ally, wanted him to try. In the end Haig said 'If you think you can

help the war by going home, then go. I trust you.' They were, Trenchard recalled, 'the most heartening words I have ever heard at a time
when I felt pretty sad and miserable'.

Haig noted in his diary that night: 'General Trenchard came to see
me on his way to his HQ from London. Lord Rothermere insists on
him going as Chief of Air Staff. T. stated that the Air Board are quite
off their heads as to the future possibilities of Aeronautics for ending
the war. I told T. that it was evidently necessary that he should become
C of S Air, much as I regretted parting with him.'[5]

The following day Trenchard sent a long letter to Rothermere
which, judging by its awkward prose, had not been finessed by Baring:

> I got back and saw Sir Douglas Haig at once. He was going away
> from G.H.Q. for a couple of days, so I just caught him. I told him
> what you wanted me to do and he will agree to it. He thought it
> would be the best thing which could be done, but he thought that
> I must still remain Chief of the Flying Corps in France as well . . .
> and that I should come here constantly to look after things, so I
> hope this is all right.
>
> I have been thinking over our long discussion a lot and I am still
> a little uneasy that as you do not know me very well you will find I
> am not altogether up to what you expect. I have very decided views
> as to how to run the Air Service, and to what extent it can and must
> expand, but at the same time I am equally decided that the expan-
> sion of the Air Service, which is necessary in a very large way and
> should be started very early, must not be allowed to jeopardise the
> whole of the Western Front.
>
> I quite think that I ought to go home under these circumstances
> – not that I want the job anyway – but I do feel that I have more
> experience than anybody else at this present moment, and that I
> have the confidence of the whole Flying Corps at present. Vast im-
> provements are necessary in the service, and they can be carried out
> and must be looked at in a large way and taken up early . . .[6]

His letter crossed with one from Rothermere expressing concern about
the 'adequacy of the preparations for the long-range bombing offensive'. Trenchard, prickly as usual, was offended. 'I am uneasy about
people being uneasy,' he replied, 'about the adequacy of preparations

for long-range bombing. I am responsible for it, and of course you will be, but if they cannot trust me then I cannot see any object in your asking me to come as C.A.S. . . .'

In fact Trenchard had already made very considerable preparations, leasing land, draining marshes and bulldozing the difficult ridge and furrow countryside of Nancy to make way for new aerodromes. He had also opened discussions with the French and the Americans about conducting joint bombing operations.

The weather in France turned bitterly cold, with thick snow on the ground, as Christmas approached that year. Trenchard was exchanging almost daily letters with Rothermere about future plans and there was a constant stream of visitors to RFC Headquarters at St Omer, among them Winston Churchill, then Minister of Munitions, who confided to Trenchard that he thought the war would last a very long time, and C.G. Grey, the splenetic editor of *The Aeroplane*, who was a persistent critic of plans to unify the air services.

After a Christmas lunch which, according to Baring, comprised 'tepid turkey, cold bread sauce, flat champagne and port made of furniture polish', Trenchard attended a concert staged by the men at which the star turn was a 'strong man' – an airman who was an enthusiastic amateur bodybuilder. Unfortunately his act went disastrously wrong when his assistants very nearly killed him by jumping on the wrong part of his body as he was straining to lift a heavy dumb-bell. Trenchard wryly reflected that he was in a not dissimilar situation – a strong man being hindered by people who did not know what they were doing.

Haig continued to press for Trenchard to be allowed to stay as GOC of the Flying Corps in France while still carrying out the duties of the Chief of the Air Staff. 'It is not just his advice on technical matters that I consider irreplaceable,' he wrote in a letter to the War Office, 'but his power to raise the morale of the squadrons and individual pilots under the strenuous conditions that we must expect in the near future.' When he was told that the war cabinet had vetoed the idea, he appealed to Lord Derby, the Secretary of State for War: 'I consider that the coming four months will probably be the most critical of the whole war in France; I therefore again ask you to reconsider this decision before ordering Trenchard to hand over to another.'[7]

'I am still corresponding with Derby over Trenchard,' Haig wrote to his wife. 'D. is a very weak-minded fellow, I am afraid, and, like the feather pillow, bears the marks of the last person who has sat on him! I hear he is called in London "genial Judas".'[8] Robertson, the CIGS, finally scotched the proposal as totally impractical and Haig was forced to concede. He reluctantly appointed John Salmond, on Trenchard's recommendation, as the new GOC RFC in France.

On 1 January 1918, the new Air Ministry came into being with a brief to prepare for the formation of the Royal Air Force on 1 April. On the same day it was announced that Trenchard had been knighted in the New Year's Honours List for 'services in the field'. He could not but be pleased by the messages of congratulation that poured in, but he typically refused to take any credit, asserting that the honour belonged to the Royal Flying Corps and was 'entirely due to the exertions of the officers under me'.

The Air Ministry was based in the grand 800-room Hotel Cecil, the largest hotel in Europe when it opened in 1896, which had been requisitioned for the war effort after the Victoria and Albert Museum and County Hall had both been considered as premises for the new Ministry and rejected. The Cecil would soon get an entirely justified reputation as a bastion of intrigue[9] and Trenchard would come to loathe the place. He had always said he was 'better in the field than in an office' and the Hotel Cecil would certainly prove that to be no less than the truth.

Almost as soon as he took up his new post he ran into difficulties with his minister. To say there was no love lost between them rather understated their strained relationship.

Lord Rothermere at once told me that he considered my job was to enhance the Air Force at all costs, regardless of how it affected the war, or the Navy or Army. I remember one of the first things he said to me was 'You will go to the meeting of the Chiefs of Staff and claim every man that is available for the RAF'. I replied that that was not my job. My job was to listen to the arguments and to see where the manpower could be most usefully employed for winning the war, and if the Navy and Army arguments were, in my opinion, sound I should have been unsound had I demanded more men for the Air Force, unless I could get more effect from using them than

they could. He said 'No, no, no, your job is to get them all' and I
said it wasn't.[10]

Immediately after this they had a vitriolic argument about whom to
appoint as director of training. Trenchard told Rothermere his choice
was 'perfectly unsuited for the job in every way'. Then, at a formal
luncheon for the French president, Trenchard got into a 'very heated
conversation' with Northcliffe about Northcliffe's plan to award '*Daily
Mail* medals' to young pilots, an idea Trenchard thought was absurd.

Accustomed to getting his own way in France, where Haig had
more or less given him a free hand to control virtually all aspects of
air policy, he found working with Rothermere an intensely frustrating
experience, mostly because Rothermere was unwilling to sit back and
let his CAS run the show. Trenchard's constant complaint was that
he was being kept in the dark, that the Secretary of State was going
behind his back, initiating plans he knew nothing about and seeking
advice from just about anyone other than his Chief of Air Staff.

> The fact remains that the S of S does not trust me and I do not
> trust him [Trenchard noted in his diary]. The broad principle is
> that when the right CAS has been chosen he should be given the
> power, without interference from irresponsible people, to carry out,
> as far as material and manpower permit, his policy of how to defeat
> the enemy in the air in conjunction with the army and navy. The
> continual meddling by irresponsible persons who have no expert
> knowledge and are not responsible for the air must be stopped or
> we shall lose the war in the air.[11]

On a visit to Haig in France he could apparently talk of 'nothing else
but the rascally ways of politicians and newspapermen', as Haig noted
in his diary on 26 January:

> General Trenchard . . . came to report how things are developing at
> home. Lord Rothermere . . . is quite ignorant of the needs or work-
> ing of the Air Service and is in great terror of newspaper criticism.
> Money is being squandered and officers and men wasted by being
> employed in creating units for performing work hitherto done by
> the Army (or Navy) for the Air Service . . . All this is very sad at a

time when officers and men are so badly needed. Trenchard thinks that the Air Service cannot last as an independent Ministry and the Air units again must return to the Army and Navy. He (T) could think and talk of nothing else but the rascally ways of politicians and newspapermen.[12]

Trenchard's disaffection was clear in a private letter he wrote to Salmond, his successor in France, on 13 February, only a few weeks after taking up the post:

I am very uneasy about the friction which will be caused between the navy and the army as we get down to the Air Service. I hope it will be all over in six months, but I am doubtful. I fear the navy will think they have joined the RFC and every department put together under two heads, either a naval man under an army man or vice versa, will cause trouble at first . . .

I come up against snags ever day in making this Air Service and the more I think of it the more I think what a ghastly mistake has been made in trying to make an Air Service during this war. It is almost an impossibility to run, and I am spending most of my time trying to bustle up the cause of delays, machines, and the development of new types . . . I miss very much the small self-contained staff in France . . .

I am still on the brink of stopping, but if I stop, I do not know if I shall be doing right to the Flying Corps . . . I am certain that I could get this show running perfectly if only I became more of a dictator at home, but of course this is impossible.[13]

Trenchard claimed he had a disagreement with Rothermere almost every day.

I remember he got rather annoyed over my views of the war. I tried to point out to him that whatever the future of the Air was, which I believed in, the fact remained that the whole British Army was practically engaged in a desperate struggle all along the Western Front, and it was no good his saying that he took no interest in it, because we could not afford to lose the war in the west, and we should do if the Air did not help the Army.

I then remember pointing out to him that never again would it be necessary to have these enormous armies locked in a death grip along a line of trenches if the Air were used properly, but we had not arrived at the proper use of Air Power then, or anywhere near it, and the Air was only trying to find its feet and find out what it could do. We had many such discussions and disagreements.

He was furious when he discovered that Rothermere had submitted a paper to the war cabinet about which aircraft to use on anti-submarine operations without informing him and that the subject had been discussed at a meeting between the Admiralty, the Munitions Department and the Air Ministry to which he had not been invited. The first he knew of the meeting was when a report was copied to him several days later by the secretary of the war cabinet. This despite the fact that he had been in almost daily discussions with the Admiralty for nearly two months on the same matter.

Another cause of friction was Rothermere making an issue of allowing Trenchard the freedom to appoint his own deputy and then disapproving of his choice, claiming another candidate was much more suitable for the post and contending that Trenchard did not have 'a very clear conception of what the duties of a Deputy Chief of Air Staff are'.

At times it seemed Rothermere was intent on almost schoolboy point-scoring. When his office received a letter from a Londoner who claimed he had heard a Gotha bomber over his house a few nights earlier, it was passed to Trenchard's office but dismissed, in a reply by a Colonel Davidson, with the blithe assertion that it was no easier to identify an aircraft by its smell than it was by its engine noise. Rothermere caused inquiries to be made, discreetly, among various aviation authorities and young airmen and ascertained that actually it was quite easy to identify an aircraft from its engine noise. When an opportunity arose he then asked Trenchard if he agreed with Colonel Davidson's opinion and Trenchard, predictably loyal, probably felt he had no choice but to support his colleague. Rothermere was delighted to play his trump card, proving his CAS was completely wrong about a simple aviation matter.

In his defence, Rothermere at this time was not a well man. On 12 February he had been informed that his eldest son, Vyvyan, a captain in the Irish Guards, had died in hospital from wounds he had sustained at Cambrai. (Vyvyan was the second of his children to die in the war: Vere, a lieutenant in the Royal Naval Volunteer Reserve, had been killed in Gallipoli in November 1916.) Rothermere was said to be utterly shattered by Vyvyan's death, so much so his family feared he was on the verge of a complete nervous breakdown.[14] Rothermere warned Trenchard on or around 1 March that his poor health might force him to relinquish his appointment, but added that under no circumstances would he leave before 1 April, when the Royal Flying Corps and the Royal Naval Air Service were due to amalgamate and become the Royal Air Force.

By then matters were coming to a head. Trenchard was astonished to be asked by the First Sea Lord, Sir Eric Geddes, why he was refusing to release the 4000 aircraft he [Geddes] had been promised by the Air Minister for anti-submarine patrolling. It was the first Trenchard had heard of it – he warned Geddes that there were not 400 spare aircraft available in the entire country, let alone 4000. He stormed into Rothermere's office spoiling for a showdown. 'You are leading Geddes up the garden,' he roared. 'You have promised him all these machines which you cannot possibly deliver.'[15] Rothermere blustered and claimed he had 'no recollection' of mentioning 4000 machines. It transpired that he had noticed from the returns put on his desk that there were 3800 aero engines in reserve and 4000 airframes without engines – putting the two together would create nearly 4000 serviceable machines. It was left to Trenchard to explain that few of the engines were suitable for the available airframes, most of which were, in any event, obsolete.

A few days later Trenchard, close to the point of throwing in the towel, decided to seek advice from 'Wully' Robertson, who had recently been forced to resign as CIGS after falling out with Lloyd George. It was a strange choice: they were certainly not close and Robertson had a reputation for being just as curmudgeonly as Trenchard. It may be that Trenchard thought Robertson could be more open now he was no longer in office. He also, he readily admitted, had no one else to turn to. 'You have-got to remember I had no intimate friends except Maurice Baring,' he noted rather sadly. 'I had many acquaintances, but had never even got to a nickname with them.'[16]

Robertson still occupied a grace and favour apartment in York

House, a wing of St James's Palace, a short walk from Trenchard's own rented flat in Park Place. It was late in the afternoon when Trenchard arrived. Robertson received him cordially, gave him a whisky and soda and listened patiently to his litany of complaints. When he had finished, Robertson said he wanted to sleep on what he had heard and asked Trenchard to return in the morning. Early next morning, Trenchard rang the bell again on Robertson's door. Robertson opened it, wearing slippers and a dressing gown over his pyjamas. He fixed Trenchard with a glare, grunted 'Trenchard, do what your conscience tells you' and shut the door in his face.

'As I walked away,' Trenchard recalled, 'I felt he meant do not hand your responsibilities on to me. Assume them yourself and decide yourself . . . and stand the praise or blame that will come of it.'[17]

Copies of the extraordinarily rancorous exchange of letters and memorandums between Trenchard and Rothermere which followed over the next few days are now lodged in the National Archives[18] stamped 'For the personal information of the Minister only'. They clearly indicate that the relationship between the two men, never good, had completely broken down by the middle of March. Both were opinionated and plain-spoken and neither could be bothered to disguise the naked antipathy each felt for the other.

On 18 March Trenchard wrote a long letter to Rothermere about what he described as the 'increasingly serious' situation. Citing various examples where the minister was seeking advice without any reference to him, he pointed out that as Chief of Air Staff he was responsible for advising the minister and was able and willing to obtain for him all the information he required.

'I am far from denying that you have a perfect right to see whom you like,' he concluded, 'but at the same time if you have not sufficient confidence in me even to tell me what is happening in the branches of my own department I consider, and I feel sure that you will agree with me, that the situation created is an impossible one.'

Rothermere's first reaction was to ignore the letter but on further consideration he decided a reply was required. He did not mince his words. 'Replying to your letter of yesterday's date,' he began, 'I hope you will pardon me if I describe it as unnecessary. There has never been any question here as to what your position is. You are Chief of Air Staff and are my principal, not necessarily sole, adviser in all

matters pertaining to the employment of personnel and material . . .'
But he then went on to explain why he could never regard the advice
of any member of the Air Council as 'polemical', citing the ludicrous
disagreement about whether or not a Gotha bomber could be identified by its engine noise. 'You and Colonel Davidson may be right, but
what I wish to make clear is that in view of a grave conflict of opinion
on such a matter as this, it is impossible in the early days of a new
Service, for a Secretary of State to accept the advice of any professional
adviser without demur.'

He utterly rejected Trenchard's complaints about seeking advice
from other quarters.

> In regard to the various matters mentioned in your letter, I must
> tell you that it is always open to the Political Heads of any Depart-
> ment to confer at any time they like with whomsoever they please
> without consultation with their Chiefs of Staff or anyone else . . .
> I am writing you this memorandum so that there may be no mis-
> understanding in the future. I had at first intended not to reply to
> your letter, but on further consideration I can see it is necessary I
> should do so.

Within hours of receiving Rothermere's memorandum, Trenchard
was dictating an embittered letter of resignation:

> I have been Chief of the Air Staff for nearly three months now, and
> during that time I have felt it is almost impossible to carry on many
> times, and as you know I have seen you on various matters which
> have been serious at the time.
>
> I fully realise the difficulties of making this Department of State,
> and I have done my best to help put it on a sound footing, but all
> through I have felt and do feel that you would rather take outside
> opinion than my own.
>
> Under these circumstances it is plainly my duty to ask to be
> relieved of my appointment as Chief of the Air Staff as early as
> possible . . .

Rothermere declared himself to be 'dumbfounded' by Trenchard's letter. 'I knew perfectly well,' he wrote later, 'that the mere rumour of his

resignation twelve days before . . . [the formation of the RAF] might have a most disastrous consequence.' He asked to see Trenchard in his private suite at the Ritz Hotel the following day and revealed that he himself intended to resign shortly and asked if it would make any difference to Trenchard's decision. Trenchard agreed it would, but that it would be for Rothermere's successor to decide whether to accept his resignation or not. Rothermere, who was clearly infuriated, told Trenchard that under no circumstances would he continue to work in the same office with him and that if his health allowed him to stay on it would be a matter for the Cabinet to choose who should stay and who should go. He then asked Trenchard if he would at least delay his departure until after the RAF had come into being, as to leave at that moment would cause great embarrassment not just to him, but to the government. Trenchard reluctantly agreed.

Another abrasive newspaper baron, Lord Beaverbrook, recently appointed as the government's first Minister of Information, was also unashamedly ill-disposed towards the Chief of the Air Staff, whom he described as a man with 'common sense but limited ability' who 'enjoyed bitter hatreds'. Beaverbrook claimed that from the start Trenchard was a disaffected and hypercritical member of the newly formed Air Council who exercised a strong influence, demanded authority to be consolidated into his own hands and 'within weeks' communicated his disloyal complaints to Salmond in France.

In London at that time it was known that a major German offensive in France was imminent. Faced with escalating demands for peace from a civilian population exhausted by war, the German High Command resolved to make a last-ditch attempt to break the stalemate on the Western Front before the overwhelming resources and *matériel* of the United States joined the battle.

Shortly before dawn on Thursday, 21 March, thousands of German stormtroopers emerged through the early morning mist and swept over the Allied lines on a 40-mile front stretching from the Somme to Cambrai. The German plan was to smash through the British and French positions, seize the Channel ports, drive the British Army into the sea and force the French, with Paris under threat, to seek an armistice. By the end of the first day, the Germans had broken through at several points and the British had lost nearly 20,000 dead. Within a few days the spearhead units had overrun the British

Fifth Army and driven an enormous wedge deep into the British positions.

Trenchard claimed that Rothermere panicked – or at least 'got into a great state of agitation' – when it seemed the German offensive might succeed, and talked about bringing as many aircraft as possible back from France for the defence of England. 'As far as I could gather,' Trenchard recalled later, 'he intended leaving the Army to its fate, but he was so excited it was hard to listen to him.'[19]

Trenchard witheringly suggested that his Secretary of State should go to the country for ten days and leave him to carry on and deal with the crisis. Trenchard's strategy was precisely the reverse of that of his boss – he ordered all available pilots and aircraft to be rushed to France. The Royal Flying Corps, soon to be reorganised as the RAF, would play an important role in stemming the enemy advance with ferocious air battles taking place over the front, fighter aircraft strafing the German troops at low level and bombing attacks on aerodromes and railways behind the front. Casualties were heavy and even eclipsed those of 'Bloody April' the previous year.

> The struggle is not over yet by any means [he wrote to Salmond in France on 25 March], and therefore I would earnestly ask you to watch as much as ever you possibly can the question of keeping your squadrons up to strength. If for any reason we cannot keep them up it is essential, in order to keep up morale, that you boldly pull a squadron bang out of it altogether so as to save being under-strength in several. I hope this will not become necessary and I hope we shall be able to keep you going, but the full breakfast table is one of the roots of confidence of the Royal Flying Corps . . .[20]

On 1 April 1918, the Royal Air Force – the first independent air service in the world not subordinate to its national army or navy – came into being with little ceremony and not much celebration among the ranks. Trenchard thought it uniquely appropriate that what he called 'the child of Smuts' should be born on All Fools Day. Many officers and men of the former RFC resented being forcibly amalgamated with 'those bell-bottomed buggers' in the Royal Naval Air Service and ridiculed their new blue uniforms as being 'the final prostitution of the RFC to the amorous advances of the sailor'.[21] To John

Slessor, a future marshal of the RAF but then a pilot in France, the uniform was 'a nasty pale blue with a lot of gold over it, which brought irresistibly to mind a vision of the gentleman who stands outside a cinema'. Some pilots claimed the RAF uniform featured a black tie because Trenchard was no longer in command. King George V was more sanguine and sent a telegram to Rothermere congratulating him and expressing the hope the union 'will preserve and foster that *esprit de corps* which the two separate Forces have created by their splendid deeds'.[22]

On 5 April Trenchard paid a lightning visit to the front, toured no less than 20 aerodromes in a single day and was very encouraged by the high morale of the pilots. '"We are giving them hell in the air" they kept saying – and so they were. . . . They said they were quite certain they would fight it out and win.'[23] On his return to London he was invited to Downing Street to brief Lloyd George and the Cabinet.

'Most of the Ministers were very uneasy,' he recalled. 'Only the prime minister, unpredictable as ever, looked and talked like a man who had not lost heart. He met me in the passage, though I knew he disliked me,[24] and said "Well, General, though we shall not win the war this year, we shall win it next instead." He showed courage at that moment far outweighing that of all the rest of them.'

While the battle was still raging in France, Rothermere furiously complained that his CAS was playing his cards so close to his chest that he (Rothermere) had little idea of what was happening. 'General Trenchard refused to supply the Air Council with any statement as to what he was doing to meet the present emergency. He did not think they [sic] should be the recipients of any information. The little information I received was doled out in small morsels, and I was really unaware of what was going on.'

Meanwhile, in an effort to find some kind of rapprochement, Lloyd George had deputed Smuts to examine the rights and wrongs of the dispute between the Secretary of State for Air and the Chief of the Air Staff. Smuts, eminently fair-minded, advised the prime minister that the simplest solution would be to let Trenchard go. Lloyd George agreed.

On the afternoon of 10 April Rothermere sent for Trenchard and formally told him his resignation had been accepted by the war cabinet. (Trenchard was convinced then, and remained so convinced for the rest of his life, that Rothermere had engineered his departure to make it appear that he had stepped down at the height of the battle in France.) At the suggestion of Smuts, Rothermere offered Trenchard the command of the Royal Air Force in France, but he indignantly turned it down, asserting that his friend Salmond was doing a very good job and that it would be quite wrong to ask him to step aside, especially in the middle of a battle.

The following morning Sir Frederick Sykes, the last person in the world Trenchard would have wanted to see, knocked on his office door, announced that he had been sent by Rothermere and that he was to take over as CAS immediately. Trenchard stiffly asked him if there was anything he wanted to know about the job; Sykes shook his head. Trenchard cleared his desk and left the building without another word.

On Saturday, 13 April, Rothermere sent Trenchard a singularly petulant letter formally accepting his resignation:

> Dear General Trenchard,
>
> I now accept your resignation tendered to me on 19th March.
> I cannot say I do so with any particular reluctance. Every man is the best judge of what he does but I believe your act in resigning your post as Chief of the Air Staff twelve days before myself and the large staff here were going into action to accomplish the gigantic task of the fusion of the Royal Naval Air Service and the Royal Flying Corps is an unparalleled incident in the public life of this country.
> Two days ago you reproached me for not accepting your resignation when proffered and suggested I had temporised. It is true. I could do nothing else. I was filled with profound anxiety lest your resignation might become public and rumour with its thousand tongues might allege you had resigned in protest against some policy of mine which would be disastrous to the interests of the 25,000 officers and 140,000 men who were just going to become the Royal Air Force.
> Under such circumstances your resignation might have jeopardised the whole scheme of amalgamation on which I and

many others had been working night and day for some months.
I can only attribute it to instability of purpose, which I have
observed in you on several occasions recently and which, in my
opinion, is due to the overstrain and work of the last three years.

For anything you have done since I have been here [unwritten
implication – little or nothing] I wish most cordially to thank you.

Yours very faithfully . . .

Rothermere's letter prompted Trenchard to submit a memorandum to
the war cabinet explaining the precise circumstances of his resignation and enclosing correspondence with the Secretary of State which
proved, he claimed, that he had been unable to carry out his work
unfettered or without outside interference and that Rothermere had
'encouraged the intervention of various people without responsibility in decisions concerning operations'. Refuting the calumny that he
had stepped down at the height of the battle, he pointed out that he
had submitted his resignation two days before the spring offensive was
launched and concluded: 'I had no wish to take any action during the
battle and I deeply regret that the Secretary of State has considered it
necessary to do so.'

Rothermere, offered the chance to reply by the secretary of the war
cabinet, dispatched a note denouncing his CAS with such vitupera-
tion that it must rank as one of the rudest documents in the National
Archives. It began 'Is it worth while replying to General Trenchard's
memorandum?' He clearly thought it was. 'As Chief of Air Staff he
was perfectly impossible. He is entirely without imagination, and
although he had been in this office for three months he had prepared
no strategic plans of any kind whatsoever. If there was ever a case of
a square peg in a round hole, it is to be found in the appointment of
General Trenchard as Chief of the Air Staff . . .'

Conveniently forgetting the meeting at the Ritz during which he
had virtually twisted Trenchard's arm to make him take the job, he
claimed that Trenchard was not his choice; he had been persuaded to
offer him the post by William Weir (then president of the Air Council). Trenchard had only accepted 'on terms', first demanding the right
to appoint all the military members of the Air Council – which Rothermere had refused – and then insisting he remained C-in-C of the

RFC in France, an arrangement the CIGS had quickly terminated. In his [Rothermere's] opinion, 'no language is too harsh to stigmatise the conduct of General Trenchard' in resigning when he did. He assumed he was 'indispensable' and nothing would satisfy him. 'As a commanding officer he has doubtless exhibited great qualities,' Rothermere conceded. 'As a Chief of the Air Staff he has not the outlook, the ability to study scientifically theoretical problems, the readiness to advance young officers of merit, or the willingness to associate others with his work, which in my opinion are indispensable in a man filling this post.'

Lieutenant General Sir David Henderson, recently appointed vice-chairman of the Air Council, soon followed Trenchard out of the door, declaring he could not work with the unfortunate Sykes, whom he still suspected of plotting against him earlier in the war. In a private letter to Bonar Law, the Leader of the House of Commons, he said he was anxious to escape from the 'atmosphere of intrigue and falsehood which has enveloped the Air Ministry for the last few months' and feared he would become 'a focus of discontent and opposition'.[25]

Reporting the resignations, the *Daily News* tartly observed that 'the list is steadily growing of acknowledged masters of their craft for whose services in the crisis of our fate the Government has no serious use'. Even the King expressed concern about what was happening at the Air Ministry. 'His Majesty's one desire,' Lord Stamfordham, the King's private secretary, wrote in a note to Lloyd George, 'is that the new Air Force should be as perfect as can be and he regrets that it should lose any of those Officers who have, since the beginning of the war, helped to build up the Royal Flying Corps and the Royal Naval Air Service respectively.'[26]

Most newspapers, with the notable exception of those owned by Rothermere and his brother, were agreed that Trenchard was a great leader, that his departure was a disaster for morale and had been greeted with dismay at the front in France. Most also reported that he had stepped down because of differences of opinion with the Secretary of State, but the strong feeling was that he had been unfairly driven from office. Only the *Manchester Guardian*, while conceding his downfall was a matter of 'lively regret', suggested that it might have had something to do with his 'autocratic bearing'.

Meanwhile Rothermere, having been relieved of the irritating thorn in his side, was said to be reconsidering his own resignation and staying on as Secretary of State, but his position soon became untenable, with too many questions being asked about why both Trenchard and Henderson had felt the need to walk out of their jobs. The final nail in his coffin was a paper he circulated on the future of the RAF which, according to one of his advisers, Major Baird, was both wildly optimistic and grossly inaccurate.

At the prime minister's personal request, Rothermere agreed to submit a revised letter of resignation omitting his initial reference to Trenchard's 'insubordination' as being a contributory factor. Instead he praised Sykes, the new Chief of the Air Staff, as being 'a brilliant officer with his singularly luminous mind, great knowledge of staff work and grasp of service organisation . . . [with] sovereign gifts, particularly necessary now, of elasticity of outlook and receptivity of mind . . .'[27] In other words, all the qualities that Rothermere felt his predecessor so singularly lacked.

News, on 25 April, that Lord Rothermere had stepped down from the government 'on the grounds of ill health and private sorrow'[28] was greeted with delight in many quarters. On the afternoon of the announcement a number of young officers were said to be seen hanging out of the windows of the Hotel Cecil cheering and waving. When a passer-by asked if there had been a victory in France, one of them shouted a reply: 'No, a victory at home. Lord Rothermere has gone.' The following morning both the *Daily News* and the *Morning Post* called for Trenchard to be reinstated as Chief of the Air Staff.

Rothermere remained utterly unrepentant on the subject of his former CAS. 'In getting rid of the late CAS,' he wrote to Sykes, 'I flatter myself I did a great public service. The mere thought of the Air Service being in the hands of someone without precision, elasticity of outlook and receptivity of mind caused me grave anxiety. Starting on such a basis there was no hope of the great Air Force being what I am now assured it will be in your hands . . .'[29]

He wrote in similar vein to Bonar Law: 'In getting rid of Trenchard I flatter myself I did a great thing for the Air Force. With his dull, unimaginative mind and his attitude of "*Je sais tout*" he would within twelve months have brought death and damnation to the Air Force. . .'[30]

On Monday 29 April the changes at the Air Ministry were the

subject of a four-hour debate in the House of Commons, during which most speakers took the opportunity to lavish praise on Trenchard and lament his departure. Sir John Simon and Lord Hugh Cecil, both former junior officers on Trenchard's staff and now MPs, insisted that Trenchard had been forced out and that his loss was having a grave effect on morale in France.

It is no exaggeration to say [Sir John asserted], that the news of the recent loss of General Trenchard struck these young men [the pilots at the front] as nothing less than a deadly blow. They wholly failed to understand it . . . Surely it was a terrible disaster that in the middle of this great battle, when so much is happening, such a distinguished soldier felt it his duty to offer his resignation, and that we should have lost the services of a man who had been, whatever else we say about him, the idol and inspiration of this great service?

Other members fervently agreed, speaking of 'complete consternation throughout all ranks', of 'disgust' in the whole air service in France, of 'unrest in the public mind' and the 'disastrous effect'. Mr William Joynson-Hicks, a future Home Secretary, talked about 'the magic personality of General Trenchard' and read out a letter he had received from a young pilot in France: 'The one man we need, the one man who has been produced by the war, and the man we really need now, is General Trenchard, because he is honest and strong and a hustler. You have no notion what the effect is upon the Corps both in France and in England.'

I know this much [declared Sir Edward Carson], I know that a great, fierce, courageous, patriotic soldier like Sir Hugh Trenchard would never have chucked his job when the great battle approached unless he felt himself driven to it. I do not think in all my long experience in the House I have ever known a case which has created such universal anxiety in a Service as the retirement of Sir Hugh Trenchard has in the Air Service.

He had spoken to many officers, he continued, and they had all told him the same thing – that the 'soul' had gone out of the service.

Lord Hugh Cecil, the member for Oxford University, compared

Trenchard with Britain's greatest military heroes. 'Supposing we were to read of another war, that the government had lost Wellington or Nelson, how angry we should be, how we should say that this improvidence of ability was the worst improvidence of all. I put it to the government that they have lost a great national asset.' When Cecil kept referring to Trenchard's dismissal, the prime minister got to his feet to protest. General Trenchard had not been dismissed, he said, he had resigned for reasons which he did not wish to go into. The Cabinet, he continued, had to decide whether it was wise to accept his resignation and asked General Smuts to look into the matter. When General Smuts came to the conclusion that General Trenchard's special qualities were not used to the best advantage in his position as Chief of Air Staff, it was decided to accept his resignation. But Lloyd George made it clear that it was the government's firm intention to retain General Trenchard's services for the Royal Air Force in some capacity, a statement that was met with ringing cheers from both sides of the House.

A number of members called for Trenchard to be reinstated and pressed the prime minister to explain exactly what post was to be offered to the former CAS, but Lloyd George would not be drawn and only referred to a statement issued by Sir William Weir, who had been appointed Rothermere's replacement as Air Minister:

He is not prepared to allow the Air Force to lose the great qualities and unique experience of General Trenchard, and proposes to offer him a position in which these qualities and experience will find an outlet of the greatest value to the force. He asks that the House will not press for a definition of the position at the present time, and asks me to say that it is not a position created for General Trenchard, but one directly associated with his own aerial policy.

14

BOOM AND BOMBERS

While the furore over the resignations at the Air Ministry was continuing, Trenchard was said to be spending much of his time, in mufti, sitting morosely on a bench in the spring sunshine in Green Park, not far from his rented bachelor apartment in Park Place. With nothing to do, probably for the first time in his life, he had plenty of time to brood about what had happened and consider his options, none of which held much attraction.

His first reaction on leaving the Air Ministry had been to apply to rejoin his regiment, even though he knew it would mean being reduced in rank from Major General to Lieutenant Colonel. The War Office refused his application and instead offered him the command of a division in France, which he turned down on the sensible basis that he did not know enough about the situation on the ground to be able to command a division competently. He was then offered a brigade, which he felt would be more manageable and accepted, but the appointment got somehow buried in Whitehall red tape and never materialised.

The problem of what to do with Trenchard was first passed to Alfred, Lord Milner, a former colonial adminstrator who had recently replaced Lord Derby as Secretary of State for War. It is probable that Milner had more on his mind than the necessity of dealing with what Sir Maurice Hankey, the secretary to the war cabinet, described as 'this tiresome Trenchard business'.[1] The situation in France remained critical; at one point the Germans had pushed the front back to within 75 miles of Paris and on 11 April Haig had issued an Order of the Day which would become famous: 'Victory will belong to the side that holds out longest. There is no other course open to us but to fight it out. Every position must be held to the last man. There must be no retirement. With our backs to the wall and believing in the justice of our cause, each one of us must fight on to the end.'

Unsurprisingly, Milner was in a foul temper, and deeply disinclined to be sympathetic, when he met Trenchard at the War Office to discuss his future. Almost the first thing he said when Trenchard walked in was that if he had had his own way he would have sent Trenchard back to his regiment immediately after he had resigned. Trenchard, taken aback, retorted that that was exactly what he had wanted but his [Milner's] office had refused him permission. Neither man recorded what passed between them thereafter, but Trenchard noted that the meeting ended 'unsatisfactorily'.[2]

Haig stepped in from France to try and rescue his friend, writing to Milner that in view of the increasing importance of aircraft he considered the time had come to attach to his headquarters a major general to act as adviser on all matters relating to the employment of aircraft. 'I understand that Major General Trenchard is now available and would ask that he may be sent out as soon as possible . . .'[3] Milner, disinclined to be accommodating, did not take the bait.

On the weekend before the debate in the House on the resignations at the Air Ministry, Sir William Weir, the new Air Minister, invited Trenchard to a meeting at his flat on the Embankment in Westminster. He had four job offers to put to him – Inspector General of the RAF overseas, Inspector General of the RAF at home, GOC of the RAF in the Middle East, or commander of the Independent Air Force (IAF), an enlarged long-range bombing force that was to be set up in France to attack German cities, which last option Weir hoped he would accept. Trenchard made it clear he was not particularly enamoured of any of them, but agreed to consider all four at the end of what proved, in Weir's words, to be a 'difficult and inconclusive'[4] meeting. Any hopes that an announcement could be made in the House about General Trenchard's new appointment were obviously dashed.

On 1 May Trenchard wrote to Weir rejecting all four offers. The first two he did not consider to be 'real work', the third was unacceptable because he viewed the Middle East as a backwater and he was opposed to the IAF because he objected to diverting any air resources in France from what he considered to be their principal task – supporting the army. In addition he remained suspicious, despite the prime minister's assurance to the House that a job would not be created for him, that

that was exactly what was happening, probably to damp down the continuing bickering about his resignation.

Further meetings followed and further letters were exchanged, with Trenchard finding endless excuses not to accept whatever he was offered, suggesting that he was only being offered a post to put an end to the agitation his resignation had provoked and putting forward proposals for a job in which he would be interested – one was being appointed GOC of the RAF with equal status to Sykes, who would handle administrative matters, while he ran operations in France. No one who knew anything about their history could believe that this arrangement would work. When Trenchard complained about certain conditions, Weir offered to alter them, but still Trenchard was not satisfied.

By 6 May Weir had run out of patience and ruled that the correspondence must cease. He reiterated the various choices available and told Trenchard the time had come for him to make up his mind.

> Now I trust I have made it clear to you that I will not create a position specially for you. The above are positions requiring men, and I want you to accept one of them so that your experience may contribute to the success of the Royal Air Force and not on any ground of quelling what you call 'the agitation'. Any of these positions in my opinion answers your test of 'being of value', and, moreover, fully covers the promise I made to the Prime Minister. If there are any points not clear in the above, I shall be available for half an hour between nine-thirty and ten tonight.[5]

Trenchard chose not to take up Weir's offer to 'clear up any points' that night since he was still completely undecided what to do. Two days later he was sitting on his usual bench in Green Park, reading the morning newspapers, when two naval officers in uniform, presumably on their way to Whitehall, approached his bench deep in conversation. They took no notice of him, sheltering as he was behind a newspaper. One of them was saying in a loud voice that he had no sympathy for any officer who abandoned his post in a crisis, no matter what the circumstances. (In fact by then the crisis in France had more or less passed – Germany's Spring Offensive had stalled through heavy casualties and lack of supplies.) Trenchard suddenly realised that the officer might be talking about him. He was. 'It's an outrage,' he continued. 'I don't know why the Government should pander to a man who threw in his hand at the height of a battle. If I'd had my way, I'd have had Trenchard shot.' The other man nodded in agreement. Trenchard heard no more as they moved out of earshot, but was obviously shocked by what had been said. It was at that moment that he realised he could not continue prevaricating about a new job. 'I remember,' he noted, 'I felt I could no longer sit about doing nothing.'

He picked up his paper, walked briskly back to his flat with a new sense of purpose and immediately wrote a note to Weir accepting command of the Independent Force, despite his reservations about it. Weir, no doubt grateful for an end to the continuing uncertainty surrounding Trenchard's future and knowing his antipathy towards his replacement as CAS, offered to allow Trenchard to report directly to him, bypassing Sykes – a facility of which Trenchard would take full advantage.

The new appointment was, unquestionably, a bitter pill for Trenchard to swallow. He was leaving the top job in the air service and returning to France to command a unit very much smaller than that he was commanding when he left the country a few months earlier. He tried to justify it by claiming it was his chance to 'help bring about the establishment of a sound air policy', but there was no disguising the appointment was a significant step down. The high-sounding title – Independent Force – was, he claimed 'all moonshine'. 'What the Independent Force was, was nothing more than the 8th Brigade which had been under my command long before. What I commanded was a few squadrons which represented a tiny part of my original command. In other words, I was not anybody much.'

Rothermere, still smarting, could not resist gloating in a letter to his brother about what he saw as Trenchard's humiliation.

I never expected my health would allow me to stay at the Hotel Cecil Air Ministry headquarters [he wrote on 20 May], but I determined to stay long enough to knock out that dud Trenchard. He was establishing a Kitchener regime in the Air Force and gave out quite openly to his intimates that he intended to be the autocrat of the new service. I simply waited for him and tripped him up. Instead of being Chief of the Air Staff he is now second string to

Salmond in France. As Chief of the Air Staff he was simply a gargantuan joke. If he is the kind of man Haig surrounds himself with, I am not surprised we have done so badly in France.[6]

Trenchard soon discovered what it was like to be 'not anybody much'. On his way to take over his new command at Nancy, in the French battle zone, towards the end of May, he stopped off at the RAF HQ.

Everybody seemed opposed to the formation of the Independent Force [he noted in his diary], as if I had anything to do with it. They were all rather difficult to deal with on the subject and I think it was due to their being rattled. They all seemed to think I had no idea there was a frightful battle going to be fought any minute. It only shows what I always expected if the Air Force was divided into two – it would do a lot of harm and that spirit will shortly spread from Headquarters to squadrons.[7]

He complained he was in a no-win situation: that the army thought he had abandoned them in favour of bombing Germany, while the 'bombing people' thought he was basically more interested in helping the army and only 'luke-warm' about bombing.

In his first confidential report to Weir he was a little more optimistic. 'Provided that the C.A.S. [the hated Sykes] lets me know what is going on, I am perfectly certain that in time I shall get the thing going as an independent show. If I am not told I shall have an impossible job . . . I have not yet got a headquarters or any staff and am doing all the work myself.'[8] At least he knew he could count on the Secretary of State's wholehearted support. Weir made no secrect of his belief that the long-range bomber was the war-winning weapon of the future, capable of 'seriously worrying' Germany. His ambition was to build the Independent Force into an arm capable of conducting a massive aerial offensive against German cities and destroying key enemy war industries. As it turned out, the 37 squadrons promised to the Force never materialised – at the end of the war Trenchard could still only call on less than a quarter of that number.

Trenchard assumed tactical command on 5 June, taking over from Newall, who became his deputy and whose views about being summarily replaced are not on record. In the eight months he had been in charge, the Independent Force had carried out 142 bombing raids on Germany – the first use of strategic air power and the first time the air war had been waged independently of troops on the ground.

The Force headquarters was set up in the handsome seventeenth-century Château d'Autigny-la-Tour, 40 miles south-west of Nancy. Baring, who had returned to Trenchard's service after a long leave, was charmed. Autigny-la-Tour, he noted, was a

> lovely little village with squat white houses and red roofs nestled on a hill and surrounded by still higher hills in the heart of the Vosges. Our beautiful and dignified old chateau was right in the village, its gates forming part of the village street halfway up the hill. In front was a courtyard down which there were two rows of acacia trees flanked by two medieval towers with pointed roofs. The house was a two-storied building in an L-shape with a terrace connecting the kitchen and flower garden with stone steps. At the far end was a long pond surrounded by trees and full of carp.[9]

Soon after he arrived, Trenchard gathered the pilots together for a pep talk. As always he presented them with the plain, unvarnished truth. He warned them that they would eventually have to be prepared to fly long distances on dark moonless nights on bombing missions into the heart of Germany and that they would have to become accustomed to 'cloud flying', since they could not afford to allow bad weather to hamper operations. He never tried to minimise the risks they would face, never left them in any doubt that he would do whatever was necessary to win the war. He concluded, as he often did, by saying: 'If I thought that by sending every one of you across the line never to return would shorten the war by just one week, I have to tell you it would be my duty to send you.' The pilots, many of whom knew they would not survive the war, were reported to have 'cheered him to an echo'.[10]

The mission of the Independent Force was to undertake 'direct action against the heart of the German industrial system', but Trenchard was privately assailed by doubts about the effectiveness of the force and he began keeping a diary to record his concerns. 'The last two days have made me think more and more what a great mistake it has been to start this bombing force in such a war as this and in such a battle,' he wrote on 10 June. 'It involves a large staff being here and less

efficiency in bombing, resulting in a waste of manpower . . . I shall
run this force efficiently and get it going, but at a great unnecessary
waste of manpower, time and energy.'[11]

In London a review had been drawn up by RAF staff officers and
submitted to the war cabinet suggesting that air power was capable of
winning the war by attacking Germany's 'root industries' and destroying the morale of the people. To politicians (and indeed the public),
any alternative to the ghastly slaughter in the trenches was a preferred
choice. Trenchard did not believe for a minute that air power alone
could win the war, but he had come round to the view that bombing
could make a useful contribution if the Independent Force was supplied with suitable and sufficient aircraft, but it was not happening.
Instead, he was being swamped by personnel.

Early entries in his diary make his frustration clear:

26 June: The bombing of Germany goes on with the number of
squadrons provided, but the total result of separating the force as
far as I can see at present is to employ about 40 officers on the staff,
about 200 men, a large amount of transport, besides building huts
for the Headquarters, etc, in order to take the place of GHQ and
HQ RAF and to carry on the work these organisations were quite
capable of carrying out . . .

1 July: The GHQ Staff continue to roll up in large numbers . . .,
but still there is too much work for the officers at present. The total
result of this increase is nil to the effectiveness of the bombing of
Germany . . . I look round and see all the personnel brought in to
make the Independent Force has not added one to the number of
bombs dropped on Germany under the old system.

13 July: It is curious to think that all the people who are so keen
on bombing Germany are actually reducing the amount of bombing that could be done and largely increasing the personnel required
to do it . . . Once more I must write in my diary that the bombing
of Germany is now a necessity, and that this Force should be increased by all the means in our power, but it is almost impossible
to explain this to anybody who does not understand the rudiments
of war. What beats me is that one moment everybody tells me I am
the only man to do it or knows anything about the Air Service and
the next moment everyone argues in every way against anything I

want, which shows they only believe their own uninformed opinion. I have stood firm for 3½ years now, first against one lot and then against another, and I have guided the development of the Air Service in battle zones and in this bombing, and I have not diverged right or left from my principles, so I shall try to carry this out to the end if they will only allow me to do so . . .

22 July: I am more convinced than ever that the shortage of machines in the Independent Force, which is now very serious, is due to it being completely separated and not under the command of one commander . . .

30 July: . . . Still more staff have arrived, but no more bombs have been dropped on Germany.

His prediction that the Independent Force would lead to divisions within the RAF proved to be absolutely correct. Because it operated outside the RAF command structure, the RAF viewed the Independent Force as a rival for desperately needed supplies.

My personal relations with RAF HQ became very strained [Trenchard admitted]. The only man who would speak to me was Game [Brigadier General Philip Game, chief of staff at RAF HQ]. I even had insulting letters. I found myself writing to Haig for things I wanted and I got peevish letters from RAF HQ saying they were worried by great battles on the Western Front and could not be bothered with my petty requests. I didn't blame them one little bit.[12]

The Force had to be located in the French battle zone because it was only from there that any significant German cities were within the range of Allied bombers. But its isolation from the BEF created more problems, not least because Marshal Foch, recently appointed commander-in-chief of the Allied Armies in France, initially refused to recognise what he described as an 'irregular air force' controlled directly from London. The matter was referred to a sub-committee of the Supreme War Council in Versailles, where General Marie Charles Duval, commander of the French air service, scoffed at the very existence of the Force. 'Independent of what?' he asked, 'Of God?' He dismissed the concept, saying that what was needed was 'unification, not dissipation'.

The French made it clear they were opposed to strategic bombing, believing that all air resources should be used in support of the army, a policy which, ironically, Trenchard had supported since the start of the war. Meanwhile Trenchard was entirely reliant on French co-operation for supplies and communication, for land to build airfields, for the installation of electric power lines to light runways and storage facilities for fuel. It required all Baring's tact and skill as a diplomat, and his fluent command of the French language, to persuade local French army commanders to help, albeit reluctantly.

'If it had not been for my friendship with General Castelnau[13] and for Maurice Baring's personal relations with France, my position would have become impossible,' Trenchard recalled. 'The French put every difficulty in my way. They would not give me land for aerodromes nor allot me roads for my supplies . . . I was in lonely isolation.'[14]

The Air Ministry in London had drawn up a lengthy list of targets within range of the Independent Force bombers about 120 miles behind the front, along a line through Cologne–Frankfurt–Stuttgart, assigning each a priority, and sent regular orders to the Château d'Autigny-la-Tour indicating which targets were to be attacked. Trenchard more or less ignored them and sent his pilots out to bomb targets he selected – aerodromes, railway junctions, ammunition dumps and the like – that would best support army operations at the front. 'Before we could bomb industrial areas in Germany,' he explained after the war, 'we had to travel over hundreds of miles of front which was peopled by enemy air squadrons. Intensive air fighting was going on in this area all the time. It was impossible for me to contemplate long-range bombing unless and until I had some measure of superiority of control over this area.'[15] Of the 416 bombing missions carried out between 6 June and 30 September only 68 were directed against industrial targets compared to 185 against railways and 139 against aerodromes.[16]

In a memorandum to Weir Trenchard justified his decision to target the railways.

I had to decide, when it was impossible to reach their objectives well into the interior of Germany, what alternative objective should be attacked and which attacks would have the greatest effect in hastening the end of hostilities. I decided that railways were first in order of importance . . . The reason for my decision was that the Germans were extremely short of rolling stock and also some of the main railways feeding the German army in the west passed close to our front and it was hoped that these communications could be seriously interfered with, and the rolling stock and trains carrying reinforcements or reliefs or munitions destroyed.[17]

Trenchard often viewed instructions he was receiving from London as absurd, like when he received a telegram ordering him to suspend operations on the festival of Corpus Christi, which fell in June that year. 'This seems to me a very dangerous practice to start,' he noted in his diary. 'If bombing is stopped for one religious festival, why should it not be stopped for another? Why should it not be stopped on Good Friday and Christmas Day? It also brings up the question of bombing on a Sunday. If the Germans agreed to stop bombing on this day [Corpus Christi], have they agreed to stop the battle?'[18]

He also protested strongly when he learned about a humanitarian initiative by King Alfonso XIII of Spain to try and persuade both sides in the war to stop bombing undefended towns and cities. Spain was neutral in the war, but King Alfonso was married to a granddaughter of Queen Victoria and was thus concerned about events in Britain and dispatched his ambassador in London to test the government's reaction to a proposition that the Germans would abandon bombing civilian targets if the Allies would do the same. The King's initiative was not welcomed. The ambassador was coldly informed that the British government had always objected to the bombardment of undefended towns, but could never give up the right to attack genuine military targets.

'If it is intended to put an end to the bombing of our towns by the enemy at the expense of allowing the enemy's towns to be immune,' Trenchard wrote to Weir, 'I can only add that we shall be deliberately depriving ourselves of our most important means of winning the war.'[19]

In reality the war at that time was actually being won on the ground rather than in the air. By July the Spring Offensive had petered out, leaving the German army severely depleted, exhausted and in exposed positions. The territorial gains were in the form of salients which greatly increased the length of the line that would have to be defended when the Allies counter-attacked. The strength of the German army had fallen from 5.1 million fighting men to 4.2 million and the superiority in numbers that it had enjoyed on the Western Front would soon be reversed as more American troops arrived. Even worse, they had lost many of their best trained men – the stormtroopers who had led the offensive and paid the price. Trenchard was at Foch's headquarters when news arrived that a French counter-attack had broken up the German advance. 'Foch turned to me,' Trenchard recalled, 'and said, with one of those phrases of which he was rather fond, "You see, when the fruit is ripe it drops into your hands."'[20]

Not long afterwards Trenchard was in an unusually expansive mood when he hosted a luncheon party at the Château d'Autigny-la-Tour for senior French officers. Conversation turned to the subject of illnesses and Trenchard, who was not unfamiliar with sickness, boomed about how he had recently not given in to measles and how he could not stand sick people and that they should just get on with it. From down the table Baring piped up, in his squeaky cultured tones, 'I agree, General, with what you say, but would myself have put it rather differently.'

'Oh yes,' Trenchard inquired, 'what would you have said, Baring?'

'I would have said,' Baring responded with a sly smile, '"I have had every illness under the sun without it affecting me, except housemaid's knee."'[21]

Trenchard joined in the general laughter.

Officers dealing with Trenchard on a daily basis never knew how they would find him – he could be generous and warm-hearted, but he could also be touchy and bad-tempered. A story went round about how, one morning over breakfast in the mess during a visit to a bomber station, the lid of a coffee pot had slipped and dropped onto his lap.

Trenchard got up without a word, strode to a window and hurled both coffee pot and lid out into the garden in a fury. Only Baring did not watch, but continued munching his toast without even turning his head.

In early August four more squadrons arrived equipped with the latest bombers – three with Handley Pages and one with de Havilland 10s – but Trenchard was still plagued by supply problems and large numbers of the promised new squadrons had failed to materialise.

On 18 August, in a lengthy entry in his diary, Trenchard let rip at the 'muddle and mess' at the Air Ministry:

> None of the day bombing squadrons are working at present owing to the shortage of pilots and machines, but if we had only two squadrons probably both of them would have been working. This is what I cannot get civilians to understand: it is better to have fewer units kept up to strength than to have a large number of units under strength. The more I see of this Independent Force and the little that has been done during the summer months and the great difficulty the Air Ministry have in keeping it up show one [the lack] of imagination of the powers at the Air Ministry. I fear the muddle and mess at the Cecil caused by people with no war experience affect very adversely the work out here.
>
> I wonder when the war is over what truth we shall get out of the enemy with regard to the actual damage done by this bombing. I am certain the damage done to both buildings and personnel is very small compared to any other form of war and the energy expended. The moral [sic] effect is great – very great – but it gets less as the little material effect is seen. The chief moral [sic] effect is apparently to give the [British] newspapers copy to say how wonderful we are, though it does not really affect the enemy as much as it affects our own people.[22]

Trenchard was right in assuming that the inexpert bombing techniques available at that time actually caused very little real damage, but wrong in his assessment about the effect on civilian morale. Although some reports spoke of a serious effect on the morale of a civilian population already dispirited and war-weary, as in the Blitz during the Second World War indiscriminate bombing of civilians tended to stiffen their resolve to resist at the same time as stoking their hatred of the enemy. What bombing did achieve was to drain the enemy's resources, imposing a need to maintain a large defence force – anti-aircraft guns, searchlights and aircraft – to protect threatened areas. At the end of the war 330 German front-line fighters were deployed to oppose the Independent Force, which never exceeded a strength of more than 130 aircraft.

On 27 August Trenchard and Baring lunched with General de

Castelnau at his headquarters and Trenchard described to the French commander a raid on a Mannheim chemical factory which had taken place a few nights previously. Two machines went down so low, below the height of the factory chimneys, that searchlights were sweeping the ground and anti-aircraft batteries fired horizontally across the works. Seven of the ten aircraft involved were lost, two on the way when the formation was attacked by 40 enemy aircraft and five on the return through rain, thick clouds and thunderstorms. 'The enemy's tactics on this occasion appear to have been to concentrate their attacks on the rear machines,' Trenchard said. 'Many of the enemy's machines were undoubtedly damaged, and some were probably destroyed, but the fighting was so close that neither pilots nor observers had time to observe results.'[23]

In August the Independent Force dropped more than 100 tons of bombs on Germany, up from a mere 70 in June, but lost 21 machines. But the bombing missions often involved return journeys of 300-plus miles. After a raid on Frankfurt, nine de Havillands had to fight all the way home and, after five and a half hours in the air, three were obliged to glide back across the lines and land wherever they could behind the Allied trenches. Every one was badly shot up, but they all made it back safely, except for one observer who was found dead in the cockpit from enemy machine-gun fire.

In his report on the operations of the Independent Force, Trenchard paid generous tribute to the crews:

The courage and determination shown by the pilots and observers were magnificent. There were cases in which a squadron lost the greater part of its machines on a raid, but this in no wise dampened the other squadrons' keenness to avenge their comrades, and to attack the same target again and at once. It is to this trait in the character of the British pilots that I attribute their success in bombing Germany, as even when a squadron lost the greater part of its machines, the pilots, instead of taking it as a defeat for the Force, at once turned it into a victory by attacking the same targets again with the utmost determination ... I never saw, even when our losses were heaviest, any wavering of their determination to get well into Germany.[24]

When he learned that 99 Squadron had lost seven de Havilland machines on a single raid, he drove straight to the squadron's aerodrome to speak to the surviving pilots. The squadron, en route to a daylight raid on Mainz, had been intercepted by a formation of enemy fighters more than 30 strong; only two machines made it back to base.

'They had a great fight,' Trenchard reported to Weir. 'I went round at once and told them that as long as they kept up their spirits it was a victory for us. This, I said, is what defeats the Huns so much: when we suffered casualties we went out and bombed again.' On another occasion when only two of eighteen aircraft sent out on a mission had returned, he discovered that another squadron had gone out, without orders, to 'have another smack'.

Trenchard still had a reputation in some quarters as being a heartless taskmaster obsessed with maintaining the offensive at any cost and blithely unconcerned about sending young men to their deaths on a daily basis. His gruff manner, his unwillingness to show any emotion and his frequent assertion that he would willingly sacrifice an entire squadron if it would shorten the war by just one day, all helped bolster that image. But Baring, who knew him better than any man alive, knew he grieved silently over so many young lives lost. His boss, he reported, was often 'frightfully upset' by the losses and would frequently sit up all night at an aerodrome, grey-faced and exhausted, waiting for the machines to return after a big raid.

> The distances were so great [Baring wrote], the possibilities of changes in the weather were so numerous and so various, the margin of safety was so narrow, the determination on the part of the pilots to attempt all there was to be attempted was so certain, that whenever one knew there was a big and long raid on hand one could not help being desperately uneasy till the machines had come back. It was not merely a question of losing one or two machines. One knew only too well that a change of weather might occur when the machines were at a great distance, and one might quite easily lose the whole formation.[25]

No one could ever doubt the courage required by aircrews on long-range bombing raids into Germany. They took off in unreliable, flimsy machines in the certain knowledge that their chances of returning were problematic; they had to endure the bitter cold in an open cock-pit several miles high at the mercy of the wind and weather; attempt to stay on course hour after hour with primitive navigational instruments; pray they did not encounter enemy aircraft; dive onto their targets, often through a hail of anti-aircraft fire, and release their bomb loads with the help of a stopwatch and the crudest of bomb sights; then expect to fight their way home, often against head winds that would reduce their speed to 30 miles an hour, as enemy fighters swarmed up to destroy them.

It was certainly not a mission for the faint-hearted, yet there remained a whiff of romance about the whole business. Standing on a hill and watching a squadron take off at dawn one morning, Trenchard turned to a French officer standing nearby and, uncharacteristically, asked him: 'Doesn't it make your heart beat faster when a machine goes up?'

'Yes,' the Frenchman replied. 'Some people call aviation a sport. I call it war.'

At that moment Trenchard saw that the last machine in the formation, which had lurched uncertainly into the air, had a problem. 'He's going to crash,' he said to Baring and seconds later the wing dipped, struck the ground and was torn off. The aircraft turned turtle and crashed in flames. Trenchard and his companions ran down the hill and found both pilot and observer had been thrown clear. The pilot was dead, lying on the ground in a crumpled heap, but the observer was staggering around with his clothes on fire. Trenchard grabbed him, rolled him on the ground to extinguish the flames then took out the small gold Asprey's pocket knife that he always carried, cut away his smouldering clothes and cradled his badly burned head until an ambulance arrived. He survived.

When he returned to his car Trenchard grunted to Chalcroft, his driver, 'Aviation is war, Chalcroft, not sport.'

'Seems like it sir,' Chalcroft replied.

A week later Trenchard and Baring visited casualties at the Flying Hospital at Chaulmes. Among them was a young pilot who had been badly hurt, shot through the chest, in an encounter with an enemy fighter 50 miles from home but had brought his machine back safely, making such a perfect landing that his squadron commander had no idea that both pilot and observer were severely wounded. At the

hospital doctors said he was hovering between life and death. Trenchard asked if it would be possible to present him with a DFC and a
doctor admitted it could just help him pull through. 'The General
went in,' Baring noted in his diary, 'gave him the D.F.C. and he was
intensely pleased. He afterwards recovered.'[26]

From London, Weir urged Trenchard to ever greater excesses. 'I
would very much like it if you could start up a really big fire in one
of the German towns,' he wrote, speculating on the effect if incendi-
aries were scattered on older districts where there were few modern
buildings. 'I can conceive of nothing more terrifying to a civilian population than bombing from a low altitude, and I was frequently very
apprehensive that the Boche would do this in London, and that the
results would be very serious.' Weir was unbothered by the prospect
of heavy civilian casualties. 'If I were you,' he added, 'I would not be
too exacting as regards accuracy in bombing railway stations . . . The
German is susceptible to bloodiness, and I would not mind a few accidents due to inaccuracy.'

'I do not think you need to be anxious,' Trenchard replied, 'the
accuracy is not great at present, and all the pilots drop their eggs well
into the middle of town generally.'[27] A week later Weir complained that
bombing railways was doing nothing to assuage the public's thirst for
revenge and that what was wanted was attacks on munitions works
and other industrial targets. Trenchard's response was to assert that
bombing was damaging German morale to much greater effect than
the material damage. Although major targets in Germany were still
beyond the range of bombers at that time, he was already thinking
about the potential of massed bombing raids to devastate cities and
spread terror. 'In any future war with Germany,' he noted, 'a sys-
tematic campaign of heavy bombing would shatter the morale of its
people.'

On Monday, 9 September, Charles à Court Repington, *The Times*
war correspondent, showed up at the Château d'Autigny-la-Tour. Repington had met Trenchard several times before, earlier in the war, and
was as impressed by him this time as he had been previously.

Trenchard the same as ever. Brilliant, full of ideas, alert, combative and a mine of information. He has 120 aeroplanes, mainly
Handley-Pages,[28] for long-range bombing, and the squadrons are

scattered round partly concealed in woods. The Huns have 600 aeroplanes for the defence of the Rhine towns . . . He does his work without escorts of fighting machines, and thinks that he will be safe when his bombers can bomb at 20,000 feet, as the enemy will have no time to rise so high and intercept the bombers before they have done their work and are 50 miles away. He thinks that he has done much morale and material damage, and showed us photographs of the bombs falling on various towns. His planes have now to fight all the way out and back again . . . T. declares that he has not changed his view that bombing is necessary . . . But he did not admit that he favoured the very large development of the IAF which the Air Ministry is set on . . .[29]

Repington also noted that while the Force benefited from Trenchard's strong personality, it was 'against common sense' for it to be independent of control by either Salmond, Haig or Foch and was thus deeply resented.

September was the blackest month for IAF casualties, with 91 machines lost – 75 per cent of the force establishment of 122 aircraft. In October the weather changed for the worse. 'Day after day attempts were made to reach the long-distance targets,' Trenchard reported to London, 'but the wind was generally too strong; or, if there was no wind, heavy rain and fog prevailed by day and dense mist by night which often lasted until ten or eleven o'clock the following morning.' Prolonged periods of mist, fog and low cloud by day and night halted even short-range operations and on 19 days and 22 nights no operations were possible during the month.

When the weather cleared sufficiently to allow operations, Trenchard's routine reports concealed, behind the dry facts, the incredible dramas that were going on in the skies above Germany:

On 21 October, 12 machines of No. 110 Squadron left to attack Cologne . . . The lines were crossed at 16,000 feet and a compass course was flown over and through cloud. The wind appears to have increased from the West during the flight, and the Rhine was crossed and mistaken for the Moselle [a common problem]. Shortly after crossing the Rhine a dense bank of cloud was encountered at 17,000 feet. The leader fired a red flare and with his formation

well closed up, endeavoured to descend in the clouds. The formation then got much split up. Two of the machines climbed and
flew south-west until they came out of cloud and dropped their
bombs on railways and a factory (apparently in the neighbourhood
of Frankfurt) and both returned safely to their aerodrome. One
other machine followed the leader and came out of cloud at about
11,000 feet, when the leader signalled the 'wash-out' and continued to descend. Three other machines returned and landed in the
darkness at various places near the front line. The remaining seven
machines did not return.[30]

At the end of October squadrons from France, Italy and the United
States were added to Trenchard's command to create an Inter-Allied
Independent Air Force (IAIAF) tasked with launching wide-scale
strategic bombing operations against Germany into 1919. He still
believed that the force would be more effective if deployed in support
of the army.

> I have received a letter confirming my appointment as Commander-
> in-Chief of the Inter-Allied Independent Air Force [he noted in his
> diary on 30 October]. It is a bit late . . . It would have been much
> better to have put the Force as I originally suggested under Sir
> Douglas Haig so that whatever the alterations in the line it would
> have worked automatically. When will the politicians understand
> that one must make an organisation in war that will meet ever
> changing conditions? Politicians do not understand the difference
> between principles and conditions.[31]

Trenchard struck up a good relationship with Brigadier General 'Billy'
Mitchell, the young colonel commanding all the US air squadrons in
France, who was as enthusiastic an advocate of air power as Trenchard and was a similarly brusque character. (Mitchell would later be
regarded as the 'father of the US Air Force', but he antagonised many
senior figures with his passionately outspoken opinions and was court-
martialled in 1925 for insubordination after accusing US military leaders of incompetence and an 'almost treasonable administration of the
national defense'. He was found guilty and suspended from active
duty for five years without pay.)

The IAIAF was to be equipped with Handley Page V/1500 bombers, the four-engined British counterpart to the German Giant. Capable of carrying a bomb load of 7500 pounds and staying aloft for more than 12 hours, only three had been delivered by early November. All three were fuelled and loaded for the first raid on Berlin when, at 11 o'clock on the morning of 11 November 1918, the guns fell silent all along the Western Front and the most terrible war the world had ever known came to an end.

'The Armistice was signed this morning,' Trenchard noted laconically in his diary. 'Thus the Independent Air Force came to an end. A more gigantic waste of effort and personnel there has never been in any war . . . It has certainly taught me what I really knew before – an impossible organisation was set up by the politicians simply in order that they could say "I am bombing Germany" . . .'[32]

Trenchard could not wait to get away. He immediately telegraphed Marshal Foch asking for permission to hand his command back to Haig, a move that irritated his friend Salmond, on whom the Force was unloaded, prompting him to cavil about the general's eagerness 'to pass on an unwanted baby and clear out with all possible speed'.[33]

On the same day, admitting that he was increasingly troubled by the migraines that had plagued him for years, he wrote to Weir suggesting he should be put on half pay for a year. 'This will give you a chance of pushing on some of the younger men,' he wrote, 'as you must not forget that although I am not old, I am forty-six, and most of the other officers are six or seven years younger. I am perfectly certain I am right in having a good long rest as my head gets very bad at times now.'[34]

Weir's solicitous response was to suggest that he should take a holiday before making any important decisions and that they should talk when he got home.

In the early morning of 17 November 1918, as he drove with Baring through the heavy iron gates and the stone arch of the Château d'Autigny-la-Tour for the last time, en route to Paris, Trenchard was astonished to find the narrow pavements of the Rue du Château lined with hundreds of cheering airmen who had come for no other reason than to bid farewell to their chief. He was almost overwhelmed with emotion and profoundly embarrassed as he waved in acknowledgement, his usually stern features relaxed into an uncertain smile.

'I can't believe it,' he muttered to Baring. 'There must be some mistake.'

MUTINY AND THE MAD MULLAH

After leaving Autigny-la-Tour, Trenchard and Baring drove to Paris, where he (Trenchard) recalled that 'great jubilations were taking place' with 'fireworks being fired everywhere and scenes that beggared description' – despite six days having passed since the Armistice.[1] He somehow managed to find a room at the Ritz Hotel but did not, he claimed, join in the celebrations. Baring loved to tell a story about a 'certain lady' who waited outside Trenchard's room and then got in an elevator with him, introduced herself and asked if he would escort her to a dance. When he curtly replied that he did not dance, she pouted and confessed she had spent all she had on her dress and hat. Trenchard gave her flimsy dress a withering look and said: 'I see – all on the hat.'

He returned to London by air on 21 November, where he continued working on his final dispatch, a typically pragmatic assessment of events: 'Between 6 June and 10 November, in the course of 239 raids, the Independent Force dropped 550 tons of bombs, 160 by day and 390 by night . . .' He only strayed from a sober recitation of facts and figures when he claimed there was a 'moral [morale] effect' to the bombing campaign, which he calculated as being in a proportion of 20 to 1 to the 'material effect' – odds that were purely subjective, more or less meaningless and would be treated with considerable scorn. 'It is not possible to estimate to what extent the mental state of the workmen affected German war production,' he continued, 'but there is no doubt that in some cases it is very considerable . . .' He further speculated that the *threat* of bombing raids was probably as effective as the raids themselves. 'It would not be an exaggeration to say that more moral effect with consequent loss of production was caused by alarms than by the actual dropping of bombs.'[2]

Trenchard tacitly accepted that bombing operations, hampered by weather, navigation problems, unreliable machines and a host of other difficulties, had probably not spread the expected death and destruction to any great extent. He was quite right. A team of experts sent to Germany after the war to assess, on the ground, the actual damage caused by bombers of the Independent Force in the 11 months of 1918 found the results to be very disappointing, even accepting that strategic bombing was in its infancy. Very few factories had suffered a direct hit and even when they had been hit the damage was superficial. The Badische steel works on the Rhine in Kehl had been attacked over and over again, yet most of the bombs fell between the buildings. 'Generally speaking,' their report noted, 'the directors did not attach much importance to air raids . . . Damage had invariably been repaired at once without any difficulty, and in very few cases had any stoppage of work resulted.' Railways, which had been specifically targeted, were rarely disrupted and even when the track had been damaged trains were simply re-routed until the damage could be repaired. Of the 1300 bombs dropped on Thionville station in north-eastern France only 100 hit the target and around a quarter of those failed to explode. 'The consensus of opinion of our bombing [of the railways] by the German officials, is summed up in the word "annoying".'

Trenchard made no mention in his autobiographical notes about what he did at Christmas that year, only that he spent it 'with a few people'. In the absence of being offered a new post, he had made up his mind to resign from the service and was thus surprised to be woken one morning in mid-January – he was still in bed, even though it was ten o'clock – by an urgent telephone call from an aide to Wully Robertson, who was then C-in-C Home Forces.[3] He was even more surprised by what the aide had to say – the C-in-C presented his compliments and asked if the general would be able to leave immediately for Southampton to put down a mutiny.

The arrangements for demobilising thousands of men in uniform at the end of the war had turned into a shambles. During the 1918 General Election campaign the previous month Lloyd George had promised quick demobilisation, but Lord Derby, the Secretary of State for War, had put together a complicated scheme which was aimed at kick-starting the economy and was manifestly unfair. Under his plan, workers in key industries were due to be released first, but since many of them had only been called up in the later stages of the war, resentment spread quickly when it looked like men who had served longest were likely to be the last to be demobilised.

On 3 January simmering bitterness turned to mutiny at Folkestone, when 2000 soldiers destined for service abroad refused to embark on their troopship and staged a protest march to the Town Hall, cheered by local residents. 'Two thousand men, unarmed and in perfect order, demonstrated the fact they were fed up – absolutely fed-up,' the *Daily Herald* reported. 'Their plan of action had been agreed the night before: no military boat should be allowed to leave Folkestone for France that day, or any day, until they were guaranteed their freedom. It was sheer, flat, brazen, open and successful mutiny.'

Unrest spread to Dover, where four thousand troops held a mass meeting to air their grievances and at Isleworth, in west London, Army Service Corps drivers refused to take out their lorries. On 8 January thousands of troops determined to go home descended on London from barracks around the country and marched on the War Office, further stoking government fears that disaffected returning soldiers would create rallying points for industrial unrest and Bolshevism. The government was keenly aware that revolutions in Russia and Germany had been spearheaded by mutinous troops, and there were real fears the same could happen in Britain.

The worst disturbances occurred a few days later in Southampton when 5000 troops due to return to France occupied the docks and announced they were no longer prepared to obey orders. Robertson clearly believed that Trenchard was just the man to deal with the situation, but Trenchard disagreed – firstly he was on leave and secondly, as far as he was concerned, he had resigned his commission. When the aide insisted that it was Robertson's personal request that the general should take charge at Southampton, Trenchard barked: 'What as?'

The aide was nonplussed. 'Sorry?'

'Am I to go as an Army general or an Air Force general?' Trenchard asked. He had, he explained, no official status – who was he to take orders from?

The aide discreetly suggested that Robertson probably 'didn't give tuppence' which general he went as, so long as he went.

Trenchard wearily agreed to go, but with the greatest reluctance. He sent a message to Baring to say that he was needed and the two men left for Southampton on the afternoon train from Waterloo, with Trenchard wearing the uniform of an army general. They found rooms, with some difficulty, at the smart South Western Hotel, close to the docks, where most of the first-class passengers had stayed before embarking on the *Titanic*.

Next morning, before breakfast, Trenchard took a stroll past the dock area, where hundreds of soldiers were brewing tea in small groups or milling about aimlessly in a large area strewn with kitbags, blankets and litter of all kinds. It was clear that discipline had completely broken down. A few dispirited officers looked on, apparently incapable of instilling any order or getting the mess cleaned up. Pickets guarded the gangways to the ships, which appeared to be deserted.

After breakfast Trenchard and Baring, in a borrowed staff car, drove to the barracks on the outskirts of the city, where three elderly officers – the commanding officer, adjutant and quartermaster – all admitted they were out of their depth handling the crisis. They told him they believed that trouble had been fomented by a small number of men due to return to France to face disciplinary charges and that they had persuaded others to join them. Most of them were holed up in the cavernous Customs Shed in the docks.

Trenchard had read newspaper reports about the spreading unrest in the army and was not unsympathetic to the men's grievances. He thought it was inevitable the demobilisation plans would cause trouble among men weary of the war and anxious to return home, but at the same time he recognised that indiscipline could not be tolerated, whatever the circumstances.

It was typical of Trenchard that he would first attempt a direct approach. Later that afternoon, with Baring at his side, he drove into the docks in his official car and ordered it to be parked in full view. Watched by every soldier in the place, he jumped out, adjusted his cap and marched straight into the Customs Shed. He could find nothing to stand on, so he called in his great booming voice for the men to gather round him. The sudden appearance of a general seemed, initially, to subdue them. They listened in sullen silence while he explained he had been put in charge to resolve the situation. He said he would personally listen to every one of their grievances, even if it took a month, but that first they must immediately return to duty or face the consequences. At this the men began shouting and catcalling, drowning out his words, and surged forward, almost knocking him over. He thought for a moment he was going to be physically attacked.

'It was most unpleasant,' he wrote later. 'They said they did not want to listen to me. They wanted either the Prime Minister or the C-in-C and they would not listen to anybody else. I told them plainly they would see nobody except me. They booed and shouted and I walked out with what dignity I could, followed by a great crowd close up behind me. It was the first time in my life I had been hustled – so to speak – by a lot of soldiers.'[4]

By the time Trenchard and Baring emerged from the Customs Shed – both quite shaken – it was dark. As words had failed so conclusively, Trenchard recognised he had no alternative but to use force. He found a small office with a telephone in the centre of the dockyard and called the local garrison commander in Portsmouth, asking for a battalion of soldiers, with rifles and ammunition, to be sent to Southampton by train immediately. The garrison commander was nervous, said he could not guarantee how reliable any battalion would be. Trenchard took the precaution of asking him to include an escort of military policemen. He then telephoned Robertson to inform him what he was doing. His final call was to the GOC Southern Command, who was clearly appalled at the prospect that a bloodbath might ensue. The GOC told Trenchard that he would not be able to give him support if Trenchard ordered his troops to fire on the mutineers.

'I'm not asking for your support,' Trenchard snapped, 'I'm simply informing you of my intentions.' Privately he was hoping that a 'theatrical' display of force would persuade the mutineers that he was prepared for anything, but he admitted he had no idea what he would do if it did not work.

Before settling down to wait for the battalion to arrive from Portsmouth, he ordered all the lights in the dockyard to be switched off. While they were waiting in the dark, there was a hesitant knock at the door. A very young and very frightened soldier, visibly trembling, stood outside wanting to give himself up. Trenchard invited him in and questioned him closely about the mood of the 'mutineers'. The boy said that most of the men did not want to get involved but they had been shamefully treated. They had been told by an officer at Waterloo that they were travelling to Southampton to be demobilised only to learn when they arrived, from the self-same officer, that they were in fact returning to France. It was this that had sparked off the revolt. Trenchard was furious that a British officer could be capable of such duplicity.

When the Portsmouth troops – 250 of them – turned up, Trenchard briefed them. 'You all know why you are here,' he told them. 'This nonsense must stop.' They were to load their magazines with ten rounds and then follow his orders to the letter. They would approach the Customs Shed in a single line, spread out three yards apart. When he gave the word, they were all to cock their rifles, making as much noise as possible. No one was to fire without his explicit order. He felt sure, he said, that everything would come all right.

The 'mutineers' had little idea what was happening, only that something was. They heard a muffled order in the dark and the un-mistakable sound of 250 rifle bolts sliding into place. Suddenly, all the lights went on and they could see a long line of soldiers facing towards them with rifles at the ready. In the centre of the line stood the general they had more or less thrown out the night before, flanked by burly military policemen. He gave them a moment to recognise him. 'Now then,' he said, 'I have come to see that each one of you goes on board to go back to France, come what may.'

A young sergeant stepped out of the crowd in the Customs Shed, marched up to Trenchard and shouted in his face 'Go to hell!' Trench-ard, expressionless, turned to one of the military policemen, a giant of a man, standing next to him. 'Knock this man down and take him on board,' he said. The sergeant was duly dragged off. Trenchard could see the 'mutineers' were looking increasingly uneasy and uncomfortable.

'Now,' he demanded, 'are you going to do what you are told?' When he identified what he thought was a murmur of assent, he said bright-ly, 'Right, now that is all settled, I will hear what you have got to say.'

He arranged for a table and chair to be brought in and said he would listen to anyone who had a reason why they should not be sent back to France. Those without a reason were ordered to embark, but the remainder formed a long queue at the table. Many confirmed that they believed they were travelling to Southampton to be demobilised; they were all released immediately. One man said he had simply been caught up in the activity at Waterloo and had been bundled on the train even though he was half deaf and nearly blind. A number told Trenchard that they had been arrested for overstaying their leave by just a few hours. Trenchard thought it was ludicrous and told them they were no longer under arrest but they should board the ship next day. In all he allowed some 2000 men to go on their way; the remainder went back to France, either willingly or unwillingly, some to face trial on serious charges.

The mutiny was not quite over. A hard core of resisters held out in a barricaded barrack room, but by then Trenchard had run out of patience. He ordered the windows to be smashed and fire hoses turned on those inside. 'In a couple of days,' he noted, 'the docks were working normally.'

Shortly afterwards unrest throughout the army was brought to an end by Winston Churchill, who had taken over at the War Office in a government reshuffle. One of his first acts was to scrap the existing demobilisation plans which had caused so much resentment and substitute a 'first in, first out' scheme, which was both sensible and fair and was accepted by everyone. He also extended service until April 1920 for the most recent conscripts so that currently serving soldiers could be demobilised.

Churchill occupied a new, dual appointment as Secretary of State for War and Air combined. Weir, who had no political ambitions, wanted to return to private life and had asked to be relieved as Air Minister and so Lloyd George had casually told Churchill to 'take the Air with him' when he moved to the War Office, as he had decided there was no need for the Air Ministry to remain a separate department. *The Times* disapproved: 'This union under such a minister as Mr Churchill,' a leader on January 11 opined, 'is asking for trouble and a sure cause of future mischief.' With the prime minister not much concerned whether the air service survived, combining the two ministries could have meant the death knell of the RAF, but Churchill liked anything new and adventurous, shared Trenchard's vision of air power playing a decisive role in imperial defence and saw the new service standing 'alone and midway between the land and sea services'.

Weir pressed Churchill to appoint a new CAS with 'a mind and a will of his own' if the RAF was not to disappear and suggested he should reinstate Trenchard, less than a year after his contentious resignation. Sykes, who was still the CAS, had damaged his reputation and chances of staying on in the job by drawing up plans for a ludicrously extravagant post-war Royal Air Force, comprising 154 squadrons for service at home and overseas with bases throughout the

Empire costing £75 million a year – an unrealistic sum far in excess of anything the Treasury would sanction.

Trenchard was still in Southampton when he received a telegram asking him to return to London on 'urgent Air Force business'. He had no idea what it was about and indeed still considered his military career to be over. Since the end of the war he had been thinking more and more about returning to Africa. From Southampton he had written twice to his friend Sir Walter Lawrence, an influential author and former civil servant, saying how much he would like a governorship in Africa. 'I should be very grateful indeed,' he wrote on 17 January, 'if you would write to Amery [Leo Amery, the Under-Secretary of State for the Colonies] about a Governorship in Nigeria or some other African colony.'[5]

It was not to be. About the last thing Trenchard expected, when he met Churchill at the War Office in the first week of February 1919, was to be offered his old job back. His immediate reaction was to turn it down, firstly because he instinctively felt he would not be able to agree with the new minister about the future of the Royal Air Force and secondly because Churchill already had a CAS – Sykes. Churchill airily waved away his second objection, saying he had already decided to put Sykes in charge of the development of civil aviation. As to the first, Churchill had a suggestion.

Winston said you go away and write down what you think your policy ought to be, and I will do the same. We will exchange our notes and then meet again the next day. I wrote down my notes very shortly and sent them over, saying that I did not think he would agree, but I got nothing from him. The next morning he rang up again and said would I go and see him. I went over and he said 'Well I have got your notes' and I said 'Yes, but I haven't got yours.' 'Well,' he said, 'I had no time to write it, but I see nothing in yours that I disagree with'. This was such a typical Winston move that I admit I was puzzled. We talked on a lot about things and it really came down to the only thing we looked as if we were going to disagree on was the titles. He said I must accept and he pressed me to, so I agreed to come back as CAS.

Sykes was made Director General of Civil Aviation. The high-sounding title of 'Director General' much appealed to him and he was also made a G.B.E., which he accepted warmly. In the same way as I never handed over to him, so he never handed over to me when I took over again. In fact, I do not think I ever saw him for months after that. I used to see his figure floating about, never saying a word to anybody and looking very sad and sore.[6]

The paper Trenchard presented to Churchill – with a covering note predicting he would probably find much to disagree with – was just two handwritten foolscap sheets with seven numbered paragraphs proposing an air ministry kept as small as possible and a similarly small air force 'not beyond the capabilities of a few carefully chosen officers to run' and more in keeping with the economic climate. It would comprise a mix of officers on permanent commissions and those seconded from the army and navy for four years. All officers would have to learn to fly and training would be specialised for fighter pilots, reconnaissance and bombing. Churchill went along with everything, only objecting to Trenchard's wish to retain the existing military rank structure – he favoured new ranks for a new service.

Only a few days after resuming work as Chief of the Air Staff in mid-February, Trenchard was struck down by 'Spanish flu', a pandemic which would infect around 500 million people around the world and kill up to 100 million, making it one of the deadliest natural disasters in human history. He had a phobia about doctors and refused to admit he was ill when the symptoms – extreme fatigue, difficulty in breathing, fever, coughing – began to appear. Exhaustion finally forced him to take to his bed and by the time Baring summoned a doctor – against his wishes – he was suffering from acute pneumonia.

On 3 March he wrote to Churchill to say he was not well enough to continue as CAS and was therefore tendering his resignation.

I do not think I have the guts to pull it through now. I am played out and I am sorry I took the job as it must be most inconvenient to you. It is worrying me very much indeed and I feel that there are many things not going right until you have put in my successor. Perhaps in six or nine months' time if I have recovered I can be of use in some small way again. But at present I feel I am not fit to work. The doctor does not think I shall be fit for three weeks or maybe longer.

[Churchill replied]:

I appreciate warmly the motive which prompts you to write as you have done. I think after all your hard work you ought to take a month or six weeks' leave and then let me know how you feel. There is not the slightest difficulty in carrying on for that time. In any case, I could not think of losing your greatly valued service until I was satisfied you were physically unfit.

I do not believe for a moment that you will not be in good health and spirits long before the six weeks I prescribe are over. I am looking forward so much to working with you; but you really must get quite fit before you come back.

Two weeks later Trenchard wrote again to say he was 'still very weak' and would not be any use until the end of April and once again offered to resign.

'There is no question of anyone taking your place,' Churchill replied, 'and I have no intention of acting upon your various offers to resign, which arise from your high sense of duty. I am sure you have the most valuable work to do for the Flying Corps, and we will hold the fort until you are restored.'[7]

Trenchard continued to work at home, dictating letters, reviewing papers and issuing instructions to a stream of visitors from the Air Ministry. Baring, devoted as always, moved into Trenchard's apartment to help take care of him when three nurses, one after another, despaired of caring for such a difficult patient and walked out.

His condition steadily worsened. Hovering between life and death, he became obsessed with a desire to see, once again, Kitty Boyle, now the widow of his friend and brother officer, James Boyle, from their days in Londonderry before the war. Messages were sent to her home in Lowndes Square to the effect that General Trenchard was seriously ill and would like to see her, but no replies were forthcoming. In fact Kitty was in France, visiting the area where her husband had been killed in October 1914, to arrange for a cross to be erected in his memory and establish the circumstances of his death.

As soon as she returned and read the messages she hurried to Trenchard's apartment in Park Place, fearful that she might already be too late. The door was opened by Baring, whom she had never met, but who she assumed was some kind of medical orderly. He looked at her Red Cross uniform – she had worn it to France – and breathed a sigh of relief. 'Are you by any chance the new nurse?' he asked. 'The patient has already got rid of three.'

Kitty explained she was an old friend and was visiting at the general's particular request. Baring seemed doubtful. The general was really too ill to receive visitors, he said, but Kitty persisted and was eventually admitted. As Baring led the way to Trenchard's bedroom several RAF officers waiting on chairs in the hall rose to let her pass. Outside the bedroom he whispered that the general was conscious but had great difficulty speaking and breathing and was very reluctant to help himself by stopping work.

As Kitty entered the room, Trenchard's eyes widened. He was dishevelled and unshaven, lying in bed with an ice pack on his head and was so ashamed of his appearance that he instinctively tried to cover himself by pulling a sheet up over his head. Kitty laughed. 'Hello, Boom,' she said, pulling the sheet down. 'How are you?' Trenchard grunted. She busied herself about the room, cleared the papers from his bed and put them to one side out of his reach, straightened his bedclothes and told him to lie still while she took his temperature. It was 104. She said she was going to ask the officers waiting to see him to leave and Trenchard just nodded, apparently happy to acquiesce with whatever she said.

For the next month Kitty visited every day. Sometimes Trenchard was delirious, babbling about the horrors of the war and his grief over the fine men who had lost their lives, and she realised how much the war had taken out of him. Very slowly he recovered. When he was at last able to sit up, he dictated a letter to Churchill explaining that he was unlikely to be able to return to work for some time and suggested again that under the circumstances it might be better if he was replaced.

Churchill still would not hear of it. 'I could not think of losing your greatly valued services until I was satisfied you were physically fit,' he replied repeating his previous sentiment. 'I am looking forward so much to working with you.'[8]

Kitty was very fond of her sick friend, but at the same time she was astonished and embarrassed when one morning, completely out of the blue, he took her hand and proposed marriage. She had always

considered him a confirmed bachelor, utterly uninterested in the opposite sex or domestic life. To cover her embarrassment she laughed
and shook her head. She was sorry, she said, she had no desire to marry
again, or to join those war widows being led to the altar out of pity
or chivalrous sentimentality. 'Start afresh with someone who can look
after you and nobody else,' she told him. 'I'm tired and have too many
other commitments.' She had three children to look after, she said, she
was busy nursing and helping other wives and she was still 'very much
in love' with the memory of her husband.[9]

Trenchard was crushed. He presumably had every hope that Kitty
would accept, otherwise he would never have dreamed of proposing
marriage at the age of 47 to a woman he had only got to know well in
the last few weeks. (He had written to her regularly all through the
war, but had not spent any time with her since his visits to the family
before the war, when the Boyles were living in Salisbury and he was
at the Central Flying School in Upavon; although he later confided
to his private secretary, T.B. Marson, that she was 'the woman I have
wanted to marry for 10 years.'[10]) Kitty learned much later – and it saddened her greatly – that Trenchard believed she had turned him down
because of the stigma on his family caused by the shame of his father's
bankruptcy. Nothing could have been further from the truth.

If she had felt she could have accepted his proposal she would certainly have done so, because she knew how lonely he was. In 1914,
shortly after he had left for France, she had been surprised to receive
a letter from him asking if she would visit his mother, who was dying.
'He had no other friends to ask,' she recalled. 'For the first time it was
fully borne in on me how lonely and friendless he was. There was a
definite sense of shame about him which put a chip on his shoulder
and made him almost aggressively determined not to accept anyone as
a real friend, however hard they tried.'[11]

(Kitty was no stranger to unhappiness herself. One of 14 children
– her father had seven children by his first marriage and seven by his
second – only three of her step-siblings were still alive when she was
born in 1885 and two would die before she was five years old. As well
as losing her beloved husband in the war, two of her brothers were also
killed.)

Colleagues observed that Trenchard was unusually despondent
when he finally returned to work at the beginning of May, but put it

down to the effects of his long illness. He was certainly not the kind of man to share with anyone his disappointment in love, so no one knew that he had been rejected by the only woman in his life that he had ever shown any interest in.

The Air Ministry had moved from the Hotel Cecil to No. 1 Kingsway, to a building renamed Adastral House, from the RAF motto 'Per Ardua ad Astra' ('Through adversity to the stars'). Trenchard was soon immersed in a multitude of problems dealing with demobilisation and managing the difficult reduction of the Royal Air Force from its wartime strength. By the end of the war the Royal Air Force was the most powerful air service in the world, with 188 combat squadrons, 291,170 officers and men, including 5182 pilots, and 22,647 aircraft. Trenchard's task was to contract the force to just 30 squadrons. Choosing which officers to keep – 300 out of 30,000 – was, he recalled 'appallingly difficult'.[12]

He was also engaged in a continuing battle to maintain the independence of the force against fierce opposition from the army and the navy, both of whom still wanted to control their own air service, and a government anxious to make drastic cuts to its defence expenditure. The CIGS, Field Marshal Sir Henry Wilson, and Admiral David Beatty, the First Sea Lord, argued forcefully that the RAF should be disbanded in the interests of economy. Beatty, the youngest British admiral since Nelson, a strikingly handsome and charismatic public figure, was a particularly formidable opponent since the Royal Navy, the 'senior service', enjoyed enormous prestige; he lobbied hard for an air service under navy control, for reasons both of economy and strategy.

Trenchard was fortunate for a time to have the unwavering support of General Jack Seely, a lifelong friend of Churchill who had been appointed under-secretary of state for air. Seely was a redoubtable character: a soldier/politician who had fought in France throughout the war, he had the distinction of leading one of the last great cavalry charges in history, at the Arne in March 1918, on his warhorse, Warrior. He had been an enthusiastic advocate of air power since the inception of the RFC, was a qualified pilot and once arrived to answer questions in the House by landing a seaplane on the Thames opposite Parliament, having flown under Tower Bridge on the way wearing a top hat. Despite his friendship with Churchill, he considered it was a mistake for his friend to try and combine jobs and resigned at the end of the year when the government refused to set up a separate Air Ministry. Seely was eventually succeeded by Lord Londonderry, a rich Anglo-Irish landowner whose wife was a noted London hostess. Like his predecessor, Londonderry was committed to the future of air power and piloted his own aircraft; he and Trenchard would become firm friends and his appointment provided the RAF with an element of social cachet it sorely lacked compared with the Royal Navy and the top regiments in the army. Joining the RAF to fly an aircraft was not seen, in some quarters, as a suitable ambition for a gentleman.

For a while Trenchard, who was always sensitive about his family background, believed the aristocratic Beatty looked down on him and was motivated by personal dislike. Londonderry assured him this was not the case. It was not due to anything personal, he said, but was caused by Beatty's 'dread' that an air officer might one day be appointed commander-in-chief. 'The navy is one hundred years behind the times,' Londonderry explained, 'and the war has not modernised it.'[13]

Despite the friction, both Trenchard and Beatty frequently played polo, with Churchill and Londonderry, before breakfast at the Hurlingham Club in west London or at Roehampton. Trenchard stabled his ponies behind Londonderry's mansion on Park Lane in Mayfair, although he was eventually forced to give up polo when his workload at the Air Ministry became too much. No one worked harder, or longer hours, than the CAS, and staff became accustomed to his great voice echoing down the corridors of Adastral House at all hours and his habit of summoning subordinates by pressing all the bells on his desk at once.

Given his contempt for politics and politicians, his lack of tact and his candid admission he was 'not good in an office', Trenchard would prove, surprisingly, to be a bureaucratic infighter of rare ability with a gift of getting his own way even against considerable opposition. On 2 July 1919, he was called before the House of Commons Select Committee on National Expenditure to justify what was seen as the extravagant use of aeroplanes by Air Ministry personnel. The tone of questioning was markedly hostile, with Sir Frederick Banbury, the chairman, sarcastically inquiring who, in the Ministry, had the use of aeroplanes for 'flying about'? Trenchard coldly replied that not only did various officers make use of aeroplanes but he actively encouraged them to do so. When he was then asked if it was necessary he bridled and said he deeply deprecated the question. In his view it was 'most necessary' for the Secretary of State and the Under-Secretary of State to have the use of machines to travel by air as it gave great confidence to the air service and helped boost morale. 'I also pointed out,' he added in a note scribbled later to Churchill, 'that if Sir Frederick became Air Minister I should strongly recommend that he too travelled about by aeroplane.'[14]

In fact the current Air Minister would have very much liked to have piloted his own aircraft. Churchill had tried to get a licence before the war when he was First Lord of the Admiralty, but had given up at his wife's request after his instructor had been killed in a flying accident. He had decided to take up lessons again, using his ministerial position as justification. On Friday 18 July, he drove to Croydon aerodrome for a routine training flight but stalled during take off and plunged nose-first into the ground from a height of about 90 feet. His life was probably saved by his instructor, Jack Scott, who switched off the engine seconds before the machine hit the ground, preventing an explosion. Scott broke his leg and Churchill was badly bruised. Subsequently Trenchard managed to persuade him to abandon any future flying ambitions on the perfectly reasonable grounds that a minister who largely shared his views was more use to him alive than dead. (When Trenchard wanted to set up an Auxiliary Air Force, Churchill frowned on the idea of 'weekend fliers' probably, Trenchard thought, because he was not one himself.)

Apart from his unrequited love life, 1919 was a good year for Trenchard. In July he was appointed Colonel of the Royal Scots Fusiliers, an extraordinary honour for someone who had left the regiment only six years previously in the relatively lowly rank of major. Around the same time he was created a baronet with a grant of £10,000 and promoted from air vice marshal to air marshal, after a tedious squabble about ranks in the new service. His portrait also appeared in a series entitled 'Flight and Men' in *Flight* magazine, although this last accolade probably meant very little to him.

It was remarkable at a time when so much was happening – mass demobilisation, peace talks in Versailles, the reordering of Europe and the threat of serious industrial unrest at home – that the leaders of the three services should expend so much energy debating the nomenclature of the RAF and that the subject should arouse so much passion. At times the discussion bordered on the absurd. Trenchard's proposal that the RAF's equivalent rank to field marshal and admiral of the fleet should be marshal of the air prompted Wilson, the CIGS, to ask, in all seriousness, if it was Trenchard's intention to bring the rank of field marshal into disrepute. When the navy objected to the RAF having a vice marshal, Trenchard quipped that he had 'no idea the Navy claimed all the vices as its prerogative'.[15]

Trenchard was finally obliged to seek an audience with the King to get Royal approval for the list of new titles for the commissioned ranks in the RAF. The King only demurred at marshal of the air, hinting that it perhaps 'infringed the prerogative of the Almighty'. It was forthwith changed to marshal of the Royal Air Force, a rank which Trenchard would be the first to hold. The King also approved the continued use of the RFC's red, white and blue roundels to commemorate the valour of all those who had died in the war.

Initially, Trenchard and Churchilll worked well together. Churchill liked and respected his CAS, soon took to calling him 'Boom' (although he liked to joke that perhaps 'Bomb' might be more appropriate) and trusted him to get on with the job with the minimum of interference. Although occasionally irritated by Churchill's inclination to become embroiled in matters which should not concern him and his tendency to be influenced by the last person to whom he had spoken on any given subject, Trenchard could not but be impressed by his prodigious energy, intellect and innate political skills. But relations between them became strained after Lloyd George introduced the 'Ten Year Rule' to tighten the government's grip on defence spending, by requiring the armed services to draft their estimates on the assumption that the British Empire would not be engaged in any great war for the next ten years.

To Trenchard's dismay, Churchill began to express doubts, for the first time, about the wisdom of maintaining an independent air service in the light of the 'Ten Year Rule'. Trenchard knew that without the support of his Secretary of State the RAF was almost certainly doomed. In early September he decided that he had no alternative but to resign, once again. Working late one night at Adastral House he called in his private secretary, Captain T.B. Marson, dictated a letter of resignation and asked for it to be delivered immediately to

Mr Churchill. Marson, Baring's successor, clearly had something of his tact and diplomacy, and quietly suggested that Trenchard should sleep on it as it was unlikely, in any case, that the letter would reach Churchill before the morning. Without a word, Trenchard slid the letter into his desk drawer and turned the key.

Next morning, he tore it up, took a taxi to the War Office and burst into Churchill's office, angrily brushing aside anyone who tried to block his path. A shouting match followed behind closed doors which could clearly be heard by the awestruck secretaries sitting outside. At one point Trenchard bellowed about the absurdity of trained airmen becoming mere chauffeurs for the army and navy, a phrase that fired Churchill's imagination, and when tempers had cooled he suggested that Trenchard should produce a memorandum developing that theme as an argument for retaining an independent air service.

Trenchard drafted a paper later that same day under the title 'Why the RAF should be maintained as separate from the Navy and the Army', emphasising the 'consensus of expert opinion' predicting an increasingly important role for air power in the future. 'It seems to me,' he concluded, 'that there are two alternatives.'

(1) To use the air simply as a means of conveyance . . . to carry out re-connaissance for the navy or army, drop bombs at places specified by them immediately affecting local operations or observe for their artillery.
(2) To really make an air service which will encourage and develop airmanship, or better still, the air spirit, like the naval spirit, and to make it a force that will profoundly alter the strategy of the future . . .[16]

There was no doubt which option he preferred. To his credit, Churchill fully supported his CAS when the paper was presented to the Cabinet, adding a note of his own:

No compromise is workable. If we are not to relegate aviation to a minor position and lose the predominance which we have won at such cost during the last five years, we must create a real air service, not necessarily large but highly efficient. The problem is not, in the first instance, one of how many service squadrons we require to meet strategical needs, as in the case of the army, but one of making a sound framework on which to build . . .'[17]

This was undoubtedly Trenchard's strategy and he was already working on a blueprint for the permanent organisation of the Royal Air Force – the first time anyone had ever attempted to draw up a constitution for a new fighting service. 'I am working night and day on permanent conditions of pay and service,' he wrote to his friend John Salmond, then Air Officer Commanding the Southern Area, 'and Mr Churchill is doing all he can to help. It is taking time, and it is so important that I cannot do half my other work.'

Drafted and redrafted over and over again at Trenchard's behest, it would become a model for other air forces around the world. It was finally published in December as a White Paper under the dry title 'The Permanent Organisation of the Royal Air Force',[18] although it would also be known as the 'Jonah's Gourd Memorandum' from the obscure biblical reference in the preface, dreamed up by one of Trenchard's 'English merchants' (his epithet for the staff officers with the unenviable task of translating his complex thoughts into cogent prose): 'The Force may in fact be compared to the prophet Jonah's gourd.[19] The necessities of war created it in a night, but the economies of peace have to a large extent caused it to wither in a day, and we are now faced with the necessity of replacing it with a plant of deeper growth . . .'

Throughout the document the emphasis was on establishing the independence of the new service, whether it was in intangibles like fostering an 'air force spirit' or in the bricks and mortar of RAF stations and training establishments. Just 7000 words long, it predicted the RAF would grow 'larger and larger and become more and more the predominating factor in all types of warfare' and covered all the major areas of future development – the need for an officers' training college similar to Sandhurst or Dartmouth, an apprentice scheme, an Auxiliary Air Force of part-time pilots and the introduction of the then revolutionary concept of short-service commissions.

While it would later be described as 'one of the most courageous and far-sighted pieces of constructive planning in the annals of air power'[20] its reception in the press at the time was lukewarm. Even Charles à Court Repington, an admirer of Trenchard, could find little of merit in it.

It is absurd to talk of any fraction of our armed forces as independent [he wrote in the *Morning Post*], since unity of conception and control is the leading principle of war . . . No evidence has been given that the Independent Air Force shortened the war by an hour, and the fact that this force was brilliantly commanded and served with the utmost heroism does not alter that . . . It is heresy for Sir Hugh Trenchard to suggest that the air force can be a substitute for part of our garrisons overseas, and these exaggerations do harm to the air force itself by turning its friends into enemies.

As a sop to the army and the Royal Navy, Trenchard indicated in the memorandum that the 'small parts' of the RAF specifically trained to work with the other two services would 'probably', at some time in the future, become an arm of that service. (This never happened and prompted Beatty, later, to indignantly accuse Trenchard of a 'breach of faith'.) If he had hoped that this concession would neutralise the threat the other services posed to the new service, or ease tension between them, he was badly mistaken, as he learned when he sought a meeting with the CIGS and Admiral Beatty in an attempt to win them over to his argument. Field Marshal Wilson, the CIGS, had never disguised his hostility towards the air service and was famously on record for describing the RAF contemptuously as 'coming from God knows where, dropping its bombs on God knows what, and going off God knows where'.

Trenchard's memories of the meeting, in Beatty's office at the Admiralty, remained undimmed for the remainder of his life. Beatty sat at his desk with Wilson standing behind him, leaning against a marble mantelpiece with a monocle screwed in one eye. As was his habit, Trenchard paced up and down as he made his case and he noticed that each time he turned Beatty was obliged to shield his eyes from the December sunlight slanting through the window. In the end Beatty became so uncomfortable he got up from his chair and he, too, began pacing the office. When Trenchard had finished, Beatty immediately launched an attack on Trenchard's oft-repeated claim that 'the air is one and indivisible', saying he certainly did not share that view and he doubted the CIGS did either, prompting Wilson to chime in 'Hear, hear.'

Towards the end of the meeting Trenchard realised he was getting nowhere and that neither Wilson nor Beatty had budged an inch. In desperation he played one last card. Clearly, he said, if the War Office and the Admiralty were determined to scupper the air service there was little he could do to stop them, but out of a sense of fair play he appealed for a temporary truce – 12 months' respite from public and private attacks on the RAF to allow him to put his plans into action. If he had failed by the end of that time they were free to do whatever they wished. Beatty could not resist a call on his conduct as a gentleman and agreed; Wilson reluctantly went along with his navy counterpart. Both men would later come to regret acceding to their gentlemanly instincts, since Trenchard used the hiatus to consolidate his position and lay down solid foundations which would make it much more difficult to disband the new service.

One of the buttresses, and the embodiment of Trenchard's determination that the RAF would be independent of the other two services, was the RAF College at Cranwell, the world's first air academy, which opened on 1 November 1919. He steadfastly resisted pressure to use the existing training and logistical facilities of either the army or the Royal Navy, arguing that the RAF needed its own institutions to develop airmanship and engender an 'air spirit'. The college, formerly a naval flying school, was near Sleaford, in Lincolnshire, surrounded by open fields and well away from the temptations of big cities. Trenchard thought the location was ideal, a place where cadets would find life 'cheaper, healthier and more wholesome'[21] and not be tempted to make nocturnal visits to the fleshpots of the capital.

Another Trenchard initiative was the Aircraft Apprentice Scheme, a three-year course to train boys between 15 and 17 as technical ground crew, at RAF Halton, formerly the estate of Alfred Rothschild, near Wendover in Buckinghamshire. The estate had been commandeered during the war and bought on Trenchard's recommendation when Rothschild died in January 1918. Graduates became known as 'Trenchard's Brats' and as many as 40 per cent subsequently won commissions. Six places at Cranwell were reserved for the students who scored top marks in the written and oral examinations, who performed well on the sports field and who were deemed potential 'officer material'.

(In 1926 Wing Commander Robert Barton, an instructor at Halton, made a special plea for one of his apprentices to be awarded a cadetship even though he scored poor marks outside the classroom.

'Having known the boy for three years,' Barton recalled, 'I was aware that he was no good at games and had a poor personality, but at the same time I realised that we had somebody whose brain was streets above any of the other boys and that if he did nothing else he would develop into a most valuable technical officer.' Unfortunately, the Personnel Branch was unimpressed and refused to make an exception for him. Barton had served with Trenchard in the Royal Scots Fusiliers before the war – he was the reluctant subaltern Trenchard had taught to ride at Londonderry – and so his request for a hearing with the great man was approved. He argued so persuasively on behalf of his student that Trenchard overruled the Personnel Branch and agreed that the boy should be given a cadetship. At the same time, he warned Barton that if he was making a mistake he would not be forgiven.[22] Thus it was that 19-year-old Frank Whittle, inventor of the jet engine, entered Cranwell and learned to fly.)

It was evident to Trenchard that he must do everything in his power to shield the RAF from criticism and three weeks before Christmas he sent a 'private and personal' letter to all RAF officers calling for them to work together to improve what he saw as the tarnished image of the new service:

As demobilisation is very nearly finished and the post-war stations have now been decided, it is most desirable and necessary that the Air Force should get a good name in England, and I feel it is up to all officers to do their utmost to improve the tone and its reputation.

It is no good mincing matters, at the present time, the Air Force in England has a very bad name, although it is, I do not doubt, greatly exaggerated, but at the same time, there is a certain amount of truth in it. Complaints are heard on all sides, of transport being used unnecessarily by officers and other ranks. Some men are allowed out all day and do no work. That officers are seen walking about with undesirable women, and also, in some cases that they are taken in to the barracks. That officers are turned out in dirty uniforms and walk about arm in arm in big public thoroughfares with women and others. That officers drink too much in the mess and outside, and drink with sergeants . . .

I know there are great hardships with which officers have to contend. They are uncomfortable and do not know where they are permanently stationed. Their quarters are badly furnished and are in many cases temporary huts, but I feel certain that they will recognise that this is almost unavoidable at present but every effort is being made to get over these difficulties and if they, for their part will help in the way I have indicated, both I and the officers working with me will do our best to help all officers in every sense.

All of you made the reputation of the Force in the field, and I ask you to do your best to get it an equal reputation in peace. I hope all officers will treat this as a personal letter from myself.[23]

Actually the reputation of the RAF, in the eyes of both the people and the government, was soon to get an unexpected boost, courtesy of a despotic Arab religious leader dubbed the 'Mad Mullah' by the British media. Mohammed Abdullah Hassan, the 'Mad Mullah', and his Dervish followers had been waging jihad against British imperialism for more than 20 years in British Somaliland, a protectorate reluctantly administered by the Colonial Office and set up to provide supplies for the nearby British Indian outpost of Aden. The British Army had launched four expensive expeditions to kill or capture him and all had failed.

In 1919 the government was seriously concerned at the continuing state of lawlessness posing a threat to British rule in Somaliland and a meeting was convened at the Colonial Office to discuss sending yet another military expedition. Trenchard was among those present. When the CIGS informed Lord Milner, the Colonial Secretary, that such an expedition would require at least two divisions and would cost several million pounds, Milner turned to Trenchard to ask if he had any suggestions. Trenchard had long visualised imperial policing as an important role for the RAF and he grasped the opportunity to make it happen, proposing that the RAF should take responsibility for the whole operation. The army, he added, would not be needed; local colonial forces in British Somaliland would be quite sufficient. Wilson, predictably, was outraged that this upstart new service should presume to upstage the venerable British Army, with its centuries of experience and tradition.

Nevertheless, a second meeting was arranged with Churchill in the chair and Leo Amery, the Colonial Under-Secretary, deputising for Milner. Wilson remained implacably opposed and at one point protested that he thought he must be the only 'sane person' present. By what right, he asked, did the Colonial Office presume to plan a military expedition independent of the War Office? He predicted the likely outcome – that the operation would be a failure and he would be required to send in troops to rescue the airmen and clean up the mess. But Trenchard stood his ground. By then he had made detailed plans and discussed them with Churchill, who was greatly attracted to the idea of striking at the Mad Mullah and his followers, few of whom had ever seen an aeroplane, from the air. At the meeting Churchill indicated he was in favour, as did Amery. Wilson finally and reluctantly withdrew his objections, having extracted a guarantee from Trenchard that under no circumstances would he ask for troops.

By the beginning of January 1920, a temporary airstrip had been constructed at Berbera in British Somaliland and a squadron of 12 DH9a bombers had arrived from Cairo, secretly shipped in crates from Britain on HMS *Ark Royal*. The pilots entered the country under the guise of being geologists. Their orders were to attack the Mullah's camps and forts, to drive his men into the open and then pursue them at will. They were supported on the ground by the Somaliland Camel Corps, 500 strong, and a battalion of the King's African Rifles from Kenya, but the Air Staff in London was adamant that ground troops should be held back until the first attack.

Finding the Mad Mullah in the vast expanse of the Somali desert proved a challenge and on the first day only one machine located its target. On 21 January the Mad Mullah was said be sitting on the balcony of his fort at Medishe with his uncle and other advisers when an RAF bomber first came into view. Word apparently went round the jihadists that it was a chariot of God coming to escort the Mullah to heaven. They soon discovered differently. The first bomb was said to have killed an amir standing next to the Mullah: the tribesmen and their terrified families ran for shelter in nearby caves. Over the next few days, aircraft bombed and machine-gunned the area, targeting the caves and forts where the tribesmen had taken refuge and scattering their livestock in all directions. When ground troops arrived all the Mullah's principal leaders were killed in the fierce fighting that ensued. In three weeks it was all over. The Mullah escaped with his family to Abyssinia and made an attempt to rebuild his forces but died, ironically of Spanish influenza, later in the year. For the next 20 years Somaliland would enjoy peace and stability.

The Governor of Somaliland praised the RAF as 'the decisive factor' in the victory, adding that the air raids 'exercised an immediate and tremendous moral effect over the Dervishes, who in the ordinary course are good fighting men, demoralising them in the first few days'.[24] Amery was able to report to Parliament that the total cost of the operation, including transport for the King's African Rifles, extra pay for the Camel Corps and fuel for the aircraft, amounted to £77,000, as opposed to the £6 million cost of the last ground-based expedition. It was, he said, 'the cheapest war in history'.

It was, also, the best possible news for the future of the RAF, which by then had been drastically slimmed down to around 3200 officers and 25,000 other ranks. By March more than 23,000 officers, 21,000 cadets and 227,000 other ranks had been demobilised. In line with the very real need to reduce government expenditure, nearly 150 aerodromes had been given up, along with 122 landing grounds, and vast quantities of surplus equipment had been sold off at rock-bottom prices.

'I used to say, in those days,' Trenchard recalled, 'that I was left with nothing but two heaps of rubble, one of bricks and mortar and the other of men, but I hoped I had kept the gems in both heaps.'[25]

16

A FIGHT FOR SURVIVAL

In the early summer of 1920 Trenchard's demeanour changed markedly; there was a spring in his step that had not been there before, he was more ready to smile, less inclined to press all the bells on his desk at once and seemed unusually content with life, despite the increasing burdens of his office. None of his colleagues at the Air Ministry could explain it. The mystery deepened when two senior RAF officers observed their chief outside the Berkeley Grill climbing into a taxi carrying a large bunch of pink carnations. The following day he was seen driving down Piccadilly in an open taxi with an unknown lady and three children holding coloured balloons.

All was made clear by a paragraph at the bottom of page 17 of *The Times*, on 16 June 1920, which announced the engagement of Air Marshal Sir Hugh Trenchard, Bt, Chief of the Air Staff, and Katherine, widow of Captain the Hon. James Boyle, Royal Scots Fusiliers. It was, perhaps, the last news that anyone expected and word spread quickly around Adastral House: two years short of his fiftieth birthday, Boom was in love! Who would believe it?

It happened almost by chance. On a warm summer Sunday several months after he had recovered from the Spanish influenza that had very nearly killed him, he was sitting on a bench in Hyde Park lost in thought, running through all the problems piling up on his desk, when a shadow fell across him and he realised that Kitty Boyle was standing in front of him. She was out for a walk with her children, one of whom had spotted him, and so she had stopped to say hello and ask how he was. He leapt to his feet, apologised and explained he had much on his mind. They stood talking for some time; Trenchard seemed so anxious to unburden himself that Kitty asked him if he would like to join them for lunch at her mother's house in Lowndes Square nearby. Trenchard accepted with alacrity.

The lunch was a success. Trenchard did his best to be a charming and amusing guest and not to be a bore about military matters. Kitty said she would be happy to see him again and he began calling ever more frequently, often with flowers, visits that frequently ended up with the Chief of the Air Staff on all fours on the carpet, playing with her children, who were then aged between seven and ten. He liked the children, liked nothing more than taking them out on shopping expeditions to the toy departments of West End stores. He asked her, once again, if she would marry him and once again she refused, but her affection for her strange friend grew; she recognised there was warmth and humour behind his stiff disposition and when he gathered up his courage to ask for her hand for a third time, she relented. 'He was so pressing and insistent and helpless, the poor darling,' she recalled.

It is likely that Kitty took over most of the arrangements for the wedding, since Trenchard was heavily involved overseeing the first RAF pageant at Hendon Aerodrome, an event he hoped would be an annual showcase for the service as well as a fund-raiser for the RAF Benevolent Fund. (He was inordinately proud of the fact that for the first six years every event at the pageant started precisely on time – not even a minute late.) Pilots had been practising aerobatic stunts, mock dogfights, races and formation flying for weeks, but the success of the event very much hinged on the fickle British weather. A story circulated, perhaps apocryphal, that on the day before the pageant Trenchard summoned the Ministry's chief meteorologist to his office for a weather update. When he revealed he was expecting low cloud, poor visibility and the possibility of thunderstorms, Trenchard frowned and told him it was not good enough; he was to go away and come back with a better prediction. Utterly mystified, he withdrew and returned 30 minutes later with an improved version, offering the possibility of sunny intervals. Trenchard approved.

Actually the day turned out to be reasonably clear and sunny and the pageant was a great success, attracting a huge crowd of some 20,000 awestruck spectators who watched bombers hitting targets in the centre of the airfield with extraordinary precision, unaware that the screech of the bombs was from recordings being broadcast over the tannoy system and technicians were artificially creating the explosions on the ground with pre-laid charges. 'The most thrilling moment of the day,' *The Times* reported, was when Miss Sylvia Boyden, 'a slender, fair-haired girl of 21', leapt from the tail of a Handley Page bomber and parachuted to the ground. Trenchard wandered through the distinguished visitors in the VIP enclosure with his fiancée at his side smiling broadly, particularly when Admiral Beatty congratulated him on an excellent show. His expression only darkened when a formation of three Handley Page bombers flew low directly over the Royal Box, from where young Prince Henry, the future Duke of Gloucester, was watching proceedings with other members of the Royal family.

Afterwards, Trenchard buttonholed Squadron Leader Sholto Douglas,[1] who had flown the leading aircraft.

He demanded to know what the devil I thought I was up to, endangering the lives of our royal guests. What would have happened, he wanted to know, if any one of the three aircraft, taking off as we did in pretty tight formation, had had an engine failure? It was the first and only time that Trenchard ever went for me, and as soon as he started wading into me I knew that he was absolutely right. Had there been an accident through an engine failure – and such failures were common enough in those days – it would have been a disaster of the greatest magnitude. I shuddered when I thought of it.[2]

Two weeks after the pageant, Trenchard married Mrs Katherine Boyle. That he wished for the minimum of fuss was clear from an announcement in *The Times* stating that the wedding would take place at St Margaret's Church, Westminster, on 17 July. 'Friends will be welcome at the church. There will be no reception afterwards.' In fact there was, inevitably, a degree of fuss, since the church was packed with friends and well-wishers and, *The Times* reported, 'a large number of RAF officers'. Mr and Mrs Churchill headed a long list of guests which included, curiously, Major General Sir Frederick Sykes and Lady Sykes.[3] The bride, who was 'unattended', wore a lavender crêpe de Chine dress with a mauve hat and veil and carried a bouquet of pink carnations. Outside the church an RAF Guard of Honour was drawn up and six pipers from the Royal Scots Fusiliers escorted the happy couple to their carriage.

The best man was, of course, Maurice Baring, who Trenchard would later say 'was the greatest personal friend I have ever had'.[4]

*

After the RAF's triumph in Somaliland, Trenchard did not have to look very far for another arena in which the air service could prove itself – Mesopotamia, the 'cradle of civilisation', where a Turkish-led insurgency against the proposed imposition of British authority had broken out earlier that year and where the British Army was sustaining alarming casualties. Trenchard had no doubt that the model of imperial air control that had worked so successfully in Somaliland would also work in the much larger and more politically charged situation in 'Mespot' and he had been given the green light by Churchill to prepare detailed plans. He was helped, immeasurably, by a man who had an unrivalled knowledge of the area – Lieutenant Colonel T.E. Lawrence, whose exploits in the Middle East had won him international fame as 'Lawrence of Arabia'. Lawrence was working as an adviser at the Foreign Office and had several meetings with Trenchard to discuss Mesopotamia.

In November 1920 Trenchard was invited to Cambridge to address the Union on the subject of air power. It was arranged that he would stay with the Duke of York, who had been on his staff at Nancy and who was then a student at Trinity College. He was in bed and asleep when a motorcyclist roared up to the house at two o'clock in the morning and banged on the door. He was delivering a note from Churchill saying the Cabinet was due to make a decision about Mesopotamia that week and asking Trenchard to confirm he was willing to 'take it on'. Trenchard scribbled a reply in the affirmative and managed to resist adding a note asking why it could not have waited until the morning.

At a crucial Cabinet meeting a few days later Lloyd George asked Trenchard to explain why he considered air policing would work when Sir Percy Cox, the newly appointed High Commissioner in Baghdad, made it clear he considered it the worst possible option, an opinion vigorously supported by the CIGS, who predicted, as he had in Somaliland, that it would end in humiliation, disaster and the irreparable tarnishing of British prestige throughout the Middle East.

Trenchard had prepared a detailed strategy showing how RAF squadrons could be deployed, how they could be used to impose peace and how quickly ground forces in Mesopotamia could be brought home – and costs saved. It was an irresistible combination for a government financially drained by a long war and facing the crippling costs of maintaining not only the Empire but the territorial mandates awarded after the end of the war. His proposals were enthusiastically endorsed by Churchill, soon to be appointed Colonial Secretary with special responsibility for the Middle East. At the end of the meeting it was agreed, to Trenchard's great satisfaction, that responsibility for security in the area should be transferred from the army to the Royal Air Force – a remarkable boost to the prestige and influence of the new service that no doubt led to much grinding of teeth in the War Office and the Admiralty. Churchill, too, was elated, since the decision cleared the way for him to put into place his long-term plans to end the British Mandate in Mesopotamia and install Faisal ibn Husayn, a member of the Hashemite dynasty, as king of the newly created kingdom of Iraq.

It was a mark of Churchill's respect for his Chief of Air Staff that he had invited him to become a member of 'The Other Club', despite his (Trenchard's) doubtful qualifications – the criteria for membership being a convivial personality and scintillating conversational skills. 'The Other Club' was a political dining society impudently set up by Churchill and his best friend and fellow Parliamentarian, F.E. Smith, before the war when both were allegedly blackballed from joining The Club, the venerable dining circle founded in 1764 by the artist Joshua Reynolds and the essayist Dr Samuel Johnson. It seemed they were both deemed to be too controversial to be considered. Membership of The Other Club, which met fortnightly in the Pinafore Room at the Savoy Hotel, was strictly by invitation only. The rules of the club were read out at every function, the last of which, added by Churchill, was 'Nothing in the rules or intercourse of the Club shall interfere with the rancour or asperity of party politics.'

It was at a gathering of The Other Club that Churchill first broached the subject of Trenchard attending the conference he was intending to convene in Cairo in March to establish a unified British policy in the Middle East. They were discussing the arrangements for withdrawing ground troops from Mesopotamia when Churchill suddenly said they were talking too much shop and in any case there would be plenty of time to go over everything when they were 'on their way to Cairo'.

Trenchard had suspected that his presence would be required although nothing had been confirmed until that moment. The problem was that he did not want to go. He had just learned he was about to become a father for the first time at the age of 48 and he did not want to leave his pregnant wife alone for the month he assumed he would have to be away. It was a very rare example of him putting personal interests before duty and testimony to how much Kitty meant to him.

He did not tell Churchill the real reason for his reluctance, but offered up a string of reasons why he thought it was a bad idea. As he talked, Churchill's expression grew darker and darker and when at last he spoke he could barely contain his anger. It was utterly ridiculous, he said, that the Chief of the Air Staff could not leave his desk for a few weeks; the conference was vitally important not just for the future of the Middle East but for the future of the RAF, too. He continued in this vein for several minutes, then got to his feet and stalked out, having made it quite clear that, like it or not, Trenchard would be going to Cairo.

They did not talk for several days, then Churchill telephoned out of the blue, strangely oleaginous and solicitous. He had just heard, he said, the very good news about Lady Trenchard and wanted to proffer his congratulations. *Now* he understood why Trenchard was so reluctant to go to Cairo, but he was not to worry because he (Churchill) was not going to let the conference drag on a minute longer than necessary. Afterwards he was going on a tour of the Middle East but Trenchard need not accompany him – he could return home as soon as the conference was finished on the same ship that took them out.

On 1 March 1921 Churchill, Trenchard, Lawrence, now Churchill's adviser on Arabian affairs, and a bevy of civil servants left London by train for Marseilles, where they boarded a French steamship bound for Egypt. Disembarking in Alexandria, they travelled by rail to Cairo, although they were obliged for security reasons to detrain outside the city and drive in through back roads. Trenchard was not pleased. 'I never felt so ashamed in my life,' he recalled, 'as when the British government could not send its Secretary of State by train to the main station in Cairo.'[5]

Delegates – military leaders and civil administrators from throughout the Middle East, jokingly branded by Churchill as 'the forty thieves' – gathered at the luxurious Semiramis Hotel, overlooking the Nile. With Churchill in the chair, the proceedings fairly ripped along. High on the agenda was the question of the British Mandate

Officers of the HQ staff of the Independent Force in France, 1918. Trenchard seated centre, front row.

Pipers escort the happy couple at Trenchard's wedding in July 1920.

Maurice Baring, 'the greatest personal friend I ever had'.

Inspecting graduates at RAF Halton, 1927

Trenchard broke the rules to allow his friend T. E. Lawrence to enlist in the RAF as an aircraftsman.

In the Royal enclosure at Hendon Air Show in 1927. Trenchard in bowler hat and spats, King George V on his right.

Talking to air crew on a visit to France, 1939

In full dress uniform as Colonel of the Royal Scots Fusiliers

On the steps of Scotland Yard on his first day as Commissioner of Metropolitan Police in 1931

(*opposite*) In full dress uniform as Commissioner of Metropolitan Police

Addressing troops on a visit to the Middle East, 1942

With Montgomery in North Africa

Prime Minister Harold Macmillan unveiling Trenchard's statue in Whitehall in July 1961

in Mesopotamia but since a decision to end the Mandate and install Faisal as king had already been taken in London, the discussion was not much more than a formality. Churchill made it clear that the proposal to make the RAF responsible for security in Iraq was not up for discussion. There was, nevertheless, considerable opposition. Both Sir Percy Cox and the GOC Mesopotamia, General Sir Aylmer Haldane, declared the policy to be unworkable and expressed fears that the RAF would not be able to keep control, without army support, in troubled areas like Kurdistan. Wilson, the CIGS, dismissed the plan as 'hot air, aeroplanes and Arabs'.

Trenchard confidently asserted they were wrong, pointing to the RAF's success in Somaliland and emphasising the psychological effect on troublemakers of the appearance, over their heads, of an RAF squadron. When the only female delegate, Gertrude Bell, asked him if his aircraft would drop bombs until their victims surrendered he replied, with a rare flash of dry humour: 'No Madam, we're going to drop bottles of Eno's Salts to sort out their livers.' Even Sir Percy Cox joined in the laughter.

The extraordinary Gertrude Bell, then in her fifties, was an English writer, traveller and archaeologist and friend of T.E. Lawrence who had been recruited by the government as 'Oriental Secretary' to act as liaison with the nascent Arab government in Iraq. Fluent in Arabic and Persian, she had travelled widely throughout the Middle East before the war and established close relationships with many Arab leaders. In 1915 she was assigned to Army Intelligence Headquarters in Cairo for war service and became the only female political officer in the British forces. She would later be memorably described as 'one of the few representatives of His Majesty's Government remembered by the Arabs with anything resembling affection'.[6]

Very early on in the conference, Bell made Trenchard laugh when she asked him how many pencils he was going to need to silence his critics. She had been sitting next to him in the conference hall and noticed that every time he stood up to speak he emphasised what he was saying by stabbing a pencil onto the desk in front of him so hard he broke the point. She then quietly picked it up and sharpened it. At the end of the debate she said: 'How many pencils do you usually get through in a conference, Air Marshal? I've sharpened at least ten.'[7]

Trenchard usually dined at the Semiramis Hotel with Gertrude

Bell and T.E. Lawrence and one evening after dinner Lawrence greatly surprised him by mentioning that he might, one day, like to join 'this air force of yours'.

Trenchard did not take him too seriously. Lawrence was 33 years old, already a lieutenant colonel and a national hero. He was an unlikely recruit to the RAF, but nevertheless Trenchard said he would be glad to have him.

'Even as an ordinary ranker?' Lawrence asked.

Trenchard was aghast. 'No, certainly not,' he said. 'As an officer or nothing.'

Lawrence smiled enigmatically and said no more.

Churchill was as good as his word about the brevity of the event: as far as Trenchard was concerned it was all over in nine days. (Churchill even found time while he was in Cairo to paint and to work on the manuscript of *The World Crisis*, his magnum opus on the Great War.) Before the conference ended Churchill, Trenchard, Lawrence, Gertrude Bell and a number of other delegates rode out on camels to the Pyramids to be photographed for posterity lined up in front of the Sphinx. Churchill managed to fall off his camel but insisted on remounting with something less than elegance, while his fellow riders tried not to laugh.

Trenchard returned to Britain to find the press deeply unenthusiastic about the newly created kingdom of Iraq and the notion of it being policed from the air by a puny and relatively untried RAF. There were many predictions of disaster and ignominy in store and serious doubts cast on the government's claim that £10 million could be saved by replacing the garrison with eight RAF squadrons supported by local levies. Trenchard was unconcerned and sent a note to Churchill assuring him that 'the risk that I said was a reasonable risk is not too great and whatever our relations may be in the future, I hope you will feel that anyhow I have not let you down'.[8]

The practicalities of the handover were made doubly difficult by obstruction from the War Office, which was disinclined to cooperate at any level since the CIGS remained implacably opposed to the new service and loud in his criticism of it. 'The sooner the Air Force crashes the better,' he noted in his diary on 7 May. 'It is a wicked waste of money as run at present.[9] When the War Office refused to supply Trenchard with armoured cars needed for security duties and routine ground patrolling in Iraq, he solved the problem in classic Trenchardian fashion – he simply ordered RAF workshops in England and Egypt to make them. By armour-plating suitable vehicles, the RAF soon had its own armoured cars driven by airmen, as Wilson also refused to provide troops for the task.

In April Churchill surrendered the air portfolio to his cousin, Freddie Guest, the Government Chief Whip, and the Air Ministry reverted to its previous separate status. Trenchard welcomed his new political boss, not just because he was an amateur pilot but because he was also a well-known polo player (he would win a bronze medal with the British polo team in the 1924 Olympics in Paris). *The Times* was not complimentary about Churchill's tenure: 'Gold braid and metal polish, acres of cantonments, establishments aping the Army, those are the fruits of his well-meaning and laborious, but wholly inadequate rule at the Air Ministry.' The criticism would have been more fairly aimed at Trenchard, who was so determined to divert much of the Ministry's budget into setting up ground establishments that the RAF was lampooned in the media as the 'Royal Ground Force'.

Regardless of political changes, the Chief of the Air Staff remained very much a law unto himself. Apart from the eight squadrons assigned to Iraq, there were further squadrons deployed in Egypt, Palestine, India and Ireland. When he wanted to increase the air strength in Egypt by sending an additional squadron to the Canal Zone he asked the Foreign Office if there would be any political objections. Sir William Tyrell, the Permanent Under-Secretary, replied that it would be quite impossible to approach the Egyptian government with such a proposition at that particular moment, whereupon Trenchard was obliged to confess that he had already moved the squadron there, albeit by way of an apology, 'in a small way and on a very low basis'.[10]

With the 12-month truce negotiated by Trenchard in December 1919 long over, hostilities between the three service chiefs had resumed and were inflamed when Trenchard circulated a contentious paper arguing that the Air Ministry should assume responsibility for the strategic defence of Britain since the main threat to national security was posed

not from a landing on these islands but from repeated incursions on a large scale by hostile aircraft . . . Unless we can put up an adequate defence we must be prepared for a dislocation of national life to a degree unthought of in the past . . . The navy and the army cannot materially assist us to face this attack and no improvements in guns or other defences will ensure our security . . . [therefore] responsibility should be assumed by the Air Ministry.[11]

Inevitably, the CIGS and the First Sea Lord had rather different views and were outraged by the notion that the army and the navy would be obliged to play subsidiary roles to this arriviste new service. The issue was hotly debated in the Committee of Imperial Defence, which had been set up 1902 by former prime minister Arthur Balfour to create a strategic vision defining the roles of the services. Ironically, it was to Balfour, by then an elder statesman, that the committee turned in 1921 to try and reconcile the bitter differences between the services on the question of national defence. After two months listening to testimony from all three sides, Balfour came down firmly in favour of an autonomous air service taking the lead role in the event of air raids on Britain. 'I am convinced,' he concluded, 'that any attempt to reduce the new force to an inferior position will seriously hamper its vigorous development and may put us at a serious disadvantage . . .'[12]

Trenchard could not have been more pleased but it was not, by a long chalk, the end of the argument. The survival of the RAF would be the subject of two more government reviews in the next two years, both of which found in favour of the continued existence of an independent air force, despite unrelenting antagonism from the other two services.

On 6 June 1921, to Trenchard's huge delight, Kitty gave birth to a son, whom they named Hugh. Soon afterwards, the family moved from London to Dancers Hill House, an ivy-covered Palladian villa with eight bedrooms standing in its own grounds near South Mimms, Hertfordshire, which was available on a long lease and would be their home for years to come. (Another son, Thomas, was born in December 1923. Kitty was pregnant again two years later, but lost the baby and was very ill for several weeks, to the undisguised consternation of her husband.)

Friends and colleagues who visited Trenchard at Dancers Hill House were often astonished by the transformation of the Chief of the Air Staff into a genial host, loving husband and affectionate father and stepfather, a man quite different from the austere, demanding, overbearing figure to be found at the Air Ministry. Kitty loved entertaining and the annual garden party at Dancers Hill, to which all the neighbours were invited, was the social event of the year in the village.

Trenchard took his role as a parent very seriously. Despite the burden of his official duties, he found time to teach all the children to ride and hunt, play hockey and tennis. (He still occasionally played polo before breakfast with Churchill and others at the Hurlingham Club.) When Hugh junior was two years old he was struck by a mysterious illness which was obviously causing him great pain. Trenchard spent hours pacing the nursery at night, cradling the boy in his arms to try and soothe him. Eventually mastoiditis was diagnosed; an emergency operation was carried out at Dancers Hill and Hugh quickly recovered. Kitty later told friends she had never seen her husband so nervous as when he was waiting outside the room while his son was being operated on.

In the spirit of post-war austerity Trenchard often eschewed the use of his official car and cycled to Potters Bar railway station with a bulging briefcase balanced on the handlebars. Kitty always waved him goodbye and watched anxiously as he wobbled down the drive at Dancers Hill House, never entirely convinced he was in complete control. He would frequently return at the end of the day accompanied by a member of Air Ministry staff and they would work late into the night, sustained by a whisky and soda. Other nights Kitty would act as his unofficial secretary and take dictation after the children had gone to bed.

Early news from Iraq seemed to confirm all the worst fears of those critics who claimed that indiscriminate bombing would result in heavy civilian casualties and provoke the Arab tribes they were intended to pacify. The first operational report submitted by Group Captain Amyas 'Biffy' Borton,[13] the interim commander in Baghdad, described how three raids on turbulent areas had produced good results on the ground, but then went on to offer an example of the 'vivid if rather ferocious glimpse of the type of warfare we have to wage' near Nasiriyah: 'The eight machines broke formation and attacked at different points of the encampment, simultaneously causing a stampede among the animals. The tribesmen and their families were put to confusion, many of whom ran into the lake, making good targets for the machine-guns.'

Churchill was horrified when he read the report and fired off an angry minute to Trenchard:

> I am extremely shocked at the reference to bombing which I have marked in red. If it were to be published it would be regarded as most dishonouring to the air force and prejudicial to our work . . . To fire wilfully on women and children is a disgraceful act, and I am surprised you do not order the officers responsible for it to be tried by court-martial . . . By doing such things we put ourselves on the lowest level. Combatants are fair game and sometimes non-combatants get injured through their proximity to the fighting troops, but this seems to be quite a different matter.[14]

Trenchard did not require the pilots to be court-martialled. An inquiry revealed that political interference was responsible – an overenthusiastic district administrator, a civilian completely unaware of the capacity of air power, had ordered that an example be made of the encampment at Nasiriyah, which had been particularly troublesome. Determined that it should not happen again, Trenchard reiterated his instructions for Iraq – that leaflet warnings were to be dropped in advance of any attack and that villages were to be given 24 hours' notice of an impending bombing raid to give their inhabitants time to evacuate their homes, although the appearance of aircraft carrying out the leaflet drop was often sufficiently alarming to persuade tribesmen to cease hostilities.

In November 1921, Field Marshal Henry Wilson, soon to retire after nearly four years as CIGS, had a final intemperate dig at the RAF. According to a report in the *Daily Telegraph*, he used the opportunity of a speech at the unveiling of a memorial to the men of the Ulster Division at Thiepval in the Somme to ruminate on how the nature of war had changed during the course of 1914–18. Towards the end, he said, it had become a war of men and aeroplanes, of bombs and gas directed against women and children. The aeroplane seemed to him to be nothing more nor less than an invention for killing women and children, and suggested there was an urgent need to ponder on the further development of air forces which as far as he could see meant explosive bombing and gas bombing of towns – something to be greatly discouraged.

Wilson's remarks infuriated Trenchard. He immediately sent a note to Freddie Guest complaining about Wilson's 'consistent and implacable animosity' towards the air service.

> He has left no stone unturned to disparage this service both openly and under the veil of humour which, in my opinion, is usually apt to pass the bounds of good taste . . . This speech is, however, only a phase of Sir Henry Wilson's protracted campaign against the RAF, a campaign in which he is prepared to use any and every weapon upon which he can lay hands and I therefore feel that I cannot let it pass without an emphatic protest.

He warned of 'disastrous consequences' of the professional head of one fighting service being considered free to 'state to the world at large' his dissent from the recommendations of another. 'How much easier our task would have been, and would be in the future,' he concluded, 'if the older services had always said "How can we help you?" instead of saying "How can we destroy you?"'

He then fired off an angry letter to Wilson from the Air Ministry:

> I do not wish you to think I am attacking you behind your back so I write this to tell you that I am asking my secretary of state to circulate to the Cabinet a statement on this speech and on your habitual general attitude towards the air service. It is impossible for me to sit still under these perpetual attacks inspired – and, as it seems to me, virtually led by you – to which considerations of dignity and good taste forbid me publicly to reply.

An insouciant Wilson protested his innocence and claimed to have been misreported. 'I am very distressed to think that you took the Daily Telegraph report as "gospel" . . .' he replied. 'I hope you will believe me when I say that until I read your letter this morning I had not dreamt that my remarks could be twisted by any friend or enemy into an attack on the air ministry.'[15]

Trenchard had little alternative but to say he was 'satisfied', even if he was not. In any case, Wilson would soon cease to be a thorn in his side. He resigned from the army in February 1922, was elected a Member of Parliament for North Down and was assassinated on the doorstep of his home in Eaton Square by two IRA gunmen on 22 June. He was in full uniform, having just returned from the unveiling of a war memorial at Liverpool Street station. Some accounts claimed that when the first shot missed, Wilson charged his attackers with his sword drawn.

By the end of 1921 it was clear that the strategy in Iraq was beginning to pay dividends. Faisal had been crowned and the kingdom was relatively peaceful – both Sir Percy Cox and General Haldane, who had argued against the policy at the Cairo conference, were now said to be converted. Air Commodore Brooke-Popham, on a visit to the country, was reminded of Wilson's contemptuous description of the RAF as a force 'coming from God knows where, dropping its bombs on God knows what, and going off God knows where'. 'You remember Henry Wilson's remarks at the Staff College,' Brooke-Popham wrote to Trenchard. 'Well, that exactly expressed the reason for the immense morale effect that aeroplanes are having in Mespot. The Arabs feel utterly impotent against them. In fact, H.W. all unwittingly paid the R.A.F. the best compliment he could . . .'[16]

The deployment of the RAF in Iraq also enabled an air bridge to be established between Cairo and Baghdad for the carriage of official passengers and mail and for switching squadrons from the Nile Valley to Iraq and from there, via the Persian Gulf, to India. To help pilots navigate across vast tracts of desert wilderness furrows were ploughed in the sand and marked by empty fuel cans painted white. Considerable dangers awaited pilots who got lost or were forced down by mechanical problems. Air Vice Marshal Geoffrey Salmond, John Salmond's brother and the Air Officer Commanding in Cairo, reported that two pilots who had crash-landed in the desert in the north of Iraq had both had their throats slit by hostile tribesmen, and he asked Trenchard if pilots should perhaps carry cards printed in Arabic and offering handsome rewards for their safe-keeping.

Trenchard did not think it was a good idea.

> To my mind [he replied], this is contrary to all British ideas of warfare. At one moment a man is dropping bombs and trying to kill the enemy, the next he has to come down and land – and then asks

his enemy not to shoot him. It reminds me of the Boer in South Africa who shot at my servant. My man was going at him with a bayonet, and the Boer opened fire at over 500 yards and missed him every time until the bayonet came within five yards of his throat. Then he dropped his rifle and put up his hands. But he did not insult us by offering us five pounds to let him off . . .'[17]

On 5 January 1922 an anonymous article appeared in the *Pall Mall Gazette & Globe* – a London evening newspaper and forerunner of the *Evening Standard* – attacking the RAF under the unequivocal headline 'CHAOS IN THE AIR FORCE' and quoting as its source an unnamed 'distinguished officer'. Trenchard immediately suspected Admiralty skulduggery and while trying to track down the source of the article learned that confidential RAF memoranda had been handed to Vice Admiral Sir Roger Keyes, the Deputy Chief of Naval Staff. Keyes was something of a war hero, having planned and led the daring raid on the German submarine pens at Zeebrugge in April 1918, which resulted in the awarding of eight Victoria Crosses. He was also, by curious happenstance, Trenchard's brother-in-law, having married Kitty's sister, Eva, in 1906. Despite their family connection, they were firmly on opposite sides of the fence with regard to air power: Keyes fervently believed that naval aviation should be under the control of the Royal Navy; Trenchard, just as fervently, did not. The tension between them made family life difficult, for a time.

When Trenchard angrily confronted his brother-in-law about the confidential documents, Keyes airily admitted he had received some 'typewritten sheets' but claimed he had no idea they were confidential. He had locked them in a drawer, unread, and then had burned them as he had no desire to become 'mixed up in any way' with RAF domestic matters. 'It did not occur to me,' he wrote to Trenchard after their fraught meeting, 'that in the happy event of our regaining control over the very small air force which we consider essential for the efficiency of the fleet, there might be something of value in them.'

Keyes hinted that perhaps Trenchard was being a little 'over-sensitive' to public criticism. Trenchard could not agree. Other newspapers soon picked up and embellished the *Pall Mall Gazette* story and the *Gazette* itself followed up with an article in which Rear Admiral Sir Reginald 'Blinker' Hall (he had a severe facial tic), the former Director of Naval Intelligence and now a Conservative Member of Parliament, claimed the Admiralty was 'seriously concerned' about the RAF's efficiency – so concerned, in fact, that it was considered imperative to reinstate the Naval Air Service as a separate force.

It was not long before rumours were circulating, to Trenchard's great alarm, in Whitehall, Fleet Street and London clubs, that the government was intending to break up the air force. Churchill soon heard about them and stepped in, writing to Austen Chamberlain, the Lord Privy Seal, with copies to Lloyd George and Trenchard, reminding him that since the RAF was constituted by an Act of Parliament, its status could only be changed by further legislation and thus it was wrong, and very damaging, for its future to be considered as an open question. To protect the RAF's reputation and curb undesirable interservice rivalry Churchill urged the Lord Privy Seal to make an unequivocal statement in the House to the effect that government policy was embodied in the Air Force Act which the government had no intention of repealing at the present time. At a Cabinet meeting two days later, he again pressed for such a statement and obtained the assent of the prime minister.

On the evening of 16 March, with Trenchard sitting anxiously in the Strangers' Gallery, Chamberlain rose to his feet in the Commons to speak during a debate on a motion put down by Admiral Hall that 'the Naval Air Service should be put under the control of the Board of Admiralty'. What he had to say stunned all those present who had been listening to the rumours. 'If the matters raised by my honourable and gallant friends related solely to the navy,' he began, 'I should not have thought it necessary to intervene.' Unfortunately, he continued, theirs was a 'rather narrow point of view' which he thought should be broadened to cover the position of the government as a whole.

The reasons which led to the birth of the Royal Air Force still held, he said.

I do not want it to be thought that the Government is blind to the real difficulties which arise out of the present system. I do not pretend for one moment that it works with perfect harmony. But our view is that the objections to the reabsorption of the air force by the army and navy are far greater than any objections which can be raised against the existence of a separate Air Ministry and Staff

. . . We consider that it would be a retrograde step at this time to abolish the Air Ministry and to reabsorb the air service into the Admiralty and the War Office . . .[18]

Trenchard caught a train back to Dancers Hill that night with a light heart. A month later he attended the opening of the RAF Staff College at Andover – another important underpinning of the service. Designed to provide specialised training for promising flight lieutenants and squadron leaders to prepare them for staff duties at the Air Ministry or command headquarters, Trenchard described the College, rather maladroitly, as 'the cradle of our brain'. He installed Brooke-Popham as the commandant and in a speech to the first course of students offered some heartfelt advice about working with the other services, weighing the balance between cost and efficiency and keeping a sense of proportion about casualties. 'Acquire the habit of clearly and concisely stating a case,' he concluded, confessing with a smile that it was a habit he was himself 'still struggling to acquire'.

It was no less than the truth. It was not unusual for officers to gather outside his office on the sixth floor at Adastral House after a briefing to try and figure out exactly what it was he wanted them to do. It could be a frustrating process.

He was not by any means a clear thinker [John Slessor, then a young staff officer at the Air Ministry, recalled]. His racing brain was always a length or two ahead of his hesitant tongue. He'd send for you and talk away and you'd go off and produce the paper you thought he wanted and bring it back next morning and by the evening you'd be sent for again and be told it was a very bad paper and that you hadn't understood him at all. And there would be your paper covered in Boom's writing, which was more or less illegible. You'd be told to go away and produce another one. Eventually you got more or less the right answer.

I remember once when he had to make a speech to a cabinet sub-committee on a subject about which he felt deeply and I and a colleague on his staff expended blood, sweat, toil and tears producing version after version of this oration on Boom's instructions. At last the great day came and when it was over I rang Pug Ismay,[19] who had been a student at the Staff College with us and was then

one of his assistant secretaries at the Committee of Imperial Defence. 'Well,' I said, 'how did it go?' 'All right', said Pug. 'No one
really understood what he was saying but somehow or the other, as
usual, he got it across.'

He had a wonderful capacity for getting people's names mixed
up. I was never sure whether I was going to be addressed as
Slessor or Leigh-Mallory or Collier; one had to be ready for anything. He was a man of strong views – almost violently so sometimes.
Many people did not always agree with him – I did not always
– but everyone recognised and admired his sincerity and single-
mindedness. He was incapable of a petty thought and however
much one might disagree with him, one could not help loving and
respecting him.[20]

Slessor often used to ghost-write Trenchard's speeches, articles and letters to the press. He was one of an exceptional group of devoted young
disciples working with Trenchard in the 1920s who would all go on to
become air marshals. They included the Salmond brothers, Jack and
Geoffrey, Hugh 'Stuffy' Dowding, Sholto Douglas, Arthur 'Bomber'
Harris, Philip Game, Charles Portal and Ralph Cochrane, commander of the 'Dam Busters' raid – a veritable roll of honour and proof of
Trenchard's extraordinary ability to inspire loyalty and nurture talent.

Another great admirer was Christopher Bullock, a former RFC pilot
who had been appointed principal private secretary to the Secretary of
State for Air in 1919, remained in that post for ten years and worked
very closely with Trenchard, whose office was just across the corridor
in Adastral House. 'Of course he had his failings, for he was intensely
human,' Bullock recalled. 'He had moods and could be intolerant and
obstinate – on occasion almost child-like in his obstinacy. But, sooner
or later, he would admit – sometimes grumblingly admit – when he
was wrong. Personally as I grew to know him better, I found these
little weaknesses endearing – without them he would have been too
good to be true.'

Bullock briefed Trenchard before he was due to appear before
the committee headed by Sir Eric Geddes, who had been appointed
by the prime minister to identify where economies could be made
in government departments. On the evening before his appearance,
Trenchard invited Bullock into his office and asked him to play the

part of Geddes and test him with the kind of questions he might expect in the morning.

I sat down in his chair and he stood in front of me. 'Sir Hugh,' I said solemnly, 'as chairman of this committee I must ask you a few questions.' I am afraid an imp of mischief entered my head and I asked him half a dozen teasers which I thought he probably could not answer and so it proved. There came a series of 'I don't knows' in an increasingly sulky voice whilst he strode about the room swinging his key chain – a mannerism of his. His brow grew blacker and blacker and I thought I was – and I should have deserved it – in for a real thunderstorm. But finally he broke into a roar of laughter and with a broad grin said something like 'All right young man, you can go, but see that clear and full answers to those questions are typed and ready on my desk by 9.30 tomorrow morning.' As it was then after seven o'clock I was up until after midnight and had to be in early the next day. He had the last laugh.[21]

In the event, the notorious 'Geddes Axe' did not fall on the RAF. Trenchard must have delivered a bravura performance before the committee, since Geddes professed himself to be impressed by the RAF's economical administration and accepted Trenchard's contention that the service provided good value for money and was vital to the long-term strategic defence of the United Kingdom. Not only that, but he could foresee 'economies to an increasing extent ought to result from the advent of the air force . . . not only by the substitution of aircraft for certain other arms of the older services, such as light cruisers and cavalry, but by a revolution in the method of carrying out certain operations'.

Trenchard himself could not have put it better. No one had any doubt that it was the Chief of the Air Staff who had saved the day. 'Without his conviction and strength of character,' one of his staff officers observed, 'the Air Force would probably not have survived.'[22]

BUILDING AN AIR FORCE

Shortly before the RAF Staff College opened, *The Times* published a series of articles revealing an extraordinary rise in the strength of the French air force. It was an unpleasant shock to the British public, conditioned by harsh economic reality to accept drastically pared-down defence forces. The French air force had grown in size to no less than 123 squadrons with 1090 aircraft – nearly ten times the size of the Royal Air Force – and there were plans to expand to 220 squadrons with more than 2000 aircraft. Twenty of the RAF's 28 squadrons were stationed overseas and only two fighter squadrons were deployed to defend the British Isles.

No one seriously expected an attack from France – Britain and the French had not fought since Waterloo – yet there remained a lingering sentiment that France was Britain's traditional enemy, despite having fought side by side in the trenches. There was talk about 'putting temptation in the way of French statesmen that they would find hard to resist'[1] and a doom-laden RAF study calculated that if just half the French air force attacked London it could deliver 100 tons of bombs in the first 24 hours and 40,000 casualties could be expected in the first week.

It was, then, hardly surprising that the government, mesmerised by what the French air force could do, began reviewing existing plans for the air defence of the British Isles and quickly concluded they were woefully inadequate. Trenchard came in for criticism for spending too much on bricks and mortar and not enough on front-line aircraft, but he remained unbothered and recognised that the so-called French threat could only be good news for the RAF. When he was asked to submit proposals for upgrading home defence, he cannily resisted demanding too much and suggested increasing the number of home defence squadrons to 20, with reserves to expand to 50 if required. He

proposed that the bulk of the force should comprise bombers in line
with his strategy that any attack on Britain would be met with a continuous and hopefully devastating counter-offensive.

> There is a big agitation on here [he wrote to Borton in Iraq in July
> 1922], the real object of which is a trifle obscure but the ostensible
> object of which is to increase the existing air force by a good num-
> ber of squadrons. Of course, everybody who has an axe to grind
> is taking part in it with a view to furthering their own ends – the
> armament firms, the Admiralty (very active), the Press, and various
> retired admirals, field marshals, etc . . . The army say they would
> sooner have the Air to deal with than the Admiralty which, al-
> though it may be a left-handed compliment, is undoubtedly true
> . . . There is now no question of breaking up the force.[2]

On 3 August, the day before Parliament rose for the summer recess,
Lloyd George announced that the government had sanctioned Air
Ministry plans for an expanded air force of 14 bomber and 9 fighter
squadrons – some 500 machines – at an increased cost of £2 million
per annum. There was an immediate howl of protest from the press,
particularly Northcliffe's papers, *The Times* and the *Daily Mail*, which
launched vituperative attacks on the Air Ministry for squandering
public money.

'Among other mares' nests,' Trenchard wrote cheerfully to a friend,
'the Northcliffe Press have found they want to get rid of me. I don't
mind, for I'm having quite good fun and the air force is becoming
stronger and stronger and doing more and more work.'

Trenchard left with his family for their annual shooting holiday in
Scotland at the end of August, but was urgently recalled to London
in mid-September when the so-called Chanak Incident raised the unwelcome prospect of Britain being drawn into a war with Turkey. The
Turkish army under Mustafa Kemal Atatürk, fresh from defeating
Greek forces and recapturing Smyrna, was advancing on Constan-
tinople in the Dardanelles neutral zone and threatening to attack
British and French troops stationed at Chanak. Ineptitude and muddle characterised the British response.

Trenchard arrived back in London on an overnight train from Glasgow on 15 September and went straight to a Cabinet meeting at which

it was decided that Chanak must be held. Trenchard promised to have three squadrons – two at home and a third in Egypt – ready to move within 24 hours. On the following day Lloyd George approved the issue of a communiqué threatening Turkey with a declaration of war by Britain and the Dominions.

Churchill, presiding over daily briefings with the chiefs of staff, was in the habit of calling meetings at any hour of the day or night to discuss the latest cables from Chanak. Trenchard was thus not surprised, but not best pleased, to get a telephone call at one o'clock in the morning, after he had gone to bed, summoning him immediately to Downing Street. There was no time to call his official car and, rather oddly, he had never acquired a driving licence, so Kitty offered to take him in her 'Tin Lizzie' – Model T Ford. She put a leather coat over her nightdress, left her hair in a long pigtail and set off for Downing Street with her husband in the passenger seat.

> It was a fine night. Hugh was very worried about what to do with me. I said nothing, I would sit in the car. He kept trying to make me go and sit by the fire with the other secretaries. I resisted, but finally I had to. After about three hours the meeting came out. Winston saw me and said: 'Lady Trenchard. What are you doing here?' I said 'You might ask. Why are you all here at this hour? Is it war or are you only keeping hard working men who get up early out of their beds, not to mention their wives?' Winston turned to Hugh and said 'Boom, she is attacking me.'[3]

The Chanak Incident fizzled out in early October when, two hours before the reinforced British positions were ordered to open fire, the Turks suddenly agreed a truce. There was widespread relief at home, but widespread dissatisfaction with the government's handling of the crisis. On 19 October a meeting of Conservative MPs at the Carlton Club voted to end the coalition, forcing Lloyd George to resign. He was replaced by Andrew Bonar Law, a development Trenchard viewed with deep misgivings since the new prime minister's son-in-law was none other than Frederick Sykes, who was by then a Conservative MP and who had married Isabel Harrington Law, the elder daughter of the new prime minister, in 1920. If, as he suspected would happen, Bonar Law consulted his son-in-law on matters of future air policy, he was virtually certain that the advice the prime minister received was hardly likely to redound to his benefit, or necessarily accord with his own views. He was absolutely correct: Sykes, who had once been a prominent supporter of an independent air force, now advised the prime minister that the RAF was an expensive luxury that should be abolished. (There was no doubting that the mutual antagonism each felt for the other was still extant. A book written by Sykes, *Aviation in Peace and War*, was published that year and contained not a single reference to Trenchard.)

Trenchard would have been even more worried had he been present when Bonar Law asked Sir Samuel Hoare, one of the leaders of the Conservative revolt against Lloyd George, to take over as Secretary of State for Air. Law made it clear that he was considering abolishing the air force and going back to the old system of navy and army control of aviation.

'I shall therefore expect you,' he said, 'if you take the post, to remember that it may very soon cease to exist.' Hoare frankly admitted it was not a very enticing offer, but it was his first ministerial post and so he 'eagerly accepted it'.[4]

He met Trenchard at Adastral House the following day, immediately after receiving his seal of office from the King at Buckingham Palace. He knew nothing about the Chief of the Air Staff except his 'reputation for great obstinacy', but it seemed he was not so much impressed by their first meeting as awestruck.

I saw at once that he was one of those men whose presence cannot be ignored, whatever be the company in which they find themselves. Very tall, broad-shouldered, with shaggy eyebrows and a deep voice . . . here was a man massive and majestic in body as well as mind. So big a man might have been mentally slow and stolid. Not so, the first Chief of the Air Staff, whose clear deep-set blue eyes were the eyes of a seer of vision, and whose words were the explosions of heaped up thoughts that took time and fermentation to break out. He was clearly a man with a mission, a fanatic according to his critics, a crusader according to his friends . . .

In his mind there was none of the doubts that Bonar Law had expressed about the continued existence of the Air Force. The very suggestion of dividing the service between the Navy and the Army

was, in his eyes, a sin against the light . . . Trenchard's words discovered for me a new world. Not a better or happier world, as he
himself admitted. For he said in so many words that the invention
of flying was a calamity for the human race. Once invented, however, it was futile to mope about it. The need was to use it to the fullest
possible degree for our own purposes. If we did so, we could make
it the predominant deterrent against future wars, provided that we
did not blunt the edge of this new power by the unskilful hands of
those who did not believe in it . . .

I listened enthralled to his words and as I afterwards reflected
upon them, I suddenly realised that I might after all have come to
the Air Ministry not to wind it up, as Bonar Law had suggested,
but to help establish it upon an equality with the Admiralty and
the War Office, and to create a peacetime Air Force as a united and
independent service in no way inferior to the Navy and Army. Each
day that followed confirmed this feeling.[5]

Hoare described Trenchard as 'the first really great man that I had ever
met in my life' and confessed that he viewed him as 'a prophet' and
that his (Hoare's) mission thereafter was 'to be the prophet's interpreter to a world that did not always understand his dark sayings'. (A not
inappropriate metaphor – Christopher Bullock once drily observed
that Trenchard's utterances 'often had all the obscurity of the more
difficult of the Old Testament prophets'.)

Trenchard could hardly have hoped, even in his wildest dreams,
for a more supportive Secretary of State. 'I think he will be a tower
of strength,' he noted, 'when he understands all the difficulties of
the subject.'[6] Hoare remained at the Air Ministry, his admiration for
Trenchard undiminished, for the next seven years, apart from during Ramsay MacDonald's short-lived Labour administration in 1924,
when he was replaced by Brigadier Christopher Thomson, a man
whose political views were anathema to the Chief of the Air Staff.
Thomson was not an MP and had to be elevated to the peerage. He
thought it would be a compliment to the service if he took the name
of an RAF station in his title and sent a list of stations to Trenchard,
asking him to tick those he thought most suitable. Trenchard ticked
Fowlmere and Cattewater.[7]

Nine days after meeting Trenchard for the first time, Hoare, presumably inspired by the Chief of the Air Staff's vision and passion, successfully argued at a full meeting of the Committee of Imperial Defence that it would be prudent to set up an impartial inquiry before an irrevocable decision was taken to scrap the RAF by decree. Later that evening he revealed to Trenchard that he had known from the start that the prime minister was intent on eliminating the air force. Trenchard was appalled, both by the information and the fact that Hoare had not told him earlier. Lord Salisbury was appointed to chair a sub-committee of the Committee of Imperial Defence to examine the state of Britain's air service. It was to drag on for months, with the Admiralty and the Air Ministry deeply entrenched in unyielding positions and neither giving ground.

On 20 February the First Sea Lord ran out of patience and warned the prime minister that he was ready to resign immediately unless naval aviation was returned to the control of the Royal Navy. Some cynics suggested that Beatty had been motivated by a leader in *The Times* the previous day hailing the first victory of the RAF over the Royal Navy in a rugby match at Twickenham, at the weekend, as a 'bright omen for the future of the youngest of the fighting services'.

Trenchard's response to Beatty's ultimatum was to threaten to resign himself if such a thing happened, prompting Bonar Law to remark, not without some justification, that Trenchard was such an expert in resigning that he would be grateful for his advice when his turn to resign came. (It came much sooner than he knew – on 22 May it was announced that the prime minister had been obliged to resign because of ill health. He was replaced by Stanley Baldwin.) In the event neither resigned: Beatty was mollified by the setting up of another sub-committee specifically to examine naval–air co-operation.

Giving evidence to the Salisbury committee, Trenchard took the opportunity to lay into the Admiralty. 'I would ask the Committee to bear in mind,' he said, 'the conditions under which the Air Ministry has had to work during the past four and a half years, and during much of that time the Admiralty has taken every opportunity of attacking us. We have had continuous attacks, not only against the principle of the existence of the Air Ministry, but by the publicly expressed attitude of senior naval officers . . .' He went on to accuse the Admiralty of publishing pamphlets asserting the Air Staff was drawing alarmist pictures of the possibility of air attack. 'It makes me bitter,' he concluded, 'to think of the criticisms that have been levelled at us by officers who have never yet been in the air.'[8]

Trenchard had a brief respite from the political infighting that now formed part of his life when he and his wife were among the guests at the wedding of Prince Albert, the Duke of York, to Lady Elizabeth Bowes-Lyon (later the Queen Mother) at Westminster Abbey on 26 April. In a break with tradition the ceremony was held in the Abbey, rather than a Royal chapel, to bolster the spirits of the nation after the Great War. To Trenchard's great pleasure, the Prince wore the full dress uniform of an RAF group captain, his senior rank at the time, and the new Duchess of York made her first appearance as a member of the Royal Family at the RAF pageant at Hendon in June – another feather in the RAF's hat.

That same month Lord Salisbury's committee found no case for a separate naval air service and recommended a further expansion of the Home Defence force to 52 squadrons by 1928 (trebling the size of the RAF), and the tedious resignation tit-for-tat resumed. The entire Board of the Admiralty threatened to resign en masse if the committee's recommendations were approved and Hoare threatened to resign if they were not. Trenchard's reaction to possible Admiralty resignations was typical: 'Let them. Good riddance.' In the end no one resigned and the government accepted Salisbury's proposals with Baldwin telling the House that the air force needed to be 'of sufficient strength adequately to protect us against air attack by the strongest air force within striking distance of this country'.[9] The Admiralty secured a number of minor concessions and was led to believe that the committee's conclusions were not necessarily a final decision, thus storing up trouble for the future.

You must be pleased that the great naval battle is over and very proud of the result [Philip Game, then AOC India and a family friend, wrote to Kitty]. The more I think of what he [Trenchard] has done in the last few years, the more I am completely overcome with astonishment. With anyone else as Chief of the Air Staff, the air force would have broken up long ago. He, on the contrary, entirely by his own efforts, has trebled it, secured its position, and induced the Government to do what no Government has dared do for a century – make a stand against the Navy.[10]

Another of the recommendations of the Salisbury report was that the chiefs of staff should form a permanent sub-committee of the Committee of Imperial Defence. Trenchard was pleased because it gave him equal status to that of the CIGS and the First Sea Lord. Salisbury's hope was that regular face to face meetings would reduce interservice tensions and generate a new spirit of professionalism and co-operation. It was a forlorn hope: the feuding continued more or less unabated, particularly between the air force and the navy. 'The only place the navy was prepared to bury the hatchet,' one historian noted, 'was in Trenchard's back.'[11]

Trenchard dominated subsequent meetings at the Air Ministry to decide the composition of the expanded force, pressing his doctrine that air power was most effective when used aggressively. When Charles Portal, a future Chief of the Air Staff but then a lowly squadron leader, suggested that efforts should be made to ascertain the correct proportion of bombers to fighter aircraft, Trenchard insisted there was no such thing as a 'correct proportion' – the best option was to have as many bombers as possible. His view was that in a 'bombing duel' the French would 'probably squeal before we did' and that the nation which could stand being bombed the longest would ultimately win.[12] It was finally decided that 35 of the 52 squadrons should be made up of bombers. (In fact the 52 squadrons had still not been achieved by the outbreak of the Second World War.)

In August the RAF notched up a notable success in Iraq when Kemal Atatürk renounced Turkey's claim on Mosul in the north of the country, where an undeclared war had been continuing for months. Air Vice Marshal Sir John Salmond had formally assumed command of all British forces in Iraq the previous October, taking over a brigade of British and Indian troops, four companies of RAF-manned armoured cars and eight squadrons of aircraft. (His predecessor commanded 33 battalions of infantry and six regiments of cavalry.) When Kurdish rebels threatened to overwhelm a garrison in Mosul, Salmond, acting on his own initiative, immediately organised an airlift of his scanty ground forces into the area – the first military troop lift in history. The sudden appearance in the area of several hundred troops so disconcerted the rebels they melted away into the mountains.

Air and ground operations, using biplanes left over from the war equipped with light machine guns and small bombs, continued for a further five months and eventually forced Turkish irregulars back across the frontier. 'I cannot emphasise too much the value your successful command in Iraq has been to us,' Trenchard wrote to Salmond.

Salmond had been able to demonstrate that what Hoare called 'control without occupation' was effective and offered the enticing prospect of upholding imperial prestige at minimum cost in lives and cash. But the human cost, in the lives of tribesmen and their families, of pacifying villages by bombing, was rarely counted and consternation was caused when Air Commodore Lionel Charlton, the Chief Staff Officer at Iraq Command, openly questioned the policy. Charlton was said to have been shocked when he visited an Iraqi hospital treating the horribly mutilated victims, including women and children, of an RAF raid. He eventually resigned and returned to England where he sought an interview with the Chief of the Air Staff. Trenchard gave him short shrift.

'Why did you want to see me?' he barked.

'About my reasons for resigning.'

'Look here, Charlton, you resigned. I accept your resignation. There's nothing more to be said.'

'Won't there be an official inquiry, then?'

Trenchard snorted. 'An inquiry? Into what? Your conscience? Certainly not.'

It was the end of the interview. To his credit, Trenchard made sure that Charlton was not victimised in any way. Although he was barred from foreign postings, he went on to serve as AOC No. 3 Group in Andover until he took early retirement, after which he became a successful children's author.[13]

Trenchard was unlikely to have given Charlton a sympathetic hearing since bombers and bombing remained at the heart of his belief that the only way to defeat an air attack was to launch a counter-offensive of overwhelming power to destroy the will of the enemy to resist. He talked about it endlessly in meetings at Adastral House, in speeches and pep talks to airmen, and he was such a dominating personality, with such a commanding presence, along with experience and authority no other man could rival, that his personal views effectively formed the basis of RAF strategy for years to come.

In a speech at RAF Buxton he spoke about war being a contest between the 'moral tenacity' of opposing countries.

> In the next great war with a European nation, the forces engaged must first fight for aerial superiority and when that has been gained they will use their power to destroy the morale of the nation and vitally damage the organised armaments for supplies for the armies and navies . . . If we can bomb the enemy more intensely and more continually than he can bomb us, the result might be an early offer of peace.[14]

He rarely mentioned the fact that with the crude sights available at the time bombing remained essentially indiscriminate, although he was delighted when he learned that four pilots of No. 6 Squadron, carrying out target practice in Mosul, notched up 100 per cent accuracy, one pilot blowing the aiming stake out of the ground with his second bomb. He sent a personal letter of congratulations to the squadron commander, Squadron Leader C.H. Keith.

'Nice of him, wasn't it?' Keith wrote home. 'And it meant quids to my men. It is little personal touches like this which have so endeared the great "Boom" to the service.'[15]

In the 1924 New Year Honours Trenchard was awarded a GCB, an honour which some observers wrongly interpreted as meaning he was on the point of retiring, either voluntarily or involuntarily. 'I was extraordinarily lucky to get it without being kicked out,' he wrote to a friend, 'and some people asked me if it had been given to me because I was going.'

Not many months passed before Trenchard and the First Sea Lord had another very serious falling out, this time over who should be responsible for the defence of the proposed naval base in Singapore. Beatty insisted that fixed 15-inch guns pointing out to sea would be adequate; Trenchard argued that torpedo bombers could attack an approaching enemy fleet at a much greater distance and with greater accuracy and would mean a saving of £3 million. The dispute rumbled on for three years and Trenchard eventually gave way. He would later consider it the greatest blunder of his career and after the disastrous surrender of Singapore to the Japanese in 1942 – the most humiliating capitulation of British military history – he never forgave himself, believing the course of history might have changed had he carried the day.

It was a view supported by Sir James Grigg, the Secretary of State for War when Singapore fell:

> I have always considered that the real tragedy of the Singapore decisions was much more that Lord Beatty's view prevailed over that of Lord Trenchard in regard to the methods to be adopted for defending the base. The naval view meant fixed defences and big guns and forts, and these turned out to be useless. But it might have been a different story if Lord Trenchard's plan of entrusting the protection of the fortress predominantly to the air had carried the day.[16]

Relations between Trenchard and Beatty steadily worsened and when Admiral Beatty lodged a formal complaint with the Cabinet about a lack of co-operation and bad faith on the part of the RAF, Richard Haldane, the Lord Chancellor in the new Ramsay MacDonald administration, was asked to look into the matter. A highly regarded lawyer and politician and influential writer on philosophy, Haldane quickly realised that both Beatty and Trenchard were firmly rooted in their respective positions and decided it was time to knock heads together – hard.

He informed the First Lord of the Admiralty and the Chief of the Air Staff that he would give them three months to establish a working relationship and settle the differences between them. If they failed to produce a written agreement in that time, he would impose a settlement. Haldane's ultimatum seemed to engender a new spirit of give and take – neither Beatty nor Trenchard wanted a third party to decide on their futures. Negotiating, once again, with his brother-in-law, Roger Keyes, Trenchard made a key concession, essentially consenting to dual control of naval aviation. Further compromises were accepted and a provisional settlement was hammered out by July, within Haldane's time limit. The only issue remaining was whether the navy or the air force should finance the fleet squadrons and that was passed to the Treasury for arbitration.

A covering letter submitted with the final report, signed by both Keyes and Trenchard, was cautiously optimistic: 'We both recognise that in trying out the scheme, amendments will no doubt from time to time be required in the light of practical experience, but we hope the main principles of the scheme will provide a lasting and satisfactory settlement of the questions which have been at issue between the Admiralty and the Air Ministry.'

While Trenchard and Keyes were wrangling, more trouble flared in Iraq and questions began to be asked, again, about the morality of terrorising civilians by bombing from the air. To appease agitation in the press, the new Colonial Secretary, J.H. Thomas, asked the High Commissioner for a considered statement on bombing policy in Iraq. Henry Dobbs, who had taken over from Sir Percy Cox as Commissioner, replied that 'terror from the air' saved more lives than it cost by preventing violent tribal conflict. Salmond followed up by pointing out that action was never taken without the closest consultation with civil authorities. 'It is a commonplace here that aircraft achieve their results by their effects on morale, and by the material damage they do, and by the interference they cause to the daily routine of life and not through the infliction of casualties. The casualties inflicted have been most remarkably small . . .'[17]

Both men were being faintly disingenuous. Trenchard had earlier instructed Salmond not to report details of bomb tonnage dropped or casualties caused as the news that 'two tons of bombs had been dropped on some little village daily' might give 'a wrong sensation of proportion at home'. The previous November he had written in similar vein:

Sometimes remarks come to my ears, not from officers but friends I meet who have evidently inside information (the ordinary back-biting that is always going on), that the policy [of air control] is becoming too brutal. The expression sometimes used is 'Why are we bombing these tribes?' and very often 'and women and children' is added. I don't want to worry you with all this. It seems to me you have kept the country quiet and saved a lot of bloodshed by your efficient handling of the show.[18]

On 20 January 1925 the *Daily Chronicle* reported that the Chief of the Air Staff had been observed going into Adastral House carrying two guinea pigs and that a dastardly rumour had circulated the Air Ministry to the effect that they were to be used to test a new poison gas.

The *Daily Chronicle* was happy to put the rumour to rest: Sir Hugh, it reported, was devoted to his children and his children were devoted to guinea pigs. In between his duties at the Ministry the Air Chief had gone out and bought two as pets for his children and they had accompanied him home at the end of the day.

By 1925 Trenchard's authority in Whitehall was more or less unquestioned and his influence extended beyond the myriad of problems, technical and logistic, involved in creating an entirely new force. In October a committee of civil servants and representatives from the three services set up to examine air raid precautions reported that 'Sir Hugh Trenchard was so emphatically of the opinion that an increase of the defence forces beyond a certain proportion would not secure greater immunity from attack, that we felt we had no alternative but to continue our investigations with a view to mitigating, so far as possible, the evils attendant upon aerial bombardment . . .' Trenchard clearly made his case, because the committee concluded: 'In our opinion the most effective reply to an attack from the air is the provision of a strong attacking force wherewith to carry the war into the enemy's territory.'[19]

Another Trenchard initiative came to fruition that year with the formation of the first Auxiliary Air Force squadrons. Churchill had originally derided the notion of recruiting 'weekend fliers' but Trenchard, typically, had persisted, setting up squadrons in London, Glasgow and Edinburgh and University Air Squadrons at Oxford and Cambridge. Speaking at Cambridge he explained the thinking behind encouraging undergraduates to take up flying. 'It will be a great means of enabling the spirit of aviation to spread . . . It will give the brains of the country a chance of being used for aeronautical purposes which will be an important factor in home defence.' (He was right. Auxiliary Air Force pilots would make an important contribution to the defence of Britain in the Second World War, shooting down the first enemy bomber over England and being heavily engaged at Dunkirk and throughout the Battle of Britain. In recognition of their achievements, the force was honoured by the prefix 'Royal' in 1947.)

Paradoxically for a man committed to building an air force, Trenchard occasionally expressed a wish that, for the sake of humanity, the aeroplane had never been invented. 'I do not want you to think that I look upon the air as a blessing altogether,' he said in the same speech at Cambridge. 'It may be more of a blessing for this empire than for any other country in the world, but I feel that all the good it will be in civil life cannot balance the harm that may be done in war by it. If I had the casting vote, I would say abolish the air. I feel it is an infinitely more harmful weapon of war than any other . . .'[20]

Towards the end of 1925 Trenchard was obliged to appear three times before a Cabinet committee reviewing defence expenditure to justify, once again, the continued existence of the RAF. He had been horrified to discover, a few months earlier, that Churchill, now Chancellor of the Exchequer, had invited Sir Laming Worthington-Evans, the Secretary of State for War, to submit proposals for creating a separate army air wing. Trenchard felt he had been betrayed – he had considered Winston to be a friend and supporter of the air service. Sir Laming was neither, and was famously on record as doubting the Arab population would acquiesce if 'peaceful control of Mesopotamia ultimately depends on our intention of bombing women and children'.

Trenchard's first reaction was to lodge a bitter complaint, but on second thoughts he decided an appeal to Churchill's notorious vanity might prove more productive:

> I am really seriously worried and alarmed. You know when you got me to come back and run the air force how very diffident I was, how I was doubtful whether I could do the job successfully, how I thought it would be too great a task for me, and how I was dubious of getting enough support to enable me to carry it through. And no one remembers better than I do your wonderful kindness and assistance, your constant assurance that I *should* carry it through and make a success of it. And now I ask you to look at the service that has been formed and is growing up . . . Wherever you go, whether it is in a Punch-and-Judy show or in grand opera [a very curious analogy, this], in the highest circles or the lowest, you will hear the opinion that the air force do better than anyone else. Yet because a few people like Worthington-Evans state to you that they can save £4 or £5 millions by taking over the air and running it differently, you think we may have made a mistake . . . You know the only true way of economy in the defensive services of this country is not to do away with the army or the navy, but the substitution of the air in part of their duties and responsibilities.[21]

In his reply Churchill confirmed that his preference would be for an independent air force, but he hoped Trenchard would understand the pressure he was under at the Treasury and that he was simply exploring the possibility of a compromise that might result in significant defence savings. Trenchard's pre-eminent concern, as he mentioned later to the prime minister, was that 'the need for economy should not become a peg on which the older services could hang a fresh demand for our abolition'.

In the end, he need not have worried. The Cabinet concluded there was no justification in abolishing the Air Ministry and the prime minister confirmed in the House, on 25 February 1926, that 'the Government has no intention of reopening the question of a separate air arm and Air Ministry'. Trenchard was required to slow down the expansion of the RAF previously agreed and reduce the number of machines allocated to home defence squadrons from 18 to 12, but they were economies which he could accommodate so long as the service survived.

Rumours were circulating around this time that he was intending to retire. He scotched them in a speech to officers at RAF Uxbridge: 'Let me tell you, as far as I know there is no limit to my time. I shall go when the government tells me they want me to go and not before . . . Be quite certain, I am not retiring now or in the near future.' His announcement was greeted with thunderous applause.

In the spring of 1926 the RAF was pressed into government service when the Trades Union Congress threatened to call a general strike in support of 800,000 mine workers who had been locked out by the mine owners after refusing to accept reduced pay and longer working hours. Frantic efforts were made to arbitrate a settlement and the strike, due to begin at midnight on 3 May, was nearly averted until printers at the *Daily Mail* refused to print an editorial under the headline 'For King and Country', condemning the action as a 'revolutionary move which can only succeed by destroying the government and subverting the rights and liberties of the people'. Baldwin promptly called off negotiations saying the printers' action interfered with the liberty of the press and free speech.

The government had had plenty of time to prepare plans to deal with the emergency and maintain basic services. Soldiers and sailors were drafted in to help maintain essential supplies while the RAF was required to organise daily communication flights between London and the major cities to deliver official mail and copies of the government's official newspaper, the *British Gazette*, edited by Churchill. Trenchard set up a co-ordinating body called 'Crisis' at the Air Ministry and during the ten days of the strike RAF heavy bombers delivered 1.3 million copies of the *Gazette*, although many were dropped in bundles from the air, particularly in the industrial north-east, where newsagents feared proletarian reprisals for selling it. The TUC claimed that up to 1.75 million workers – mainly dockers, railwaymen, lorry drivers and steelworkers – supported the action, but it achieved nothing. Miners maintained their resistance for a few months but they, too, were eventually forced back to work and had to accept lower wages and longer working hours.

In 1927 Trenchard was promoted to marshal of the Royal Air Force, the first person to hold the RAF's highest rank, but as far as he was concerned there was little to celebrate, since stringent government economies were really beginning to bite. On the morning of 11 February he arrived at 11 Downing Street with Sir Philip Sassoon, the Under-Secretary of State for Air, for a crisis meeting with Churchill to warn him that the RAF could not stand further cuts. Trenchard pointed out that the Bristol fighters used by army co-operation squadrons were completely outdated, being more than ten years old, and at least a third of the bomber force comprised similarly outdated DH9-As, which had entered service in 1918 and were long overdue for replacement in an age when aviation technology was advancing rapidly.

'Winston started, as usual, very difficult,' Trenchard later told Hoare. The meeting turned even uglier when Sassoon politely inquired if the army and the Royal Navy had carried out the agreed cuts in their budgets. Churchill turned on him angrily, grunted that it had nothing to do with them and he would not allow it to become a subject for discussion. After a great deal of argument back and forth, he grudgingly agreed to allocate a miserly £100,000 for new aircraft and approved a budget for the air force of £15½ million. 'He was more peaceable at the end,' Trenchard reported, 'but said he had his back to the wall and no money.'

Always anxious to beat the drum for the RAF, in May Trenchard gave his full support to an attempt by a Hawker Horsley torpedo bomber fitted with long-range fuel tanks to make the first non-stop flight to India, a distance of 4500 miles. The aircraft took off from Cranwell with a crew of two, was briefly sighted over Wiesbaden in Germany but was not seen again until 34 hours later when it made a forced landing at Jask in the Persian Gulf, as a result of a fuel blockage. The flight, 3420 miles, was nevertheless a record but sadly no one noticed. A few hours later on 21 May Charles Lindbergh landed in Paris, having made the first successful transatlantic flight from New York, a distance of 3600 miles, in his Ryan monoplane, Spirit of St Louis in 33½ hours. His achievement dominated the headlines around the world for weeks to come and transformed Lindbergh into the world's most famous aviator.

Later that year an RAF team, funded by the Air Ministry at Trenchard's insistent prompting, won the Schneider Trophy – a seaplane race – in Venice in the face of strong Italian competition. Flight Lieutenant Sidney Webster, at the controls of a Supermarine S5, won the race over the lagoons with a world record average speed of 281.66 mph. Webster and his fellow RAF competitor, Flight Lieutenant Worsley, were lauded as heroes in the media when they returned home. (RAF pilots won the trophy again in 1929 and 1931.)

Much less welcome publicity were the frequent reports of fatal accidents – 1927 was a bad year – both at home and abroad. Hoare was pressed in the House to reveal the precise figures but refused, increasing suspicion that the Air Ministry had something to hide. To Trenchard's irritation, newspapers often published details of those killed before the next of kin had been informed – the result of airmen passing on the names to reporters in return for 'a drink'. He was persuaded, against his better judgement, to meet with members of the Newspaper Proprietors' Association to discuss the matter and was treated to a lecture by Lord Burnham, the owner of the *Daily Telegraph*, about the freedom of the press and the principles under which it operated. It was too much for Trenchard. 'Don't talk to me about your precious Press principles,' he exploded. 'All you are interested in, the whole pack of you, is your miserable Press pence.' He glared round at the assembled press barons, got to his feet and stalked out without another word.

During the winter of 1928/29 the British Resident in Kabul warned the Foreign Office that 600 European civilians were at risk of being trapped by rebels advancing on the Afghan capital intent on the overthrow of King Amanullah. There was grave concern for their safety – in 1841, when the British Army was besieged in Kabul, 4500 troops and 12,000 non-combatants were allowed to leave and set out for Jalalabad. Six days later a single survivor reached the city; the entire column had been massacred. The foreign secretary asked Trenchard if the RAF could intervene. The Kabul operation – the first major civilian airlift in history – took nine weeks to accomplish but all 600 men, women and children were brought out safely. RAF aircraft flew a total of 28,160 miles with the loss of only one machine, a Victoria transport which crash-landed without casualties. It was an impressive demonstration of air power in a peaceful role and would further enhance the RAF's reputation.

At home Admiral Sir Herbert Richmond, first commandant of the newly created Imperial Defence College, put forward a proposal that the rules of war should be defined in identical terms in the manuals of all three services since the 'situation as regards aerial warfare is still indeterminate'. Trenchard fundamentally disagreed: on the contrary, he had a very clear idea of the RAF's role and went on to produce a polemic absolutely guaranteed to enrage his counterparts in the army and navy.

The military aim of a Navy is to destroy in battle or to neutralise and weaken the opposing navy including its directing will and morale . . . As far as the army was concerned the ultimate aim was the destruction of the enemy's main forces on the battlefield whereas it was not necessary for an air force, in order to defeat the enemy nation, to defeat its armed forces first. Air power can dispense with that intermediate step . . .

He went on to argue that the object to be sought by air action was to paralyse from the very outset the enemy's productive centres of munitions and to stop all communications and transportation. He accepted that civilian casualties would result but claimed that was no reason to regard bombing as illegitimate, providing reasonable care was taken to confine the scope of bombing to military objectives.

'What is illegitimate, as being contrary to the dictates of humanity, is the indiscriminate bombing of a city for the sole purpose of terrorising the civilian population. It is an entirely different matter to terrorise munitions workers . . .'

His conclusions were grim.

> There can be no question – whatever views we may hold in regard to it – that this form of warfare will be used. There may be many who, realising that this new form of warfare will extend to the whole community the horrors and sufferings hitherto confined to the battlefield, would argue that the air offensive should be restricted to the zone of the opposing armed forces. If this restriction were feasible, I should be the last to quarrel with it, but it is not feasible . . .
>
> Whatever we may wish or hope, and whatever course of action we may decide, whatever the views held as to the legality or the humanity or the military wisdom and expediency of such operations, there is not the slightest doubt that in the next war both sides will send their aircraft out without scruple to bomb those objectives which they consider the most suitable.
>
> I would, therefore, urge most strongly that we accept this fact and face it; that we do not bury our heads in the sand like ostriches, but that we train our officers and men, and organise our services, so that they may be prepared to meet and counter these inevitable air attacks.[22]

Both the First Sea Lord and the CIGS not unnaturally objected strongly to the implicit suggestion in Trenchard's memorandum that their services were being reduced to an ancillary role and both poured scorn on the potential of bombing. 'It is ridiculous to contend,' the CIGS pointed out, 'that the dropping of bombs has reached such a stage of accuracy as to ensure that the bombs would only hit military targets.' The inevitable outcome of accepting Trenchard's strategy, he said, would be that the government was advocating 'indiscriminate bombing of undefended towns and of their unarmed inhabitants'.

The final nebulous agreement, that the aim of the air service should be defined as breaking enemy resistance 'in concert with the Navy and the Army' by 'attacks on objectives calculated to achieve this end', left Trenchard plenty of room to promote the strategy he had espoused from the start.

By then he had made up his mind to step down at the end of 1929 to make way for a younger man – his friend Air Chief Marshal John Salmond, who was not yet 50, was in line to succeed him. But before leaving he insisted that a long and contentious memorandum titled 'The Fuller Employment of Air Power in Imperial Defence', expounding his 'personal views' about the future responsibilities of the RAF, should be circulated to members of the Cabinet.

After reviewing RAF operations in the Middle East and India, Trenchard laid out extraordinarily ambitious plans for the air force to take over from navy and army forces across the Empire and at home.

> I contend that the case for air control has now been fully proved, that our Imperial Defence arrangements should be extensively overhauled and our methods modernised and that the new and improved form of control which air power provides should be used as the means of effecting considerable economies in defence expenditure and reduction in armaments, and of keeping order without having to maintain large mobile military forces and from time to time embark on long drawn-out military operations.[23]

The memorandum became known as Trenchard's 'last will and testament' and provoked a furious reaction from the CIGS, the First Sea Lord and Maurice Hankey, the Cabinet Secretary, who considered it a grave breach of protocol and claimed it had damaged interservice relations. 'Things were going well,' Hankey wrote to the prime minister, 'until Sir Hugh Trenchard's "swan song" was circulated. This greatly irritated the older services and fanned the missionary zeal of the Air Ministry. Ever since then co-ordination has been going from bad to worse.'[24] Trenchard's friends, too, viewed its publication as a blunder, since it caused unnecessary difficulties for his successor and did no good to his cause.

Trenchard retired as Chief of the Air Staff on 1 January 1930 and was raised to the peerage, becoming the RAF's first peer. He chose for his title Lord Trenchard of Wolfeton, commemorating the family seat in more prosperous times before his father's bankruptcy. At the time of his retirement it was safe to say that no individual had had more impact on the forging of British defence strategy in the air. The Royal Air Force was not his creation – in fact he had been opposed to its formation at the time – but it became his creation. He fought mightily to prevent its disintegration, fashioned its structure, defined its role and safeguarded its future by strength of will and a dogged determination that it would survive. Almost all its senior officers owed their positions to his patronage. Such was his prestige and authority that what would become known as 'the Trenchard doctrine' dominated strategic thinking within the air force for years to come.

He had, inevitably, made enemies along the way. His obsession with bombing and his unswerving belief in what bombing would do to an enemy's will to resist would open him to criticism both at the time and particularly later, when Bomber Command set out to ravage Germany in the Second World War. His insistence that an aircraft was an offensive weapon meant little attention was paid to defensive tactics or to realistic training in aerial combat. Some critics claimed his greatest failure as Chief of the Air Staff was to allow the quality of the RAF's fighting equipment to deteriorate by not keeping up with technological advances. Sir Maurice Dean, a former Under-Secretary of State for Air, complained that the fighting equipment was not very different when Trenchard left than when he started, that the RAF was still stuck with fixed-undercarriage, fabric-covered biplanes at a time when they were increasingly regarded as obsolete by other air forces.

Nevertheless, Hoare paid him a generous tribute in a statement to the House: 'I do not suppose that any Service had ever been so closely identified with its Chief of Staff as has the Air Force with Sir Hugh Trenchard. What it owes to his wise guidance, his consistent foresight and his resolute purpose I have had perhaps a better opportunity of judging than anyone else. Trenchard was beloved throughout the Service.'

At a dinner in his honour after his retirement Trenchard could not resist a final kick at the politicians with whom he had had to deal for a decade. 'I have served in my time under six different Secretaries of State and fourteen or fifteen Under-secretaries,' he said in his speech. 'I see that most of them are here tonight. [Pause] I hope none of you will take offence if I say that I never saw much difference between any of you.'

THE CHIEF OF AIR STAFF AND THE AIRCRAFTSMAN

It was, perhaps, the most unlikely friendship in the world – between a man in the highest rank in a service and another in the lowest – but there was no mistaking the warmth and admiration each felt for the other, clearly evident in the frequent letters they exchanged. Although it appeared at first sight that there was little in common between Hugh Trenchard, the Chief of the Air Staff, and Aircraftsman John Ross, there were, in fact, significant similarities. Both, in their own ways, were visionaries; both were obsessives; both were impatient with bureaucracy; and both lived with embarrassing family burdens – Ross that he was illegitimate, Trenchard that his father was a bankrupt. Ross was, of course, better known as T.E. Lawrence – 'Lawrence of Arabia'.

In his autobiographical notes Trenchard claimed he first met 'little Lawrence of Arabia' on the ship taking them to the conference in Cairo in March 1921. His memory failed him: it is clear from the records he had several meetings with Lawrence in London in the weeks before the conference to discuss plans for the RAF to take control of Mesopotamia. At that time Lawrence, a lieutenant colonel in the British Army at the age of 32, had been recruited by Churchill to work as political adviser in the newly formed Middle Eastern Department at the Colonial Office, after his spectacular adventures leading Arab irregular troops in operations against the Ottoman empire during the war.

Ironically he had only become world famous as 'Lawrence of Arabia' through the acumen of an American war correspondent by the name of Lowell Thomas, who had travelled briefly with him in the Middle East, accompanied by a cameraman. After the war Thomas embarked on a lecture tour recounting his experiences, supported by moving pictures of mysteriously veiled Arab women and exotic

Bedouin warriors on camels thirsting for battle. Invited to London, he opened at Covent Garden in August 1919, with braziers burning incense outside and dancers performing in front of images of the Pyramids. At first Lawrence only had a small supporting role, but when Thomas realised that it was Lawrence's enigmatic figure in Arab robes that captured the public's imagination, he relaunched his presentation with a new title: *With Allenby in Palestine and Lawrence in Arabia*. It was an enormous success and turned Lawrence into a household name. (Lawrence claimed to dislike the film intensely, although he saw it three times. He also agreed to pose in London for a series of portraits, in Bedouin robes, to promote the show.)

If Trenchard was mistaken about when and where he first met Lawrence, there is no doubt that it was during the Cairo conference, after dinner in Churchill's suite at the Semiramis Hotel, that Lawrence first raised the prospect of joining the RAF as an aircraftsman. Trenchard understandably thought it was preposterous that a man like Lawrence, a legendary figure who had been instrumental in shaping the Middle East, should consider joining the RAF as an other rank. A number of biographers have tried to explain Lawrence's strange decision to enlist. He had returned from the Middle East disillusioned that many of the promises he had made to his Arab friends had been broken by the British government; he often talked unhappily about having 'prostituted' himself. While his personal celebrity as 'Lawrence of Arabia' was soaring it was also becoming burdensome and it is likely he sought an escape, and oblivion, in the ranks.

After the Cairo conference Lawrence became a frequent and welcome visitor, on his motorcycle, to Dancers Hill House. Kitty was fascinated by him and her husband was intrigued, and slightly mystified. 'He was the sort of man,' Trenchard recalled, 'who, on entering a roomful of people, would have contrived to be sick on the spot had everyone stood up to applaud him. Yet if, on entering the same room, nobody stirred or showed the faintest sign of recognition, Lawrence might well have reacted by standing on his head.'

They quickly became firm friends. Trenchard was not quite old enough to be Lawrence's father, but he nevertheless came to treat him like a wayward son he was happy to indulge and for whom he harboured particular affection. Lawrence, on his part, would come to

positively idolise the Chief of the Air Staff as a giant among men, a
man who, in his eyes, could do no wrong.

Lawrence was working by day at the Colonial Office and toiling
late into the night revising and re-revising the manuscript of his major
opus, *Seven Pillars of Wisdom*, the soon to be celebrated autobiographical account of his adventures fighting with Arab rebels in the last two
years of the war. Friends worried that he was in a state of severe mental
turmoil, but throughout this period he was becoming more and more
determined to join the RAF as an airman.

On 5 January 1922, he sent a handwritten and impassioned plea to
Trenchard for help:

> You know I am trying to leave Winston on March the first. Then
> I want about two months to myself, and then I'd like to join the
> R.A.F. – in the ranks of course. I can't do this without your help.
> I'm 33 and not skilled in the sense you want. Probably I couldn't
> pass your medical. It's odd being too old for the job I want when
> hitherto I've always been too young for the job I did . . .
>
> You'll wonder what I'm at. The matter is that since I was 16 I've
> been writing: never satisfying myself technically but steadily get-
> ting better. My last book on Arabia [*Seven Pillars of Wisdom*] is
> nearly good. I see the sort of subject I need in the beginning of your
> Force . . . and the best place to see a thing is from the ground. It
> wouldn't 'write' from the officer level.
>
> I haven't told anyone, till I know your opinion: and probably
> not then, for the newspapers used to run after me and I like being
> private. People wouldn't understand.
>
> It's an odd request this, hardly proper perhaps, but it may be one
> of the exceptions you make sometimes. It is asking you to use your
> influence to get me past the Recruiting Officer! Apologies for mak-
> ing it: If you say no I'll be more amused than hurt. Yours sincerely,
> T.E. Lawrence.[1]

Trenchard had clearly given up trying to persuade his friend to apply
for a commission as he replied within a few days:

> I am prepared to do all you ask me, if you will tell me for how
> long you want to join; but I am afraid I could not do it without

mentioning it to Winston and my own Secretary of State and then
whether it could be kept secret I do not know . . .

What country do you want to serve in, and how? I would make
things as easy as anything . . .

Yours, H. Trenchard.

(Their correspondence remained formal throughout; Trenchard never
signed himself Hugh and Lawrence never addressed him, like other
friends, as Boom.)

Lawrence was not able to leave the Colonial Office on 1 March
because Churchill was difficult and did not want to lose him. In fact
the notion of Lawrence wasting his talents in the ranks of the RAF
irritated Churchill so much that he did his best to scupper the whole
idea, but Lawrence persisted and Churchill eventually acquiesced,
albeit with great reluctance, to him leaving the payroll of the Colonial Office while retaining him as an honorary adviser. On 21 July
Lawrence wrote a jaunty note to Trenchard: 'Winston very agreeable
[to him enlisting in the RAF]. Hope your Lord [Freddie Guest, the
Secretary of State for Air] was the same.' Trenchard replied 'Yes, my
Lord very agreeable . . .'

During a visit to Dancers Hill House, Trenchard made one last
attempt to persuade Lawrence to change his mind, but he remained
resolute. On 16 August Trenchard signed a secret, and entirely un-
lawful, memorandum giving Lawrence a privilege to which no other
enlisted man was entitled: 'It is hereby approved that Colonel T.E.
Lawrence be permitted to join the Royal Air Force as an aircraft hand
under the alias of John Hume Ross. He is taking this step in order to
learn what is the life of an airman. On receipt of any communications
from him through any channel, asking for his release, orders are to be
issued for his discharge forthwith without formality.'[2]

Special arrangements had to be made for him to enlist in the RAF
under an assumed name and Trenchard passed the task to his chief
personnel officer, Air Vice Marshal Oliver Swann, much to Swann's
discomfort. 'I disliked the whole business,' he recalled later, 'with its
secrecy and subterfuge.'[3]

When Lawrence presented himself to the RAF Recruiting Centre
in Covent Garden for enlistment as Aircraftsman J.H. Ross something close to a farce ensued. The recruiting officer (who happened to

be Captain W.E. Johns, later the author of the popular *Biggles* books) was immediately suspicious when 'Ross' turned up without his birth certificate, or any references. His first thought was that Ross might well have been on the run from the police and after he had sent him home to find the required documentation he checked the photographs of wanted men he kept in his desk drawer. Ross was not among them, but Johns put in a call to Somerset House and discovered that no John Hume Ross had been born on the date Lawrence had supplied.

When Ross turned up next day with his documents they were so obviously forged that he was once again sent packing. The Air Ministry was only a few minutes' walk away and Lawrence went there immediately to give the bad news to Swann. Shortly afterwards Johns received a telephone call from the Ministry ordering him to recruit Ross without delay: 'This man is Lawrence of Arabia,' he was told. 'Get him into the Force or you'll get your bowler hat.' Both Trenchard and Lawrence had hoped that his entry into the RAF could be kept a secret, at least for a while. In fact the secret was out before he had got his uniform. After some difficulty finding a doctor willing to pass him as fit for service, Ross was finally signed in as AC2 No. 352087.

He was sent to the RAF training depot at Uxbridge where he found the regime senselessly brutal, but he managed to endure it and in November was transferred to the RAF School of Photography at Farnborough. By then many officers knew who he was. Most of them could not understand why he was serving in the ranks and some suspected that he had been sent by the Air Ministry to spy on them. Inevitably word got out to Fleet Street and reporters were soon discovered snooping round Farnborough. On 27 December 1922 the *Daily Express* broke the sensational story that Lawrence of Arabia, Britain's most famous war hero, was serving in the ranks of the RAF.

Under a headline

'Uncrowned King' as Private Soldier

LAWRENCE OF ARABIA
Famous War Hero Becomes a Private

the story began: 'Colonel Lawrence, archaeologist, Fellow of All Souls, and king-maker, has lived a more romantic existence than any man of the time. Now he is a private soldier.' In a follow-up piece next day he was identified as AC2 Ross and his location was revealed, by which time a great mob of reporters and photographers was gathered outside the gates of the School of Photography hoping to get a glimpse of its most famous student.

At the Air Ministry, Trenchard came under increasing pressure to discharge this troublesome recruit. He made an unprecedented visit to Farnborough to warn Lawrence his position in the RAF was becoming untenable. Both men might have hoped it would all blow over but in January the new Secretary of State for Air, Sir Samuel Hoare, who had never been enthusiastic about the whole arrangement in the first place, decided that Lawrence would have to go. When an aggrieved Lawrence wrote to Hoare asking for the reasons for his discharge, Trenchard replied on Hoare's behalf: 'As you know, I always think it is foolish to give reasons! But this case is perhaps different. I think the reason to give is that you had become known in the Air Force as Colonel Lawrence instead of Air Mechanic Ross and that both you and the officers were put in a very difficult position, and that therefore it was considered inexpedient for you to remain in the service.'

Lawrence did not give up without a fight. On 28 January 1923 he wrote to Wing Commander T.B. Marson, Trenchard's private secretary, from Frensham Ponds Hotel near Farnham asking the Chief of the Air Staff to give him another chance, perhaps by posting him to a remote station where his presence would not be an embarrassment to the commanding officer:

Dear Marson,

This is for the C.A.S., when he is not momentarily burdened with big politics.

I've been looking round, these last few days, and find an odd blank – there is nothing I can think of that I want to do and in consequence nothing that I will do! And the further I get from the R.A.F. the more I regret its loss.

So I'm writing, not hopefully, to ask whether he thought (and turned down the idea) of giving me another chance? The newspaper chatter I don't take seriously (and you won't still it much by throwing them the fresh tit-bit of my discharge) so it seems the real difficulty must be the disturbance I caused, unwillingly and unwittingly, at Farnborough. I can't help thinking that it must have been, in large part, because the finding me out happened there, and I don't see why there should be further discomfort over me if I were posted, openly, to a more remote place . . .

The C.A.S. said the other day (when I was too bothered with the news) that I was an unusual person and inevitably embarrassing to a C.O. – but I don't agree. I've had a lurid past, which has now twice pulled me down, and of which I'm beginning to despair but if my C.O. was a decent size he'd treat me as average and I'd be average.

As I say, this isn't very hopefully written. I fear it's too late, and the business closed. If you know it, please tear it up and tell me so in a note from yourself: but the contrary chance would be worth so much to me that I'm trying it. The last thing I wish is to seem important but I'm so sure that I played up at Farnborough and did good, rather than harm, to the fellows in camp there with me, that I venture to put in a last word for myself.

Yours ever,

T.E. Lawrence.[4]

Trenchard replied two days later with a sweetly sympathetic letter:

My dear Lawrence,

Marson has shown me your letter. I am never burdened with big politics, it is always that the little politics are the burden to me. I would like to agree with all you have written but the trivial circumstances have been too much for me and for you. It is the smallness of it that has brought about the decision to finish it, and I know you will accept it however much you hate it. To my way of thinking, the only thing that would be of any use would be an armoured car officer – short service. One of the drawbacks to you is that you have been a bit of a friend of mine, and that has made it so hard for me to deal with. I will think things over and if you could come and see me I will talk over what I can suggest for you, providing my Secretary of State agrees, and you want it . . .

Lawrence was still dead set against taking a commission. All he really wanted was to get back into the RAF, but he accepted for the moment that it was not possible and began looking round for something else to do. He was not short of high-placed friends and an officer with whom he had served in the Middle East persuaded the War Office to allow him to slip into the ranks of the Royal Tank Corps under the name of T.E. Shaw. Trenchard, perhaps feeling a little guilty about his friend, wrote him a cheery note on 19 March: 'I hope before you join up in your new Tanks Corps you will come and see me, so that you can say if there is anything you want me to do or look after. Mind you, at all times, you have only to write to me and I will do anything I can to help you in any way you require.'

In fact Lawrence had already started training at Bovington by then and he wrote Trenchard a long letter describing his life there, trying to minimise the fact that he hated the place, hated the other men and hated the army. After he had finished basic training he was assigned a job as a clerk in the quartermaster's stores, which at least left him time to continue work on the revisions of *Seven Pillars of Wisdom*.

On Armistice Day Trenchard was due to lay a wreath at the Cenotaph. A few days beforehand he wrote to Lawrence suggesting he should take some leave and inviting him to join the party he was arranging at the Army and Navy Club in the evening. Lawrence replied that he was unable to comply as he was confined to barracks as a defaulter. Trenchard was furious and quite ready to break the rules for his friend. He had a word with General Sir Philip Chetwode, the Adjutant General to the Forces at the War Office, and the military authorities at Bovington were swiftly instructed to arrange for Private Shaw to be sent on leave without delay. Then Trenchard dispatched a gently chiding letter to Lawrence, addressing him as 'T.E.': 'The Adjutant General has arranged your leave most carefully. At the same time, you must not be a defaulter or you will be kicked out. Don't be an ass! If you start being a defaulter it will be impossible for me to help you or for you to help yourself . . . I wish I could see you again and have a talk with you. Do not forget I am always ready and anxious to help you. Best of luck . . .'

In March 1924 Lawrence met Trenchard in London and pleaded to be allowed back into the RAF. He followed up with a letter the next day:

Dear Sir Hugh,

Forgive this letter. I'm ashamed of it already, since I know you sacked me for good, and it's perverse of me not to take it so. Yet the hope of getting back into the R.A.F. is the main reason for my staying in the Army . . . I've served exactly a year in the Army now, and been found amenable to discipline. Don't say that the Army can more easily digest an oddity than can the R.A.F. It isn't true. The Air has twice the vitality – with good reason.

Whenever I get one of your letters I open it excitedly to see if your mind has changed. It seems to be so plain that the presence in the ranks of a man as keen on the air as myself must be generally beneficial . . .

He goes on to talk about difficulties he had with his commanding officer at Farnborough and concludes: 'It's all difficult to write. If you'd been a stranger I could have persuaded you: but my liking for your Force and its maker make it impossible for me to plead properly. Do think of the many hiding-holes there are (India, Egypt and Mespot and seaplane-ships) before you tear this up! Yours sincerely, TEL.'

Trenchard, ever willing to pull strings for his friend, took up Lawrence's case with his then Secretary of State, Lord Thomson, to no avail. As an alternative he suggested that Lawrence might like to complete the official history of the Royal Flying Corps in the Great War. The author of the first volume, Sir Walter Raleigh, Merton Professor of English History at Oxford, had died after contracting typhoid on a research trip to Iraq. Lawrence turned it down, saying he did not want the responsibility.

On 6 February 1925, writing from his cottage in Dorset, Lawrence tried again:

Dear Sir Hugh,

February is 'supplication' month . . . so for the third time of

asking – Have I no chance of re-enlistment in the R.A.F., or
transfer? It remains my only hope and ambition, dreamed of every
week, nearly every day. If I bother you only yearly it's because I
hate pestering you on a private affair . . .

He went on to say he had a clean conduct sheet, had kept his job as a
storeman in the quartermasters stores, had lived carefully and 'am in
clean trim, mind and body'. He concluded:

Please don't turn me down just because you did so last year and
the year before. Time has changed us both, and the R.A.F. since
then. I could easily get other people to help me appeal to you: only
it doesn't seem fair, and I don't really believe that you will go on
refusing me for ever. People who want a thing as long and as badly
as I want the R.A.F. must get it some time. I only fear that my
turn won't come until I am too old to enjoy it. That's why I keep
on writing.

Yours very apologetically,
T E Shaw, ex TEL, JHR.

Unfortunately Sir Samuel Hoare was back in office as Air Minister
and absolutely refused to allow Lawrence to re-enlist, saying he was 'a
person with altogether too large a publicity factor for the ranks'. When
Lawrence got the news he threatened suicide, although Trenchard,
for one, did not take it too seriously. Once, while staying with the
Trenchards at Dancers Hill, he had spoken of 'ending it all' if he was
unable to return to the RAF. Trenchard called his bluff. 'All right,' he
said without raising an eyebrow, 'but please go into the garden. I don't
want my carpets ruined.' Lawrence laughed and the incident became
a private joke between them.

Not everyone dismissed Lawrence's suicide threat so lightly. His
friend George Bernard Shaw, who had already written once to Prime
Minister Stanley Baldwin urging him to end the 'shocking tomfoolery'
of Lawrence's service in the ranks, wrote again in July pointing out
that a major scandal would result from the suicide of the country's
most celebrated war hero simply because he had been refused permission to transfer to the RAF. The notion resonated powerfully with the

prime minister, who promptly overruled Hoare. Trenchard was the first to give Lawrence the glad news and on 16 July 1925 he signed the order approving his transfer back to the RAF, still with the name of Shaw.

Lawrence, absolutely delighted, was posted to Cranwell, from where he kept up a regular correspondence with the Chief of the Air Staff. 'I've got everything I want,' he wrote at one point 'and nearly every morning when I wake up a little rush of delight comes over me, at finding myself still in the R.A.F.'

In the summer of 1926 Lawrence volunteered for service in India, partly to escape the commotion which he rightly guessed would surround the publication of a subscribers' edition of *Seven Pillars of Wisdom*. Two days before he sailed for Karachi on the troopship *Derbyshire* he sent a copy to Trenchard, specially bound in air force blue leather and inscribed 'To Sir Hugh Trenchard, from a contented, admiring and, where possible, obedient servant. T.E.S.'

Trenchard thanked him for the gift as 'being a delightful touch from the most disobedient mortal I have ever known'. He went on to assure Lawrence he remained available to help him in any way he could.

> I hope you keep fit but if you get seedy you may get sad and if you do, do write and let me know, so that if necessary I can bring you home . . . I would very much like to have seen you before you actually sailed, but I suppose that is not possible, and perhaps it would be inadvisable from your point of view: but if you want to be put up for a night, my wife and children would be delighted to see you before you went out at Dancers Hill. Let me know.

The voyage from Southampton to Karachi took a month and was, Lawrence reported, utter misery. Even India, with its heat, squalor and poverty, seemed like a deliverance when he arrived. He was posted to an RAF depot outside the city and assigned a job as a clerk in the Engine Repair section.

Six months passed before Trenchard got round to reading *Seven Pillars of Wisdom*.

My dear Lawrence, How are you? [he wrote from the Air Ministry on 7 June 1927] I hear you are at Karachi, and I hope you are well and enjoying yourself . . . Have read your book and I must say that once I took it up, I didn't put it down again until I had finished it, or nearly did. It is splendid, I could see the blowing up of the bridges you describe! I have insured it and left it to my little son in my will . . . No time for more, but let me know how you are, and if you are happy and contented, or if you would care to come back to the Air Force in England for a bit and enjoy yourself in the cooler climate. I could do it quite easily if you want to . . .

Yours sincerely, H. Trenchard.

(Cutting short Lawrence's overseas tour would have been contrary to regulations, but Trenchard was never a stickler for doing everything by the book and was not in the least bothered about bending the rules for his friend.)

Lawrence replied on 30 June with a long letter expressing surprise that Trenchard had managed to 'wade' through his book, describing his life in Karachi and assuring Trenchard he was perfectly content: 'I'm sure I was wise to come overseas. There is no local press, and I arouse no interest in camp. Karachi I haven't visited. So nobody outside the depot has seen me. Service character still good, and I've not yet been in real trouble: nor sick.'

He rarely let more than a few days pass before replying to letters from Trenchard. 'You see, I have for you one of my unreasonable regards,' he explained. 'So when a letter from you turns up, the border line between my chest and stomach gets suddenly warm; and it would take an uncommon convulsion of nature to stop me from answering you.'

When a problem cropped up in the Middle East, Trenchard did not hesitate to ask Lawrence for guidance – possibly one of the few instances in recorded military history where someone in the highest rank sought advice from someone in the lowest. King Faisal of Iraq had fallen out with Ibn Saud, the King of Hejaz and Nejd (later Saudi Arabia) and when the two sides began raiding each other's territory, Trenchard wrote to ask Lawrence what he would do about it in his place.

Lawrence replied with a long letter explaining both the background and how he would tackle the situation:

> An accommodation between Ibn Saud and Faisal could be arranged, but would not cure your trouble, at the moment. I don't think they are the main people, or the parties with the initiative. Ibn Saud is a fine company-commander, who's a bit out of his depth with a battalion. He's trying to bestride two worlds, the desert and the towns. It has never been done so far, except episodically. Faisal wanted to attempt it, in 1918: and I broke him away, then, from the nomads, roughly. I don't believe you can yet unite, or federate, or crush into one tyranny even, any two Arab-speaking districts.
>
> The fellow you need to influence is Feisal el Dueish, or whoever is the driving force behind the raiders . . .

Throughout this period Lawrence had been revising the notes he had written under a blanket on his bed, 'between Last Post and lights out', during his basic training at Uxbridge. He planned a book entitled *The Mint* because, he would explain later to Trenchard, 'we were all being stamped after your image and superscription'. Although Trenchard had known from the start that it was Lawrence's intention to write a book about the RAF, he did not relish the prospect and could not have been pleased to learn it was well advanced.

Worried that Trenchard would be upset, Lawrence wrote to assure him he had no intention of publishing it in his lifetime:

> After I'm dead someone may censor out of it an edition for publication . . . It's a worm's eye view of the R.A.F. – a scrappy, uncomfortable thing. I've been an uncomfortable thing while I wrote it. The ranks, even of your incomparable force, don't make for easy living or writing. Every word of this has been done in barracks . . . The general public might be puzzled, and think I didn't like the R.A.F., whereas I find it the only life worth living for its own sake. Though not the Depot. Uxbridge was bad, and I'd have written and told you so, only that it seemed implicit in your letting me join, that I should take my stuff quietly.

Trenchard replied to say he was mainly worried the press would get hold of it and use it to attack the RAF, but he was also at pains to reassure Lawrence that he was not angry: 'I do not feel a bit annoyed with you. I feel I always thought you would do it, though I hoped you would not . . . I may feel hurt at this, but you should not be, as I am not hurt at all about it. You know it is not for myself I care twopence, but for the Air Force, that I have tried so hard to get going in the right way . . .'

On receipt of Trenchard's letter Lawrence immediately dispatched a telegram reassuring him, once again, that *The Mint* would not be published: 'Copyright remains mine therefore impossible anyone publish without my permission which will never be granted.' He followed up with a long handwritten letter denying, even, that he planned a book:

> I am distressed that the news of my having re-copied the Uxbridge notes should have caused you worry . . . If you read ten pages of the notes you'll see there has never been in the writer's mind an idea of its coming out, in whole or in part, as a book. It is written without reserve for the private eyes of understanding people. I have treated the R.A.F. as a full-grown show, said my best and worst of it. Sincerity is the only written thing which time improves . . . There are too many fools in the streets to broadcast it safely. They'd think I didn't like the R.A.F., whereas I'm as stoutly its lowest number as you are its highest. You get a God's eye of it, I a worm's eye view. The worm, let me assure you, hugs himself with happiness on his good days in it . . .

He may have thought a little judicious flattery would help placate Trenchard, since he continued:

> Do please credit your most experienced A/C, who has, in his time, been a man of action, and even made a tiny fighting service out of nothing, when he assures you that the R.A.F. is the finest individual effort in British history. As this is a private letter, I'm going to let myself go and tell you (what I'll never say in print, unless I survive you and write your life, which God forbid!) that the R.A.F. is your single work: that every one of us, in so far as he is moulded to type, is moulded after your image; and that it's thanks to your being head and shoulders greater in character than ordinary men, that your

force, even in its childhood, surpasses the immemorial Army and Navy. No other man in the three or four continents I know could have done what you've done . . .

Nevertheless Lawrence remained concerned that *The Mint* would overstep the bounds of their curious friendship. 'I hope *The Mint* will not make Trenchard hate me,' he wrote to his friend Charlotte Shaw, the wife of George Bernard Shaw. 'He is so very kind and large: but it offends against the tradition of loyalty, and perhaps he will think me a scab for betraying my service.'

Several weeks passed before Trenchard was able to obtain a copy of the manuscript. When he at last got round to reading it, he can only have been appalled by Lawrence's stark, unexpurgated account of his days as a recruit – the bullying, the cruelty, the inhumanity, the mind-numbing drills and fatigues and being screamed at by NCOs: 'LOOK AT ME! LOOK ME IN THE FACE YOU SHORT-ARSED LITTLE FUCK PIG!' The passages extolling the many virtues of the Chief of the Air Staff – 'the pinnacle and our exemplar' – can have done little to minimise his consternation or the effect it would have on the reputation of the RAF if it ever got out.

Nevertheless his response to Lawrence – four typewritten pages on Air Ministry paper – was a model of restraint:

I know I shall not hurt your feelings: it was what I expected to read. I feel I understand everything you put down at the time and your feelings, but I feel it would be unfair to let this loose on a world that likes to blind itself to the ordinary facts that go on day after day. Everything you have written – I can see it happening – the way you have written it as if it was happening, but the majority of people will only say 'how awful! how horrible! how terrible! how bad!'

There are many things you have written which I do feel we know go on and we know should not go on, though what you have written does not hurt me one bit – far from it, and yet, if I saw it in print, if I saw it being published and misunderstood by the public, I should hate it, and I should feel my particular work of trying to make this force would be irretrievably damaged and that through my own fault. I wonder if you understand what I have written. I think you do; try to. I read every word of it and I seemed to know what was coming in each line, and I feel no soreness, no sadness, about your writing; and yet again I feel all of a tremble in case it gets out and into the hands of people who don't know life as it is. But as the Air Force gets more and more of the spirit I want it to get, so a lot of what you have written will automatically leave the Air Force without there seemingly being any alteration in the eyes of the public . . .

I am perfectly certain I am not really uneasy about *The Mint*, so don't think any more that I am. Your letter reassured me and I am certain you will understand my views, so I am pleased at having read it, and shall not probably remember it again in my life and time, though it will interest many people in many years to come.

'I was glad to get your letter,' Lawrence replied, 'and to learn that *The Mint* had not decided you to cast me out of the R.A.F. again. Also to see that you do not think it a dreadful work. I do not think it is, any more than you do: – though the fools of the public (numerous creatures these are) would howl and say "How DREADFUL" if it was published.'

In the meantime, Lawrence's CO, Wing Commander Reginald Bone, had belatedly discovered that one of his aircraftsmen was 'Lawrence of Arabia'. (It was said everyone in the camp knew Shaw's true identity except the aptly named Bone.) He was not pleased, and he was even less pleased when he learned that Aircraftsman Shaw was in regular correspondence with the Chief of the Air Staff. Shaw was ordered to report to the adjutant and show him recent letters he had received from Trenchard – an outrageous breach of his privacy, but Lawrence complied without protest. His public 'outing' caused some dissension among the officers and Lawrence heard that one had boasted about 'laying a jump' on him. Anxious to keep his record clean he applied, to Bone's great relief, for a posting up-country. He was transferred to Miranshah, the smallest RAF station in India only ten miles from the border with Afghanistan in an area frequently raided by hostile tribes, where he was assigned the job of orderly office clerk.

On 11 September 1928 Lawrence wrote a long letter to Trenchard describing his life in Miranshah: '. . . so tiny and so remote and so shut-in a place was exactly what I needed to be quiet in. We are behind barbed wire, and walls with towers, and sentries and searchlit every night. It is like having fallen over the edge of the world. A peace and hush which can be felt. Lovely. I hope to stay here for the rest of my overseas spell.'

This was but a preamble to the real purpose of the letter – Lawrence wanted Trenchard to approve a five-year extension to his service.

> The only thing, since 1925, that has happened to make you feel sorry I am in the R.A.F. is, possibly, the Uxbridge Notes . . . However, I have told you that I will not publish them, whatever happens to me, in the R.A.F. or out of it. So this is not blackmail.
>
> You have never been reconciled to my serving, as I am quite aware. The Senior officers all hate it. My immediate C.O.s (perhaps I've been fortunate) have all been exceedingly good to me, and have defended my harmlessness when I have been absently discussed. I think, if you were the F/Lieut, Commanding Miranshah that you would lose your nervousness regarding me. I am nearly always cheerful; and work quite hard, and – amazingly – distract the other fellows in camp. For them I am almost an education, for I have done and read so much, and seen so many people and places, that they use me as a reference library. And I think that the spectacle of a semi-public character contented in their ranks does tend to increase their self-respect and contentment.

Trenchard did not reply until 30 November, the day on which he issued formal instructions to the AMP (Air Marshal Personnel) allowing Lawrence to extend his service, adding the ingenuous comment: 'This, as you know, is quite illegal and informal. At the same time this is in no way to cancel the orders given that if at any time Lawrence asks to leave the service he is to be allowed to do so at once without any question . . . This matter must be quite plain, and must be kept confidentially in a drawer by the A.M.P. together with all previous letters from me on the subject.'[5]

> I did not answer your letter on the subject of your re-engagement [he wrote to Lawrence], because you said if I did not reply you would assume I agreed. I do agree to your extension for 5 years. I have also agreed that if you want to stop out there [in Miranshah] until 1930 or 1931 you may do so. At the same time, I am quite ready

to bring you home of course, if you are at all seedy, and station you
again at a place like Cranwell or somewhere similar.

I have cabled to Sir Geoffrey Salmond [commander of the RAF
in India] telling him I agree to your extension, and to tell you, so
you will probably be told before you receive this. Let me know how
you are and how things are going.

Now let me tell you this. Various people at home have been to see
me, rather to implore me not to allow you to re-engage, but to bring
you back to England. I have said that when you like to write to me
or my successor and say you are tired of the Royal Air Force, I will
agree to your going, but I will not take it from any of your friends
that you really want to go out. This much I know you will do (and
you owe it to me) – you will tell me when you want to leave . . .

I should much like to see you and talk over things. My little boy
is growing up fast. There is one thing you will hear by the time you
get this letter, or very soon after, and that is that my resignation has
been definitely accepted, and I leave at the end of December 1929.
It is not, of course, decided who will succeed me, but I shall have
done nearly 12 years by that time, and I think it is time for the good
of the Air Force that I should clear out. You will probably agree,
but may think it necessary to write and say you don't agree. Do not
do this, because you must not get dishonest by stopping in the Air
Force. It is supposed to be an honest Service, and I think it is.

He signed the letter simply 'T' – the nearest he ever came to informality.
In fact Lawrence had already heard of Trenchard's impending
resignation over the station radio and immediately wrote a touch-
ing valedictory note. His letter, dated 11 December, crossed with
Trenchard's.

So it's all over, and I can't tell you how sorry I am. Of course, I
know it's your wisest move, and you have finished, and all that:
but here I've just been able to take on for five more, as you go out.
You'll feel it hard: for you have never really been in the R.A.F. at all.
You've made it; and that means you are not in it. People can't make
things bigger than themselves: not bigger enough to get into. I'm
sorry, because it feels nice, to be in it, like I am.

I think you have finished the job. A man would be slow, who

couldn't exhaust all of himself into a thing in ten years. You were lucky to have the chance for ten years. No other man has been given a blank sheet and told to make a Service, from the ground up. Neither the Army, nor the Navy have a father in the sense of the R.A.F. Now you'll see the child tumbling down and hurting its knees, and getting up again. Don't worry, more than you need. It's a very healthy, and tolerably happy child . . .

You'll feel exceedingly lonely and tired for a long time: and I wonder what you'll do: for you aren't old enough to settle down. Perhaps you'll go and govern somewhere. That will be only the shadow of power, after what you've had: but shadows are comfortable, after too fierce a light. So possibly you will be contented.

You'll be rather shocked to find that three weeks after you're gone (about the time you're reading this) your past services haven't any interest or value in the Government's eyes. It's what we can do, yet, which makes us regarded.

I've said to you before, that in my eyes (very experienced and judgmatical [sic] eyes) you have done the biggest and best thing of our generation: and I'd take my hat off to you, only at Miranshah I do not wear one. There'll never be another King like you in the R.A.F., and I'll feel smaller under whoever it is takes your place. Allenby, Winston, and you: that's my gallery of chiefs, to date. Now there'll be a come down.

You know that I'm at your disposal (except in disposing of my body) at all times and circumstances.

Lawrence's hopes of staying at Miranshah would soon be dashed. On 16 December 1928, the *Empire News*, a long since closed British Sunday newspaper, published a ridiculous story claiming that Colonel Lawrence, 'the most mysterious man in the Empire', had been in Afghanistan where he had had interviews with the king, the chief of police and the war minister and was currently travelling in the country disguised as a holy man on a pilgrimage. The story was a complete fabrication and although the *Empire News* was forced to publish a retraction, the damage was done. On 3 January 1929, the chief of the British Legation in Kabul telegraphed Sir Denis Bray, foreign secretary to the Government of India in Delhi, asserting that rumours about Lawrence were creating an 'ineradicable suspicion in the mind of the Afghan Government that he is scheming against them in some mysterious way'.

Two days later the *Daily Herald* splashed another completely fictional story claiming that the Afghan authorities had ordered the arrest of Colonel Lawrence on the grounds that he was believed to be assisting Afghan rebels to cross the border. On learning that the Foreign Office in London considered 'Lawrence's presence anywhere in India under present conditions is very inconvenient', Sir Geoffrey Salmond, A.O.C. India, cabled Trenchard for advice. Trenchard, with his usual consideration for his troublesome friend – 'I want to help him as much as I can,' he told Salmond – agreed that Lawrence should be transferred out of India and asked Salmond to ascertain whether he would like to go to Aden, Somaliland, Singapore, or return to England. Lawrence plumped for going home.

Lawrence left Bombay on 12 January on the SS *Rajputana* with orders to report to the Air Ministry after the ship had docked in Tilbury, but when the *Rajputana* stopped at Port Said he was given a message from Trenchard ordering him to disembark at Plymouth to avoid the crowd of reporters that were expected to be waiting to meet him at Tilbury. 'On your arrival the Press will, I am afraid, meet you and as much as possible will try and interview you and photograph you. Endeavour as much as you can to avoid being interviewed. Disembark at Plymouth, where I am sending someone to meet you who will be in plain clothes. From Plymouth you can then go off on leave, but as soon as you can come and see me.'[6]

The *Rajputana* dropped anchor off Plymouth on 2 February 1929. A naval launch with Wing Commander Sydney Smith on board in plain clothes was sent out to meet the ship and Lawrence, in his RAF uniform, climbed down a rope ladder thrown over the side. But the Air Ministry had seriously underestimated his celebrity. Word had got out that Lawrence was leaving the ship at Plymouth and the *Rajputana* was surrounded by circling boats packed with reporters, photographers and newsreel cameramen recording every moment. In the cabin of the naval launch, Smith handed Lawrence a 'welcome home' note from Trenchard containing two pound notes 'in case you may want it' and an invitation to stay at Dancers Hill House.

Smith, aware that Plymouth railway station had probably been staked out by the media, arranged for a car to take them to the station at Newton Abbott, where they boarded a train for London. But by the time they arrived at Paddington, a rabble of reporters and photographers was waiting for them. A cavalcade of cars followed their taxi to a flat in the Cromwell Road where Lawrence was hustled inside. Next day his arrival back in Britain made headlines around the world. The *New York Times* reported the car chase on its front page under the headline 'LAWRENCE OF ARABIA HIDES IN LONDON: FLEES REPORTERS ON ARRIVING FROM INDIA'.

Lawrence spent his first weekend at Dancers Hill House, with the Trenchard family, miraculously undisturbed by the press. On Monday morning, in civilian clothes, he accompanied Trenchard in his official car to London. They parted at the Air Ministry. Trenchard had emphasised to Lawrence the need for him to maintain the lowest possible profile and was astounded when, several hours later, he received a telephone call from Hoare, in a state of some agitation, to inquire if he realised that Lawrence was in the House, in uniform, 'holding court' with a group of Labour MPs. It seems he had gone straight from the Air Ministry, changed into his uniform, marched into the lobby of the House and asked to see Ernest Thurtle, the Labour member for Shoreditch, who had been asking provocative questions about why Lawrence had been allowed to enlist in the air force as an airman under a false name.

Trenchard got a message to Lawrence summoning him to return to the Air Ministry immediately. Lawrence was not in the least contrite and explained to Trenchard that the MPs had listened to him with considerable sympathy and that he had dissuaded them from asking any more 'foolish questions' about him. (One of the reasons he had begged them to desist was because he was apprehensive the circumstances of his illegitimate birth would be revealed.) Trenchard was only partly mollified. 'Why,' he asked in despair, 'must you be more of a damned nuisance than you need to be?'

(Thurtle and Lawrence subsequently became close friends and worked together on a successful campaign to bring about the abolition of the death penalty for cowardice or desertion.)

It was evident to Trenchard that the sooner Lawrence was extracted from London the better and so he was rapidly posted to RAF Cattewater, a flying-boat station on Plymouth Sound. From there he took advantage of Trenchard's last few months in office by urging him to tackle the little irritations of life in the ranks – the 'trifles' he had mentioned in one of his letters which 'irritate and do the most harm', ranging from the compulsory fastening of the top button of uniform greatcoats to the abolition of bayonets. He lobbied for scrapping compulsory church parades, posting servicemen closer to their homes, increased wearing of civvies, permission for pillion-riding on motorcycles, and permission to leave the service voluntarily. Trenchard listened carefully to his friend, and enacted many of the reforms he suggested – in the case of buttoning greatcoats, within weeks.

In September 1929 Lawrence managed to get on the wrong side of Lord Thomson, who was briefly back in office as Air Minister after Ramsay MacDonald had replaced Baldwin as prime minister. Lawrence was helping out at the Schneider Trophy Race which was being held that year over the Solent. One of the most glamorous events of the sporting calendar, it was attended by innumerable dignitaries and celebrities, many of whom were friends of Lawrence and stopped to chat with him. At one point he was seen talking animatedly with Lady Astor. Thomson may have understandably felt aggrieved that an airman was receiving more attention from the great and good than the Air Minister himself. The crunch came when the leader of the Italian team, who was also a friend of Lawrence, asked if it might be possible to get their slipway, which was covered in green algae, cleaned up. Lawrence duly got it organised but the sight of British airmen cleaning the Italian slipway enraged Thomson, who demanded to know who was responsible. The inevitable altercation which followed took place in front of the world's media and photographs of the Air Minister 'in conversation' with Lawrence of Arabia went round the world, to Thomson's intense embarrassment.

Shortly afterwards Thomson got his own back on the wayward airman. Lawrence had asked Trenchard if he could spend his leave taking part as crew in a seaplane tour of Europe. Trenchard, always indulgent to his friend, had agreed, providing it was approved by the Air Minister. But Thomson was in no mood to accommodate the aircraftsman who had effectively upstaged him at the Schneider Trophy Race, and instructed Trenchard to inform Lawrence that permission for him to go on the seaplane jaunt was withheld. Lawrence was summoned to the Air Ministry, where Trenchard warned him he had come very close to being kicked out of the RAF again and that henceforth he was to 'confine himself to the duties of an aircraftsman'. Not only that, but he was also forbidden from visiting, or even speaking to, any 'great men' or women, among them Churchill, Birkenhead, Austen Chamberlain, Philip Sassoon and Lady Astor. George Bernard Shaw later confessed that he was rather 'piqued' not to have been included on the banned list.

Lawrence recognised that Trenchard was only following his minister's instructions and this little contretemps in no way affected their relationship. A few days before Trenchard's retirement, Lawrence wrote him another affectionate letter:

> The fact that we are all sorry you are going shows your rightness in going. The R.A.F. should be (and I feel it is) now big enough to stand on its feet. You are too big to be the father of a grown-up child. Let the beast go and make its own mistakes. It's going to be a very splendid service, and will always be proud of you. When you have been away from it, a while, you'll be very proud of it . . . After you are 'out', may I come and see you, if you stay in England?

Lawrence stayed on in the RAF, professing happiness, until the end of his enlistment in March 1935. Two months later, riding his beloved Brough Superior SS100 motorcycle in Dorset near his cottage, Clouds Hill, he swerved to avoid two boys on bicycles who had been obscured by a dip in the road. He lost control and was thrown over the handlebars. He died in hospital six days later, on 19 May 1935.

The Mint, edited by his brother, Professor A.W. Lawrence, was eventually published in 1955.

THE POLICE COMMISSIONER

Trenchard more or less disappeared from public life for some months after his retirement, retreating to Dancers Hill to spend precious time with his family. He was 58 years old and had been, mostly unwillingly, in the public eye for more than a decade; it was little wonder he welcomed the obscurity of retirement as 'that happy fate'.

He had had numerous offers to join the boards of different aircraft manufacturers, but had made it a strict rule that he would never make 'a penny piece' out of his position as the most senior officer in the RAF, although he accepted a directorship of the Goodyear Tyre and Rubber Company. His friend Sir Edward Peacock, a Canadian merchant banker who had been appointed a director of the Bank of England, put his name forward, along with Leo Amery, a former Colonial Secretary in the Baldwin government. 'Goodyear were looking not so much for seasoned businessmen,' Peacock explained, 'as men who knew their way around Government departments. I had no hesitation whatever in recommending Trenchard and Leopold Amery, both of whom I knew and both of whom happened to be free.'[1] He might have added that both also needed the money – neither had independent means and Trenchard's two sons, Hugh and Thomas, were destined for Eton.

In March 1931, 15 months after stepping down as CAS, he was surprised to get a call from Ramsay MacDonald, the embattled Labour prime minister, inviting him to Downing Street. It was not a social call. Trenchard's name had been suggested to take over from Lord Byng as commissioner of the Metropolitan Police. Byng, former commander of the Third Army in France during the Great War, was in poor health and anxious to retire. MacDonald was concerned that unrest in the police might lead to a disastrous strike and the breakdown of public order and the Cabinet was agreed that another strong-minded military man was needed to take charge of the Metropolitan Police.

MacDonald explained to Trenchard that the government was looking for a 'Militarist' as commissioner. 'The militarist we want, of course, is you,' he said.

Trenchard's response was terse to the point of rudeness. 'The militarist you're not getting,' he grunted, 'is me.'

MacDonald begged him not to make a decision there and then, but to think it over and discuss it with Sir John Anderson, the Permanent Under-Secretary of State at the Home Office. Trenchard agreed, but warned the prime minister that he was very unlikely to change his mind. He chose not to mention the fact that he had been offered a job in the City with the possibility of earning up to £20,000 a year – an astonishing sum for the time – and which might have enabled him to realise his long-held dream of restoring Wolfeton to the family.

Finding a replacement for the police commissioner was the least of Ramsay MacDonald's problems. His government was virtually overwhelmed by the economic crisis following the Great Depression and the Wall Street crash and split by demands for cuts in public spending. Unemployment had doubled to more than two and a half million. As the economic situation rapidly deteriorated, MacDonald struggled to cope and found himself attempting to reconcile two contradictory aims – achieving a balanced budget to maintain the value of the pound and maintaining assistance to the poor and unemployed at a time when tax revenues were falling. A Cabinet committee urged savage cuts in welfare benefits and public-sector wages, a move bitterly opposed by the trade unions. News that the government was considering imposing a 10 per cent pay cut did nothing for the morale of the 20,000 members of the Metropolitan Police Force, already at a low ebb, battered by a series of scandals reported in salacious detail by the popular press.

The Metropolitan Police Force, known to most Londoners as 'the Met', was established by Sir Robert Peel in 1829 and for the first 100-plus years of its existence commissioners were always chosen from the ranks of retired army officers or senior civil servants. The commissioner for much of the 1920s was Brigadier General Sir William Horwood, a good administrator but an aloof, humourless and arrogant figure who made no attempt to get to know the men under his command. When he began filling senior posts with other retired officers he stoked left-wing fears that there was an agenda to militarise the police force. In November 1922, he survived an assassination attempt when a mentally ill individual sent him a box of chocolates – walnut whips – laced with arsenic. Assuming they were a present from his daughter he ate one and only survived because of the prompt attention of a police surgeon. Thereafter he was known throughout the force, disdainfully, as 'the chocolate soldier'.

In 1926 the patience, fortitude and tolerance of police during the General Strike had so impressed the country that *The Times* opened a subscription list and a grateful public contributed nearly a quarter of a million pounds. A year later, everything had changed. From 1927 onwards the popular newspapers were increasingly running stories about misconduct and corruption in 'the Met'. Horwood failed to act, dismissing the stories as gossip and scandal-mongering unworthy of his attention, even when Station Sergeant George Goddard of 'C' Division was convicted of taking bribes from night club owners (he was said to have 'secured for himself a sum more than sufficient to bribe a whole Division').[2] Towards the end of his time in office, Horwood found himself facing a full-blown scandal when the curious Money–Savidge affair erupted.

On the evening of 23 April 1928, Sir Leo Chiozza Money, an Italian-born politician, journalist and writer, was said to have been observed by a police constable in Hyde Park kissing a young woman, Miss Irene Savidge, a 'radio valve tester' from North London. Both were arrested and charged with indecent behaviour. Sir Leo vigorously protested his innocence, claiming he had only been giving Miss Savidge advice about her career. At the police station he protested he was not 'riff-raff' but 'a man of substance' and insisted on being allowed to telephone the Home Secretary, Sir William Joynson-Hicks, to apprise him of events.

The arrest of a prominent public figure, 58 years old, apparently caught canoodling with a 23-year-old girl in Hyde Park, inevitably made headlines, as did their subsequent acquittal in court and remarks by the magistrate commenting unfavourably on the reliability of police witnesses.[3] The case could have ended there, except the police sniffed an 'establishment' conspiracy and hauled the luckless Miss Savidge in for further questioning – an interrogation that lasted for five hours, without a female officer being present, and at which she was required to show the officers her pink petticoat, the colour and brevity of which was duly noted. Miss Savidge, not unreasonably, complained about her treatment and her case was the subject of an adjournment debate in Parliament followed by a public inquiry which criticised the excessive zeal of the Metropolitan Police and led to reforms about the way female suspects were treated, along with a long-running media discussion about whether the police should concentrate on law and order, rather than trying to be 'censors of public morals'.

Sir William Horwood retired at the height of the media firestorm, leading many people to assume he was quitting in disgrace, but in fact he had always been due to leave that year, as he turned 60. His successor was Lord Byng. Known to his friends as 'Bungo' (his elder brothers were 'Bingo' and 'Bango'), Julian Byng was a very different sort of character. The scion of a distinguished family (his grandfather, the first Earl of Stafford, had commanded a brigade at Waterloo), Byng had recently completed a notably successful stint as Governor-General of Canada, where he had travelled the length and breadth of the country meeting Canadians wherever he went and immersing himself in the culture of the country, becoming a devoted fan of ice hockey. When he was appointed commissioner of the Met, his first question was to ask if the force was a 'happy family'. On being told that that was far from the case, he set about trying to make it so, introducing a number of popular reforms, including a system of promotion based on merit rather than length of service and the extensive use of police cars working through a radio control room.

Byng quickly realised that the constant stream of bad publicity following the Goddard scandal and the Money–Savidge affair was having a very damaging effect on *esprit de corps* and so he sought a meeting with the Newspaper Proprietors' Association to plead for moderation and balance in the coverage of the Met's activities. Relations with the media steadily improved, but most of the good work that Byng put in was undone by the threat of a pay cut and the increasing militancy of the Police Federation, the 'trade union' of the force, with alarming talk about the possibility of a police strike.

Sir John Anderson no doubt ran through the Met's history and problems when he met Trenchard a few days after Trenchard had been summoned to Downing Street. He emphasised why a man of Trenchard's calibre was needed to take over the force and institute a

much-needed reorganisation and further sweeping reforms, someone
who would not be deflected by opposition or unpopularity. Sir John
referred to the Royal Commission set up in 1927 to investigate the
powers and procedures of the police and which had recommended
an end to the traditional method of advancement. Any system which
limited appointment to the higher posts to those who had entered the
police as constables was, it concluded, 'inimical to the public interest'.
The Home Office was already working on plans to set up a police college. It was the government's view that there was no better man than
Trenchard to see the job through.

Despite all Sir John's blandishments, Trenchard remained unmoved
and insisted that he was not interested.

Meanwhile Ramsay MacDonald's government was falling apart.
With senior ministers threatening to resign if the government went
ahead with drastic reductions in public spending, MacDonald submitted his resignation in August but was urged by the King to form
a National Government with the Conservatives and Liberals. The
following month around 1000 disgruntled sailors from the British
Atlantic Fleet began refusing orders when their ships returned to
Invergordon from autumn manoeuvres and they learned that their pay
was going to be cut by around 10 per cent. The so-called Invergordon
Mutiny, one of the few strikes by the military in British history, caused
panic on the London Stock Exchange and a run on the pound, forcing
the new National Government to suspend the Gold Standard.

Although the strike only lasted a few days and all the ships sailed
on time when they were ordered to return to their home ports, the
incident shook the Cabinet and there were fears that the police, facing
similar pay cuts, might follow suit. Sir John Anderson still held to the
view that Trenchard was the right man to take charge of the Metropolitan Police at this critical juncture as did the new Home Secretary,
Sir Herbert Samuel, who wrote to Trenchard on 2 October to say he
had discussed the matter with the King who 'very warmly' approved
the proposal and greatly hoped 'that you will be able to see your way
to accept the appointment. I should be very grateful if you would
come and talk over the matter, and if you are not ready to give your
acceptance, I trust you will at least keep an open mind until you hear
what is to be said'.[4]

The following day, Sir Warren Fisher, the head of the Home Civil

Service, one of the most influential civil servants of his generation and a close friend of Trenchard, telephoned to 'urge him to the utmost of my power' to accept the position and suggested they should meet. During the course of a long weekend at Dancers Hill Sir Warren laid out the government's situation. 'In my talks with him on Saturday and Sunday,' he reported to the Cabinet later, 'I made it clear that in my deliberate opinion his undoubted duty is to accept the position; in fact he had no alternative. I assured him that it was the earnest wish of the King, the Prime Minister, Mr. Baldwin [Lord President of the Council] and the Home Secretary that he would assent.'[5]

At the end of a weekend of sustained pressure, Trenchard finally, and 'with the utmost reluctance', agreed to accept the offer and abandoned all hope of acquiring Wolfeton. He made two conditions. The first was that he would have the right to resign at short notice if he felt his 'life's work' at the Air Ministry was in any way endangered, and the second was an oblique reference to a long-standing and unfulfilled ambition – to be Viceroy of India. Opposition to British rule in India was fomenting and Trenchard said that if the government felt he would 'be more useful there' he would also want to be allowed to step down as commissioner. Sir Warren assured him of his belief that the Cabinet would accept both conditions without difficulty as part of a 'gentleman's agreement'. Sir Warren also promised that his salary as commissioner would be bumped up from £2700 per annum to £4000, which was what Trenchard claimed he was earning by 'various forms of work'.

A few days later Ramsay MacDonald invited Trenchard to Downing Street to thank him for taking the job. Trenchard thought the prime minister, whose health was declining rapidly, looked 'dreadfully tired – a woolly-haired, sad old man, with watery eyes that seemed to be giving him a lot of trouble, and a tongue that rambled more than ever'. MacDonald assured his visitor that he would be given a free hand to institute much-needed reforms at the Metropolitan Police.

'Even if it means turning the force upside down?' Trenchard asked.

'If that's necessary,' MacDonald replied, 'we'll support you.'

'Is this a good time for wholesale reforms?'

'If life has taught me one thing,' the prime minister said with a wan smile, 'it's that there's never a good time for doing things that are unpleasant.'[6]

Three weeks after accepting the position, Trenchard was amused to receive a letter at Dancers Hill from the Home Office asking for a cheque or postal order in the sum of ten shillings 'for the defrayal of the Stamp Duty on the Royal Warrant for your appointment as Commissioner of Police of the Metropolis'.[7]

The news that the new commissioner of the Metropolitan Police Force was to be Lord Trenchard was released to the press on 7 October 1931 and was generally applauded. Even Harold Laski, Britain's most influential intellectual spokesman for socialism at that time, and a man very unlikely to agree with Trenchard on anything, welcomed his appointment in a long, not entirely complimentary, profile in the *Daily Herald* under the headline 'Lord Trenchard – Give Him a Job and He Never Lets Go'.

'He looks precisely what he is – blunt, direct, self-confident, determined,' Laski wrote.

Lord Trenchard's gifts are not those of the subtle man, or of the intellectual. He is of the type whom you ask to do a piece of organisation in the knowledge that he will do it well. You do not expect innovation from him; his mind is not experimental. He has neither vision nor eloquence. His qualities are good, ordinary intelligence and real moral power. You cannot be in his presence without the sense that he will drive directly to his goal . . .

Lord Trenchard is of the type of which the supreme example is the Duke of Wellington. Where other men talk of courage, he will talk of duty. His praise is economical and abrupt, but when you get it you feel as though you really have been singled out from other men . . . He does not argue very well; he has no small talk. But you cannot move him from the performance of his job. There goes into the doing of it a certain grim earnestness that has almost religious intensity about it . . . Reserved, taciturn, liable to sudden explosions, he never lets go of the task in hand. He sets himself a limited task, but you cannot budge him from its accomplishment. He has little imagination and no nerves. He is slow, but very sure, somewhat dour, but just to the bottom of his being. And like most men of his stamp – Lord Kitchener for example – behind the external wall of steel there is a surprising veil of tenderness for the few who are his intimates. An accident in the air will wring from him two or three awkward sentences; but behind the appearance of impenetrability there is a wound within, which he would rather die than disclose . . .

Laski's main concern about the appointment was whether the new commissioner would have the patience or insight to grasp the 'psychological aspect' of the police complaints. 'He will not, I hope, lack the imagination to see that the way to meet grievances is not by repression but by the removal of its just causes. On another side, his stern sense of the need for obedience to orders need not prevent him from asking fundamental questions.'

Trenchard was actually halfway across the Atlantic on a long-planned trip to North America when the announcement of his appointment was made. As Colonel of the Royal Scots Fusiliers he was due to inspect the affiliated Canadian regiment in Kitchener, Ontario. He also took the opportunity to visit the Goodyear factory at Akron, Ohio, where he watched the maiden flight of an airship being built for the United States Navy. Before heading home he was invited to pay a courtesy call on the police commissioner in New York and afterwards endured a press conference at which one reporter asked 'What are your plans for cleaning up London's underworld?'

'What underworld?' he replied somewhat ingenuously. 'I didn't know London had one.'

On Monday, 1 November 1931, Trenchard had an audience with the King at Buckingham Palace. He stayed, the newspapers reported, 'for some time'. King George V kept a careful finger on the nation's pulse and was well acquainted with the problems in what he called 'my police'. He encouraged the newly appointed commissioner to confide in him and not to hesitate to ask to see him if there was anything he needed to discuss with him. The following day Trenchard was photographed in a Homburg hat, one hand thrust into his overcoat pocket, the other carrying a walking stick, on the steps of Scotland Yard smiling broadly on his first day as commissioner of the Metropolitan Police.

He was shown round the building and introduced to department heads by Sir Trevor Bigham, the deputy commissioner, an Eton-educated barrister who had served with the Met for more than 20 years. Trenchard's reputation as a stern taskmaster had preceded him and his appearance and demeanour on his first day as commissioner did nothing to dispel the apprehension many officers felt. It was clear from the start that his regime was going to be very different from that of his predecessor, the amiable and easy-going 'Bungo'. Trenchard missed nothing, asked innumerable questions and expected straight answers, with no obfuscation.

He was profoundly depressed by much of what he found. Morale was at rock bottom due to pay cuts, discipline was poor, corruption was rife and many constables were still patrolling beats which had been laid down by Sir Robert Peel a hundred years earlier. Their facilities were wretched: totally inadequate provision for sport and recreation; police section houses were appalling and married quarters even worse; and the provident fund was so badly administered there was a very real risk that policemen who had contributed to it for years would get nothing out of it. The Police Federation, which was allowed to convene 12 meetings a year in police time, was actually holding many times that number.

Three weeks after his arrival Trenchard addressed a meeting of 2500 Metropolitan officers packed into Queen's Hall, a concert venue in central London. The meeting did not start well. Trenchard marched in and immediately ordered the hall to be cleared and all the windows opened to dispel the fug of pipe and tobacco smoke which had accumulated while the men were waiting for him to arrive. 'Be back in five minutes,' he barked, 'when I can breathe.' When the meeting finally got under way, according to a report prepared by an official shorthand writer, he adopted an avuncular, self-deprecating tone, first apologising for his lack of oratorical skills. 'I am not good at speaking with long sentences and long words,' he said after introducing himself, 'but I thought it would be a good thing that you should see me and I should see you.' He said it was his intention to hold two or three such meetings every year in order that problems at all levels could be aired. He would be asking constant questions of everyone and wanted straight answers, and he asked for forgiveness if he was unable to remember names. He spoke of honesty, discipline, fairness and 'playing the game' and appealed to them all to look on him as a friend always ready with advice. He even managed to raise a laugh at his own expense when he told them a story of his recent visit to New York. At the press conference after the meeting with his American counterpart, he responded to so many questions by saying he did not know the answer that next day one New York newspaper dubbed him 'Chief Dunno'.

But at the same time he left his audience in no doubt that his management style was going to be very different from that of his predecessor. Restoring public confidence in the force and rooting out corruption were going to be priorities. Providing each of them did their duty, he said, they would not find him too harsh or unreasonable a person to deal with, but any abuse of the rules would not be tolerated. He regarded the Police Federation as mischievous and irresponsible in the way it flouted regulations. Officers must immediately cease airing their grievances in the press. 'If any unauthorised account of what I'm saying to you here gets into the papers,' he warned ominously, 'the culprits will regret it.'

Trenchard spoke for less than 15 minutes and then called for questions from the floor, most of which he ruled out of order since they mainly revolved around the threatened pay cuts. He could not answer them, he said bluntly, because he knew no more than they did.

It soon became clear that Trenchard could not wait to 'turn the force upside down', the phrase he had used at his meeting with the prime minister. By Christmas 1931, less than two months after he had started work, he had summarily abolished one of the four main departments – the 'Legal and Civil Business' branch – and divided its work between the three remaining departments. He had also established on a permanent footing an experimental 'Ideas' department and tasked it to analyse, as a matter of urgency, exactly how a force of 20,000 men, distributed over an area of 700 square miles and 180 police stations, actually spent its 50 million man-hours during a 12-month period. It was his intention it would be the genesis of a fundamental restructuring of the force.

'Trenchard did not arrive so much as burst on the scene,' Ranulph Bacon, a detective at Scotland Yard, recalled. 'He was the nearest thing to a human typhoon this century has seen. Twenty-four hours in the day were not enough . . . He saw at once that lethargy and apathy had to be overcome.'[8]

Among the initiatives Trenchard inherited from his predecessor was a plan to completely reorganise the Met's system of patrols – the 'beats' pounded every day by policemen throughout the capital which had been laid down by Sir Robert Peel and were so predictable that

criminals could safely arrange their activities to avoid clashing with a
patrolling policeman. Byng had been trying unsuccessfully to push
the plan through for two years. Trenchard recognised its importance,
took it up as a matter of priority and put together a working group of
senior officers with instructions to come up with a practical solution
by the end of the year. He characteristically refused to listen to pro-
tests that there was insufficient time and was unconcerned to learn
that the group had been obliged to work through the Christmas holiday to meet the deadline. In the first week of January 1932, a press
release was issued by Scotland Yard announcing that a new system of
patrolling was now in force, a communiqué greatly unwelcome in the
criminal fraternity.

Meanwhile, senior officers at Scotland Yard were struggling to get
accustomed to the new regime. A chief constable whose habit was to
arrive at the Yard in mid-morning, after having exercised his horse
on Rotten Row, suddenly remembered one day he had an appointment with the commissioner in less than five minutes. He was still
pulling on his uniform tunic when he burst into the corridor leading
to Trenchard's office. To his dismay he could see the tall figure of the
commissioner waiting outside his office at the end of the corridor. 'All
right,' Trenchard boomed. 'I can see. Go back and dress properly. I
said 11 o'clock and it's two minutes past. I'll expect you at 11 o'clock
tomorrow morning.'

Settled in his ways as a military man, he expected his orders to be
obeyed without question and resented tentative suggestions that he
should perhaps discuss them first. Although he worked hard to improve the average policeman's lot – providing greatly improved sports
facilities and housing accommodation, for example – he remained a
feared and resented figure, suspected throughout his tenure of wanting
to 'militarise' the force. He was also a gift to newspaper cartoonists,
one of whom portrayed him as a moustached charlady cleaning out
the dusty corners of Scotland Yard with a mop, pail and duster.

Those dealing directly with the new commissioner on a day to day
basis had to rapidly accustom themselves to his peculiar inability to
express himself clearly and try to understand what he wanted by a
process of elimination or intuition. If they could not do so, they often
took the problem to the amiable Hamilton Howgrave-Graham, the
head of the Metropolitan Police secretariat. Howgrave-Graham was

a civil servant, not a police officer, and had been a great admirer of Trenchard's predecessor, but he would later judge the four years of Trenchard's regime as the 'most exciting period' since the foundation of the Force in 1829.

> Even the most ardent opponents of some of the things he did must agree that life was never dull when Lord Trenchard was around; and those who were privileged to work in close daily contact with him developed a wholesome admiration for his quite astonishing powers . . . When he was engrossed in a subject – and that was his normal condition – his thoughts seemed to travel faster than his words. They appeared to be a lap or two ahead, and the poor words, trying madly to catch up, tripped and stumbled to such an extent that an almost unbelievable incoherence occasionally resulted . . .
>
> It is often said (and I had before those days always believed) that a man who cannot express himself clearly is unlikely to have any powers of clear or logical thought. This may be generally a sound proposition, but Lord Trenchard was an exception to this rule. Not only could he think with the greatest clarity, he had also quite unusual powers of discriminating between the essentials and the non-essentials, between the important and the unimportant, between the permanent and the ephemeral. He could drag the 'guts' out of a complicated problem in a remarkably short time and, when he had done it, and held them up for one to see, one realised at once that they were indeed the real and only guts and that nothing else mattered very much . . .[9]

Howgrave-Graham considered one of his most important duties – as Baring and Marson had done before him at the RFC and the Air Ministry – was to 'translate' Trenchard's wishes into official language. But for his own amusement he kept a note of some of the commissioner's more memorable verbal circumlocutions and tangled metaphors:

> 'Have we got men really to do this sort of work? It seems to me that this place is an ordinary fair, like coconut shies, with the question of a competition for cigarettes. Is it any worse than coconut shies, or hitting a bat to hit bells, etcetera?'

'You can't see the wood for the weeds.'

'If you do that, you'll put the soup in the cart – I mean the horse in the soup.'

'We must have plenty of ammunition up our sleeves.'

'Really, it is not seriously intended that we should waste our time in running them in on the subject of what is called greyhound racing, or the game of darts and shoot darts and the gun.'

Trenchard had a habit of walking about his office, swinging his key chain, thinking aloud and often ending a sentence with 'd'you see?' or 'and everything'. 'Yes, I want you to do this,' he said one day, 'so that I can hang my peg on it, d'you see?' A little later he referred to a parade and said 'The route was lined by boy guides and everything.'

At one point Trenchard told Howgrave-Graham he intended to send each of the assistant commissioners on leave for a day or two and sit in their offices to understand what they did. He asked Howgrave-Graham if he saw any difficulty in this and Howgrave-Graham replied 'None whatsoever, provided you don't do the same to me.'

'And why not?' Trenchard demanded.

'Because,' the other man said, 'you'd spend half your day running into the Commissioner's office and always finding it empty.'

Trenchard laughed as if it was the funniest thing he had heard for days. He had, Howgrave-Graham admitted, a peculiar sense of humour. It was a complete waste of time to tell him a 'funny story', either proper or improper; he would simply grunt. But if some unexpected remark suddenly struck him as comical he would roar with laughter.

Howgrave-Graham recalled a conference in the commissioner's office with about eight senior officers present when Trenchard suddenly decided he needed the advice of Baker, the solicitor to the commissioner. Baker was duly summoned.

Howgrave-Graham carefully noted the exchange that followed.

'Now, Baker,' Trenchard said, 'as a man and not a lawyer, what is the defence if they have the thing and you take it and they have it here, d'you see? It's wrong and we got to stop them, d'you see?'

'What is the thing?' Baker inquired, not unreasonably.

'Kendal has it in his room. Will the law help us? Ask Foster why we are and see the Attorney and put it right.'

'But what is the thing?' Baker persisted.

'Please don't interrupt, Baker. Now leave me everybody.'

Howgrave-Graham was also intrigued by Trenchard's peculiar inability to remember names. Three colleagues named French, Trench and Frere became so accustomed to the commissioner muddling them up that they answered to whichever name he happened to choose. When Trenchard told his secretary to book a table at a restaurant he called 'Moussini', she knew he really meant Monseigneur; similarly Malmaison was invariably called 'Dalmatian'. Sir John Moylan, the receiver of the Met, with whom Trenchard was in almost daily contact, was always called 'Moylam'. Working late with him at Dancers Hill one night, Howgrave-Graham ventured a correction. 'Excuse me for interrupting,' he said. 'It isn't Moylam, it's Moylan, and I'm not Howard Graham, I'm Howgrave-Graham.' Next morning he noticed the first item on Trenchard's aide-memoire was 'Find out what Howard-Graham's name is.' He found out, but it made little difference – he continued to be Howard-Graham.

None of these foibles detracted from Trenchard's complete mastery of the task at hand.

His output was enormous [Howgrave-Graham recalled]. He was a ten man-power man. He accomplished in four years more than anybody else I've ever met could do in a dozen years. There was hardly a feature of police activity or organisation that he did not tear up by the roots, examine with a microscope and re-plant – generally improved. If anybody was ever fool enough to justify a practice on the ground of its long acceptance, his immediate reaction was that that was the best possible reason for investigating it drastically.

Saturdays, traditionally a half day, were particularly hectic since he wanted everyone to cram in as much work as would be done on a full day. One of his favourite aphorisms was that he had 'never yet met a man who killed himself from overwork'. He had no time for sickness and was irritated rather than sympathetic if any of his staff fell ill. If things were not going well he was said to be 'like a bear with a sore head', best avoided.

The press observed what was going on at Scotland Yard with bemusement. 'The monthly reorganisation of the Metropolitan Police,' the incomparable Beachcomber noted in the *Daily Express*, 'will take place weekly in future.'

> No matter what you were doing and no matter who you were [one of his private secretaries recalled], you came at the double when he called. In Lord Byng's time any official, senior officer or secretary who entered the commissioner's room in a hurry would be quietly asked what the fuss was about and invited to recover his or her breath. Trenchard was different. He kept his finger pressed hard on the bell until the person he wanted appeared. And he'd start dictating before you'd time to collect your wits.[10]

Trenchard continued his predecessor's practice of convening a meeting at Scotland Yard every Wednesday morning of all senior officers to grill them, unrelentingly, about crime in their districts and what they were doing about it. It could be an uncomfortable experience for those unable to provide direct answers supported by facts and figures. In the same way he used to tour aerodromes in France, he would make unannounced and unexpected visits to police stations at odd hours. Whereas Lord Byng tended to chat informally to the men, often asking about their families, Trenchard showed little interest in their personal lives or indulging in small talk and would fire questions at them about station routine and working practices.

He cracked down hard on corruption (accepting bribes, or 'tips', from street bookmakers, publicans and prostitutes was, he was appalled to discover, commonplace), ended the practice of uniformed constables raising funds by going door to door and selling tickets to concerts and sports games, stopped off-duty policemen providing security at greyhound race meetings and ended 'proficiency pay' of half a crown a week being paid routinely; henceforth it would have to be earned. None of these measures did anything to increase his popularity, not that it bothered him in the least.

No matter was too small for his attention. The Met organised as many as 120 'minstrel concerts' during the winter months every year, the tickets for which were sold door to door. Trenchard argued that many tickets were bought under duress and that the concerts could be profitable if they were organised properly. He contacted a London impresario who offered to provide theatres for the police minstrel concerts free of charge, but the Police Federation refused to co-operate. Trenchard thus decided he had no alternative but to 'regretfully allow the minstrels to cease'.

The *Bystander* magazine, later one of the commissioner's most persistent critics, lampooned him in this almost affectionate piece of doggerel:

I'm terrible Trenchard, the King of the Cops
I'm always on duty, my work never stops
I've been highly successful at wiping out crime
Hardly anyone now has a drink after time.
I'm as fearless and bold as my brave boys in blue
Who think nothing of a raid on a nightclub or two.
I'm the motorists' menace with no peace of mind
'Til we've had every car owner, summoned and fined.
Assassins and burglars had better beware
I shall be after them, when I've more time to spare.

In April 1932, Trenchard attended the first meeting of a Cabinet sub-committee convened to discuss police expenditure. High on the agenda was the problem of police pay. Due to a misunderstanding, the police had been led to believe that their pay would only be cut by 5 per cent, rather than the 10 per cent that was to be imposed on the military and civil servants. The government was determined the police would be treated no differently from the military and was understandably concerned how they would react. Neville Chamberlain, the Chancellor of the Exchequer, asked Trenchard how he thought the London police might react if they were told the concession on their pay was a mistake. Would they respond, he inquired, to an appeal for restraint? Trenchard shook his head. An appeal for restraint, he said, would be pointless.

Chamberlain then voiced the fear they all felt and asked if the police might strike. Trenchard agreed it was a possibility, particularly as the reforms he was intending to introduce were likely to be unpopular. A

decision was deferred for six months on the assumption that Trenchard would be better placed to handle a strike in the autumn if given
time to prepare for such an eventuality.

In early May Trenchard had another audience with the King during
which he outlined the problems still faced by the Met and the reforms
he proposed. Later the same day he sent a confidential memorandum
to the King via his private secretary, Sir Clive Wigram, explaining the
difficulties being created by the Police Federation. 'It does not put forward any scheme but shows what are the chief matters that are wrong,'
he wrote in a covering note. 'It is a very hush-hush paper, and nobody
here has seen it, and only one or two Ministers know of its existence
. . . I hope you will keep it very secret as it would do untold harm if it
became known.'

Two days later Wigram returned the paper and said the King had
read it 'with the greatest interest'. He said he had impressed upon His
Majesty the need for discretion and continued, 'Doubtless you are up
against an immense problem and it will be difficult to get Parliament
to face the facts of the situation. They would probably prefer to blink.'

The following week Trenchard wrote again after particularly vituperative attacks on him in the press.

> You may probably have seen a very bitter criticism against me
> and mine in some illustrated paper last week, called, I think, the
> *National Graphic*. And this morning I see there is very hot crit-
> icism against me and all my works in the *Daily Express*. I hear
> personally there are one or two people behind the scenes who are
> boiling up as much agitation as they can on this subject. I thought,
> in case you had not seen this, that you might just like to know
> about it.

Wigram replied by return of post: 'We did indeed see the monstrous
attack upon you in the *Daily Express* and the King and everyone are
more than disgusted. Cannot you catch the agitators who are trying
to stir up trouble?'

Trenchard had no doubt that the most scurrilous agitators could be
found in the ranks of the Police Federation and when he was invited
to address the Federation's annual meeting in London at the end of
May he vigorously defended his reforms as essential in rehabilitating

the Met and restoring public confidence in the force. He was heard in stony silence.

By the autumn of 1932 Trenchard had gone through innumerable drafts to produce what became known as the 'Police Book' – his confidential analysis of what was wrong with the Met and how it could be put right. The Police Federation was, inevitably, blamed for many of the ills: 'Grievances are ventilated through this organisation rather than through the officers whose business it should be to prevent and remedy them. Esprit de corps is almost entirely lacking. There is an atmosphere of suspicion and lack of confidence. Discipline is wooden, repressive and unintelligent. The standard of conduct is low and incidents of actual dishonesty occur at regular intervals . . .'

He went on to point out that only 18 per cent of the force had been educated beyond elementary level, only 11 of the 759 officers on the establishment belonged to what he described as 'the educated classes' and only one constable in the entire 100-plus year history of the force had ever attained the rank of assistant commissioner. The rank and file were ageing, poorly trained and ill equipped to deal with modern criminals; it was little wonder the crime rate in London had been rising steadily for several years. There had been too rigid adherence to Peel's doctrine of filling senior posts from below, but long experience and good service in the lower ranks were not necessarily suitable qualifications for promotion; it was imperative that recruitment was broadened to attract better-qualified candidates. Twenty-five years' service with little prospect of promotion, but a pension at the end of it, produced plodding policemen unwilling to show initiative.

His solution was to push through the setting up of a police training college. The idea had been around for some time, despite being contemptuously dismissed by the Police Federation as 'offering short cuts to promotion for a pampered few'. One of the obstacles was obtaining agreement from the large number (181) of autonomous police forces spread around the country. Trenchard solved the problem very simply: he proposed that there should be a college solely for the Metropolitan Police.

On 20 October Trenchard summoned all the Met's district and divisional officers to a meeting at Scotland Yard to warn them that the government intended to revoke the 5 per cent pay concession that had been offered to the police months earlier. Trenchard had secretly prepared squads of 'specials' – civilian volunteer constables – to stand by in the event of a police strike but it proved to be unnecessary. The pay cut was accepted with a great deal of grumbling, but there were no calls to strike.

Trenchard was lucky. A Metropolitan Police strike at that moment would have been a disaster, since 3000 angry unemployed workers from economically depressed areas in Wales, Scotland and the north of England were converging on London in what became known as the 'Great Hunger March', organised by the National Unemployed Workers' Movement. The strain of the economic crisis, social unrest, the spread of Fascism, and government policies which had plunged thousands into extreme poverty had generated serious social unrest – more than a million people had signed a petition protesting against government policies which the marchers intended to deliver to Parliament. They arrived in Hyde Park on 27 October and were met by media hostility (the *Daily Mail* called the marchers 'dupes of the Communist party') and the biggest police deployment for more than 100 years – almost 2000 constables, including 108 mounted police. Despite Trenchard's appeal for ordinary citizens to stay away, huge crowds gathered, some of them Communists intent on inciting disorder. Serious violence erupted in and around the park with mounted police charging the demonstrators wielding long batons. The unrest continued for several days, resulting in 75 people being injured.

The organisers were prevented from delivering their petition to Parliament by the presence of 1200 police officers deployed around Parliament Square, and they later protested that the police were using plain-clothes officers to spy on them, an accusation that was probably correct, since Police Sergeant A. Davies took shorthand notes of the speeches in Hyde Park, now lodged in the National Archives. Oscar de Lacy, one of the leaders, was reported as saying:

> Comrades I want to say this, that the national government and Lord Trenchard must take warning and understand that before they can depend on the marchers being batoned down, they will have to reckon with the seething discontent inside their own ranks. I suppose that is sedition, but it is common knowledge that through

the cuts in their pay the police are seething with discontent, and they have a right to be discontented.[11]

In November Trenchard received the first of what would be a number of death threats. It was in the form of an anonymous letter written in Morse code which when transcribed read 'U have 4 days to live so beware. A warning from the speed k 8. Bye bye.' Not long afterwards a letter addressed to Lady Trenchard was delivered to Dancers Hill House: 'This is to let you know that you will soon be a woman without a husband as he is useless in this country and is asking for trouble he is going to get it. If we do not get him in a certain time then your life will have to be taken and has [sic] we have been well paid to do the job we are going to carry it out perhaps it will be both of you . . . killing is our motto we have done four murders and not caught yet.'[12]

Lady Trenchard was completely unconcerned. She was a very resilient character, as opinionated as her husband (she believed people with thick necks and little ears were unreliable), full of energy and always in a hurry. Despite the fact that her husband was the police commissioner, she blithely ignored speed limits, showed precious little regard for other road users and not infrequently drove the wrong way down one-way streets. In her sixties she could vault a five-bar gate and when an intruder unwisely broke into the family home one night he was confronted by Lady Trenchard, in her nightdress, who wrenched a ceremonial sword from a display on the wall and so frightened him that he leapt through a plate glass window to escape.

Trenchard did not keep a diary during his time as Metropolitan Police commissioner but an insight can be gleaned into his private life by the regular letters his formidable wife wrote to her son [Trenchard's stepson], John Boyle, then serving with the Royal Scots Fusiliers in the Middle East. Kitty presented a very different picture of her husband from the austere image known to the public. She wrote to say how nice his stepfather looked on a white horse at the State Opening of Parliament. 'Father refused to be slow paraded this year and trotted about and kept warm and enjoyed himself, then got off and went inside and told naughty stories to the Prince of Wales . . .'

'Lots of insults in the Press for Father,' she wrote cheerfully in January 1933, 'saying he is arming the Police, etc. Actually he found some 6,000 police were armed with out of date revolvers and no one could shoot, so he altered it to 300 and those to be able to shoot very well, so off the Press went, militarising the Police, etc. No shadow of truth, as usual.'

In another letter she described a happy family moment during a rare break in Scotland: 'Father caught a salmon, seven pounds, his first, all of us watching and telling him how to do it – he had his pipe in his mouth and a broad pleased grin but never spoke a word till the fish was landed. Little Hugh and Tom were hopping about with excitement, great fun.'[13]

It was while the family was staying in Scotland – at Teviothead Lodge Hotel in the Borders – that Trenchard picked up a copy of the *Daily Express* to read a sensational 'exclusive' story on the front page that an attempt had been made on his life by a man with a revolver waiting for him outside Scotland Yard. Later that morning he received a telegram from Howgrave-Graham saying the story was 'quite untrue'. The informant was an unemployed labourer living in a Salvation Army hostel who was known to be unreliable. A *Daily Express* reporter had been told by the police three times that there was no truth in the story, but they published it anyway. The following day a grudging retraction was published on an inside page.

In February 1933 there was another protest rally against government policies in Hyde Park.

Sunday today [Kitty wrote from Dancers Hill], and supposed to be great trouble in London – unemployed and Communists and Labour all to process from everywhere – the wireless says 300,000 people – anyway the Specials took over the traffic and it was all peaceful, they all got to Hyde Park and away again without damage. Father went to see and put on a Burberry and an old brown hat as a disguise and walked about the Park to see all the fun, rather naughty of him, but he poked about to see if the police were doing all they ought, etc, and came back tonight amused and pleased with himself having seen a lot of things.[14]

(Actually he was not quite as incognito as he had hoped because he was pictured mingling with the demonstrators in the *Daily Express* the following day.)

In May Trenchard's second annual report was published with

details of sweeping plans to reorganise the Met. At the request of the new Home Secretary, Sir John Gilmour, Trenchard had gone through the report to moderate the language and expunge terms like 'the educated classes' and 'officers and gentlemen' or anything that would hint at the militarisation of the Met – a red rag to many policemen. Nevertheless the report bore the unmistakable imprint of his personality, in both its content and language, and generated a storm of controversy, particularly since it indirectly called into question the reliability of the police in a major emergency. Blame was again heaped on the Police Federation, which he accused of deliberately stirring up trouble, distributing mischievous propaganda, encouraging insubordination and misrepresentation. Significant among his reforms was a proposal to prevent new 'short-service' recruits from joining the Federation and to bar membership to all officers from the rank of inspector upwards.

Trenchard's report was swiftly transformed into a White Paper which provoked a heated debate when it was presented to the House. Fears were expressed that the new police college would create an elite 'officer class', but it was his proposal to change the constitution of the Police Federation that most enraged the Left. Frederick Cocks, the recently elected Labour MP for Broxtowe, saw no need to mince his words:

> [The Bill] is essential to the design of the government to militarise, or rather Hitlerise, the Police Force of this country and to render the Police Federation absolutely useless at the bidding of a self-advertising autocrat, a militarist, who, unfortunately, is now in command of the police force, whose bidding the Home Secretary obeys and who is now doing his utmost to destroy the morale of the finest police force in the world . . .

It was all too much for Brigadier General John Nation, who leapt to Trenchard's support:

> At last we have a Commissioner who is a man of proved ability and great organising power. With great respect I say that I think he is comparable with Lord Kitchener in his best days . . . That our Air Force today is second to none in efficiency, in organisation and in

up-to-date methods is almost entirely due to Lord Trenchard. He has produced a report which we have all read and I think that for clarity and honesty of purpose that report is hard to beat.

A young backbencher by the name of Aneurin Bevan begged to differ and accused the government of wanting to segregate 'the officer class' from the Federation. 'It is entirely a Fascist development,' he claimed. 'It is to make the Police Force more amenable to the orders of the Carlton Club and Downing Street if there is a disturbance . . . They want to militarise the upper hierarchy of the police force because they cannot trust the police force . . . [they] must have the janissaries of the State who can be relied upon to carry out the orders of the Government.'

Clement Attlee, then deputy leader of the Labour party, perceived similar dark motives:

I do not think I recall another report by the head of such a body as the Metropolitan Police Force in which one can search in vain for the slightest appreciation by the author of the report of the men serving under him. I have never seen a more coldly clinical document . . . The whole thing breathes a spirit of distaste for the ordinary constable . . . He [Trenchard] is trying to change the character of the force altogether . . . from a force that acts with the people and in sympathy with the people, and believes in the liberty of the people, to a force in the hands of the Home Secretary or the Government to use exactly as they please. It is not the danger from the higher types of criminals of which the right honourable gentleman is thinking, but the possibility of danger from the working class, and he wants a force to use against them.

Several Labour members commented on Trenchard's 'obvious hostility' towards the men he commanded and 'the many occasions he went out of his way to insult them'. One slyly asked the Home Secretary if the commissioner's appointment was full-time (almost certainly knowing the answer), and when it was confirmed that this was indeed the case asked why it was that the commissioner was recently reported to have spent a day inspecting an RAF base.

George Lansbury, leader of the Opposition, claimed that the Home

Secretary had not put forward a single reason why 'these revolutionary changes' needed to be introduced and went on to lampoon the commissioner mercilessly:

> Now, all of a sudden, comes Lord Trenchard. This wonderful genius of the air has discovered that this police force wants revolutionary treatment. I have great admiration for people who fly, whether that person be Lord Trenchard or anyone else, but what police experience has Lord Trenchard had? When did he ever arrest a drunk and disorderly? I have no doubt that if it came to fighting on the Continent, or putting down a riot with a few bombs from the air, Lord Trenchard could organise with the best of them . . . but as to experience as a police officer . . .[15]

Trenchard did not attend the debate. As always he seemed to be untroubled by self-doubt and viewed his critics as either wrong, or simply wrong-headed, or both. But he may not have been as unconcerned as he appeared – he confessed to several close friends that taking on the job of commissioner had made him 'the loneliest man in Britain'.[16] Notwithstanding left-wing fears and alarmist rhetoric, the Metropolitan Police Act 1933 was passed with a comfortable majority and greeted with considerable hostility by the men of the Met, who could see their already limited prospects of promotion being eclipsed by the influx of college graduates earmarked for fast-track advancement. All the old fears about 'militarising' the force were aired once more; there were even rumours that the whole thing was a plot to divide the force, with the 'officers' deemed to be more reliable in times of industrial unrest.

Trenchard, meanwhile, began searching for suitable premises for the new college. It was a coincidence that they were found at Hendon Aerodrome, where the first RAF pageants were held in the Twenties. The aerodrome's clubhouse had been taken over by Hendon Country Club, but the venture had failed. It offered sufficient accommodation for the college and there was enough land all around to provide space for some of Trenchard's other plans – a forensic laboratory, a police driving school and detective training facilities.

To advise on the best ways of training police drivers, Trenchard called on the services of Sir Malcolm Campbell, the celebrated racing driver and holder of the world land speed record in his famous Blue

Bird. Sir Malcolm's view was that a properly equipped advanced driving school was needed; it was promptly set up in the college grounds. Under Trenchard's regime more cars were fitted with radios and a central control room was established. In a short time he was able to report to the Home Secretary an increase in the number of cases of criminals being apprehended miles from the scene of the crime. 'Once it is known among the criminal fraternity that movement on the roads in an identifiable car is a risky business, this type of crime will be checked.'

In February 1934 another hunger march organised by the National Unemployed Workers' Movement – the largest so far – descended on London after the government imposed a further cut on benefits, and rumours spread that 'slave camps' – unpaid labour camps for unemployed men who had become idle from lack of work – were to be set up. Trenchard was so concerned about the prospect of public disorder that he wrote to Buckingham Palace, the Duke of York and the Prince of Wales asking that members of the Royal Family avoid public and semi-public engagements in the week following the arrival of the marchers. Trenchard said in his note that he did not want 'in any way to be alarmist', a view clearly not shared by the Home Secretary who hinted that bloodshed was likely and issued a public warning for children to be kept off the streets, shop windows to be boarded and Londoners to stay at home. There was a heavy police presence when the marchers converged on Hyde Park with bands and banners for a mass rally; the threat of violence was palpable, but in the end the event was entirely peaceful. A number of protesters were later observed marching round Trafalgar Square chanting 'One two three four five, we'll have Trenchard dead or alive.'

We dined with the King last Thursday, a party of thirty, quite fun, lots of friends, and everyone very friendly and cheery [Kitty wrote to her son on 20 March]. The Queen said she had quite forgiven Father for 'confining her to Barracks' while the marchers were here, though she was pretty bolshie at the time about it! Father is up to his neck in papers, plans and works for the future, as well as getting out his police report, and is carrying on a good row with all the Cabinet because they implored him not to speak in the House of Lords debate on Defence last week, which he had intended to do.

He got certain things out of them, so gracefully agreed not to this once, but is returning to the charge that he must and will speak when he considers it of importance, they are all scratching their heads over this now. Actually he is quite ready to leave his police job any time that is convenient for them now – the reforms are done, the Federation broken, totally reorganised from top to bottom, staff appointed, legal department, wireless department, laboratory, maps, and fleet of cars all going, they had none of this before. Recreation grounds all bought and going, and clubs running, quarters made habitable, canteens cleaned up and the decrease in crime quite wonderful this year and very satisfactory number of captures. The police themselves are now civil and nice to us, and smile and salute on all occasions, it is a marvellous change, of course there is more to be done, more cleaning up within still, but that will go on for a good many years yet and could be done by others, so if Father feels there is better work for him I'm all for him moving on. He hates the sordid, sad and dirty cases and is really upset by them, so I think someone else might do them now.[17]

By the spring of 1934 Trenchard was certainly ready to move on. He had already served six months beyond the two years he had originally agreed and wanted to be free to influence defence policy. On 13 March 1934, he wrote to the prime minister asking to be allowed to retire at the end of the year:

I have for some considerable time been thinking how and when I could resign the post I was asked to take in October, 1931. I do not want to comment on the work I have tried to do since I have been here. It will be for others to judge . . . It will be remembered that when I became Commissioner the first cut in pay had been made, and the men were objecting to the imposition of the second cut (as well as objecting to the first). Further, at that time the state of discipline, in my opinion, could not be characterised in any other way than as extremely serious; also corruption was much too prevalent.

Now I feel that my work is really completed, that is so far as it could ever be completed by me, let me summarise briefly what has been done . . .

It was an impressive list – getting the pay cut accepted, improving discipline and working conditions, curbing the Federation and more or less reorganising the force from top to bottom.

> I don't want the above summary [he continued], to be read as meaning what a lot I think I have done because I know quite well how much was done by those who assisted me in the general work of reorganisation . . . It seems to me that I shouldn't be letting the Government or the Home Secretary down if I asked to be relieved of my office at the end of this year.
>
> A large number of the changes will only achieve their full result in about twenty years' time, and as it is impossible for me to remain here for much longer than another three or four years – even if the Government wanted to keep me – it appears to me infinitely preferable that I should retire at the end of 1934. There will have to be a general election in 1935 at the latest. It would be impossible for me to resign just before it, and probably very difficult to do so just after.
>
> I feel also that my interest and my keenness now lie elsewhere. I am very interested in the question of Imperial Defence – not that I want to make speeches, but I want to take a more active part than I can at present. I feel very strongly that this is a question of really national importance . . .[18]

MacDonald was not inclined to accede to Trenchard's request, perhaps because there was no obvious candidate to replace him or perhaps because he did not want the commissioner stirring up trouble on defence issues. In the end it was the King, who had first persuaded Trenchard to take the job, who persuaded him to stay on. The King pointed out that there was to be a Royal wedding later in the year – his son George was due to marry Princess Marina of Greece in November – and the Silver Jubilee would be celebrated in May the following year. Both events would attract huge numbers of visitors and the King was anxious that the arrangements would be handled efficiently – he asked Trenchard to 'reflect carefully' before deciding to resign. Trenchard agreed to delay his departure at least until after the Silver Jubilee.

It was a testament to Trenchard's energy and drive that the Metropolitan Police College at Hendon was opened by the Prince of Wales in May 1934 – less than a year after it had been approved by Parliament. In fact the first 32 cadets – 20 already serving policemen and 12 new recruits – had already started their course earlier that month. Kitty was at the opening ceremony, of course:

> It all went very well [she wrote to her son], the Prince in very good form, most Cabinet ministers turned up, bankers and others of Father's friends and a lot of RAF people, all the old superintendents and wives, over 6,000 for tea. Sir John Gilmour having been well primed brought in the police motto, which is 'Watch and Ward'. Maurice Baring whispered to me I thought for police it was 'watch and chain' which was very funny . . .[19]

Kitty made a point of talking to Jack Hayes, a Labour MP and ex-policeman who was one of her husband's most trenchant critics. She said she was pleased to meet him as she had kept all his criticisms in her scrapbook and asked what he was going to write this time. He laughed and said he had come to have a look. 'Good, I'm so glad,' she replied. 'It is always better to write about what one sees and knows than guesswork isn't it?' He said he had been on the end of some straight talking from Lord Trenchard and felt he would not be able to disagree with him at all soon. 'That's a pity,' Kitty responded. 'We must all have our own criticisms. For instance, I don't like your buttonhole nearly as much as mine, yours being a bolshie red, while mine are lilies of the valley.'

With the college up and running, Trenchard found time to tackle other issues. He had been shocked by the condition of the married quarters and section houses in which the constables lived. 'They really are a disgrace to civilisation,' he wrote to Gilmour. 'The canteens are in basements with practically no heating, and they are dark, smelly, dirty and worse almost than coal cellars . . . In one case I came across six families with a communal bathroom . . . it is hard to raise the status of the decent man if we do this sort of thing to them.'[20]

Trenchard had a simple philosophy that 'nice things make nice men'. 'By this,' he would explain much later, 'I mean that by living in decency and fair comfort, they obtain a higher degree of character than if they live in squalor surrounded by vicious and adverse conditions.' He called for a capital building programme to be prepared for some 800 married quarters and 20 or more section houses each with separate rooms with washing facilities for each constable. Funds were not immediately available for such an ambitious programme, but Trenchard insisted that the question of rehousing the Metropolitan Police was mentioned in the King's speech at the State Opening of Parliament in 1934; a government loan of £4 million was eventually authorised and building began the following year.

Meanwhile a new challenge to law and order had emerged in the strutting form of Sir Oswald Mosley, founder of the British Union of Fascists, whose uniformed 'blackshirts' were frequently involved in violent confrontations with Communist and Jewish groups in London. Six months earlier Trenchard had suggested to the Home Secretary that the 'wearing of uniform' by private citizens for political purposes ought to be banned, but nothing was done. Trenchard warned that 'grave riots' were possible and in June 1934 mass brawls broke out at a BUF rally in Olympia when blackshirts began removing hecklers. In September Trenchard had to deploy some 7000 policemen, more than a third of his total force, to prevent the risk of trouble when Communists and Fascists staged rival rallies in Hyde Park within insulting distance of each other.

In October he took a day off to attend the official opening of RAF Cranwell by the Prince of Wales. A special train from London had been laid on for the occasion and Kitty was intrigued by the German air attaché, who she said was an enormous man 6' 5" tall, made even taller by his ceremonial uniform and who clashed his heels together and threw up 'the most tremendous salute' whenever he got near her husband. The first time he did it, in the dining car on the train, it made everyone jump. Trenchard looked up and murmured 'That man quite frightens me.'

Kitty often acted as her husband's unofficial secretary, taking dictation from him at Dancers Hill and later typing out his notes. Shortly before the Duke of Kent's wedding to Princess Marina in November she was making notes about issues he was to discuss at his next audience with the King when he suddenly said: 'Beer in the park for the police and use motor vans liberally at night to get them home.' His thoughts had jumped to arrangements for refreshments for the police, who would be on duty for 12 hours on the day of the wedding. 'Being a dutiful wife,' Kitty said, 'I merely added a few exclamation marks and shoved it in with the rest for the office.'[21]

Huge crowds gathered in London for the wedding, Kitty reported to her son:

London quite mad ... I drove down the Mall where we found Father actively employed as a policeman shooing the crowd with his white horse and talking with his hand up in the approved manner ... There have never been such crowds to cope with before and really not enough police, the RAC took the traffic and only by Father's new wireless and motor reserves to be rushed from place to place could it be coped with, but fortunately all went marvellously well and Father does deserve the congratulations that are coming from all quarters ... You will have seen all about the wedding, it was a marvellous sight and we had very good places in the Abbey, close up. Father got off his white horse and joined me and ran out just before them and got on again. I then gathered up the family when the crowd had dispersed a bit and we all went to Scotland Yard for half an hour and so to lunch at the Rag [the Army & Navy Club]. The night before the Queen suddenly said she must go to a play and take Marina and George and drive down Bond Street to see the decorations – poor tired Father managed to gather two police cars and a few police and he and I went in his car and we piloted them down Bond Street with police on the steps of her car to shove people away, terrific excitement and crowd, no other vehicles, but it all went well . . .[22]

During the Silver Jubilee celebrations in May 1935, Trenchard wanted to see what was going on so once again donned an old raincoat and cap and joined the crowds in St James's Park. There were so many people about that the police had created one-way pedestrian traffic on a bridge over the lake. Trenchard didn't notice and when he attempted to cross against the stream, a policeman tapped him on the shoulder and said 'Hey Daddy, you can't go that way.' Legend has it that when Trenchard turned round the policeman was so shocked to see who it was that he fell into the lake.

Trenchard gathered a fund of stories from his time at Scotland

Yard, like opening a letter which began 'Last Sunday my wife called my mother a barmy cow, and I threw her over Hungerford Bridge near Charing Cross,' or another from a youth in Belfast who asked if he could be put in touch with a reliable racing man to supply him with a few winners every day in return for a commission on his winnings. His favourite story, however, was about a dinner party he attended in June, the day after the death of his predecessor, Lord Byng, had been announced. The lady sitting next to him turned to him and said: 'Oh Lord Trenchard, isn't it too sad that dear Lord Byng should have died? Who will they find to succeed him as Commissioner of Police?'

Those who thought Trenchard had no sense of humour should have been at a one-man show at the Savoy when an Italian illusionist and conjuror demonstrated his skill picking pockets and relieving members of the audience of their wallets and watches. When he was informed the commissioner of the Metropolitan Police was in the audience the temptation to invite him up onto the stage was obviously irresistible. Trenchard accepted, convinced he could protect his possessions and after a few minutes the Italian admitted defeat. 'It's no good, you are too clever for me,' he said. Trenchard smiled in triumph and as he went to leave the stage his trousers fell about his ankles. Archibald James, who was present, recalled that he had 'seldom heard a greater roar of laughter' and that Trenchard happily joined in.[23]

When Trenchard finally stepped down in November 1935, the newspapers generally praised his performance.

'Lord Trenchard's reign at Scotland Yard has left an indelible mark on the police organisation of London,' the *Daily Herald* reported. 'When he took over, in 1931, bandit reign threatened to turn London into a second Chicago. Lord Trenchard changed all that. He brought it to such a pitch that it began to work with the sureness of a machine.'

The *Daily Telegraph* went further: 'He retires from the Metropolitan Police Force after carrying out with extraordinary skill his revolutionary scheme of reorganisation . . . Probably no Englishman of our time has evoked, through leadership and exceptional organising ability, a deeper respect . . .'

THE UNOFFICIAL INSPECTOR GENERAL

Throughout his time as police commissioner Trenchard had obviously maintained his interest in defence issues, although he recognised his position made it unwise for him to interfere. There were, nevertheless, occasions on which, being the man he was, he simply could not resist. In the spring of 1932, when Singapore was under threat from an increasingly bellicose Japan, he incurred the displeasure of the government by submitting an unsolicited private paper to the Air Staff once again arguing forcibly for the RAF to take over the defence of the island. John Salmond, his successor as Chief of the Air Staff, was said to be less than pleased by his presumption and Trenchard was similarly less than pleased when his proposal was summarily rejected.

Later that year, when he heard that disarmament negotiations in Geneva were to include the consideration of an international treaty banning all bomber aircraft, he drew up a six-page memorandum for the Committee of Imperial Defence outlining what he considered to be the disastrous consequences for the defence of the United Kingdom.

I would ask those who may read this paper to believe that I have no wish to add to the difficulties of the Government [he began], nor to attack the Government in any way; neither have I any desire to try to prevent the reduction of armaments or the mitigation of the brutalities of war – far from it. Also, I am not thinking of this as a question of saving the Royal Air Force from extinction. I would therefore ask you to believe me when I say that I am writing solely in the interests of humanity, economy in expenditure, and the safety of our peculiarly vulnerable British Empire . . .

He listed the successes of air policing in various parts of the Empire and warned that a ban on bombers would mean a return to policing with punitive columns at vast cost and much greater loss of life. 'I do not write as a die-hard militarist (whatever that term may mean),' he concluded, 'but . . . I say definitely that if bombing is abolished then expenditure on armaments for the next 50 years will be far greater to produce the same results, loss of life and treasure will be far heavier and the policing of the Empire will become an intolerable burden.'

In a covering letter to Sir Maurice Hankey, the secretary of the Committee, Trenchard attempted to justify his intervention: 'It is with some feeling of diffidence that I add to your worries, especially on a subject which you may say, quite rightly, has nothing to do with me any more . . .' That was exactly what Hankey did think. 'I do not see,' he replied tersely, 'how you could talk about defence matters [in his position as police commissioner] any more than I could talk about the police so long as you hold that office.'[1]

Thereafter Trenchard chose to maintain a dignified silence, although he often vented his frustration 'fervently if rather incoherently'[2] at frequent lunches with Captain Basil Liddell Hart, the military historian, who kept copious notes of their meetings, now lodged in the Liddell Hart Centre for Military Archives at King's College, London.

Once Trenchard had resigned from his position as police commissioner, however, he felt free to speak his mind and within days he was embroiled in a bitter row with Hankey after writing a letter to *The Times* suggesting that the chiefs of staff sub-committee was not operating effectively as a forum for debate:

> I fear that under pressure of work and from other causes unanimity has been too often reached by tacit agreement to exclude vital differences of opinion . . . What is wanted in the higher examination of the Defence Policy is not that the Government should get unanimous reports but that means should exist for the examination of defence requirements untrammelled by Department compromise. We want to promote free discussion and not to drive differences of opinion underground.

He also proposed that when Hankey stepped down he should be replaced by a minister.

The letter was published on 16 December 1935 and on the same day Hankey scrawled a furious note to Trenchard from the United Services Club in Pall Mall:

Dear Boom,

It took me two or three years to get over the damage you did to the C.O.S. Committee by your Swan Song.[3]

Now that we have got the thing going better than ever you weigh in with this deplorable letter to *The Times*.

Has your memory gone? Have you forgotten how disastrously the Committee failed when Salisbury, Haldane and Curzon tried successively to act as Chairmen . . . ?

Only today I heard from Paris that the French are so impressed that they are talking of adopting our system. And you want to throw us back to a discredited system that has been tried and failed . . . [4]

The two men met several times during the following days to try and sort out their differences, but the rift between them was too deep to be healed. Trenchard pointed out that he had tried to talk to Hankey before he sent the letter to *The Times* but Hankey had been too busy to see him. Hankey could not be won over, bitterly complained that he had been 'stabbed in the back', told Trenchard that 'no one who counted' agreed with him and accused him of listening to 'too much club gossip'.[5]

(The row did not, it seems, affect Trenchard's standing in high places and in February it was announced that he had accepted a second peerage, becoming Viscount Trenchard.) Hankey, meanwhile, refused to let the matter drop. A full two months after the letter had been published, Trenchard received a note from Hankey saying the prime minister's attention had been drawn to it and 'He would like to know what were the vital differences of opinion that in your time were excluded by tacit agreement or otherwise.'

Trenchard replied promptly from Dancers Hill claiming it was well known that the Chiefs of Staff Committee avoided contentious issues and that the government invariably received unanimous reports even though there was a great divergence of views between the three services. He quoted a number of examples and went on to express surprise that his 'Swan Song' memorandum should have caused harm or been resented 'unless, again, I was infringing a convention in initiating a controversial question'.

Hankey would not let that pass. There were no more 'Dear Boom' letters; now it was 'Dear Trenchard'. It seemed to him, he replied,

> and it still seems to me, a mistake on your part to have circulated this paper at the moment of your departure. Remember you assembled in this one paper all the most controversial questions affecting your Department in relation to the other Service departments. You launched them at the moment of your departure when you could no longer promote or forward them in any way. The sudden dropping of this bomb into the Government Departments naturally caused an explosion and a good deal of irritation. This was bound to make things difficult for your successor . . .

Trenchard remained unrepentant and subsequently raised all the issues in a speech in the House of Lords, although privately he was conciliatory towards Hankey.

> I noticed that the beginning and ending of our letters were getting more and more frigid [he wrote on 27 February], and I was wondering whether we shouldn't be writing soon in the third person. I am, frankly, sad at what has happened between you and me. You must remember that I tried to see you twice before I sent my letter last December, and twice since. I do not doubt in any way that you were too busy to see me, and especially when you were seedy once, but you did not think it was necessary to see me and take any further initiative, so what could I do?[6]

At the age of 62 Trenchard was not in the least interested in the prospect of retirement and that month he accepted an invitation to join the board of the United Africa Company, part of the Unilever Group, which had extensive interests in Nigeria, a country for which he retained considerable affection after his service there with the West African Frontier Force. Three months later he was appointed chairman, a position he took very seriously and would hold for 17 years, attending the office almost every day and making several trips to West Africa, where he was delighted to see how the bougainvillea he had had planted in front of the officers' mess in Lagos had grown. He named his own salary – £2000 a year – and throughout his time with the company refused to accept more. 'His ability to analyse a complicated situation,' a fellow director noted, 'to elucidate the essential factors and to see the principle which must determine the decision, made him a tremendous asset and secured him ready acceptance in the business world.'[7]

His responsibilities as chairman of the United Africa Board did not distract him from his self-appointed commitment to protect his beloved RAF and when he suspected the Air Ministry was showing signs of buckling under increasing pressure from the Admiralty to regain control of the Fleet Air Arm he lobbied hard to prevent it from happening. He had, of course, no official position; his influence emanated solely from his status as the longest standing Chief of the Air Staff and a member of the House of Lords. In November 1936 he delivered what the *Morning Post* described as an 'astonishingly vehement' speech arguing against any change.

If you divide the command of the air into two in this island, what is going to be the result? You can imagine on a dark night or in bad weather a squadron going up and asking 'Are those other machines our own?' In the last war there was a good deal of fighting between our own aircraft and there will be continuous fighting between our aircraft in a future war if you have a divided command . . .

The claim by the Admiralty shows that, instead of realising the importance of the air, they are still thinking in terms of land and sea power. There is no getting away from that . . . The views put forward by the naval partisans obstinately ignore the inescapable consequences of the fact that the operations of the air know no frontier between the sea and the land . . . I know what the Navy has meant to the Empire and that the prestige of the Empire is bound up with it . . . but the efficiency of sea power and air power must rest on partnership between the Services and not on rivalry, nor on separation.

He followed up with a letter to *The Times* claiming that separating the Air Force would be 'disastrous'. His letter generated a flurry of correspondence, including a robust response from his brother-in-law, Admiral of the Fleet Sir Roger Keyes, which made no concessions to family sensibilities and accused Trenchard of being 'obsessed' with maintaining the status quo. 'As Lord Trenchard was mainly responsible for the present system,' he wrote, 'I suppose it is only natural he should be anxious to perpetuate it.' But, he added, it was 'inherently unsound', had utterly failed to provide the navy with the air service it needed, had had 'deplorable consequences' for both the navy and the army and was 'bitterly resented'.

On the day[8] Keyes' letter appeared in *The Times*, Trenchard left Britain for a three-month tour of West Africa on behalf of the United Africa Company. By the time he returned he recognised that events were moving against him and that the battle to keep the Fleet Air Arm would probably be lost. At a Buckingham Palace garden party in July, Trenchard and his wife ran into Sir Edward Ellington, then Chief of the Air Staff, who was soon to retire. Trenchard did not think that Ellington had fought sufficiently hard to keep the service unified and when he [Ellington] expressed the hope that the Cabinet would come down on the side of the RAF, Trenchard exploded. 'Do you never leave your office, Ellington?' he snorted. 'The thing's over. It's been decided over your head, which is well buried in the sand, as usual.[9] (The Fleet Air Arm was formally returned to Admiralty control in May 1939.)

Ellington was replaced in September by Sir Cyril Newall, who had been Trenchard's deputy at the Independent Force in France in 1918. Trenchard shamelessly made use of their former relationship to exert influence over RAF affairs. When he heard that Sir Thomas Inskip, the new Minister for Defence Co-ordination, was pressing for fighters to be given priority over bombers – absolute sacrilege to Trenchard – he bombarded Newall with letters denouncing the proposition and then began writing to members of the Cabinet in such vociferous language that Newall implored him to be more discreet. It was wasted effort – he could never see the point of mincing words.

In the spring of 1937 he returned from a second visit to West Africa almost blind in one eye. A blood vessel had burst in the centre of the retina while he was on a steamer travelling down the Congo River and medical help was not available in sufficient time to repair the damage.

It caused severe distortion of his vision; he could no longer hit a tennis ball except when serving and had to have his guns altered so that he could take aim with his good left eye, but his sight continued to deteriorate, making it difficult for him to get about; towards the end of his life he would become totally blind.

That summer, on a business trip to Germany, he was invited to the magnificent Charlottenburg Palace in Berlin to dine with Hermann Goering, the commander-in-chief of the Luftwaffe. It was not an honour usually accorded to visiting businessmen but Goering, an ace fighter pilot in the Great War, obviously wanted to meet the man known as the 'Father of the RAF'. After dinner Trenchard was taken outside to watch a firework display. It was a cool evening and he borrowed a German general's greatcoat to keep warm. The atmosphere, too, was frigid, with Goering talking, through a translator, about the ability of German might to make 'the whole world tremble'. Trenchard was unimpressed. 'You must be off your head,' he growled. 'You said earlier that you hoped we would not have to fight each other. I hope so too, for your sake. I warn you, don't underestimate the RAF. It may take time, but we will win.' When Trenchard got home he reported the exchange to his wife, who was thrilled.

Trenchard had long believed war with Germany was inevitable. In July 1938 he submitted a memorandum to the Cabinet warning of the danger of a 'knock-out blow' from the air by an attack on London and arguing that it would be necessary to 'bomb Germany with sufficient force to undermine their morale in as great, or a greater, degree than they are undermining ours'. Reliance on the primacy of fighters to defend the country from air attack would be a grave, perhaps fatal, mistake. 'I maintain with all the power at my command that it might well lose us the war.'[10]

Three months later, with war clouds gathering, he wrote to Prime Minister Neville Chamberlain during the Munich crisis to offer his services to the government. Chamberlain passed his letter to Inskip, who replied: 'I don't think you will have many more days to wait. There are so many posts . . . that we shall most certainly want someone with your experience.'

Trenchard waited and waited, but no call came. By then the family had moved from Dancers Hill to The King's House, a grace and favour property with a large garden adjoining a golf course at

Walton-on-Thames. It was at The King's House that Kitty, in her nightdress, dispatched an intruder with a ceremonial sword. Her grandsons remember visiting and watching her shoot grey squirrels from the trees with unerring accuracy. In anticipation of a job that would require his presence in London, Trenchard rented a pied-à-terre in Ennismore Gardens, South Kensington.

In August, with war virtually inevitable, he sent a prepaid telegram from his rented holiday home in Scotland to Sir Kingsley Wood, the Secretary of State for Air, asking if he would be wanted at the Air Ministry or some other government department. Sir Kingsley's reply was vague: 'Will wire if I hear of suitable appointment.'

When war finally broke out in September 1939, Trenchard was 66 years old but with his experience he not unreasonably expected he would play some significant role in helping the war effort. He was keen to serve but turned out to be extraordinarily difficult to accommodate. He was offered no less than five government positions – and refused every one.

At the beginning of October, Neville Chamberlain sent for him and asked him if he would be willing to go to Canada to organise an advanced training course for RAF pilots. Trenchard turned down the offer and explained his reasoning in a private letter to the prime minister: 'I am not the man for this job. It requires a young man up-to-date in training. My experience and qualifications are more for the shaping of the broad policy of how to use air power. I still feel that one day I may be of more use at home in England than I should be if I went to Canada . . .'[11]

Chamberlain accepted his decision and replied with a note saying he did not feel it would be right to put further pressure on him to take the job. The next offer was to take charge of camouflaging potential Luftwaffe targets in Britain, which he had no hesitation in rejecting. 'I answered at once that nothing would induce me to do it,' he noted, '[as] I did not believe in defensive warfare.'[12]

Trenchard's desire to 'shape broad policy' with regard to air power largely comprised continuing pressure on the government to step up the bombing of Germany. Although RAF bombers had attacked German warships off Wilhelmshaven within hours of the UK and France declaring war on 3 September, and operations continued against enemy ports and shipping, along with dropping propaganda leaflets,

Trenchard argued that an all-out bombing offensive against Germany offered the best chance of bringing the war to an end sooner rather than later. He dismissed humanitarian objections that women and children would be killed – he told the Archbishop of Canterbury that protesters were simply 'protecting their so-called reputations as guardians of humanity' – by claiming that the lives of millions of young men would be saved and whole populations would be 'spared untold misery'.

In October he sent a twelve-page memorandum to Chamberlain with a covering letter apologising for adding to his 'terrific workload' but added: 'As I am the last Englishman alive who was a Chief of Staff and a Commander-in-Chief in the last war . . . I feel it my duty to submit these views.' Under a heading 'THE PARTICULAR METHOD OF WINNING THIS WAR', he argued for the necessity of bombing Germany without delay, advocated sending 50–100 bombers over Germany every day, night and day, and talked about 'germinating the seed of discontent that is in Germany . . . through the physical fear of seeing their homes destroyed, their own people killed, and, however unintentional, not their soldiers only, in their own country – in other words to win the war on the home front in Germany as the quickest and the best way of ending it.'[13]

Chamberlain replied with a polite note thanking him for his 'interesting and important memorandum' and promising that it would be fully considered. Three days after Christmas Trenchard submitted a second memorandum, ten pages long, entitled 'Memorandum on the Advantages of an Early Air Offensive', in which he reasoned that 'since bombing from the air is going to be a form of warfare adopted by one side or another sooner or later' it would be preferable to make it sooner, particularly as Germany 'with its carefully regulated collective mentality' was less able to stand up to such an attack than the stalwart British. 'The conclusion to which I have come is that we should not defer the inception of an air offensive against Germany. The outcome of this novel, and admittedly terrible, form of warfare must finally rest on the ability of our two nations to stand up to interference which it will cause in national life, and in this respect I say we may await the result with confidence.'

In February he tried another tack, writing to ask if the prime minister had any objection to him writing to the press suggesting that

Germany should be given 72 hours' warning of bombing raids so that women and children could be evacuated. 'Must we wait until the Germans kill non-combatants on land as well as at sea?' he asked. 'To me it seems vital to seize the advantage while it rests with us.'

Chamberlain hastily replied that publication of such a letter would be embarrassing since it would be interpreted as criticism of the government and would 'provide ammunition for Goebbels to declare we are disunited'.[14]

Trenchard despaired that his views were being ignored. He was convinced, correctly, that it was only a question of time before Germany would launch a massive aerial onslaught on Britain. 'Make no mistake about it,' he told the House of Lords, 'when the time comes, and it suits Germany's book, she will hit us by air – open towns and military objectives alike – mercilessly and thoroughly. Why should we await her convenience before striking at German military might in Germany?'[15]

Six days later the Luftwaffe demonstrated its terrible capability by 'carpet-bombing' the Dutch port of Rotterdam, destroying most of the historic city centre, leaving 900 people dead and 85,000 homeless.

By then Chamberlain had resigned as prime minister after the Allied retreat from Norway and been replaced by Churchill. Soon afterwards Lord Beaverbrook, recently appointed Minister for Aircraft Production, approached Trenchard with a third job offer – to organise the defence of aircraft factories and aerodromes. After meeting Beaverbrook and inspecting the defence arrangements at two factories outside London, Trenchard recognised that both were badly organised but claimed it would be 'child's play' to put them right. To his surprise Beaverbrook agreed and told him to forget the whole thing because Winston had 'something else in mind' for him.

On 23 May 1940, shortly before the first troops of the British Expeditionary Force would be evacuated from the beaches at Dunkirk, Churchill invited Trenchard for 'dinner and a chat' at Admiralty House. He was surprised, and not pleased, to discover that Anthony Eden, the Secretary of State for War, whom he disliked, had been invited. Churchill's wife, Clementine, and their youngest daughter, Mary, were also present. According to Trenchard's account of the evening, he and Churchill immediately got into a lengthy argument about a recent debate in the House, frequently interrupted by urgent telephone calls from Dunkirk. At one point Trenchard turned to Mrs Churchill and apologised. 'Don't worry about me,' she said. 'I like to hear the two of you arguing. I want to see which one of you will get the better of it.'

'It will be Winston, as usual,' Trenchard replied, 'but that won't alter the case.'

After dinner, when the ladies had retired, Churchill came to the point. He asked Trenchard how he would feel about becoming General Officer Commanding all land, sea and air forces at home in the event of a German invasion. He was explaining the various responsibilities involved when Trenchard interrupted and, to Churchill's undisguised astonishment and considerable irritation, began making extraordinary demands, insisting he would need to be appointed deputy Minister of Defence and 'generalissimo' with the power to make decisions without being at the beck and call of various ministers and chiefs of staff.

Trenchard had the grace to admit, later, that he had probably put his argument badly. The discussion ended with Churchill completely losing his temper. Almost incoherent with rage, he spluttered about not wanting dictators or 'Mussolinis' on his staff making 'unwarranted attacks' on politicians and the need to curb 'stupid generals'. When he had calmed down somewhat he stood up and suggested they should join the ladies. Trenchard demurred and said he thought it might be better if he left. Churchill made no attempt to persuade him to stay. 'He seemed to think we had called him in to help us out of a plight,' Churchill recalled later. 'Going up in the lift, he said to Mr Eden, "So this is the time when they call me in", or words to that effect. We neither of us liked Lord Trenchard's attitude.'[16]

Later that night, Trenchard wrote to try and make amends.

I did think when you began 'What do you feel about becoming G.O.C.?' that I must explain what I felt was the best way I could help. You of all men know that I am very bad at putting my case, and you probably quite rightly resented the way I said it. Had our discussions continued, I feel you would have agreed that whoever is appointed must be given as free a hand as possible and more power than has ever been carried in that post, owing to the speed and rapid changes in this war which must be met at the same speed or faster. Believe me, I did not want to be a dictator.[17]

Kitty must have recognised how worried her husband was because she wrote to Lady Churchill in an attempt to smooth things over. Churchill did not reply to Trenchard's letter and no more was said about the appointment, but their previously warm relationship was soon reinstated. In early September, when the Battle of Britain was at its height, Trenchard wrote to the prime minister with ideas about how to counter a possible German invasion: 'To my mind the only way to wrest the initiative from the Germans at this present moment is to hit Germany in Germany to induce the Germans to attack this country. When they have launched their attack, and not until then, should the whole bombing force be diverted to attacking the German army of invasion.'

Churchill replied that he had passed Trenchard's letter on to the chiefs of staff, but added drily: 'Few people, I think, would care to court an invasion in the hope of being able to deal with it satisfactorily once it had been launched.'[18]

Admirers of Trenchard would later claim he was largely responsible for the success of the Battle of Britain, that only the unified, independent air service he had created could have provided the gallant pilots capable of defeating the Luftwaffe. His detractors dismiss such a notion. 'The Battle of Britain was won by Fighter Command and radar,' the eminent historian A.J.P. Taylor wrote. 'Trenchard despised the one and knew nothing of the other.'[19]

Sir Arthur Harris, C-in-C of Bomber Command, understandably disagreed: 'For nearly twenty years, I watched the army and the navy, both singly and in concert, engineer one deliberate attempt after another to destroy the Royal Air Force. Time after time they were within a hairbreadth of success; time after time Trenchard, and Trenchard alone, saved us. If they had succeeded they would have abolished our air power . . . and we should have lost the Battle of Britain.'[20]

On 30 November 1940, Churchill's sixty-sixth birthday, he invited Trenchard to lunch at Chequers and made one last attempt to recruit him to government. After lunch Churchill said he was looking for a 'big man' to reorganise Military Intelligence and could think of no one better qualified for the task than Trenchard, particularly in the light of the 'wonders' he had achieved as Metropolitan Police commissioner. Trenchard promised Churchill he would give the proposal serious consideration but after two days thinking it over he decided, probably wisely, he was not the right man for the job. 'The work would require very delicate and tactful handling,' he explained in a personal letter to Churchill on 2 December, 'and I feel I am not the right type of man to carry it out enthusiastically and satisfactorily.'[21]

In fact Trenchard had already carved out a role for himself as a kind of self-appointed, unofficial, inspector general of the RAF, touring squadrons in his marshal's uniform to raise morale. He had taken on the position during the Battle of Britain, visiting fighter squadrons and chatting informally with the hard-pressed young airmen. At the height of the battle he had received an unexpected letter of congratulations from the King, writing from Windsor Castle:

> Having served in the Royal Air Force on your staff in France in the Great War, and having followed with much interest the growth of the service in the last twenty years, I feel I must tell you how much the wonderful spirit and efficiency of the air force which we see daily at this moment are due to your leadership and foresight in laying well and truly the foundations in the early days. You must feel proud of them, and that all your hard work has borne such good fruit . . .

'You give me credit for much more than I deserve,' Trenchard wrote in reply. 'I have also been round nearly every squadron . . . The spirit they are all imbued with is wonderful . . . They are what I had not thought possible – better than in the last war. On the R.A.F. I feel will fall the heavy burden of fighting all through the winter in very hard conditions, but I know their spirit will pull us through whatever happens . . .'[22]

For the remainder of the war, Trenchard spent much of his time touring squadrons deployed across Europe and North Africa, giving what he called 'pep talks'. Relieved of command responsibility, he was transformed from austere leader into an avuncular old gentleman with considerable charm, a twinkle in his eye and a fund of self-deprecating funny stories. He eschewed military formality and liked to gather the men about him and chat about his life and his beliefs, emphasising what he was saying by waving his walking stick and exhibiting a sense of humour that produced gales of laughter and would have amazed many of the subordinates who served under him when he was Chief of the Air Staff.

This is Aircraftsman Stephen Rew describing a visit by Trenchard to an RAF station in Skellingthorpe, Lincolnshire, the preparations for which had caused some resentment:

What irked us was that we had to scrub out a hangar with petrol, and practise drill, marching into this hangar and forming a hollow square around a dais built on one side, and since most of us had done little or no drill since training, we found it thoroughly 'cheesing'.

At last the great day came. We duly marched into the hangar in our Best Blue and formed up on three sides of an impeccable hollow square. The officers fell in wearing their No. 1 uniforms, which looked as if they had been specially hired from Moss Bros for the occasion. We were stood at ease, and, as is usual on these occasions, we waited. In due course, a car pulled up outside the hangar, we were called to attention, and the officers came up to the salute. Out of the car stepped an elderly gentleman with a walking stick, in a uniform which, though absolutely immaculate, was obviously well-worn, and a cap which, apart from the badge, the 'scrambled egg' and its cleanliness, might easily have belonged to one of the Squadron pilots. The contrast between this uniform, with its four or five rows of ribbons, and the Station Commander's very new-looking outfit, with its row and a half of medals, was quite funny.

He acknowledged 'Groupy's' salute and started chatting to him as the latter conducted him to the dais. When he saw it, complete with table, chair, water carafe and glass, he is reputed to have said 'Good God, man, I'm an Air Force Officer, not a bloody politician.' He forthwith walked in front of it and turned and looked at us fallen in, six deep, the nearest airman to him being about ten or twelve yards away. He surveyed us in silence for a moment and then boomed 'Good God, I can't talk to you chaps right out there, close in, close in, come on round here.' There was a moment of horrified silence, and then we broke ranks and clustered like wolf cubs round their Akela, all rank and formality forgotten. He introduced himself to us something like this: 'My name's Trenchard, some of you may have heard me called the father of the Royal Air Force, but looking at you chaps, I think doddering old grandfather would be a better description. I don't do much these days, except go round different stations like this, damaging morale, but that's what they tell me to do, so there you are!'

By this time, he was sitting on the steps of the dais – 'Old age, y'know.' He then preceded [sic] to tell us some rather nice stories against himself, one of which went like this: 'As some of you know, the Air Force threw me out and I became a Bobby during the 1930s and after some years of it, I naturally became quite well known in the force. When the war broke out, the Air Force found an office at the Air Ministry and asked me to fill it and look busy. One morning, after a raid, I was walking to the office along the Embankment, and turned up one of those streets running up to the Strand, but found it roped off, with a constable standing there. We passed the time of day, I looked at him questioningly and he nodded, so I ducked under the rope and walked up to the Strand, where again there was a rope barrier and another officer. Again I passed the time of day and enquired the reason for the ropes and he replied that there was a big, unexploded bomb in the street. I said, "Well, why did the officer at the other end not stop me?" To which he replied: "Perhaps he recognised you, sir!"'

As may be guessed, this and other stories in the same vein, had the whole station in fits of laughter, and our morale improved no end, and when he finally said 'Well, chaps, I must be going' something occurred which I personally have never heard before or since. Somebody cried, entirely spontaneously, 'Three cheers for Lord Trenchard!' and we nearly lifted the roof off the hangar.

It appears that Trenchard might have also indulged in a little play-acting to raise a laugh by persistently failing to recognise his own pilot, an incident that allegedly had happened in London earlier in his career and was perhaps the inspiration for its repetition. Wing Commander Walter Shewry was present when Trenchard visited a remote RAF station in the Shetlands.

All the personnel were out on the tarmac to greet him on his arrival in a light plane. On landing, he suggested the officers retired to the mess while he talked with the men. Later all the officers, including myself, formed a semi circle to greet him in the hall. Still a fine-looking, though elderly, man with piercing blue eyes, he said to my neighbour (a young pilot officer) 'I think I have met you before?' at which the young man went red and looked very embarrassed and said 'Yes, sir, I am your pilot.' At this the Air Chief Marshal burst out laughing and the rather awestruck atmosphere immediately changed into informal friendliness . . .[23]

In May 1941, agitated by plans to withdraw squadrons from Bomber Command to assist in the battle of the Atlantic, he submitted a bizarre memorandum to the chiefs of staff entitled 'The Present War Situation Mainly In So Far As It Relates to Air'. In it he claimed, with very little justification, 'all the evidence' showed that the German nation was 'peculiarly susceptible' to bombing. 'Virtually imprisoned in their shelters or within the bombed area, they remain passive and easy prey to hysteria and panic without anything to mitigate the inevitable confusion and chaos . . . it is at this point that we should strike and strike again . . .'

He went on to point out that only 1 per cent of bombing raids on ships hit the target and therefore 99 per cent of bombs were lost at sea and wasted, whereas 100 per cent of bombs dropped on Germany, even if they missed the target, would still kill or frighten Germans. 'We should therefore exploit to the uttermost this vulnerable spot in the German nation and we should bomb persistently military targets in every town in Germany and never let up on them. What do I mean by persistent bombing? I mean that on every single night, and most days, some bombing of military targets in Germany must take place . . .'[24]

The chiefs of staff received the memorandum with little enthusiasm. Sir Dudley Pound, the First Sea Lord, dismissed the paper as 'a complete over-statement' and warned of 'the danger of hard and fast priorities unintelligently interpreted', Sir John Dill, the CIGS, insisted the Battle of the Atlantic should take priority and Sir Charles Portal, the Chief of the Air Staff, while agreeing with the general thesis, asserted that building a big bomber force capable of reaching all parts of Germany had to take second place to creating a minimum force of aircraft capable of providing security at home.[25]

Trenchard, undaunted, asked Churchill for permission to publish the memorandum, but was curtly informed by Sir Archibald Sinclair, the Secretary of State for Air, that it would 'not be in the national interest' for his views to appear in print. Trenchard protested to the prime minister that it was his duty to express publicly 'my convinced and considered view as to what I regard as a vital issue in these tremendous days' but did not take the matter further.

At the end of 1942 Trenchard was briefly distracted from the war by the publication of *From Many Angles*, the autobiography of Sir Frederick Sykes, which roused him to a fury. Sykes was by then a Conservative MP and businessman, having served as Governor of Bombay, but his distance from Air Force matters had not erased Trenchard's deep antipathy towards him. 'I have never read a book so egotistical and smug as this,' he fumed. 'My recollection is exactly the opposite of everything that is written in this book . . .' He described Sykes' claims that he was the moving spirit behind the formation of the RFC and had been promised command in 1912 as untrue and 'grotesque'. As far as he was concerned he was convinced there was 'not a single man in the old RFC' who thought that Sykes was of any importance; the man was 'colossally conceited', secretive and never tried to help anybody but himself. 'From start to finish the book is full of inaccuracies. He points out the enormous number of difficult jobs he had to undertake, whereas the majority of people at that time will recollect that he was continually being moved out of one post to another because he was so difficult to deal with and useless . . .'[26]

Trenchard was tempted to vent his rage with a letter to *The Times*, but was restrained, probably fortunately, by his reluctance to give the book undue prominence.

Although Bomber Command was in the safe hands of a true believer – Air Marshal Arthur 'Bomber' Harris was a protégé of Trenchard's who precisely shared his views about strategic bombing – Trenchard continued his efforts to convince both public and politicians that bombing could win the war. In October 1943 he published a 15-page pamphlet entitled '*The Effect of the Rise of Air Power on War*' which he had had privately printed and, in response to a concerned inquiry from the government, agreed it circulated to 'a few people'.

Realising that the war is not yet won [the pamphlet began], I feel it is highly desirable, in the exuberance of our recent success,[27] to reflect calmly before we launch other operations that might bring about terrible losses, when the same victories can be more swiftly won at a lower cost by using the right weapons at the right time. Correct thinking about air power is vital to the world and in particular to the British Empire both for this war and the future . . .

After running through his familiar thesis on the importance of strategic bombing, he delivered a sly dig at politicians reluctant to accept his views: 'I am confident that the majority of the population of England will broadly agree with a great deal of what I have tried to imply, although Whitehall and Washington may not yet do so; for as I have often said, probably 80 per cent of the people of Britain and America believe in the claims for air power made by airmen, while 80 per cent of Whitehall and Washington do not.'

In March 1943 Trenchard received the telegram that every parent with a son serving in the war dreaded – his first-born son, Hugh, had been killed while serving with the Guards Brigade in North Africa. He was 21 years old. His mother took the news stoically. Kitty was no stranger to tragedy: she had lost her husband and two brothers in the First World War; three of her sons and no less than eight nephews would fail to survive the second. Trenchard's youngest stepson, Edward, who was mad keen on flying and had successfully applied for a transfer to the RAF, died, ironically, in a flying accident in August 1938 and his brother, John, was reported MIA (missing in action) while serving with the Royal Scots Fusiliers in Italy in May 1944. Trenchard subsequently discovered that he had been shot through the head by a German sniper near Anzio. John was married with three small children, but Kitty kept the news from their mother until the children had been put to bed so that they did not see her upset.

Archibald James, then an MP, remembered receiving a summons to meet Trenchard soon after James' own son had been reported missing after his MGB had been sunk off the Dutch coast in May 1944.

When I met Boom in the Lords lobby he signed for me to follow him, without a word. We walked up and down the long corridor that runs the length of the Lords on the river side of the chamber three times. He said nothing but I thought he wanted to commiserate with me and I said 'You may have heard that my son, David, is reported missing but as he is a very strong swimmer we think there may be a good chance that he was picked up and is a prisoner.'

Boom replied 'I have already apprised myself of this and I think your chances are good. What I wanted to tell you was that my eldest son [his stepson John] is missing and is almost certainly dead.' With that he turned on his heel and with bowed head slowly strode away.[28]

Trenchard did his best to get to Normandy as soon as possible after D-Day, but despite pulling every string he could, he was not able to make it until the end of July. He was delighted to be able to report that the Allies had complete mastery of the air. 'I spent two days there and never once saw anyone look up to see if the aircraft above was theirs – they knew they were always ours.'

After the firestorm at Dresden in February 1945, when upwards of 20,000 people were killed in Allied bombing raids, Churchill tried to distance himself from the strategy, sending a memorandum to the chiefs of staff: 'It seems to me that the moment has come when the question of bombing German cities simply for the sake of increasing the terror, though under other pretexts, should be reviewed. Otherwise we shall come into control of an utterly ruined land ... The destruction of Dresden remains a serious query against the conduct of Allied bombing ...'

Harris's response was robust and uncompromising:

Attacks on cities like any other act of war are intolerable unless they are strategically justified. But they are strategically justified in so far as they tend to shorten the war and preserve the lives of Allied soldiers. To my mind we have absolutely no right to give them up unless it is certain that they will not have this effect. I do not personally regard the whole of the remaining cities of Germany as worth the bones of one British Grenadier ...[29]

Trenchard would have agreed with every word. Even after the war he was still lobbying for more bombing capacity, writing a ten-page typed letter to the prime minister in January 1949, apologising for troubling him – 'I feel some qualms at writing to you and bothering you when you have so much to do' – and arguing for the formation of

an 'Air Striking Force' to meet the new threat from Russia. 'I venture
to say in my old age,' he concluded, 'that if we had not fought bitterly
to have a separate Air Force supported by all political parties in those
years between 1919 and 1929 then I should not be writing this letter to
you now, because if the Air Force had not been formed, the disasters
that would have ensued are too awful to contemplate.'[30]

Although his eyesight was deteriorating, he remained an inveterate
letter writer, still frequently spoke on defence matters in the Lords
and was diligent in carrying out his responsibilities as chairman of the
board of the United Africa Company. Kitty usually drove him – reck-
lessly – into the office. At weekends he pottered about in the garden
at The King's House, pruning the roses, and enjoyed family visits,
banging on a metal bowl he had brought back from Nigeria while his
grandchildren played. His son Thomas always remembered his father
as being 'full of fun'.

On 3 February 1953, a dinner was held at 'The Rag' – the Army &
Navy Club – to celebrate his eightieth birthday. Among the guests
were Churchill, five marshals of the RAF and four air chief marshals.
In August of the following year the Trenchards left The King's House
and moved to an apartment in Cranmer Court, just off Sloane Avenue
in Chelsea. By then he was almost totally blind and deaf, although
mentally alert. Typically, he refused to accept his growing infirmity.
He meticulously organised two rooms in the apartment so that he
knew where everything was and made a point of attending all the defence debates in the Lords, speaking without notes he could no longer
read.

Trenchard died on 10 February 1956, a week after his eighty-third
birthday. Four air marshals, four Royal Fusiliers, four police officers
and four airmen took it in turns to stand at the corners of his cata-
falque at the Air Ministry's assembly hall for the lying in state. On the
day of the funeral, 21 February, his coffin was borne on a flat trailer
pulled by an RAF vehicle to Westminster Abbey, where an RAF ensign flew at half mast and a Valiant bomber flew overhead and dipped
its wings in salute. Among the pall-bearers were leading airmen whose
careers owed much to his support – Marshal of the Air Force Charles
Portal, Marshal of the Air Force Arthur Tedder, Marshal of the Force
Arthur Harris and Marshal of the Air Force Sholto Douglas. His ashes
were lodged in the RAF Chapel in the Abbey.

On 19 July 1961, Prime Minister Harold Macmillan unveiled a bronze statue of Lord Trenchard in front of the new Air Ministry building in London. The nation, he said, owed him a 'debt beyond measure'.

Trenchard shares with the monarch the unique distinction of having his birthday commemorated annually by the Royal Air Force.

ACKNOWLEDGEMENTS

I would first like to thank the late Lady Trenchard for allowing me access to her father-in-law's extensive private archive – six large filing cabinets packed with papers and correspondence – at her home in Hertfordshire. The archive includes Trenchard's invaluable 'autobiographical notes' dictated a few years before his death; I have attempted to identify those small areas where his memory failed him.

Secondly I must place on record my gratitude to Lady Trenchard's son, the present Viscount Trenchard, for making himself available for numerous interviews, for providing further important documentation and for all the time he set aside for me from his exceptionally busy life. He read through the draft manuscript and made numerous helpful comments, as did his younger brother, John Trenchard. David and Simon Boyle the grandsons of Trenchard's redoubtable wife, Kitty, were also extremely helpful and provided me with access to Kitty's fascinating letters to her children, some of which are included.

The following individuals also provided generous assistance: Professor Richard Overy of the University of Exeter, author of *The Bombing War*; Christina Goulter and David Jordan at the Defence Academy of the United Kingdom at Shrivenham; Rear Admiral Jonathan Westbrook RN; Mrs Katherine Thimbleby at Wolfeton House; Min Larkin at RAF Halton; Robert Borton.

The librarians and archivists at the following institutions were invaluable: the British Library; the Bodleian Library; the Department of Manuscripts at Cambridge University Library; the Churchill Archives Centre at Churchill College, Cambridge; the RAF Museum, Hendon; Durham County Record Office; Glasgow University Archives; Royal Air Force, Halton; Imperial War Museum; House of Lords Records Office; the Liddell Hart Centre for Military Archives, King's College, London; the National Archives, Kew; the Parliamentary Archives;

Somerset Heritage Centre; the West Sussex Record Office.

My incomparable agent and long-time friend, Michael Sissons, made this book happen (as he made my eleven previous books happen) and I am very grateful for the enthusiastic support of Alan Samson, my publisher.

Finally, as always, I want to pay loving tribute to my wife, Renate, my invaluable first-line editor, for patiently reading through many drafts of the manuscript, for her wise counsel, and for cheerfully putting up with the vicissitudes of living with an obsessive author.

A NOTE ON SOURCES

TFA = Trenchard Family Archive
CUL = Cambridge University Library
CAC = Churchill Archives Centre, Churchill College, Cambridge
LHCMA = Liddell Hart Centre for Military Archives, King's College, London
NA = National Archives
IWM = Imperial War Museum
BL = British Library

Chapter 1
1 Autobiographical notes, TFA
2 Autobiographical notes, TFA

Chapter 2
1 Autobiographical file, TFA
2 Genealogy file, TFA
3 Autobiographical file, TFA
4 Kitty notebooks, TFA
5 Autobiographical notes, TFA
6 Ibid
7 Autobiographical notes, TFA

Chapter 3
1 Autobiographical notes, TFA
2 Buchan
3 Boyle
4 Autobiographical notes, TFA
5 Autobiographical notes, TFA

6 Implying he was a representative of Cook's the travel agent
7 Autobiographical notes, TFA
8 The Amritsar massacre, in 1919, when the army fired on a crowd
   gathered in the Golden Temple, became a seminal event in the
   British rule of India and contributed to the demise of the Raj.
9 Autobiographical notes, TFA
10 Ravenhill had to forfeit his medal in 1908 after he was imprisoned
   for the theft of scrap iron and could not afford to pay the ten shil-
   ling fine.
11 Autobiographical notes, TFA
12 CUL Add.9429/13/1584 (i)
13 Ibid

Chapter 4

1 Unattributed interview, Saunders file, TFA
2 Autobiographical notes, TFA
3 They were known as 'Judas Boers' and were ostracised by their
   community after the war
4 Autobiographical notes, TFA
5 Kaffir was the word commonly used at that time to refer to blacks.
   It is now considered to be a deeply offensive racial slur.
6 Autobiographical notes, TFA
7 Autobiographical notes, TFA
8 Autobiographical notes, TFA
9 Now Polokwane
10 Autobiographical notes, TFA
11 Ibid
12 76/1/62 RAF Museum

Chapter 5

1 Autobiographical notes, TFA
2 Ibid
3 Autobiographical notes, TFA
4 *London Gazette*, 25.8.1905
5 Autobiographical notes, TFA
6 Hansard, 2 June 1904
7 Autobiographical notes, TFA
8 Ibid

9 Autobiographical notes, TFA
10 Antiquated muzzle-loading rifles said to have been introduced into
   Africa by Danish traders
11 Autobiographical notes, TFA
12 76/1/63 RAF Museum
13 76/1/63 RAF Museum
14 Steel, *A Memoir*
15 Autobiographical notes, TFA
16 Autobiographical notes, TFA
17 Autobiographical notes, TFA
18 Autobiographical notes, TFA
19 His paper was marked 'too colloquial for a military essay'"
20 *London Gazette*, 18 September 1906

Chapter 6
1 *London Gazette*, 18 Sept 1906
2 Autobiographical notes, TFA
3 Ibid
4 Autobiographical notes, TFA
5 Autobiographical notes, TFA
6 Steel, *A Memoir*
7 76/1/63, RAF Museum
8 76/1/63, RAF Museum
9 Saunders file TFA
10 Add 9429/1B/1218 (i) CUL
11 Unnamed file, TFA

Chapter 7
1 Gollin
2 AIR 1/1608/204/85/36 NA
3 AIR 1/728/176/3/33 NA
4 Budiansky, *Air Power*
5 Jones, *Origins*
6 *The Aeroplane*, 23 November 1911
7 Knights of the Air, *Time-Life*
8 Morrow
9 Dickson had the unwelcome distinction of being the first pilot
   to be involved in a mid-air crash. At an air meet in Milan on 1

October 1910 his Farman biplane was rammed from above by an
Antoinette monoplane. Both pilots survived the crash but Dickson
did not fully recover from his injuries and died in 1913.

10 Per Ardua

11 Gollin

12 The site of the crash, less than a mile west of Stonehenge, is still
marked by a stone cross.

13 Bramson

14 Autobiographical notes, TFA

15 Copland Perry was killed in a flying accident in France in August
1914.

16 Autobiographical notes, TFA

17 Official history

18 Bramson

19 Saunders file, TFA

20 Baker

21 Autobiographical notes, TFA

22 Boyle

23 Longmore was the first British pilot to make a successful landing
on water, on the river Medway, in December 1911. After the Great
War he transferred to the RAF and rose to the rank of air chief
marshal.

24 Add 9429/1B/303 (i) CUL

25 Boyle

26 Biard won the Schneider Trophy in 1922 and became a well-known
test pilot.

27 Biard

28 V/1/10, TFA

29 Unnamed file, TFA

30 Autobiographical notes, TFA

Chapter 8

1 Henderson had learned to fly in 1911 at the age of 49 and was the
world's oldest pilot at that time and was the first director of the new
Department of Military Aeronautics.

2 Saunders file, TFA

3 Catalogue 24, IWM

4 Ironically, the two front pews of the RAF Church in London are

dedicated as memorials to Trenchard and Sykes – a companionship they never enjoyed in life.

5 Gollin

6 Sykes, *Aviation in Peace and War*

7 Pilots at Netheravon had pinned notices on their doors asking for everything to be left untouched until they returned.

8 Autobiographical notes, TFA

9 Skene was the first Englishman to loop the loop in an aeroplane

10 Norris

11 Autobiographical notes, TFA

12 Macmillan

13 Autobiographical notes, TFA

14 Baring

15 Joubert de la Ferté

16 'Air' was the term in common use at that time for aviation matters.

17 Gough had won a VC in British Somaliland in 1903; he was killed by a sniper at Neuve Chapelle on 20 February 1915

18 Sykes

19 Autobiographical notes, TFA

20 After the war Moore-Brabazon became a Conservative Member of Parliament, was elevated to the peerage and chaired the Brabazon Committee which was set up to develop the British aircraft industry after the Second World War.

21 Brabazon

22 Brabazon

23 By the end of the war the RFC had taken more than 400,000 aerial photographs

24 Cat 27 IWM

25 Autobiographical notes, TFA

26 His only son, also called William, joined the RAF, trained as a fighter pilot and was killed during the Battle of Britain.

27 The opening verses of 'Archibald Certainly Not!' ran:
It's no use me denying facts I'm henpecked, you can see!
'Twas in our wedding day my wife commenced to peck at me
The wedding breakfast over, I said 'We'll start off today
Upon our honeymoon'
Then she yelled, 'What! Why waste time that way?'
'Archibald, certainly not!'

Get back to work at once, sir, like a shot
When single you could waste time spooning
But lose work now for honeymooning,
'Archibald, certainly not!'
28 Autobiographical notes, TFA

Chapter 9
1 Autobiographical notes, TFA
2 Baring, 'Dear Animated Bust'
3 Autobiographical notes, TFA
4 Brabazon
5 Baring, *Flying Corps Headquarters*
6 Brabazon
7 V/1/6 TFA
8 Fredette
9 Letley
10 76/1/114, Trenchard papers, RAF Museum
11 Autobiographical notes, TFA
12 Cat 9, IWM
13 Autobiographical notes, TFA
14 Immelmann, Franz, *Immelmann:The Eagle of Lille* (John Hamilton, London 1935)
15 Divine
16 Baring, Flying Corps Headquarters
17 Baring, Flying Corps Headquarters
18 AIR 1/138 NA
19 V/1/10 TFA
20 Hansard, 16 February 1916
21 Baring, *Flying Corps Headquarters*
22 Ibid
23 Only the archway remains – the château was bombed and destroyed in the Second World War
24 PP/MCR/C15 IWM
25 Saunders file, TFA
26 Hansard, 22 March 1916
27 *Flight*, 30 March 1916
28 MFC 76/1/5
29 FC 76/1/5, RAF Museum

30 Saunders file, TFA
31 Hansard, 17 May 1916
32 MFC 76/1/76 RAF Museum

Chapter 10
1 Cat no 24, IWM
2 Add 9429/1B/1214 CUL
3 After the war he would become a Conservative MP and a close friend of Trenchard
4 War in the Air, Vol. V
5 Saunders file, TFA
6 Lee
7 The RFC's workhorse, the B.E.2, had been designed before the war
8 Lewis *Sagittarius Rising*
9 Baring, *Flying Corps Headquarters*
10 Lewis *Sagittarius Rising*
11 Macmillan
12 Gibbs
13 Trenchard Paper, RAF Museum MFC 76/1
14 Autobiographical notes, TFA
15 Stewart
16 Orange
17 Douglas
18 Baring, *Flying Corps Headquarters*
19 Fry. Fry rose to the rank of Wing Commander and was one of the few Great War airmen to survive in the 1990s.
20 Boyle
21 Baring, *Flying Corps Headquarters*
22 Trenchard papers, RAF Museum
23 Jones, Vol 2
24 Staff at RFC HQ kept a book of cuttings called 'What the Germans say about the RFC', which included letters retrieved from the bodies of enemy soldiers describing the misery being inflicted on them by the RFC and which supported Trenchard's conviction that his strategy was damaging enemy morale.
25 AIR 1/718/29/1 NA
26 Cooper
27 Sykes

28 DC 76/43/586 TFA
29 Wrench
30 Lewis
31 Autobiographical notes, TFA

Chapter 11
1 V/1/10 TFA
2 V/1/10 TFA
3 V/1/10 TFA
4 Bishop went on to win a VC, claimed to have shot down 72 enemy aircraft during the war and became a national hero in Canada, but some historians cast doubt on his story.
5 The song's dark humour referred to risk of the crew being crushed by the engine when pusher aircraft crashed.
6 Baring, *Flying Corps Headquarters*
7 A future air marshal
8 Groves
9 VI/10 TFA
10 V/1/10 TFA
11 Hansard, 29 April 1918
12 Blake
13 Baring, *Flying Corps Headquarters*
14 Repington
15 CU Library Add 9429/1B/12167 (ii)
16 Lewis, *Sagittarius Rising*

Chapter 12
1 Robertson, *Soldiers and Statesmen* (Cassell, London, 1926)
2 Cooper
3 *Aeroplane* 27/6/1917
4 Fredette
5 *War In The Air*, Vol V
6 V/1/10 TFA
7 Jones, War in the Air Appendix 11
8 AIR 1/521/16/12/3 NA
9 Autobiographical notes, TFA
10 Blake
11 AIR 1/678 NA

12 *Aeroplane*, 10/10/1917
13 AIR 1/970/204/5/1108
14 Baring, *Flying Corps Headquarters*
15 AIR 8/167 NA
16 V/1/10 TFA
17 Divine
18 Slessor
19 Terraine, J., *The Road to Passchendaele* (Leo Cooper, London 1977)
20 MFC 76/1/17 RAF Museum
21 Ibid
22 AIR 8/167 NA
23 The War Cabinet denounced Northcliffe's letter as 'mischievous'.

Chapter 13
1 Autobiographical notes TFA
2 CUL Add.9429/1B/209(ii)
3 C1/16 TFA
4 V/1/10 TFA
5 Blake
6 V/1/10 TFA
7 Unnamed fie, TFA
8 Blake
9 It became known as 'Bolo House' after Bolo Pasha, the code name of a German agent whose job was to spread alarm and despondency among the troops in France.
10 Autobiographical notes, TFA
11 C 1/16 TFA
12 Blake
13 RAF Museum, Trenchard papers, MFC 76/1/92
14 Pound
15 AIR 8/167 NA
16 CUL Add.9429/1B/204(ii)
17 CUL Add.9429/1B/209(v)
18 CAB/24/49
19 Autobiographical notes, TFA
20 TREN 1 CAC
21 Wallace
22 AIR 8/167 NA

23 Autobiographical notes, TFA
24 Lloyd George had been hearing rumours of a conspiracy, allegedly directed by Asquith, the leader of the Liberal opposition, to drive him from office. Asquith was said to have been drumming up support among senior military figures, including Trenchard. In fact it was extremely unlikely that Trenchard would have become involved in political intrigue.
25 Bonar Law Papers, Parliamentary Archives
26 Beaverbrook, *Men and Power*
27 MFC 76/1/92, Hendon
28 Hansard, 29 Apr 1918
29 Sykes papers, MFC 76/1/19
30 Bonar Law Papers, Parliamentary Archives

Chapter 14
1 Beaverbrook
2 Autobiographical notes, TFA
3 AIR 1/533/16/12/121 NA
4 Weir papers, CAC
5 Ibid
6 Pound
7 C1/10/1 RAF Museum
8 MFC 76/1/94 RAF Museum
9 Baring, *Flying Corps Headquarters*
10 Barrett, William, *The Independent Air Force* (War Birds)
11 Trenchard papers, MFC 76/1/32 RAF Museum
12 Air 8/167 NA
13 Édouard de Castelnau, commander of the Eastern Army Group
14 Air 8/167 NA
15 Air 8/167 NA
16 Air 1/415/15/312/20 NA
17 *London Gazette*, 1 January 1919
18 C1/11/12 RAF Museum
19 MFC 76/1/94 RAF Museum
20 MFC 76/1/20 RAF Museum
21 CUL Add 9429/1B/1216 (ii)
22 C/1/10/3 TFA
23 Baring, *Flying Corps Headquarters*

24 CAB 24/70/64 NA
25 Baring, *Flying Corps Headquarters*
26 Ibid
27 MFC 76/1/94 RAF Museum
28 Remington got his figures wrong – of the Force's 341 aircraft, only a quarter were Handley Pages.
29 Repington
30 CAB 24/69/35 NA
31 C1/10/3 TFA
32 Ibid
33 Joubert
34 MFC 76/1/94 RAF Museum

Chapter 15
1 Autobiographical notes, TFA
2 AIR 10/1214, NA
3 Robertson had 'resigned' as CIGS in February 1918 after a disagreement with Lloyd George and been replaced by Sir Henry Wilson.
4 Autobiographical notes, TFA
5 MSS Euro F143/101 BL
6 Autobiographical notes
7 MFC 76/1/164 RAF Museum
8 Ibid
9 Add 9429/1B/1218 (i) CUL
10 Add 9429/1B/1216 (ii) CUL
11 Ibid
12 Autobiographical notes, TFA
13 Montgomery Hyde
14 TREN 1 CAC
15 Kitty notebooks, TFA
16 AIR 1/718/29/2 NA
17 TREN 1 CAC
18 Archive file 1X/5/9 LHCMA
19 Jonah's gourd 'came up in a night, and perished in a night'
20 Montgomery Hyde
21 Boyle
22 Add 9429/1B/7 CUL

23 MFC 76/1/101 RAF Museum
24 AIR 10/1367 NA
25 Add. 9429/1B/210 (ii) CUL

Chapter 16
1 A future air chief marshal
2 Douglas, *Years of Command*
3 Sykes had married the elder daughter of Bonar Law, prompting Trenchard to joke, when he heard the news, 'I suppose that means Megan Lloyd George [the prime minister's 18-year-old daughter] wouldn't have him.'
4 Private letter, TFA
5 Unnamed file, TFA
6 Meyer, Karl E. and Brysac, S.B., *Kingmakers: The Invention of the Modern Middle East* (W.W. Norton, New York, 2008)
7 9429/1B/406 CUL
8 II/27/50 TFA
9 NMFC 76/1/36 RAF Museum
10 Slessor
11 AIR 5/552 NA
12 II/27/50 TFA
13 Borton was said to be the officer who coined the term 'Archie' for anti-aircraft fire in the Great War.
14 Churchill/Tren CAC
15 C/11/27/163 TFA
16 Brooke-Popham 1/5–7 LHCMA
17 II/27/50 TFA
18 Hansard, 16 March 1922
19 Later Lord Ismay, the first Secretary General of NATO
20 Cat 3176 IWM
21 Add 9429/1B/1267 CUL
22 Probert

Chapter 17
1 'Air Policy & Strategy', Staff College lecture, 14 February, 1938, RAF Museum
2 MFC 76/1/138 RAF Museum
3 Kitty Notebook No 2, TFA

4 Hoare
5 Ibid
6 MFC 76/1/77 RAF Museum
7 Thomson chose Cardington, the airship base near Bedford. Ironically, he was killed when the R101 airship crashed on its maiden flight to Karachi in 1930.
8 AIR 8/66/254 NA
9 AIR 2/1267 NA
10 Unnamed file, TFA
11 Smith, Malcolm
12 AIR 5/416 NA
13 Kitty notebooks, TFA
14 RAF Museum 11/5/1–57
15 Montgomery Hyde
16 Grigg, P.J., *Prejudice and Judgement* (Jonathan Cape, London, 1948)
17 Omissi
18 AIR 1/1997/204/273/245 NA
19 AIR 9/69 NA
20 Unnamed file, TFA
21 TREN 1 CAC
22 CAB 53/14 NA
23 CAB 24/207 NA
24 CAB 63/44 NA

Chapter 18
1 Copies of the Trenchard–Lawrence correspondence are held in the Bodleian Library, Oxford, under reference MSS d48
2 Bod MSS d48
3 Montgomery Hyde
4 AIR 1/2693, NA
5 AIR 1/2692 NA
6 AIR 1/2692 NA

Chapter 19
1 Boyle
2 Moylan
3 Five years later Sir Leo was in court again on asimilar charge

– attempting to kiss a young lady in a railway compartment. On this occasion he was found guilty and fined 50 shillings.
4   C/iii/i TFA
5   C/iii/i TFA
6   Autobiographical notes, TFA
7   C/iii/i, TFA
8   Ciii/30 TFA
9   Howgrave-Graham
10 Boyle
11 HO 144/18186 NA
12 File Ciii/20, TFA
13 David Boyle files
14 Boyle family archive
15 Hansard 23 May 1933 & 26 June 1933
16 Letter to Lord Swinton, TFA
17 David Boyle files
18 MEPO 2/5698 NA
19 David Boyle files
20 MEPO 5/351 NA
21 Kitty notebooks, TFA
22 David Boyle files
23 AJMS3, CAC

Chapter 20
1   TREN 1 CAC
2   LH 11/1935/86 LHMA
3   Trenchard's 'Last Will & Testament' when he stepped down as Chief of the Air Staff
4   Tren 2, CAC
5   LH 11/1936/39 LHCMA
6   TREN 2, CAC
7   Unmarked file, TFA
8   25 November 1936
9   Boyle
10 File marked 'Outbreak of war', TFA
11 MEP 19/60 NA
12 Ibid
13 PREM 1/398 NA

14 Ibid
15 Hansard, 8 May, 1940
16 Add 9429/1B/219-257 CUL
17 TREN 2, CAC
18 CAB 80/19/35 NA
19 TAYLOR, A.J.P., *From Boer War to Cold War* (Faber, London, 2011)
20 Harris
21 Ibid
22 Trenchard papers, RAF Museum
23 88/52/1 IWM
24 CAB 80/57 NA
25 AIR 8/929 NA
26 76/1/542, RAF Museum
27 He was referring to the bombing of Hamburg in July 1943, the heaviest aerial assault in history at that time, which killed 42,600 civilians and practically destroyed the entire city.
28 'Recollections of Lord Trenchard' by Sir Archibald James, TFA
29 Taylor, *Dresden*
30 PREM 8/927 NA

SELECT BIBLIOGRAPHY

Allen, Hubert Raymond ('Dizzy'), Wing Commander. *The Legacy of Lord Trenchard* (Cassell, London, 1972)

Armitage, Michael. *The Royal Air Force* (Cassell, London, 1993)

Ash, Eric. *Sir Frederick Sykes and the Air Revolution, 1912–1918* (Frank Cass, London, 1999)

Baker, Anne. *From Biplane to Spitfire: The Life of Air Chief Marshal Sir Geoffrey Salmond* (Pen and Sword Books, Barnsley, Yorks, 2003)

Balfour, Harold. *An Airman Marches: Early Flying Adventures, 1914–1923* (Greenhill, London, 1985)

Baring, Maurice. *Flying Corps Headquarters 1914–1918* (Heinemann, London, 1930)

——*Dear Animated Bust: Letters to Lady Juliet Duff, France, 1915–1918* (Michael Russell, Salisbury, 1981)

Barker, Ralph. *The RAF at War* (Time-Life Books, Alexandria, Va, 1981)

——*The Royal Flying Corps in France: From Mons to the Somme* (Constable, London, 1994)

Beaverbrook, Lord. *Men and Power 1917–1918* (Hutchinson, London, 1956)

Biard, Henry. *Wings* (Hurst & Blackett, London, 1934)

Bishop, William Arthur. *The Courage of the Early Morning: The Story of Billy Bishop* (Heinemann, London, 1966)

Blake, Robert (ed.). *The Private Papers of Douglas Haig, 1914–1919* (Eyre & Spottiswoode, London, 1952)

Boyle, Andrew. *Trenchard, Man of Vision* (Collins, London, 1962)

Brabazon, Lord. *The Brabazon Story* (William Heinemann, London, 1956)

Bramson, Alan. *Pure Luck: The Authorised Biography of Sir Thomas Sopwith* (Patrick Stephens, London, 1990)

Browne, Douglas. *The Rise of Scotland Yard* (George G. Harrap, London, 1956)

Brunskill, Ian, Liardet, Guy and Tillotson, Michael (eds). *Great Military Lives: A Century in Obituaries* (Times Books, London, 2008)

Buchan, John. *The History of the Royal Scots Fusiliers, 1678–1918* (Thomas Nelson & Sons, London, 1925)

Budiansky, Stephen. *Air Power from Kitty Hawk to Gulf War II* (Penguin Books, London, 2003)

Burge, Major C. Gordon. *The Annals of 100 Squadron* (Naval & Military Press, London, 1975)

Carver, Sir Michael (ed.). *The War Lords: Military Commanders of the Twentieth Century* (Weidenfeld & Nicolson, London, 1976)

Charlton, L.E.O. *Charlton* (Faber & Faber, London, 1931)

——*Our War in the Air* (J.M. Dent & Sons, London, 1941)

Charteris, J. *Field Marshal Earl Haig* (Cassell, London, 1929)

Clark, Ronald W. *Tizard* (Methuen, London, 1965)

Collier, Basil. *Heavenly Adventurer: Sefton Brancker and the Dawn of British Aviation* (Secker & Warburg, London, 1959)

Cooper, Malcolm. *The Birth of Independent Air Power: British Air Policy in the First World War* (Allen & Unwin, London, 1986)

Cumming, Dr Anthony J. 'The Saviour of the RAF' (History of Airpower Series – Paper 2: Trenchard, The Phoenix Think Tank, 2011)

Davidson, Sir John. *Haig: Master of the Field* (Peter Nevill, London, 1953)

Dean, Sir Maurice. *The Royal Air Force and Two World Wars* (Cassell, London, 1979)

Divine, David. *The Broken Wing: A Study in the British Exercise of Air Power* (Hutchinson, London, 1966)

Dixon, Norman F. *On the Psychology of Military Incompetence* (Jonathan Cape, London, 1976)

Douglas, Sholto. *Years of Combat* (Collins, London, 1963)

——*Years of Command* (Collins, London, 1966)

Fitzroy, Almeric. *Memoirs* (Hutchinson, London, 1925)

Franks, Norman L.R., Guest, Russell and Bailey, Frank W. *Bloody April . . . Black September* (Grub Street, London, 1995)

Fredette, Major Raymond. *The First Battle of Britain, 1917–18 and the*

Birth of the Royal Air Force (Cassell, London, 1966)

Fry, William. *Air of Battle* (William Kimber, London, 1974)

Garnett, David (ed.). *Letters of T.E. Lawrence* (Jonathan Cape, London, 1938)

Gibbs, Sir Philip. *Realities of War* (William Heinemann, London, 1920)

Gollin, Alfred. *No Longer an Island: Britain and the Wright Brothers, 1902–1909* (Heinemann, London, 1984)

———*The Impact of Air Power on the British People and Their Government, 1909–1914* (Macmillan, London, 1989)

Grey, C.G. 'On the departing chief' (*The Aeroplane*, 37 (1929), pp.1402–16)

Groves, Brigadier-General P.R.C. *Behind the Smoke Screen* (Faber & Faber, London, 1934)

Harris, Sir Arthur. *Bomber Offensive* (Greenhill Books, London, 1990)

Hart, Peter. *Bloody April: Slaughter in the Skies over Arras, 1917* (Weidenfeld & Nicolson, London, 2005)

———*Aces Falling: War Above the Trenches, 1918* (Weidenfeld & Nicolson, London, 2007)

Hastings, Max. *Bomber Command* (Michael Joseph, London, 1979)

Havard, Cyril. *The Trenchard Touch* (Countrywise Press, Chichester, 2000)

Haywood, A. and Clarke, F.A.S. *The History of the Royal West African Frontier Force* (Gale & Polden, Aldershot, 1964)

Hoare, Sir Samuel. *Empire of the Air: The Advent of the Air Age 1922–1929* (Collins, London, 1957)

Hooton, E.R. *War Over the Trenches: Air Power and the Western Front Campaigns 1916–1918* (Midland Publishing, Hersham, Surrey, 2010)

Howgrave-Graham, Hamilton Maurice. *Light and Shade at Scotland Yard* (John Murray, London, 1947)

Hughes, Matthew and Seligmann, Matthew (eds). *Leadership in Conflict* (Leo Cooper, Barnsley, 2000)

Hyde, H. Montgomery. *British Air Policy Between the Wars 1918–1939* (Heinemann, London, 1976)

———*Solitary in the Ranks: Lawrence of Arabia as Airman and Private Soldier* (Constable, London, 1977)

James, John. *The Paladins: A Social History of the RAF up to the Outbreak of World War II* (Macdonald, London, 1990)

Johns, R. Trenchard Memorial Lecture (*RUSI Journal*, Vol. 142, No. 5 (October, 1997), pp.10–16)

Johnson, J.E. ('Johnnie'). *Full Circle; The Story of Air Fighting* (Cassell, London, 1964)

Jones. H.A. *Official History of the War: The War in the Air, Vol. II* (Clarendon Press, Oxford, 1922–1937)

Jones, Neville. *Origins of Strategic Bombing: A Study of the Development of British Air Strategic Thought and Practice up to 1918* (William Kimber, London, 1973)

——*The Beginnings of Strategic Air Power: A History of the British Bomber Force 1923–1939* (Frank Cass, London, 1987)

Joubert de la Ferté, Sir Philip Bennet. *The Third Service: The Story Behind the Royal Air Force* (Thames & Hudson, London, 1955)

Keegan, John and Wheatcroft, Andrew. *Who's Who in Military History: From 1453 to the Present Day* (Routledge, London, 1996)

Kemp, J.C. *The History of the Royal Scots Fusiliers 1919–1959* (Robert Maclehose, Glasgow, 1963)

Knightley, Phillip and Simpson, Colin. *The Secret Lives of Lawrence of Arabia* (Thomas Nelson & Sons, London, 1969)

Korda, Michael. *Hero: The Life and Legend of Lawrence of Arabia* (Harper Collins, New York, 2010)

Laffin, John. *Swifter Than Eagles – The Biography of Marshal of the Royal Air Force Sir John Salmond* (William Blackwood and Sons, Edinburgh, 1964)

Lambert, Andrew. *Admirals: The Naval Commanders who Made Britain Great* (Faber & Faber, London, 2008)

Lawrence, A.W. (ed.). *Letters to T.E. Lawrence* (Jonathan Cape, London, 1962)

Lawrence, T.E. *The Mint* (Jonathan Cape, London, 1973)

Lee, Arthur Gould (ed.). *No Parachute: A Fighter Pilot in World War One* (Jarrolds, London, 1968)

Letley, Emma. *Maurice Baring: A Citizen of Europe* (Constable, London, 1991)

Levine, Joshua. *Fighter Heroes of World War One* (Collins, London, 2008)

——*On a Wing and a Prayer* (HarperCollins, London, 2008)

Lewis, Cecil. *Sagittarius Rising* (Peter Davies, London, 1936)

Mack, John E. *A Prince of Our Disorder: The Life of T.E. Lawrence* (Weidenfeld & Nicolson, London, 1976)

Mackersey, Ian. *No Empty Chairs: The Short and Heroic Lives of the Young Aviators Who Fought and Died in the First World War* (Weidenfeld & Nicolson, London, 2012)

Macmillan, Norman. *Sir Sefton Brancker* (Heinemann, London, 1935)

Manchester, William. *The Last Lion, Winston Spencer Churchill: Visions of Glory, 1864–1932* (Michael Joseph, London, 1983)

Marson, T.B. *Scarlet and Khaki* (Jonathan Cape, London, 1930)

Meilinger, P.S. 'Trenchard and Morale Bombing: The Evolution of Royal Air Force Doctrine Before World War II' (*The Journal of Military History* (April 1996), Vol. 60, No. 2)

——'The Historiography of Airpower: Theory and Doctrine' (*The Journal of Military History* (April 2000), Vol. 64, No. 2)

Morris, Alan. *First of the Many: The Story of Independent Force, RAF* (Jarrolds, London, 1968)

Morrow, John H. *The Great War in the Air: Military Aviation from 1909 to 1921* (Smithsonian Institution Press, Washington, DC, 1993)

Moylan, Sir John. *Scotland Yard* (Putnam, London, 1929)

Murray, Williamson. *The War in the Air 1914–45* (Cassell, London, 1999)

Norris, Geoffrey. *The Royal Flying Corps: A History* (Frederick Muller, London, 1965)

Omissi, David. *Air Power and Colonial Control: The Royal Air Force 1919–1939* (Manchester University Press, Manchester, 1990)

Orange, Vincent. *Coningham: A Biography of Air Marshal Sir Arthur Coningham* (Methuen, London, 1990)

——*Dowding of Fighter Command: Victor of the Battle of Britain* (Grub Street, London, 2008)

Overy, Richard. *The Bombing War* (Allen Lane, London, 2013)

Patrick, M.M. *The United States in the Air* (Doubleday, Doran, New York, 1928)

Pelling, Henry. *Winston Churchill* (Macmillan, London, 1964)

Penrose, Harald. *British Aviation: The Pioneer Years 1903–1914* (Putnam, London, 1967)

Philpott, Wing Commander Ian M. *The Royal Air Force; An Encyclopedia of the Inter War Years* (Pen & Sword, Barnsley, 2005)

Pound, Reginald and Harmsworth, Cecil. *Northcliffe* (Cassell, London, 1959)

Probert, Air Commodore Henry. *High Commanders of the Royal Air Force* (HMSO, London, 1991)

Ray, John. *The Battle of Britain: Dowding and the First Victory, 1940* (Cassell, London, 2000)

Reader, W.J. *Architect of Air Power: The Life of the First Viscount Weir of Eastwood 1877–1959* (Collins, London, 1968)

Repington, Charles à Court. *The First World War* (Constable, London, 1920)

Ross, Wing Commander Anthony (ed.). *Through the Eyes of Blue* (Airlife Publishing, Shrewsbury, 2002)

Shaw, John. 'Dwarsvlei, a Highveld Farm: Forgotten Battle of the Anglo-Boer War' (*Military History Journal*, South African Military History Society, Vol. 11, Nos 3/4)

Shores, Christopher, Franks, Norman and Guest, Russell. *Above the Trenches* (Grub Street, London, 1990)

Slessor, Sir John. *These Remain* (Michael Joseph, London, 1969)

Smith, Malcolm. *British Air Strategy Between the Wars* (Clarendon Press, Oxford, 1984)

Smyth, Ethel. *Maurice Baring* (William Heinemann, London, 1938)

Steel, Colonel J.P. *A Memoir of Lieutenant Colonel A.E. Steel* (Simpkin, Marshall, Hamilton, Kent, London, 1921)

Stevenson, John. 'The Police and the 1932 Hunger March' (*Bulletin of the Society for the Study of Labour History*, Issue 38 (Spring 1979), p.24)

Stewart, Oliver. *Words and Music for a Mechanical Man* (Faber & Faber, London, 1967)

Sykes, Sir Frederick. *Aviation in Peace and War* (Edward Arnold, London, 1922)

——*From Many Angles* (Harrap, London, 1942)

Taylor, Frederick. *Dresden: Tuesday 13 February 1945* (HarperCollins, New York, 2004)

Taylor, H.A. *Fairey Aircraft Since 1915* (Putnam, London, 1974)

Taylor, John W.R. *C.F.S., Birthplace of Air Power* (Putnam, London, 1958)

Taylor, S.J. *The Great Outsiders; Northcliffe, Rothermere and the Daily*

Mail (Weidenfeld & Nicolson, London, 1996)

Terraine, John. *The Right of the Line* (Hodder & Stoughton, London, 1985)

Thompson, J. Steve and Smith, Peter C. *Air Combat Manoeuvres: The Technique and History of Air Fighting for Flight Simulation* (Ian Allan, Hersham, Surrey)

Trenchard, Lord. *Three Papers on Air Power* (Air Ministry Publication 229 (1946))

Turner, Major Charles Cyril. *The Old Flying Days* (Sampson Low, Marston, London, 1927)

Van Wyngarden, G. *Early German Aces of World War I* (Osprey Publishing, Oxford, 2008)

Vincent, Air Vice Marshal S.F. *Flying Fever* (Jarrolds, London, 1972)

Wallace, Graham. *R.A.F. Biggin Hill* (Putnam, London, 1957)

Webster, Charles and Frankland, Noble. *The Strategic Air Offensive Against Germany, 1939–1945* (4 vols) (HMSO, London, 1961)

White, Jerry. *Zeppelin Nights: London in the First World War* (Bodley Head, London, 2014)

Williams, George K. *Biplanes and Bombsights: British Bombing in World War I* (Air University Press, Maxwell AFB, Alabama, 1999)

Wise, S.E. *Canadian Airmen and the First World War: The Official History of the Royal Canadian Air Force* (University of Toronto Press, Toronto, 1980)

Wrench, John Evelyn. *Geoffrey Dawson and Our Times* (Hutchinson, London, 1955)

INDEX